THE DANCER, THE DREAMERS, AND THE QUEEN OF ROMANIA

HOW AN UNLIKELY QUARTET CREATED AMERICA'S MOST IMPROBABLE ART MUSEUM

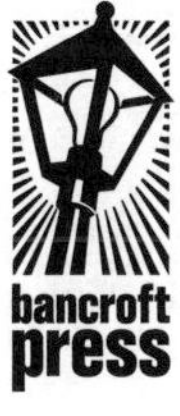

STEVE WIEGAND

Cover & Interior design: Tracy Copes

Author Photo: Hollywood Photo Studio

978-1-61088-494-5 (HC)

978-1-61088-495-2 (PB)

978-1-61088-496-9 (ebook)

978-1-61088-497-6 (PDF)

Published by Bancroft Press "Books that Enlighten"

410-358-0658

P.O. Box 65360, Baltimore, MD 21209

www.bancroftpress.com

Printed in the United States of America

To my wife Cecilia,
who is living proof that some human beings
can endure almost anything—or anyone.

TABLE OF CONTENTS

INTRODUCTION

If you travel three miles west from where U.S. 97 meets the Columbia River in Central Washington, you will come to a narrow shelf of land that separates the steep treeless hills from the north bank of the river, about 300 feet below. The shelf is occupied by a massive three-story sand-colored concrete building. It is as disconcerting in its setting as a naked person in church. And every bit as riveting.

The building is the Maryhill Museum of Art.

A 2014 survey by the Institute of Museum and Library Services listed slightly more than 35,000 museums in the United States—or about 9,500 more than the number of McDonald's and Starbucks outlets combined. Of those 35,000-plus museums, 1,605 were classified, like Maryhill, as art museums. But it is reasonably safe to say none of the other 1,604 art museums is quite like Maryhill.

For one thing, it would be difficult to name another American art museum that owns the 5,300 acres surrounding it—or a full-sized concrete replica of Stonehenge. Or derives more revenue from wind turbines and alfalfa fields than it does its paying visitors. Or that has a 10-mile-long pretzel-twist of asphalt built in the early 1900s to demonstrate road engineering techniques and is now routinely rented out for car commercials and skateboard races.

Then there is the museum's setting. Encompassed by an oasis of greenery that includes a sculpture garden, the structure boasts mesmerizing views up and down the spectacular Columbia River Gorge. The hills that crowd behind it are baked an unvaried golden hue. The color evokes thoughts of van Gogh paintings from the south of France, and/or Twinkies, depending on one's artistic/gastronomic predilections. Its isolation—105 miles to Portland, 223 to Seattle, 90 to the nearest town with more than 15,000 people (Troutdale, Oregon.) and 13 miles to the nearest town of any kind (Goldendale, Washington., population 3,428)—coupled with sometimes-nasty winter weather, compels the museum to shut down from mid-November to mid-March.

And there is the building itself. It has been variously described as a "Beaux Arts chateau," "Flemish mansion," or even a "Neo-Gothic castle." Its unlikely presence, as a 1987 *New York Times* piece aptly noted, is "oddly fitting - it brought the better works of man near one of the better works of nature."

The fascination factor spills over to the museum's eclectic contents: A gallery of 87 works by the master sculptor Auguste Rodin. Scores of exquisite chess sets from around the world. A collection of American Indian art and artifacts that rivals the best in the country for its breadth and depth. A piece of wood purportedly from the *Mayflower.* A three-set exhibit of one-third life-size mannequins, wearing the haute couture of French designers from 1946, in theatre-style settings. Eastern Orthodox religious icons. A collection of paintings from the American Classical Realist school. Art Nouveau glass by Gallé and Lalique. A lock of Queen Victoria's hair.

Blended into the mélange are bits and pieces from the lives of four people whose dreams came together to create the museum, and spurred scores of others to nurture it over the succeeding decades. The four were wildly different from each other, with widely divergent backgrounds, talents and temperaments. One was a dancer who had dreamed of becoming beautiful by creating beauty. Another was a socialite who dreamed of being accepted for who she wanted to be rather than who she was. The third was a rich man who dreamed of being a great man. And the fourth was a real-life queen who dreamed of being a fairy-tale queen.

Their supporting cast has been just as varied and equally as fascinating: A small-town lawyer conflicted by big-time plans and an overabundance of caution; a taciturn cabinet maker with peculiar ideas about art and a razor-sharp survival instinct; a flashy wheeler-dealer who loved Maryhill so much he almost destroyed it; a rich art patroness who led an unsuccessful bid to take over the museum, then returned as its financial angel, and a trio of women who turned Maryhill from a scandal-plagued curiosity to an internationally respected institution.

I first encountered the Maryhill Museum of Art on a drizzly morning in September 2014. My wife and I were driving home to California from British Columbia. A vague paragraph in an automobile club guide and a nondescript roadside marker morphed into a whim to enter a building that clearly had been misplaced.

But it was there on purpose, insisted the woman who took our admission money. She launched into a string of phrases explaining the museum's origin, which we were certain had no relationship to each other: "cars could drive right through;" "sleep on the roof;" "Dracula's castle;" "Stonehenge, down the road;" "most beautiful woman in the world."

A bit groggy from both the driving and the explanation, we spent a few hours savoring the museum's offerings, and began little by little to grasp the bits of information with which we had been gently assaulted. On our way out, we stopped for a debriefing with the admissions lady. As we talked, other museum workers joined us—it wasn't very busy—and Maryhill's story began to assume a clearer outline. Four people had created a repository of beauty and memory in the middle of nowhere. Their dream became a continuing reality through the determination and toil of generations of others who faced formidable—and sometimes bizarre—obstacles to keep the museum going.

"It would make a great movie," the admissions lady said. "Or," said my wife, "a book."

A note or two on names: In some cases, I've used the first names of people not from a sense of familiarity, but for clarity: There are, for example, three Dolphs, two Brooks and an entire range of Hills. Also, I've used the modern spelling for "Romania," except in titles or direct quotes. Call it author's privilege.

CHAPTER ONE
"This curious and interesting building"
NOVEMBER, 1926

The queen spent most of Election Day in Montana. Being a queen, she had little interest in elections. Being the queen of Romania, she had only a tourist's interest in Montana.

Marie Alexandra Victoria was on the 16th day of her historic tour of the United States and Canada. It was historic in the sense that very few queens had ever visited North America. In 1887, the queen of Hawaii had traversed the United States on her way to England, and in 1919, the queen of Belgium had toured the country. But those queens had nothing on this queen.

This queen was a war heroine, an author, a diplomat—and a well-paid spokeswoman for perfumes and cold cream. She was the granddaughter of both the late Queen Victoria of Great Britain and the late Czar Alexander II of Russia. She was related to royalty in nearly every country in Europe. And she was, in the vernacular of the time, "the bee's knees" when it came to her looks.

The passing years—she had celebrated her 51st birthday five days before—and the toll of having borne six children had added a few inches to what had once been an impossibly slender 16-inch waist. But her figure was still curvaceous, her honey-blonde hair still luxuriant, and her sky-blue eyes still simultaneously guileless and beguiling. Marie had an easy, genuine smile, and she exuded a heady mix of maternal warmth and school-girl coquettishness. She also didn't lack self-confidence.

"Yes, I know I am said to be the most beautiful woman in Europe," she told an admiring interviewer in a book published the year of her tour—and unblushingly subtitled "The Intimate Story of a Radiant Queen." "About that, of course, I cannot judge because I cannot know. But about the other queens, I know I am the most beautiful queen in Europe."

She was also, at least seemingly, coming to America at just the right time. With the "Great War" behind them, and awash in waves of consumerism and mass media, Americans in the 1920s were suckers for ballyhoo. Hundreds of magazines and some 2,000 daily newspapers printed millions of words of news, gossip, commentary, speculation and innuendo. They were supplemented by 20,000 movie theaters and 500 radio stations (compared to zero radio stations in 1919). And nothing stirred up the interests of the reading/watching/listening public more than celebrities.

When movie star Rodolfo Alfonso Raffaello Pierre Filibert Guglielmi di Valentina d'Antonguella—better known by his screen name of Rudolph Valentino—died two months before Marie's visit, an estimated 100,000 fans showed up at his funeral. The surrounding publicity helped his estate grow from "broke" to $600,000. More than two million people lined the streets of Manhattan in August for a ticker tape parade to honor Gertrude Ederle for being the first woman to swim the English Channel. And a real live queen was worth every bit as much of a fuss as a dead actor or a female athlete.

"The Democrats and the Republicans were trying to have a little election," observed Will Rogers, America's beloved cowboy sage, "and striving to get a little publicity on it, but lord, she (Marie) landed right in the middle of it, and everybody that did even remember the names of the candidates has forgotten them by now...don't ever say Americans ain't cuckoo over titles and royalty."

Then, as now, celebrity sold: As part of what had become a $3-billion-a-year advertising industry, baseball hero Babe Ruth pitched Old Gold cigarettes, Hollywood sex symbol Clara Bow modeled Chiniquy silk-embroidered hats, and Queen Marie put her royal imprimatur on Houbigant perfumes and Pond's skin creams.

"In every town I come to, I have been received like a conquering hero returning from war," she wrote her husband, King Ferdinand. "Everywhere the whole state has been put on its feet and I am absolutely overwhelmed."

But if 1920s America adored its celebrities, it also loved it when celebrities got involved in public rumpuses. And Marie's visit had been the subject of intense international scrutiny and controversy even before she left Europe. Many Romanian government officials were unhappy with her leaving the country, especially because her eldest son had recently abdicated as crown prince in order to marry a woman generally regarded as a gold-digging "commoner."

Many in the U.S. press were speculating that Marie was in the New World to do a little gold-digging of her own: She was here either to get Uncle Sam to provide hefty financial aid to her country, or to marry off her 17-year-old daughter Ileana to a rich American. Or both. There was even speculation that the real purpose of Marie's visit was to star in a movie.

There had been a lavish ticker-tape parade in New York City—during which the city's mayor had openly admired her bosom. There were uncomfortable meetings with President Calvin Coolidge in Washington D.C. There were two embarrassing stage performances of a fairy tale, written by the queen and produced by Marie's close friend, a faded American dancer/choreographer named Loie Fuller. And there had been ceaseless bickering and scheming among the sizeable retinue of politicians, society dowagers and other groupies anxious to get as close as possible to royalty.

As her luxurious private train—dubbed *The Royal Rumanian* by the press—rolled slowly through Montana, climbing the Rocky Mountains across the Idaho panhandle and into Eastern Washington state, Marie was relieved to be clear of the hordes of reporters and silk-hatted dignitaries, or at least most of them, and made it into the countryside she had come to see.

She found it lovely. "It much resembles certain parts of Roumania and Transylvania," she noted in her journal. She even enjoyed the short whistle-stop ceremonies at towns along the route. At Helena, she stood on the train's rear platform and exchanged pleasantries with a crowd of hundreds. The crowd included the state's governor, who had taken an 11-hour train ride to be there in time to greet the queen. At Missoula, she cheerfully listened to the University of Montana student band gamely struggle through the Romanian national anthem.

Several times the train stopped so the royal party could gaze at herds of bison or flocks of sheep. "If I had not the duty to be queen," Marie wistfully declared as she watched one flock, "I would want to be there. I would want to be a shepherd or a cowgirl. I look over this rugged West of yours and understand why this country is a land of freedom."

Part of the day was spent with youngest daughter Ileana and second son Nicky, who were accompanying her on the tour. They chatted about their adventures in North Dakota the day before. There had been an impromptu rodeo at Medora, and Ileana's favorite American expression—which she repeated somewhat annoyingly—had become "ride 'em cowboy." Marie periodically admired a small scar on one of her fingers. It marked where her royal blood had been mingled with a Lakota chief at a ceremony in Mandan. That made her an official sister of the tribe, with the entirely appropriate name "She Who Was Waited For."

But the queen also spent part of the day away from the others on the train. She washed her hair, dictated to the secretary/ghostwriter who was helping her write articles about her trip for an American newspaper syndicate, and spent some time alone with her thoughts.

It was cold and rainy, and the weather didn't help to lighten her mood, or distract her from brooding about several issues. The day marked the 10th anniversary of the death of her youngest son. Mircea had been just four years old when he contracted typhoid fever. He died after 10 days of agony, while Marie wept helplessly by his bedside. Time, other family crises, and the convulsions and revulsions of a world war had dulled the sharp edges of her pain, but spending the anniversary away from home jabbed at her.

There were also the constant—and confusing—reports from home that her husband was seriously ill. Despite persistent rumors in the papers that Marie would cut her trip short to rush home to his deathbed, the king had assured his wife in a telegram a few days before that he was feeling fine. "I am utterly pleased at your success," he added.

However reassured Marie was about her husband's health, there was an event looming on the royal itinerary the next day that caused her no small concern. It was the single official reason she had traveled 5,000 miles. In a piece written before she left Europe, entitled "Why I Am Coming to America," Marie said she hoped *"to help found a sort of 'Prix de Rome' for artists of the world to compete at home for the privilege of gaining the right to go there and exhibit their art and participate as nationals in the achievement of each of the nations to whom rooms have been consecrated and accepted."*

Translated into something closer to reality, the Queen of Romania was here to dedicate an art museum, as a favor for a man whom she had only met a couple of times and who didn't really want her there, at least not yet. His name was Samuel Hill.

Depending on whom you asked, 69-year-old Sam Hill was either a visionary or crazier than an outhouse rat. Southern-born, Northern-raised and Harvard-educated, Sam wasn't the source of the popular phrase "who/what/when/where/why/how-the-Sam Hill?" The expression predated him by decades. But it was often used when people talked *about* him—and people often talked about Sam Hill.

Physically, Sam Hill tended to dominate his environs. He was tall, and his broad shoulders, large head and thick hair made him seem even taller. In his younger years, he was considered one of the most handsome men in Minneapolis. Now, in his seniority, a woman traveling with Marie described him as "a perfect giant of a man, with his shaggy white head and his ruddy kindly face, reminding me more of a childhood dream of Santa Claus than anyone I had ever seen (with) his rosy face and shaggy white eyebrows. He looked like a hero who had stepped out of a book of legends, his great broad shoulders and kindly smile vivified and exalted with his delight."

A lawyer, railroad executive, utility company owner, world traveler and transportation pioneer, Sam had made and spent fortunes. He had been decorated by the leaders of four nations for his contributions to promoting peace, building roads and supporting humanitarian causes. He was a master of the grand gesture, such as when he hired a special train and brought 88 public officials to his estate to see a road-building demonstration. Even his occasional tantrums were outsized, once angrily kicking his hat back and forth across the lobby of a posh hotel for 15 minutes because his room wasn't ready.

Sam had a penchant for quixotic projects. These included a "peace arch" that straddled the U.S.-Canada border, a full-size replica of the ancient British monument Stonehenge on the banks of the Columbia River, and a 5,300-acre, almost entirely unpopulated, agrarian community on the Washington-Oregon border, which he called Maryhill—after his daughter, wife and mother-in-law. All of them were named Mary Hill.

Part of Sam's Maryhill dream was an immense three-story block of concrete, situated on a ledge a few hundred feet above the Columbia on his vast acreage. The locals jokingly referred to it as "Sam Hill's Folly." Once, he had planned it as a home for his mentally ill daughter, a gathering place for his friends, and a refuge for himself. But World War I, financial reverses, and other distractions meant the mansion had never been finished, let alone lived in. Now, at the urging of Loie Fuller—the very same ex-dancer who was Marie's friend and one of the trip's top sources of controversy—the plan was to turn it into a center for the world's artists, an oasis of beauty, a beacon of world peace. Or something like that.

"Years ago, I invited Queen Marie to come and open the museum," Sam wrote to a friend, two weeks before the queen's train was to arrive at Maryhill. "I tried to get her to put it off until 1927. She preferred coming now." And she was bringing 21 crates of art, artifacts and memorabilia for the museum.

There were very good reasons for Sam wanting to delay the royal arrival. For one thing, most of his money was tied up in land that no one wanted and investments that were mostly tenuous. He was writing, he explained with some hyperbole, from a tent in which he was living near the town of Nauvoo, Alabama, about 60 miles northwest of Birmingham. He was "working 19 hours a day," trying to make a go of a coal mine in which he had invested heavily. "I mean to get back on my feet again," he assured his friend.

Just before Marie's ship arrived in America, Sam had gone to New York to help establish her itinerary, and then headed west to deal with some formidable logistical problems before the queen's visit. One of them was the problem of access to the structure Marie was coming to dedicate. A long-delayed road on the Washington side of the river linking Maryhill to the urban areas to the west was nowhere near complete. The Oregon side boasted a splendid highway all the way to Portland. Sam had been a key figure in its construction. But the ferry services—the biggest of which Sam owned—connecting the Oregon highway to Maryhill were at the mercy of the often-brutal weather in the river gorge. And while there was a railroad bridge crossing the river, train service was limited and the local station pitifully inadequate for large groups.

The most vexing problem for Sam with Marie coming now to dedicate the museum, however, was this: There was no museum.

Passing through the tiny timber town of Sandpoint, Idaho, the *Royal*

Rumanian picked up an unexpected passenger. Prodded by his buddies, Lester Brown had climbed onto the balcony of the train's observation car as it crawled through the depot. It was bold move for a 10-year-old, but Lester's bravado turned to terror when the train suddenly picked up speed. Lester quickly found himself in the presence of royalty—and quite possibly wondering if Romanian custom dictated beheadings for interlopers.

"Like a poor little bird caught in a room without finding the window to fly out again, he was in a terrible state of fright and upset and burst into tears," Marie recalled in her journal. "I wonder what Mother will think," the boy wailed.

The queen reacted with maternal instinct and experience: She quieted the youthful intruder with candy. Prince Nicholas gave him a sweater to wear, Princess Ileana engaged him in a game of beanbag, and little Lester ended up dining on trout and duck with the royals. Marie sent a telegram to his mom, assuring her "he will be returned to you at the earliest possible moment and be taken care of until he is put in your hands by a representative of mine. We are happy to have him with us."

"The earliest possible moment" turned out to be 75 miles away, in Spokane, Washington, where Lester was put on a train for home, carrying an autographed copy of a fairytale book written by Marie. "I wasn't scared, only I kept thinking what Mama would say," the boy told reporters. And even at 10, Lester wasn't immune to the queen's charms: "She was the finest lady I ever saw,' he solemnly said.

Spokane gave the royals a tumultuous welcome. The local newspaper, the *Spokesman-Review,* estimated as many as 50,000 people turned out to watch Marie's entourage roll down the city's main street from the railroad station. That was an impressive number considering the entire town numbered just a bit more than 100,000 and it was a pretty cold night. American and Romanian flags were strung across the thoroughfares, a military band played and National Guard troops and police held back the cheering throngs.

The newspaper also gave Marie high marks for her queenliness. She "wore everything a queen should wear—pearls, ropes of them, diamonds and ermine. Her blonde hair is bobbed, but it was confined in a Juliette cap that framed her face tightly and accentuated the beauty of her heavy-browed deep blue eyes. Caps from now on will be the rage."

At the city's finest hostelry, the Davenport Hotel, Marie and her children were escorted to a makeshift throne in a large reception hall, and hundreds of lucky citizens were permitted to march past and have a look at them. Members of the Nez Perce and Coeur d' Alene tribes, in ceremonial dress, danced, presented gifts of apples and trout, and adopted Ileana ("Red Bird") and Nicky ("White Whirlwind").

"Suddenly, old Sam Hill was in our midst," Marie later recalled in her journal. "The 'White Lion' as I call him, a quaint old fellow with an over-big head and a tower of white hair. Exactly where he had come from, and how, I was not able to grasp; but there he was in a tremendous sombrero (cowboy hat), with his old-world, rather disconcerting courtesy and over-low voice…". After gazing rapturously at the queen, Sam knelt and kissed her hand.

"No one with an understanding heart or a sense of drama could witness that scene entirely unmoved," wrote an onlooker. "… Here was Don Quixote at the feet of Dulcinea."

Where Sam had suddenly come from was a private rail car that was being attached to the *Royal Rumanian* during the ceremonies. He wasn't alone. With him were two women familiar to the queen.

The first would have stood out in almost any crowd. Alma Spreckels was six feet tall, without heels, at a time when the average height of an American male was 5'9". At 45, her youthful voluptuousness had given way to a more matronly appeal, but her visage still boasted clear blue eyes and a creamy complexion. She was expensively, if not extravagantly, dressed. Her physical appearance alone commanded attention.

Her personality was equally outsized. "Big Alma" spoke to be heard, often in the next room. Her favorite drink was martinis, by the pitcher. She loved to swim in the nude, sometimes with an audience. When she went shopping for furniture, in France, she told reporters "I'm going to find me a bed that kings have made love in." Her San Francisco mansion—the most palatial in the city—reportedly had bridge tables in some of its 27 bathrooms, just in case a foursome of guests got two urges at the same time. She was routinely profane, and often witty. When the popular gossip columnist Elsa Maxwell once cattily asked her how old she was, Alma snapped back, "old enough to remember when there was no Elsa Maxwell."

She was also very, very rich. The week before Marie arrived in America, the California Inheritance Tax Office estimated with bureaucratic precision that Alma and her children were heirs to a $14,944,495 estate left by her late husband, sugar baron Adolph B. Spreckels. That translated to roughly $205 million in 2017 dollars, making Alma one of the wealthiest women in the country.

Just now, in the presence of the queen, Alma was also more than a little annoyed. She had met Marie seven years before. The queen appreciated the relief work Alma had done on behalf of Romania during the war, and had reciprocated by promising art pieces for San Francisco's Palace of the Legion of Honor Museum, which Alma had founded with her late husband. When Marie's U.S. trip had been announced, Alma's old friend Sam Hill had asked her to serve as the queen's official hostess for the West Coast leg of the tour.

But Alma had been snubbed, first by railroad officials who refused to allow her to hook up her own private car to the queen's train, and then by Portland and Seattle society matrons who had no intention of allowing a San Francisco interloper to dictate who got to sit closest to the queen in *their* cities. If Alma smiled while greeting the queen in the Davenport Hotel ballroom, it was almost certainly through clenched teeth.

The other woman with Sam Hill was Alma's close friend—and physical and emotional antithesis. Loie Fuller was barely 5 feet tall, overweight, and most decidedly unfeminine. As a young actress, she often played a boy. As she matured and became known for her dancing rather than her acting, she was "not a sylph, but built like a column—round and firm and compact." Even at the height of her fame, she usually dressed as if she had been caught in a thrift store explosion. Now, as she approached the age of 65, Loie was in the words of an interviewer "a fat, vivacious, charming lady she looks like a gypsy, with kindly blue eyes and energetic, nervous hands—a Bedouin in a sandy-colored veil and tortoise shell goggles."

Her life overflowed with exclamation points. She was wildly ambitious, but rarely finished one project before dashing off to another. She was bubbly, naïve and overwhelmingly charming, so much so that she made many people nervous. But her ditzy demeanor belied a scientific bent that had led her to innovations in stage lighting, costuming and choreography. She was one of the first women to produce a motion picture. And despite her unimpressive physical appearance, her dancing was the inspiration for sculpture, paintings and posters by masters that included Auguste Rodin and Henri de Toulouse-Lautrec.

Through a set of absurdly unlikely circumstances, Loie had become an overnight sensation at the fabled Folies Bergère in Paris. Draped in hundreds of yards of gauzy material and using her own lighting system, Loie performed night after night to sold-out houses and rave reviews. Not only was she the most famous American woman in France and most of the rest of Europe, she was making unheard-of money.

But money and Loie never stayed in the same room long, unless it was in someone else's pocket. She thus became adept at befriending those with deep pockets. As her career faded, she often coaxed funds from wealthy folks she had befriended—such as Queen Marie, Sam Hill and Alma Spreckels.

It was Loie who had pushed Sam into turning his unfinished mansion into an art museum, and who cajoled Marie into coming to dedicate it. But Romanian officials viewed her influence on the queen with great suspicion, America's upper crust viewed her status as a washed-up performer with disdain, and most of the public had only a vague memory that she had once been famous. Now, powerless, ill and embarrassed, Loie remained in the background as Sam performed his knightly gallantries at the hotel.

Once the reception had concluded, Marie was led to the hotel's somehow-appropriately named Marie Antoinette Room, where she gave a brief live radio address that was broadcast simultaneously over stations in Spokane, Portland and Seattle. Then she was taken to the local newspaper offices, where editors implored her to read election results from the balcony to the throngs waiting below.

"I however gently declined giving Spokane that thrill," Marie wrote in her journal. "Strange people! Like big children, disconcerting indeed."

Roughly 250 miles southwest of the Davenport, people in a decidedly more rustic hotel were preparing for the queen. The Meadowlark Inn had been built by Sam as part of the "town" he had also built. Neither actually functioned as an inn or a town.

The nearest real community, which was a mile down the hill on the river, had in essence been taken over by Sam when his own town failed to attract anyone to live in it. The village, which had been known as Columbus but was now known as Maryhill, was described by a frequent visitor as "mostly sand and boulders, covered with sagebrush, inhabited by lizards, with an occasional rattlesnake." There was a railroad station that was basically a shed, a few residences, a schoolhouse, a church, a gas station, a small building that served as a post office, and an abandoned barn. The unsightly barn had been burned down in an effort to remove it from the queen's view. Now she could view the charred remains of an abandoned barn instead.

The inn was a drab two-story wooden building with a columned porch, lit by kerosene lamps and warmed by wood stoves. Originally dubbed the St. James, the inn had been moved by Sam from its original site a few hundred feet away to make way for a war memorial he was building—in the shape of a full-scale concrete model of Stonehenge. The Meadowlark had been closed to the public for two years, and the sign above the door was so worn, the old "St. James" name could be seen. "It resembles," one reporter wrote, "some country hotel of a generation ago."

Undaunted—or resigned to the lack of another choice—an unlikely team of locals and society matrons from Portland's upper crust had done their best to gussy up the inn to receive the royal party. Then, while Marie's train made its way from Spokane, they stayed up most of the night playing cards and listening to election returns on the radio.

It had been a busy two weeks since Sam had telegrammed friends and officials in the area asking them to get things ready for the queen. In the town of Goldendale, which was about 13 miles from Maryhill and the only nearby community of any size, a committee was formed to provide transportation for the royal party of about 40 from the train station to the inn, and then to the mansion/museum. A hotel owner was given the honor of driving the queen, mainly because he had the newest car in town. The prince and princess would ride in the local undertaker's car.

Committees were also established to handle traffic control and parking, find U.S. and Romanian flags, and provide enough trucks to transport local school kids, who were being let out of class for the day, to the dedication ceremony. Even the railroad rails had been polished for two miles in each direction from the Maryhill station.

Three miles from the Meadowlark, Sam's unfinished edifice was also a beehive of activity, as local volunteers and hired workmen frenetically labored at putting lipstick on a three-story pig. Newspaper reporters who wheedled or bribed their way into the mansion in the week before the royal arrival were variously stunned and appalled at what they saw. Exterior walls were cracked, and interior walls had never been finished. Iron rods stuck out of the floor. Windows were heavily barred and admitted little light. The only thing that could be construed as art was a single piece of carved marble.

A reporter for the *Oregon Journal* wrote that a workman told him "six to nine inches of dirt and dust had accumulated, and the floor had become the burial ground of many rats. He need not have told me the latter, for my nose was in perfect working order that day."

"It has been guarded against vandalism," United Press reported, "but the greatest vandal of all, Father Time, has exacted his toll, until today the great concrete structure is hardly a fit place in which to entertain a queen."

But with the dirt and rodent carcasses removed, a team of eight Goldendale women worked heroically. They draped the interior with the official Romanian colors of red, yellow and blue. Pine boughs, and chrysanthemums imported from Portland florists, were used to brighten, and obscure, the unfinished columns. A speakers' platform, complete with robed throne, was installed. A huge floral wreath that contained intertwined U.S. and Romanian flags was placed opposite the stage. Someone even cadged a worn red carpet from a Portland hotel, which would be used at the railroad station, then rushed ahead of the queen to the Meadowlark Inn and on to the mansion.

"The last frontier, a bit rough in its infancy, combed its hair and filed its nails for a spiffy occasion, the like of which has never been seen before," crowed a local newspaper.Then everyone held their breath to see if all the grooming was fit for a queen.

On the train, Marie awoke to strange scenery and an unusual breakfast. The breakfast, concocted by a railroad chef at the request of Sam, consisted of a round piece of toast topped with white chicken meat cooked in cream and butter. On top of that was another piece of toast, on which was perched a "dropped" egg wrapped in bacon, and then covered with a cream sauce. The chef called it "Breakfast a la Imperial." The queen called it delicious, gave him a $10 tip and offered him a job in Romania. He took the $10.

The scenery, Marie noted in her journal, was "a curious formation of hill and rock, with the magnificent Columbia river flowing beneath. At places, stretches of sand-like patches of desert. Everything was buff-coloured and brown, with violet-inky shadows, impressive and rather grim."

First off the train at the Maryhill station was the queen's fat black spaniel, Crag, accompanied by his constant attendant, a Romanian soldier. Then came Sam, greeted by a coterie of reporters. Much of the press was giddy at the prospect of what promised to be a public relations disaster when the queen got a look at "Sam Hill's Folly."

"The museum has been the butt of considerable jokes during the trip," a United Press correspondent reported. "Since the train left New York, no one has been able to find out just what the Maryhill Museum was. Her Majesty herself was ignorant of its plan and state of completion, and her attaches shrugged their shoulders when questioned."

Before anyone could ask a question, Sam launched into parallel-but-unrelated monologues on the effects of frost on railroad ties, and how Maryhill would someday be a thriving agricultural community.

Undeterred, reporters pointedly asked him whether he truly intended to finish the mansion/museum. Sam somewhat petulantly demurred. "That depends solely upon what cooperation I get from the people of the Northwest. My building will be dedicated today to the purpose for which I built it, I want to finish it—to fulfill all the plans I made for it. But I shouldn't be expected to build roads all through this part of Oregon and Washington to get to it, should I? Why should I go ahead if the people won't make the museum accessible through highways to this section? Is it quite fair? Isn't it time I was being shown a little cooperation?"

Sam's speech over, the royals were driven up the hill to the Meadowlark for a brief reception with about 20 eminent locals and Portlandians. Conspicuous by their absence were Loie and Alma, who stayed on the train. The former was sick, and afraid her presence at the dedication would embarrass Marie. The latter was still in a snit about her recent social snubs.

At the inn, Marie was introduced to Portland Mayor George Baker, whom

Marie thought also governed all the way to Maryhill. After gently explaining Portland was a hundred miles away, Baker added that Portland had great love for Sam, who was standing nearby, "and we would like to love you too if you will let us." "I'll let you," Marie replied with a smile.

Then it was on to the mansion—and directly into it. The building had been constructed so that cars could drive into one end, drop off passengers in the center of the great hall, and drive out the other end to the underground garage.

Outside, a crowd estimated at 4,000 people by the local newspaper (but probably closer to 2,000) had gathered in crisp temperatures under a brilliantly clear sky. Hundreds of cars were parked around the grounds, causing Klickitat County's first traffic jam. Overhead, two planes dipped and swooped over the proceedings, taking movies and photographs. Later, they would rush the film back to Seattle and Portland, where it was shown in movie theaters that night.

Inside, Marie was initially unnerved by what she later wrote were "dark concrete walls, nothing finished, something grim and utterly undecorated about it, a lonely, sad, gray place." But as she listened to a handful of speeches by Sam and various officials, she was stirred by the promise behind the reality.

"As I stand here today in this curious and interesting building, I would like to explain why I came," she extemporaneously said to the crowd of about 50 inside, and the throng outside listening on a loudspeaker system. "There are great dreamers in this world, and there are great workers in this world. When a dreamer is also a worker, he is working for today and tomorrow as well. For he is building for those who come after us. Samuel Hill is my friend. He is not only a dreamer, but he is a worker. Samuel Hill once gave me his hand and said if there was anything on earth I needed I had only to ask so when Samuel Hill asked me to come overseas to this house built in the wilderness, I came with love and understanding. Samuel Hill knows why I came, and I am not going to give any other explanation. Sometimes the things dreamers do seem incomprehensible to others, and the world wonders why dreamers do not see the way others do."

Marie then turned defiantly to the controversy surrounding her friendship with Loie. "Some have wondered at the friendship of a queen for a woman some would call lowly. That woman is Loie Fuller. Her name has often been slighted. That woman stood by me when my back was to the wall She went all over America getting aid for my people. This has almost been forgotten by the rest of you, but I can no longer be silent. In this democracy, there should be no gap between the high and the lowly."

At the end of her remarks, she turned to Sam and extended her hand. "Mr. Hill, I would very much like to shake your hand." Tears in his eyes, Sam bowed his head and kissed her hand, and then grasped it in both hands.

The press, most of whom had been mirthful at the prospect of Marie dedicating an unfinished, empty building, reacted with surprised respect. The Portland *Oregonian* noted the "audience visibly gasped as they sensed the fact that the woman was baring her own heart and defying the world to speak ill of a friend who had shown devotion in time of need." The Associated Press called the speech "an impassioned defense of her mission to this country and of her friendship for an old man and woman invalid who made her visit possible." In the *New York Times*, the well-known journalist Harold Denney noted "it is doubtful if any American public official could have the wit and courage to seize a disaster as she did and turn it into a triumph."

Outside, the crowd gave Marie "three rousing American cheers," and a fourth when she released carrier pigeons to 10 western cities bearing messages from the queen. The bird bound for San Francisco, "Princess Drifted Snow," staggered into Portland the next day with a gunshot wound. But a replacement was pressed into service, and the pigeon princess eventually recovered.

Back on the train, Loie wept when told of the queen's remarks. "I never dreamed she would do anything like that," she sobbed. "I never dreamed it." Marie was also moved. "That was the most touching experience I ever had except where there was suffering," she said to no one in particular as she boarded the train.

Never one to miss a minute in the spotlight, and presumably out of earshot of Sam and Marie, Loie then concocted a tale of how she had convinced not only Sam, but a group of the region's prominent leaders, to build the museum as the seed for a new Athens-on-the-Columbia. "On that day the museum was born, and the roadway movement was started and a movement for a (motor vehicle) bridge across the Columbia received birth," she claimed. "Since that day, activities have been unceasing. It (the planned museum) is the only one of its kind in the world. Let it grow!"

On the way across the river to Oregon, the royal train stopped on the railroad bridge so the occupants could eat lunch while gazing at the scenic waterfalls and rapids below Sam's estate. Queen Marie would never again see the museum she had crossed an ocean and a continent to christen.

"Last night, Maryhill was dark," the *Oregonian* said the next day. "The mansion stands again a grim sentinel high above the Columbia, above all the inland empire. What the future holds in store for Maryhill depends on many things. But that is another story."

NOTES FOR CHAPTER 1

"Yes, I know" Mabel Potter Daggett, *Marie of Roumania: The Intimate Story of the most Radiant Queen,* 1926, p. 48.

When movie star While there are dozens of books about 1920s America, two of the most engaging are Lucy Moore's *Anything Goes: A Biography of the 1920s* (2010), and Frederick Lewis Allen's *Only Yesterday: An Informal History of the 1920s.* (1931). A handy statistical source for the era is *Who We Were in the 1920s*, by Grey House Publishing (2014).

"The Democrats and" *Albuquerque (NM) Journal*, Oct. 31, 1926, p. 13.

"In every town" Queen Marie, *America Seen by a Queen* (1999), p. 170.

Several times the train *New Castle (Pa.) News*, Nov. 2, 1926, p. 5.

However reassured Marie *Minneapolis Tribune,* Oct. 15, 1926, p. 1.

Physically, Sam Hill Constance Lily Morris, *On Tour with Queen Marie,* 1927, p. 123.

"Years ago, I" Sam Hill to Annie Whelan Ehrens, Oct. 19, 1926, Maryhill Museum of Art archives (MMA)

"Like a poor" Queen Marie, op cit., p. 93.

"The earliest possible" *Ogden (UT) Standard-Examiner,* Nov. 3, 1926, p. 7.

The newspaper also *Spokane Spokesman-Review*, Nov. 3, 1926, p. 1

"Suddenly, old Sam" Queen Marie, op. cit., p. 94.

"No one with" Morris, op. cit., p. 123.

Her personality was Bernice Scharlach, *Big Alma: San Francisco's Alma Spreckels.* (revised ed., 2016), p. 75.

The other woman *St. Paul (MN) Globe*, Oct. 4 1886, p. 2; *San Francisco Chronicle*, Nov. 13, 1896, p. 14; *San Francisco Call*, Aug. 29, 1925, p. 4.

"I however gently" Queen Marie, op. cit., p. 94.

The nearest real community Henry L. Gray, *Frontier Times*, July 1967, pp. 36-38.

The inn was a drab Portland *Oregonian*, Nov. 4, 1926, p. 11.

A reporter for *Oregon Daily Journal*, Oct. 31, 1926, p. 1.

"It has been" *Oakland (CA) Tribune*, Oct. 28, 1926, p. 3.

"The last frontier" *Oregon Daily Journal,* Nov. 4, 1926, p. 1.

On the train *Oregon Daily Journal*, Feb. 6, 1955, p. 8.

The scenery, Marie Queen Marie, op. cit., p. 95.

"The museum has" *Santa Ana (CA) Daily Register*, Nov. 3, 1926, p. 4.

Undeterred, reporters pointedly Portland *Oregonian*, Nov. 4, 1926, p. 1.

At the inn Ibid.

"As I stand" Queen Marie spoke without a written text at the dedication. This version of her remarks, which are the most detailed and the most often quoted, is from the *New York Times*, Nov, 4, 1926, p. 1.

The press, most Portland *Oregonian*, Nov. 4, 1926, p. 1; *Los Angeles Times*, Nov. 4, 1926, p. 1; *New York Times*, Nov. 4, 1926, p. 1.

Back on the train Portland *Oregonian*, Nov. 4, 1926, p. 11

Never one to miss *New York Times*, Nov. 4, 1926, p. 8.

"Last night, Maryhill" Portland *Oregonian*, Nov. 4, 1926, p. 1.

CHAPTER TWO

"A dancer of pictures"

Loie's Story

MARCH, 1902

The world's most famous dancer was broke. This in itself was not a particularly unusual situation for Loie Fuller: She routinely careened from lucrative contracts to IOUs. But this time she was broke in Romania. Loie knew only one person in the entire country she might turn to for help, and she had known that person for only a few days.

Fortunately, that person was the crown princess. Since timidity was never one of Loie Fuller's character defects, she ambled off to the palace, at nine in the morning, to ask Marie Alexandra Victoria about getting a check cashed.

The princess and the dancer had first met the day after Loie gave a bravura performance at Bucharest's Grand Opera House. In the royal box, Marie was mesmerized. "Your dances are a dream come true," she wrote in a note delivered to Loie in her dressing room after the performance. "I never dreamed I would see my visions of beauty realized here upon earth." Marie also asked if Loie would give a private performance at the palace. The dancer happily accepted.

"When I arrived at the palace, I was taken up a great staircase and then introduced into a little room," Loie wrote in her autobiography. "…In a most delightfully arranged room I saw a young woman, tall, slender and extremely pretty I actually forgot where I was, and I fancied myself in the presence of a legendary princess in a fairy-tale chamber."

The princess was 26, and already the mother of four. Her nine-year marriage had most decidedly not been the stuff of fairy tales. Born in England and raised on Malta and in Germany, Marie seemed to Loie to be as out of place in the Romanian court as "a lily planted in a field of wild poppies."

Still, Marie was a gracious host. The two women chatted for more than an hour about art, dance, depression, homesickness and painting chairs. In short, they both wrote later, they took an instant and intimate liking to each other. That night, Loie performed before the royal family for four hours, on an improvised stage set up in the palace's dining hall. When she was done, Marie presented Loie with a large photograph of herself. She inscribed it "in memory of an evening during which you filled my heart with joy."

But the royal command performance was not a paying gig. When promised funds from a promoter failed to arrive, Loie couldn't pay for moving her crew of 12 and her several thousand pounds of equipment and baggage to a scheduled performance in Rome. So, she went back to the palace.

Marie was only too happy to help. "She rang a bell and gave an order to let M. X______ know immediately that Miss Fuller would come to see him with a card from her," Loie recalled, "and that M. X______ would kindly do everything in his power to assist Miss Fuller."

Loie got the money with no problem. But the train arrived late in Rome, the baggage was misplaced, and a crowd of 3,000 left without seeing a performance. "That certainly was hard luck," Loie later philosophized. Still, she noted, if she hadn't had to borrow the money from Marie in the first place, "I should not have discovered what an admirable woman she is." Before the two parted, Marie pledged to visit Loie at the dancer's studio if she ever got to Paris. Eleven years later, the princess kept her promise.

For someone so careless with money, Marie Louise Fuller could be exceedingly economical with facts about her own life. During her career, for example, she gave at least nine different answers when asked about her birth date, ranging from the mid-1860s to the mid-1870s.

The correct answer was Jan. 15, 1862. It was bitterly cold in Fullersburg, Illinois that morning, so cold that the bed Loie was born in was moved to the floor of her grandfather's tavern so the birth could take place close to an enormous stove. "I am positive of all these details," she recalled with tongue in cheek, "for I caught cold at the very moment of my birth, which I have never got rid of."

Both of Loie's parents could trace their families back to the Revolutionary War. Her father, Reuben Fuller, came west as a small boy in the 1830s from upstate New York. The Fuller family reached a spot about 16 miles southwest of the small-but-growing-fast town known as Chicago, bought some land from the federal government, and started a farm.

The farm eventually became a village, populated mainly by Fullers. In 1850, Reuben married Delilah Eaton. Soon thereafter, he joined tens of thousands of other young men and left for the California goldfields. Two years later, Reuben was back, with enough money to buy a large farm and indulge his passion for breeding and training horses for harness racing. His other passions were music and dancing. He was good enough at the former to be in constant demand as a fiddler at local events, and at the latter to eventually open a dancing academy.

But the Fullers fell on hard times when a much-anticipated railroad line bypassed Fullersburg. When Loie was two, the family moved to Chicago. During the rest of her youth, the Fullers would move to two small Illinois towns, then back to Chicago. Her father tried his hand at occupations ranging from horse trader to dancing instructor to boarding house owner, usually with financially mixed results.

Loie, meanwhile, was apparently born not only with a cold, but also with a fever for performing. At 2½, she surprised her parents by climbing onto a Sunday school platform, solemnly reciting "Mary Had a Little Lamb," then bouncing down the steps on her bottom. At 13, she was giving temperance lectures, cleverly enlisting one of the local drunks to stand on stage with her as a compelling prop. And at 16, she was off on a months-long tour of the Midwest with a theatrical company, playing bit parts in melodramas and comedies.

Although her family nickname had been "Louie," she referred to herself as the more feminine-sounding "Loie." It didn't always help: One of her first mentions in the press noted that "among the members of the cast are *Mr.* Loie Fuller." Actually, given that she wasn't particularly feminine anyway, Loie often appeared as a boy. "She looks like a boy, as few women do in breeches," one reviewer noted, "and she acts like one, which is still less frequently accomplished."

Jumping between genders added to Loie's stage versatility, which was vital in 19th-century show business. "Variety shows," which eventually came to be known as "vaudeville," were a staple of every city's entertainment. Chicago had 20 vaudeville theaters by 1880. The shows ran almost around the clock. And for 25 cents (about $5 in 2017 dollars) a person could see as many as 20 widely varied acts.

So it wasn't unusual for Loie to find herself listed on the December 1880 bill at Chicago's Olympic Theater as "the dashing young artist and singer," alongside "Miss Ida Siddons, the celebrated skipping-rope dancer," and "Billy Arnold, the Prince of Ethiopians and unrivaled tambourinist." The trouble with variety shows, from a performer's perspective, was that it was extremely hard to stand out. The trick to achieving stardom, and big money, was in finding a special act that was both excellent and hard to duplicate. The second-best thing was to find steady work. Loie found the latter, for the first time in her career, with an American hero.

By the autumn of 1881, William Frederick "Buffalo Bill" Cody was in the midst of trading in his very real hunting/scouting/Indian-fighting past for a future full of greasepaint, nostalgia and romantic illusion. He was still two years from establishing the fabled Wild West show that would make him, after Mark Twain, the most famous American in the world by the start of the 20th century. In the meantime, he was starring on the stage. Cody knew his limitations. "I'm a star," he often said. "All actors can become stars, but not all stars can become actors." To shore up his onstage deficiencies, and feed the audience's hunger for variety, Cody threw a bit of everything into his presentations.

On Sept. 5, 1881, Cody began a one-week run at Chicago's Olympic Theater, the very same place Loie had appeared 10 months before, with the rope dancer and the tambourine virtuoso. Cody's show included a rifle-shooting exhibition by Buffalo Bill himself; songs and dances by "four chiefs of the Winnebago tribe," and the antics of a donkey named Jerry. There was also a "soul-stirring, blood-curdling" drama called "The Prairie Waif." In the role of the banjo-strumming waif was Loie Fuller. She apparently got the job when the actress originally cast in the part was fired or quit.

The show played to standing-room-only crowds. Critics generally praised it for being a kinder, gentler version of the usual melodrama. One reviewer noted it was "shorn of much of the blood and thunder that characterized Cody's former plays." Loie's performances were generally described as "adequate" and "pleasant." They were good enough to get her signed on as a permanent cast member. By the time the troupe reached Brooklyn, Loie was being billed above Jerry the donkey. This was fine with the rest of the cast, because Jerry bit, butted and kicked, while Loie was cheery and well-liked.

But Loie's luck never lasted. While performing with Cody's show in New York, she contracted a mild case of smallpox. By the time she was fully recovered, Cody was on his way to establishing his circus-like outdoor Wild West extravaganza. Loie was looking for a job.

For the next eight years, Loie's life was on a treadmill: She toiled diligently yet never seemed to get far. After regaining her health, she hooked up with a singing group, touring mostly in second-tier cities in the Midwest. That was followed by a series of jobs with various traveling theater companies. Loie was often the best thing about a bad play. In a typical review, a Chicago critic called her "a bright, pleasing little soubrette, but her acting is the only notable feature of the performance." She also got good marks for her versatility: "There is a good deal of neatness in the dancing and sweetness in the singing of Miss Loie Fuller."

In 1886, after good reviews in Boston, Loie made it back to New York City, then as now the heart of the American theater. In a six-week run in a farce called *Humbug*, she was good enough to attract the attention of a popular comic actor and producer named Nat Goodwin. A master of burlesque—parodying a serious work—Goodwin cast Loie in the title role of a play called *Little Jack Sheppard*. The play was based on the life of a notorious 18th-century English thief who had a knack for prison breaks. With her hair cut short and darkened, Loie looked like either a very pretty young boy or sort-of cute young girl.

The play proved popular, running for three months. Loie's reviews were mixed. One critic wrote her performance was "a neat and spirited presentation," while another found it "painfully coarse and crude." But Goodwin liked her, enough to cast her in two more plays as well as a road tour of *Little Jack*.

It was work at a breakneck pace, in more ways than one. At one point in February 1887, the company performed a play in Boston in the afternoon, then caught a train to put on a different play in New York that night. In another performance, Loie—for an extra $10—agreed to roll down the steps of a high stage pyramid each night. She was making a living, but she wasn't content to be a mid-level actress in forgettable plays; she wanted to be a star. So she took two bold steps, both of which proved to be disastrous: She became her own producer, and she got married.

The second mistake came about because of the first. In late 1888, Loie went to see a man named William B. Hayes about getting a loan for a theatrical production she wanted to stage, and perform first, for reasons unclear, on the island of Jamaica. Hayes, who like to tell people—falsely—he was the nephew of former President Rutherford B. Hayes, was in his fifties. He was fat, and luxuriously mustached. He was a dapper dresser, a railroad lawyer, a New York stockbroker, and a Florida real estate speculator.

He was also smitten with Loie Fuller. Loie, who at 27 was pretty, if plump, was not one to spurn the attentions of people with money. Hayes gave her the financial backing for her play. As a sort of collateral, she gave Hayes a set of photographsin which she was wearing nothing but very tight tights. On one of the photos was written the saucy inscription "Pardon monsieur. I am not dressed."

Before she left for Jamaica, Hayes proposed. Of course there was the little obstacle posed by the fact that he was already married. But, he promised Loie, he would be divorced by the time she got back. From Jamaica, Loie wrote Hayes that while waiting for his divorce, maybe they could get together under the guise of business. For example, he could put $2,500 in a production company she was putting together. "If you only had an interest in the company," she wrote, "that would be enough excuse for you to follow me around. You wouldn't be after me, but after your own interests."

That worked for Hayes. He met Loie in New Orleans after the moderately successful Jamaica run of the play was over, and they eventually returned to New York City. There, Hayes produced what he said was a divorce decree. On May 11, 1889, Hayes and Loie were ostensibly married in her boardinghouse room, with her mother as a witness and documents they both signed saying they were married to each other. But Hayes insisted that the marriage be kept secret. He was starting a bank, he explained, and it would scare off investors if it were known he had just wed a burlesque actress.

However much that might have bothered Loie, she didn't let it stand in the way of her next enterprise: She would take her play to England. With her parents at her side and Hayes' money seemingly at her command, Loie rented London's historic Globe Theatre and set about staging a play called *Caprice.*

It didn't go well. On opening night in October 1889, a cow that was being used to make a barnyard scene more realistic ate some of the scenery and got sick on stage, as only cows can do. Reviews were also a bit sickly. "Our fair visitor is a little woman, full of dainty graces, plump and personable, gifted with a pleasant pathos and humor," noted a critic, "but she threw herself away in this long, spun-out tepidity."

Loie's hopes for a three-month engagement were over in three weeks. Worse, Hayes turned off his emotional and financial support. This infuriated Loie's father. Reuben Fuller returned to New York to confront Hayes, while Loie and her mother remained in London and struggled to make ends meet.

In June, the Fuller women received shocking news. Reuben had suddenly died after dining with Hayes at a New Jersey hotel the night before. The death certificate listed typhoid fever as the cause, but Loie suspected her husband had poisoned her father, especially because Hayes had immediately arranged for the body to be embalmed.

For the next year, Loie scratched out a living in various plays and shows in London. Finally, in the summer of 1891, she and her mother sailed for home. In a shipboard interview, an admiring New York reporter described Loie as "the bright, happy, sympathetic little creature that she was when local theatergoers knew her." For her part, Loie claimed the real reason she had gone to London was "to study the different methods employed by artists in my particular line of stage work, with a view to perfecting my art." Just what her "art" was hadn't yet become clear.

It was fairly common in the American theater of the late 19th century for dancers to become singers or actors because they couldn't make a living just dancing, particularly as they got older. Loie, on the other hand, became a dancer because she couldn't act or sing well enough to become a star.

It was a risky move for a woman who, while having a pretty smile and sparkling blue eyes, was short and stout. Theater managers were generally more concerned with how attractive a woman's legs were, and how much of them she was willing to show on stage, than how well she moved them around. Audiences, which were mostly male, heartily concurred.

But Loie took her dancing in an entirely different direction. Instead of selling sex, she sold spectacle. The story of how she came up with what would become her trademark performance had almost as many versions as her birth date. The most consistent account began with her role in yet another bad play, this one called *Quack, M.D.* In one scene, Loie's part called for her to dance while under a hypnotic spell. As she recounted it in her autobiography, she concocted a costume from "a skirt of very thin white silk, of a peculiar shape, and some pieces of silk gauze." The outfit "looked thoroughly original, perhaps even a little ridiculous."

Onstage, Loie avoided tripping on the costume by holding it up and flitting around with raised arms, while pale green stage lights followed her movements. The audience went nuts about the dance, not so much about the play. It closed quickly. But Loie thought she was on to something. She spiffed up her costume, inserted rods in her sleeves to extend the robe's reach, added to her dance steps and incorporated different colored lights for different routines. Then she went knocking on New York City theater doors.

At first, no one answered. Loie Fuller, managers told her repeatedly, was a comic actress. Audiences wouldn't pay to see her dance. Undeterred, she wheedled an audition with an old acquaintance who managed the Casino Theatre, one of Broadway's top showplaces. An accomplished conductor and producer, Rudolph Aronson wasn't a big fan of Loie Fuller. A few years before, she had reneged at the last minute on a deal to perform at the Casino, opting for the Little Jack Sheppard role instead. But prodded by his brother, Aronson agreed to sit through her routine. He liked what he saw.

Aronson persuaded Loie to change the music she danced to, agreed to pay her $50 a week (about $1,300 in 2017 dollars), and came up with a name for her act: "The Serpentine Dance." From then on, any conversation about Loie Fuller was almost certain to contain some variation of the name.

Before opening at the Casino, Loie took her dance on tour for six weeks, performing between acts of a forgettable play called *Uncle Celestin*. Reviews ranged from pleasantly surprised to wildly enthusiastic, both on the road and in New York. "It is a dance for the gods on high Olympus," said the *Atlanta Constitution*. Moreover, the *Constitution* noted, "the new dance is a novelty.

Men and women are both enthusiastic over the dance. This is one time where ladies are permitted to express their admiration; they don't have to confine their gaze to peeps from behind their fans, for there is no leg show in this."

Whether it was for publicity or revenge, or both, Loie chose the start of her serpentine dance success to go after her "husband." William Hayes had doubled down on his abandonment of Loie in London by spreading stories about how she was a bit of a tramp, and he claimed he had "nude" photos to prove it.

Loie realized she lacked the evidence to charge Hayes with the murder of her father. Instead, she charged him with bigamy. She based her case on a letter she had received from a woman claiming to be Hayes' legal wife. Hayes was arrested, and the New York press had a field day with the resultant trial. Hayes denied he had anything to do with the death of Loie's father. He denied he had ever married her, or was even romantically interested. He also characterized Loie as someone who seemed to be "a playful innocent thing to all appearances, but in reality is wide awake."

The day after Loie's smash debut at the Casino, the judge dismissed the bigamy charge on the grounds that Loie had no proof she and Hayes had ever been legally married. But Loie got a double helping of revenge anyway. Fearing a slander suit, Hayes was forced to issue a sworn, public apology to Loie, retracting his remarks about her honor, denying the existence of any nude photos and saying that "I firmly believe that Loie Fuller is free from all taint of immorality or misconduct of any kind."

Worse, at least from Hayes' perspective, it was eventually revealed he had impregnated a 17-year-old girl, then lied about having signed a promissory note to pay her $2,000. He was convicted of perjury, and served two years in Sing-Sing prison, making men's trousers. "Loie Fuller is happy," the *New York Evening World* somewhat snarkily reported. "Her bigamy sensation worked very nicely."

Loie, however, was just getting started with the courts. First came a falling out with the Casino Theatre's manager, Rudolph Aronson. Loie wanted triple the $50 weekly salary they had agreed on, and much better billing than she was getting. Aronson refused. Loie quit. Aronson substituted another dancer in Loie's place, but kept using Loie's name in his advertising. Loie sued. She lost the case when her lawyer ineptly filed the suit against the theater company rather than Aronson himself. Since the deal had been between dancer and manager, the case was dismissed.

Shortly thereafter, Loie was hit with a restraining order that prevented her from being under contract with two theaters at the same time. Still reeling from those legal blows, she lost again when she sued another dancer for imitating her serpentine dance, which Loie had copyrighted. In June, 1892, a federal judge ruled that Loie's dance "was solely the devising of a series of graceful movements telling no story, portraying no character, depicting no emotion." In other words, her copyright was worthless. With three legal misses in a row, Loie decided to strike out for Europe.

"I was born in America," Loie Fuller often said, "but I was made in France." The manufacturing process began in late summer, 1892. Accompanied by her mother (who until her death in 1908 would remain almost constantly at Loie's side), Loie left behind her spectacular but brief success in New York for a continent where she hoped to encounter fewer lawyers and double-dealing managers, and even more appreciative audiences. She was drawn by one city in particular.

"The notion of going to Paris possessed me," she later wrote. "I wanted to go to a city where, as I had been told, educated people would like my dancing and it would accord me a place in the world of art."

She got there by way of Germany, and it proved to be a very bumpy route. A promised appearance at the Berlin opera house fell through. Her mother became desperately ill and had to be hospitalized for a while. Her manager quit and took most of her money with him. Loie was left with just enough to pay her hotel bill. A new agent got her a job in Hamburg, which provided enough funds to get her to Cologne, where, she indignantly recalled years later, "I had to dance in a circus between an educated donkey and an elephant that played the organ. My humiliation was complete."

The good news was that the next stop was the city of her dreams. The more-bad-news was that, once again, a hoped-for engagement had fizzled, this one at the Paris Grand Opera. Desperate, and with her mother still ailing, Loie went looking for a job at Paris' most celebrated—and notorious—night spot.

The Folies-Bergère first opened its doors in 1869. Like America's vaudeville, it featured everything from jugglers and wrestlers to dancing bears—and dancing girls. The performances of this last group of entertainers, along with the fact that it was a hangout for high-priced prostitutes, limited the Folies' clientele almost exclusively to men.

When Loie arrived at the theater, she was stunned to see the playbill included a woman named Mabelle Stuart, performing a "danse serpentine." After watching Stuart's mediocre performance, however, Loie hatched an idea. She persuaded the Foiles manager to let her perform one night, on the condition that if she danced better than Stuart, she was in and Stuart was out. He agreed, Loie danced, and Mabelle Stuart was unemployed.

On the evening of Nov. 5, 1892, Loie Fuller conquered Paris. She performed four dances over 45 minutes, and the enthusiastic audience followed her into her dressing room, still applauding. By her fourth evening, Loie's shows had sold out for 10 days in advance. *Le Figaro,* France's largest newspaper, marveled that "never has there been such enthusiasm on the part of the Paris public."

As it had in America, Loie's dancing appealed to women and children as well as men. The Foiles-Bergère was suddenly respectable, and matinee audiences were as overflowing as those after dark. By March, 1893, Loie was celebrating her 150th appearance and making $500 a week. That was more than the average American day laborer made in a year. She was known now as "La Loïe." The "la" signified she was "the real Loie," and not a Mabelle Stuart or other imitator. The diacritical dots helped differentiate her name from a French term for "goose."

The reasons for Loie's success were more than just the novelty of her act. There were plenty of alluring and skilled dancers in Paris. But Loie's dances were more than trim ankles and nimble steps. Behind her performances were not only precise, grueling choreography, but science.

Stage lighting was a key element. The incandescent light had been patented by Thomas Edison in 1879, and by the 1890s electric lights were being used in many theaters. But Loie went far beyond the standard yellow or white spotlights and stage lamps. Employing as many as a dozen electricians at a time, Loie used multiple lights and arc lamps, with rotating color disks coated with special gelatins that she made herself and kept a closely guarded secret.

Maneuvering the lights required a complex system of platforms and ladders in front of, behind and above the stage. She also used early slide projectors, referred to as "magic lanterns," to cast images and shadows on screens behind her, as well as off her body.

Then came her costumes. She designed and patented outfits that consisted of hundreds of yards of silk, kept in constant motion by strategically placed aluminum or bamboo wands that were sometimes curved at the ends to generate even more movement. One later outfit was reputed to contain 1,036 yards of material, and to have taken three years to make at a cost of $5,000.

"With continuous but gentle movements of arms, feet and form, the outline of which is sometimes veiled and other times revealed, and the folds of her gauzy garments of ever-changing rainbow-like tints, she appears like a supernatural being, sent to teach us the poetry of motion," rhapsodized a British journalist.

Loie liked to tell a self-deprecating story about her on-stage metamorphosis. After one performance, a woman brought her star-struck young daughter backstage to meet the dancer. When the girl saw Loie, however, she shrank back in astonishment, even after mother explained that this was the dancer she had just seen. "No, no, this isn't her," the child exclaimed. "I don't want to see her. This one here is a fat lady, and it was a fairy I saw dancing."

In addition to her technical and artistic skills, Loie was also—for once—in the right place at the right time. Europe was at the beginning of what became known as the Art Nouveau Movement. It took its inspiration from the shapes, colors and motion of natural things, particularly plants and animals. Moreover, it argued that "natural" beauty should be reflected in every aspect of life, from architecture to serving spoons.

Loie's dance style was considered the epitome of Art Nouveau. Artists flocked to the Folies-Bergère to see her, and she quickly—and quite literally—became the movement's poster child. Her likeness, usually greatly idealized, appeared everywhere, from coins to art posters and lithographs by such masters as Henri de Toulouse-Lautrec.

"La Loïe has been done in marble, in oils and pastels and chalk and water color," noted a New York writer, "and as for stained glass—one could fill a fair-sized cathedral with stained-glass Loie Fuller windows, provided the clergy didn't object."

Unfortunately, becoming famous and successful did nothing to negate Loie's knack for combining bad luck with expensive decisions. The bad luck came when her mother suffered a stroke in the spring of 1893, just as Loie was set to leave for performances in Russia. The costly decision came when Loie opted to stay with her mother, despite a contractual clause that required her to pay a whopping $40,000 if she reneged on her promise to appear.

The Russian manager sued and succeeded in attaching her salary at the Folies-Bergère. Desperate once again for money, Loie got a temporary release from her Paris contract—for a $3,200 fee—and took her act to England, then New York. The English tour did relatively well, but the New York appearances did not. By October, Loie was back at the Foiles, still drawing rave reviews and good-sized audiences. Only now she was doing it for nothing.

"We often had hardly enough to eat," Loie wrote. "But for the manager's wife, who at times sent us things to eat in a basket, I should often have danced on an empty stomach."

It was time, Loie decided, to leave the Folies-Bergère and try something new. This time she turned to the Bible for inspiration. With money from a quick-but-profitable tour of Belgium and the Netherlands, Loie began production of her version of the story of Salome. Loie's Salome wasn't the lusty and bloodthirsty wench who connived to get John the Baptist beheaded, as she had often been dramatically portrayed. Instead, Loie envisioned her as dancing before the evil King Herod in a vain effort to save John's life.

As it turned out, no one much cared about Loie's dramatic take on a biblical figure. But for most of the next three years, audiences from Paris to San Francisco to Mexico City loved the dances that formed the heart of the production. To stage them, Loie added even more technical tricks. Sometimes she used a semi-circle of mirrors to give her image the illusion of infinity. Her staff of electricians sometimes swelled to thirty-four, chief among them her two brothers, Frank and Bert. Some dances were performed on a stage with frosted glass panels inserted, through which colored lights could be projected. The result was breathtaking.

"Powerful red lights were thrown on Loie Fuller as she danced above the glass plates in the stage," gasped a Detroit reviewer. "Waving an enormous scarf, a great flood of flame seemed to envelop her, illuminating her drapery beneath, from the interior of her skirts as well as exteriorly. She seemed a mass of living fire and her scarves tongues of flame."

If the impact of Loie's performances was enormous, so were the box office receipts. A four-week run in New York City alone resulted in a $74,000 (about $2 million in 2017 dollars) gross profit for Loie. But "gross" was most definitely not the same as "net." In addition to paying salaries and room and board for her staff of 12, she faced enormous costs for not only moving and setting up tons of expensive equipment, but also for tearing up and then repairing theater stages that her crew specially modified for her shows.

Trying to stay in the black meant a physically and mentally exhausting schedule, and it took its toll. In Philadelphia, Loie broke down in tears on stage after the lighting system balked. In Boston, she broke down completely. "Miss Loie Fuller, the celebrated dancer, is dangerously ill with nervous prostration," the press announced in early May, 1896. "It is said that her condition is due largely to overwork."

It was first reported that she was being taken to a sanitarium in Maine, but whether she was or not is uncertain. In June, sporadic reports had her suffering from a condition called locomotor ataxia, which is an inability to control body movements, especially of the limbs. Other reports were more vague, including one with the reassuring headline "Loie Fuller Not Insane."

By October, she had recovered enough to make her first appearance on the West Coast, where she was routinely billed as "the world's most famous dancer." A reporter for the *San Francisco Chronicle* who interviewed her in November, found her relaxed and amiable, "petted but unspoiled, a woman of culture and originality," with a waistline that "has never been drawn down by a corset and is soft and natural," and "a pair of bright expressive blue eyes bubbling over with good nature and friendliness."

The reporter also noted she wore no jewelry, and her clothes and shoes were "not too new" and "have traveled for two years." And he offered a summary of Loie that would have almost certainly pleased her: "She is a plain, plucky American girl, whose road to fame has been by no means a smooth one. But her purpose has been definite and unwavering these many years. As a dancer of pictures and an embodiment of dreams, she is unique."

After her West Coast swing, Loie went south for a brief tour of Mexico. Then it was off to Texas, Washington D.C., Cuba, and back to New York. Finally, after nearly three years away and at the height of her international fame, Loie went "home" to Paris and the Foiles.

Prior to coming to Europe, Loie had never been in an art museum, and thought statues were made in factories. But as she developed her dances and attracted the admiration of artists from all disciplines, she in turn developed a deep appreciation for art. The work of one man in particular inspired her. "At the Loïe Fuller studio," recalled the French artist and furniture designer Francis Jourdan, "there was only one god: Rodin."

François Auguste René Rodin was born in 1840. By the time he met Loie in the 1890s, the short, heavy, intense artist was world-famous, although not universally admired. Rodin's sculptures were disturbingly realistic and physical, and represented a major break from the decorative, cookie-cutter approach taken by his more traditional contemporaries.

"Rodin is the sculptor most discussed, most condemned, most admired and most copied at the present day," said a *New York Times* reviewer in 1903. Like the music of German composer Richard Wagner, "it seizes one and carries one along despite all protests; it excites and disquiets one. But it makes one think and, in the end, compels one, however reluctantly, to acknowledge its power."

Loie was enthralled by both the artist and his work, referring to him in person and in her letters as "the Master." Just visiting his home, she wrote, "one feels oneself leap for joy, like the dog that precedes one in quest of the master of the house."

For his part, Rodin greatly liked but didn't always trust Loie. In a letter to a friend, reprinted with the artist's permission by Loie in her autobiography, Rodin called her "a woman of genius." At one point he planned to leave her one-fourth of his estate. On the other hand, he refused to speak to her for three years when he thought she had conned him after taking some of his pieces to New York for a showing and then publicly implying she owned them.

The arts of the dancer and sculptor were on display almost side by side at the Paris Universal Exposition of 1900. The equivalent of a World's Fair, the exposition marked the pinnacle of the Art Nouveau Movement. It also may have marked the apex of Loie's career. After returning from America, she had performed almost non-stop at the Foiles, dancing every night of the week as well as two or three afternoons. At the expo, she was the only performer to have her own theater, complete with a Loie Fuller museum.

In true Loie fashion, she managed to turn artistic triumph into financial flop. The theater, which she paid for, was supposed to cost $10,000 to build. But Loie, a New York paper noted, "with a magnificent disregard for the principles of finance, signed about $50,000 worth of checks."

Undeterred as always, Loie toured Europe after the expo, dancing, managing a troupe of Japanese actors that featured a four-foot-tall ingenue named Sada Yacco, and losing more money. Then she returned to the United States. The tour's highlights included breaking a 10-week contract with a New York City theater in a dispute over who owed whom; traveling across the country with a Broadway theatrical company that went broke and disbanded in San Francisco; and then touring on her own to rave reviews and paydays that reached as high as $2,475 for a single performance.

But as Loie entered her forties, her eyesight diminished as her waistline expanded. She toured South America and drew crowds of thousands at an exposition in Marseilles in the years after meeting Crown Princess Marie in 1902, but it was increasingly clear Loie's dancing days were numbered. She turned to teaching, giving technical advice, and dodging creditors. She founded a school for dancing, which at its peak had as many as fifty students ranging in age from five to twenty-nine. Loie dubbed them her "muses," and draped them in white robes. Her curriculum stressed "natural" dancing that called for expressing emotions rather than learning set routines. "I am training them to think and feel and express their thoughts and feelings in dancing," she explained. "I don't teach them the steps, but only suggest ideas to them."

In addition to touring with her muses, Loie was retained by the new Boston Opera House to help them set up their lighting system. But every paycheck had a line of creditors waiting for it. In New York, deputy sheriffs showed up at her suite with judgements against her totaling $1,100. She promised them she'd pay after an upcoming tour; "the sheriffs left empty-handed."

By 1912, Loie was back in Paris in much the same situation she had been in 20 years before: broke and looking for steady work. Bookings for her dance troupe were few and far between, and rarely profitable. Financial backers came and went. Loie was often ill, or said she was, with headaches and bronchitis and other ailments that periodically drove her into bed for days at a time.

"Loie Fuller is now considered passé in Paris, a city where the people are feverishly looking for something new and chic," an American correspondent wrote. "So this once famous serpentine dancer passes her time teaching classes of children the art in which she once excelled, and traveling with them to the fashionable resorts of Europe, giving performances at their kurhauses (spas) on the green."

One such performance came in the summer of 1913, in the private Paris garden of a wealthy French aristocrat. Among the guests was a woman Loie had not seen in more than a decade: Crown Princess Marie. "Princess Marie was in her greatest beauty, like a rare flower," wrote a wealthy American businessman who was in attendance. "Her golden hair was in waves down either side of her face to just above the ears, like a fair Madonna: tall and slender, a little girl of eight said 'she is like an angel!'"

Angel or not, it had been a rough year for Marie. It began with the birth of her sixth child, followed by a serious bout with phlebitis and months of bed rest. It would get rougher when Romania went briefly to war with Bulgaria and Marie heroically tended to cholera-stricken soldiers at great risk to her own health.

But the Paris visit was indisputably a bright spot. It was Marie's first visit to the city. King Carol, her uncle-in-law, considered Paris "a place of perdition," and had forbidden the princess from seeing it for herself. The king relented only because she had been so sick, and then for only two weeks.

Marie and Loie were delighted to see each other, albeit for only a short time. They had begun corresponding the year before, with Loie asking Marie to smooth the way for her troupe to visit Spain, where Marie's cousin Eugenia happened to be the queen. After their brief meeting in Paris, they continued to write each other frequently. Loie sent Marie a bronze work that Rodin had asked her to give the princess. Marie sent back a photograph of herself to give to Rodin. She described the horrors of the cholera camps. She also said that she had been writing a fairy tale and that Loie's idea "about my fairy story being produced on the stage enchants me." They both agreed they needed to see each other more often.

Unfortunately for everyone, a world war got in the way.

NOTES FOR CHAPTER 2

The princess and the dancer Diana Mandache (ed.), *Later Chapters of My Life: The Lost Memoir of Queen Marie of Romania,* 2004, p. 80.

"When I arrived" Loie Fuller, *Fifteen Years of a Dancer's Life,* 1913, p. 152.

Still, Marie was a Ibid, p. 161.

Marie was only Ibid, pp. 162-63.

Loie got the Ibid., p. 164.

The correct answer Richard Nelson Current and Marcia Ewing Current, *Loie Fuller: Goddess of Light* (1997), p. 17.

Although her family *Chicago Inter Ocean,* Aug. 31, 1878, p. 6; *New York Times*, Sept. 24, 1886, p. 5.

Jumping between genders added Scholarly and entertaining accounts of 19th century American theater include Gillian M. Rodger, *Champagne Charlie and Pretty Jemima: Variety Theater in the Nineteenth Century* (2010); John Hanners, *It was Play or Starve: Acting in the Nineteenth Century American Popular Theatre* (1993), and Frank Cullen, *Vaudeville Old and New: An Encyclopedia of Variety Performers, Vol. I* (2007).

So it wasn't unusual *Chicago Daily Tribune,* Dec. 12, 1880, p. 16.

By the autumn For more on the theatrical career of Buffalo Bill Cody, see Sandra Sagala's *Buffalo Bill on Stage* (2008); Robert Carter's *Buffalo Bill Cody: The Man Behind the Legend* (2000), and Don Russell's *The Lives and Legends of Buffalo Bill.* (1960).

For the next eight *Chicago Inter Ocean*, March 12, 1884; *Burlington (Vt.) Free Press*, Oct. 6, 1885, p. 4.

The play proved popular *New Orleans Times-Picayune*, Oct. 3, 1886, p. 8; *New York Tribune,* Sept. 14, 1886, p. 4.

The second mistake For a detailed account of Loie's marital escapades, see Current and Current, *Loie Fuller: Goddess of Light* (1997), pp. 24-44.

Before she left Ibid, p. 25.

It didn't go well Ibid, p. 27.

For the next Ibid, p. 31.

It was a risky Elizabeth Kendall, *Where She Danced: The Birth of American Art-Dance* (1979), p. 6.

But Loie took her *Loie Fuller, Fifteen Years of a Dancer's Life, With Some Account of her Distinguished Friends* (1913), p. 28.

Before opening at the Casino *Atlanta Constitution*, Feb. 28, 1892, p. 5.

Loie realized she lacked Current and Current, op. cit., p. 38.

The day after Loie's smash Ibid., p. 40.

Worse, at least from *New York Evening World*, Feb. 11, 1892, p. 2.

Shortly thereafter *New York Times*, June 19, 1892, p. 20.

The notion of going Fuller, op. cit., p. 46

She got there by way Ibid., p. 50.

On the evening of Current and Current, op. cit., p. 50.

"With continuous but" M. Griffith, "Loie Fuller, the inventor of the Serpentine Dance," *The Strand Magazine,* Vol. 7, No. 415, May. 1894.

Loie like to tell Fuller, op. cit., pp. 141-42.

"La Loïe has" *New York Sun*, Jan. 6, 1901, p. 24.

"We often had" Fuller, op. cit., p. 92.

"Powerful red lights" *Detroit Free Press,* April 12, 1896, p. 23.

Trying to stay in *Pittsburgh Press*, May 3, 1896, p. 2.

It was first reported *San Francisco Chronicle*, June 21, 1896, p. 5; *Columbus (Ind.) Republic*, June 6, 1896, p. 1.

By October, she had *San Francisco Chronicle,* Nov. 13, 1896, p. 14.

Prior to coming In Frederic Grunfield, *Rodin: A Biography*, (1987), p. 445.

"Rodin is the sculptor" *New York Times,* May 9, 1903, p. 5.

Loie was enthralled Fuller, op. cit., p. 122.

In true Loie fashion *New York Sun*, Jan. 6, 1901, p. 24.

But as Loie entered *New York Times,* Feb. 14, 1909, p. 8.

"Loie Fuller is now" *Louisville Courier-Journal*, July 5, 1912, p. 5.

One such performance *Baltimore Sun,* Aug. 10, 1913, Part 3, p. 4.

Marie and Loie Current and Current, op. cit., pp. 218-220.

CHAPTER THREE

"This estimable lady"
Alma's Story
MARCH, 1914

She was rich, attractive, alone and afraid. She liked the first two of those conditions and wasn't bothered much by the third. But the fourth was definitely an unfamiliar feeling, and as Alma Spreckels stood at the restaurant doors, she didn't like that afraid feeling one bit.

Ciro's was a swanky establishment. Located on the ground floor of the posh Hotel Daunou, it was considered one of the smartest dining spots in Paris. It attracted a heady mix of theatrical, artistic, and society types—some of whom would soon be dining with Alma. These were important people, and Alma Spreckels was just a former nude model who happened to have married very, very well. Still, she had the blood of French aristocracy coursing through her veins, and the two diamond clips her husband Adolph had given her for luck pinned to her tastefully expensive gown. So in she went.

Alma's dinner companions included Mitchell Samuels, from the prestigious New York art firm French & Co. The company had been retained by Alma's husband to help in her quest to find art and furniture for the Spreckels' fabulous, new 55-room mansion in San Francisco. Samuels put the dinner together to introduce Alma to people who might advise her on what to buy and where to buy it. Among the guests was James K. Hackett, the wealthy and well-known classical actor. There was Dr. Cornelia Sage Quinton, director of the Albright Art Gallery in Buffalo, N.Y., and the first woman to oversee a major American art museum. There was Hermen Anglada Camarana, the noted Spanish artist. And then there was Loie Fuller:

"There they stood, face to face, these two women," Loie wrote in her memoirs, for some reason in the third person. "… One of them was tall, of the Juno type, the other petite and looking for all the world like a little plump figure out of a Dresden china group (and they) stood there facing each other for quite a minute before either of them spoke and the little one putting out her hand said 'you are sensitive. You must not let people hurt you.' The tall beautiful woman smiled and said 'it is true, but how could you tell?' 'Instinct,' the other replied, 'and we can't explain instinct, can we?' And the ice was broken!"

Loie talked Alma's language, albeit at a mile a minute. Both were at heart working class American women who had labored hard to attain their dreams in a male-dominated world. Of course Loie was famous, or at least had been, so Alma mostly listened.

"I used to be a student at the Mark Hopkins Art School," Alma recalled, "(but) I knew nothing of art and imagined that all things antique were worth owning. Loie Fuller and I became great friends and she taught me that ugly things were also made in the old days and you had to learn to distinguish. One must admire furniture with beautiful lines and workmanship."

In the months that followed the dinner, Loie guided Alma's protracted shopping spree. Her purchases ranged from an 18th-century-style bed (made in the 19th century,) to exquisite glass pieces by the French artist Émile Gallé (which would someday become part of the Maryhill Museum collection.) Above all, Loie wanted Alma to buy from "the Master," Auguste Rodin.

It wasn't easy even setting up a meeting. They failed to find Rodin at home or his studio. By July, Alma had left for England on her way back to America, when Loie finally tracked the artist down at his doctor's country house. Loie phoned Alma in London and begged her to return. "I did," Alma later wrote, "and I sat up all night on the boat crossing the channel." Who she saw when she got back to France was a 74-year-old "little man" sporting a long white beard and a black velvet beret.

It had been a rocky year for Rodin, starting with a serious bout of pneumonia. His memory was becoming unreliable. In January, he had called the police to report a Rodin forgery was being offered for sale by a local art dealer. After the piece's provenance was established, Rodin had to publicly acknowledge that he had indeed sculpted the piece, and just forgot about it. And there had been a protracted fight with the French government over his offer to give France his precious personal art collection, in return for a museum to put it in and a lifetime job as its curator. The government took the offer, but only after Rodin had petulantly threatened to move to Rome and give his art to Italy.

The artist was therefore more than a little guarded when Loie showed up with a tall American woman and began talking about how Alma wanted to buy some of his best pieces. "'Master, Mrs. Spreckels has a museum in San Francisco, and I want you to let her have some of the works. And here is a photo of the museum,'" Alma remembered Loie telling Rodin while showing him a picture of what was actually Alma's new mansion. "I was on the spot and did not like to tell Rodin that Loie had a vivid imagination, and that it was our home. He said 'softly, softly, Miss Loie. You leave the picture here and I will think about it.'"

Loie left the photo, and Alma left Europe in late July. By the time she reached home, the continent was engulfed in a war that would drag on for years, devastate Europe and change the course of world history. Even so, in Alma's eyes it had been a very good trip. After all, America wasn't likely to get involved in the war. And she not only brought back all kinds of beautiful things for the mansion, she told reporters on her arrival in San Francisco, but had met all kinds of noteworthy people.

She proudly showed them a thank-you letter from the former French Empress Eugénie, for a copy of a painting Alma had sent her. The painting depicted the empress' son and a French general who happened to be Alma's great-uncle. However afraid she had felt about being over her head on her way into Ciro's, she was now feeling pretty confident that, at least in Europe, Alma Spreckels was a somebody.

For most of her first 35 years, Alma Emma Charlotte Corday le Normand de Bretteville hungered to become important. She was born on March 24, 1881, on a farm on the sandy outskirts of San Francisco, the fifth of six children of Danish immigrants, Mathilde and Viggo de Bretteville.

Alma's parents were the personification of the adage "opposites attract." Mathilde was a hard-working, energetic woman who shortly after Alma's birth convinced her husband to move the family from the largely unfarmed farm into a modest flat in the city. There, she adroitly but strenuously operated a bakery in the front room, a massage parlor in one of the bedrooms and a laundry service in the kitchen.

Viggo, on the other hand, was as lazy as he was arrogant, which was saying something. He came to San Francisco in 1866, 17 years too late for the start of the Gold Rush. He brought with him an expectation that a well-educated man who spoke several languages could prosper without actually working. When his expectation didn't pan out, the rest of the family was forced to compensate for the fact that he simply refused to find a job.

Viggo did provide Alma with a fiercely deep appreciation of her lineage, which he puffed up more than a little. The de Brettevilles, he told her, had once been a very big deal in France, at least until the French Revolution forced them, as aristocrats, to flee to Denmark. Their ancestors had fought in the Crusades, and their contemporary Danish relatives included admirals and diplomats and art collectors and explorers. The great Hans Christian Andersen had courted Alma's grandmother and written a lullaby for Viggo. There was even a family crest! Alma clung to the stories like a barnacle to a rock, even as she delivered the laundry her mother had cleaned to the back doors of San Francisco's elite.

When not looking after other people's clothes, Alma was an excellent student. At the age of 14, she was valedictorian for her eighth-grade class at the Spring Valley Grammar School. Unfortunately, except for some night art school classes, that was as far as her formal education would go. Her father had decided it was time for her to go to work fulltime.

Viggo wasn't fussy about what kind of work it was, so after a stint as a stenographer, Alma began posing as an artists' model. She was well-equipped for it, even in her mid-teens. Already six feet tall, she had luxuriant tresses, a strikingly attractive face and a voluptuous body. She was also not shy about posing nude, and she became a favorite subject for artists whose paintings adorned the walls of the city's numerous saloons.

Many of the saloons weren't much older than Alma. Neither was San Francisco. But both the artist's model and the city were growing up fast. In 1841, San Francisco was a village of six houses and one store, and called Yerba Buena ("Good Herb"). By 1901, it was the ninth-largest city in America, more than thrice the size of rival Los Angeles to the south. It was a city brimming with opportunity if one could reach out and grab it. So, Alma did, in the diminutive form of a fellow named "Klondike Charlie" Anderson. More accurately, she let Charlie grab her.

Charles J. Anderson was a short, 42-year-old Swedish immigrant with a fat wallet and an active libido. He had struck it rich in the Alaska Gold Rush, then married and divorced a dance-hall performer who took him for a reported $150,000—and he apparently didn't learn much from the experience.

In the fall of 1901, Anderson began courting 20-year-old Alma. Over a six-week period, he showered her with gifts that included diamond rings, ruby-studded garters and a box for her family at the San Francisco Opera. According to Alma, he also proposed marriage in early November, then reneged. An indignant Alma promptly slapped him with a $50,000 breach-of-promise suit.

The ensuing jury trial in February 1902 entertained the city for days. Anderson's lawyers took care to pick older jurors who wouldn't be swayed by the plaintiff, "a young woman, divinely tall and most divinely fair, with straight level brows and rosebud mouth, in aspect of a Greek goddess." They also advised their client to look less wealthy by removing "a diamond on his shirt not quite so big as his fist."

On the witness stand, Alma testified that Anderson had threatened suicide if she turned down his proposal. She added that she turned down his offer of a horse, because of a premonition that it would throw her. When a defense lawyer asked if she had any such premonition about the diamond rings, Alma snapped "I didn't think the rings would throw me."

Anderson, who seemed to take the trial as something of a joke, cheerfully admitted that he had shown Alma a good time but denied he had proposed. He also denied he had kissed Alma back after she first kissed him: "I couldn't reach up to her." In the end, the jury put a relatively paltry price on Alma's virtue, awarding her $1,250 instead of the $50,000 she had sought. Anderson never paid anything anyway and went back to the Klondike. But Alma claimed she was happy with the legal victory, referring to it in later years as "the time I sued for personal defloweration, and by God, I won!"

The legal romp with Klondike Charlie was Alma's first taste of high living and celebrity, and it suited her just fine. Her next would come posing again, this time in a diaphanous gown for permanent public display. The payoff would be a lot more than $1,250.

One day in May, 1899, San Francisco Mayor James D. Phelan made an announcement: He was forming a committee of leading citizens to plan construction of a monument to honor the U.S. Navy. More specifically, it was to commemorate the Navy's victory, under Admiral George Dewey at Manila Bay during the Spanish-American War the year before.

The committee quickly raised $40,000 from private contributions, and then slowly decided on what the monument should look like. Eventually, it settled on an 83-foot-tall granite column, to be topped by a 12-foot bronze statue and located in the city's Union Square. The committee chose a 31-year-old local sculptor named Robert I. Aitken to make the statue.

Aitken, whose career would include works at the U.S. Military Academy, the state capitol of Missouri and the U.S. Supreme Court building, picked the most statuesque model he knew: Alma Spreckels. Aitken posed Alma as the Goddess of Victory, in a gown thin enough to display her nipples and navel. She was poised on one foot, holding a laurel wreath in her right hand (symbolizing President William McKinley, who had led the monument's ground-breaking ceremony in May 1901 and then was assassinated four months later), and a trident in her left (symbolizing Dewey.)

The monument, which is still a prominent Union Square feature, was dedicated by McKinley's successor, Theodore Roosevelt, before an estimated crowd of 200,000 in May, 1903. Aitken got $2,500 for his work. Alma got the attention of a short, jowly, extremely wealthy man who was nearly twice her age and widely known for breeding thoroughbred horses, racing yachts, and shooting a newspaper editor.

Adolph B. Spreckels was chairman of the San Francisco Parks Commission, and as such played a role in completion of the Dewey Monument, thus meeting Alma. He was "the most popular of his family and in his younger days he was also the best-looking." Known to his friends as "Dolph," Spreckels "cared little for, if he did not hold in absolute contempt, the conventionalities of society." He was also a confirmed bachelor and a notorious ladies' man, so it wasn't surprising he soon began having quiet assignations with Alma around town and at his secluded ranch in nearby Napa County.

Both Adolph and Alma were the offspring of immigrants. Unlike Alma's dad, however, Adolph's father was an engine of ruthless energy. After coming to New York from Germany in 1848 as a common laborer (and draft dodger), Claus Spreckels moved to San Francisco in 1856 and opened a grocery store, then a brewery, then got into the sugar business. At first, Spreckels grew and refined beet sugar from fields south of the city. But in 1876, when Congress dropped the tariff on more desirable cane sugar from the kingdom of Hawaii, Claus invaded the islands.

By 1886, Spreckels had used legal maneuvers, shrewd and sometimes shady land purchases—and outright bribery—to become, in his own words, "the emperor of the sugar industry." While he was feared and loathed by many people in Hawaii, Claus was admired and respected in San Francisco for his civic largesse. In fact, he had contributed $10,000 of the $40,000 raised to build the Dewey Monument.

His sons were equally industrious. The eldest, John D., founded his own empire in San Diego, which included real estate, a railway, a ferry system and two newspapers. At one point, he owned so much property (including the Hotel Del Coronado and the rest of Coronado Island), that he paid 10 percent of the entire county's property taxes. Another son, Rudolph, broke away from the family at the age of 19 and became a leader of California's Progressive Movement, which successfully fought political corruption and established reforms such as the initiative and referendum processes.

For his part, Adolph began as a clerk in a family sugar refinery. He formed various partnerships with his brother John, including a lucrative steamship line. In 1884, Adolph took it on himself to defend the family name. For years, the *San Francisco Chronicle,* under the ownership of a nefarious shakedown artist and all-around jerk named Michael de Young, had editorially blistered the Spreckels family, mostly inaccurately, for everything from cheating stockholders to employing lepers as field workers. After one such attack, Adolph stormed into the *Chronicle* offices, informed a clerk that "Mr. Spreckels is here to shoot Mr. de Young," and did so.

De Young was slightly wounded, as was Adolph when the clerk returned fire in defense of his boss. Swayed by his plea of temporary insanity and the fact that de Young was widely despised, a sympathetic jury acquitted Adolph. But enmity between the two families lasted for decades. In the 1950s, Alma walked by a restaurant table occupied by Michael de Young's daughters. In a loud stage whisper she told a companion, "you know, these de Young women are nice. But of course we've never been intimate since my husband shot their father."

When Claus Spreckels died in late 1908, Adolph became president of the family sugar company. Although it's uncertain that the now-familiar term originated with him, Adolph also formally became Alma's "sugar daddy." By that time, she had been his mistress for more than five years.

During what the press later euphemistically called their "courtship," Adolph showered Alma and her family with gifts that ranged from expensive clothes to opera tickets to a trip to Denmark to visit their relatives. But he stayed far away from all the de Brettevilles in public, including Alma.

That was okay with Alma—for a while. "I'd rather be an old man's darling than a young man's slave," she told a companion. But at 27, she wasn't getting any younger, and at 51, neither was Adolph. In May, 1908, after a barrage of pleading and threats, Adolph agreed to take Alma with him on a business trip to Philadelphia. When they got there, they got married. But they kept it secret for a month, and would have done so longer if they hadn't run into some people they knew in New York while preparing to leave on an indefinite honeymoon abroad.

San Franciscans were therefore stunned in early June 1908 by the front-page news about the marriage between the "bachelor millionaire, yachtsman and breeder of fine horses," and a woman "famed for her beauty even in this city, where feminine charms are the rule." Adolph's family members were among the stunned. His nephew, who had assumed he would be his uncle's heir, refused to believe it: "This is a good joke on Uncle Adolph," he told a reporter. "Uncle Adolph will never marry."

The family—and much of the Bay Area's upper crust—were also privately disgusted that a Spreckels had stooped to wed a blatant gold-digger from a socially and financially insignificant family. But newspaper gossip columnists, who variously and incorrectly described Alma as "an accomplished pianist and gifted artist," delightedly pointed out that she had claim to more blue blood than her spouse's family.

"The de Brettevilles were 'emigres' when the heads of the many families who hold up their hands in horror at the misalliance were working in the fields or as street laborers in New York," the *Oakland Tribune* opined. "Adolph has always been the most human of all the Spreckels lot, and it is more than probable that he has made a selection that will ensure a happy and lasting union."

Adolph was also no fool. Before they left on what would be a six-month honeymoon, he had Alma sign the equivalent of a pre-nuptial agreement, limiting what she would receive if their union proved to be less than "happy and lasting." As it turned out, the agreement didn't make it through the honeymoon. Adolph tore it up on the way home, after Alma informed him she was pregnant.

The most noteworthy thing Adolph did on returning to San Francisco was begin a long legal battle that ultimately blocked two of his brothers from sharing in their father's estate. The most noteworthy thing Alma did was give birth to a baby girl "reported to have a fine pair of lungs and a healthy appetite." Over the next four years, Adolph and Alma had two more children. The night that her third child was born, Adolph, whose health had not been good, was suddenly stricken with a seizure. After prodding the doctor about its cause, Alma was stunned to learn the real reason Adolph had been hesitant to marry her: He had syphilis.

Fortunately for Alma and the children, the disease was long past the communicable stage. The seizure also rendered Adolph impotent, which meant no more children, which was just fine with Alma. She was not overburdened with maternal instinct. As her son and two daughters grew, they were looked after by a string of nurses and governesses, in whose care Alma left them for weeks or months at a time.

While she didn't particularly care for motherhood, Alma loved spending Adolph's money, mostly in a quest for the social status her past and reputation had so far denied her. In December 1910, she set her sights on the ultimate status symbol—the grandest house in San Francisco. But first she had to build it.

The neighborhood Alma chose was Pacific Heights, where the city's movers and shakers had lived for decades. In the heart of San Francisco's North Side, the community enjoyed magnificent views of the bay, the Golden Gate, and on clear days, parts of four different counties. With Adolph's encouragement, or at least his acquiescence, Alma picked out a nice Victorian home on Washington Street, and then had it demolished. She followed up by buying eight surrounding houses and having them moved. That created the equivalent of an entire city block on which to build.

Next, she hired a 35-year-old architect named George A. Applegarth. Born in Oakland and trained in Paris, Applegarth designed a Beaux-Arts-style mansion of reinforced concrete, with a two-story Corinthian-columned entry, a five-limousine underground garage, coffered ceilings and large symmetrical rooms. Marble and bronze abounded. Equally impressive were the immaculately landscaped grounds that afforded sweeping views in all directions.

"The new Spreckels home will crown the city like a royal palace," gushed a reporter who was afforded a preview of the house. "Nowhere in America has the builder before attempted anything in such large magnificence."

The home, which was finished in late 1913, cost an estimated $700,000 (about $17.6 million in 2017 dollars), It was reported Adolph intended to let Alma spend another $1 million on art and furnishings. Naturally, it was soon dubbed "the Sugar Palace." To show it off, the Spreckels threw parties. Some of the city's smart set continued to snub Alma as an upstart, while some came at least once to satisfy their curiosity. Notable guests included the writer Jack London and the Persian minister to the United States.

Another guest was a friend of Adolph's, whom he had met through a mutual acquaintance in Portland. The friend was Sam Hill, who was best known for being an inveterate traveler, a national leader in the crusade to build a reliable U.S. road system, and for being the son-in-law of the legendary railroad tycoon James J. Hill. Sam and the Spreckels became such good friends that the couple chose Sam to be godfather to their son, Adolph II. Then one day Alma answered the door to a guest she hadn't exactly invited and wasn't really expecting.

"Quite unheralded to the public, La Loie Fuller, the famous American dancer, arrived in the city last week to be the house guest of Mr. and Mrs. Adolph B. Spreckels," the *Oakland Tribune* reported in mid-August, 1914. Her visit, the paper noted, was not just social. Loie was there to explore the possibility of her dance troupe performing at the 1915 Panama-Pacific International Exposition—and perhaps put together a Rodin exhibition for the expo as well: "Miss Fuller is one of the most ardent admirers in the world of the genius of Rodin."

As far as the sculptor was concerned, Loie was also a pest. After Alma's European shopping trip ended, her ship home had barely cleared the horizon when Loie Fuller started working on Rodin: The tall American woman was absurdly rich. She had lots of rich friends. She wanted to put The Master's works on permanent display. Rodin could make a lot of money and ensure his fame would be permanently ensconced even in the wilds of the U.S. West Coast.

At first, he resisted. A dozen years before, Loie had taken some of his work to the New York Metropolitan Museum of Art and given him a promissory note for them that proved to be worthless. He eventually got his pieces back, but he had to make good on the note, which he had deposited in a bank. Afterward, Rodin refused to speak to Loie for several years.

"I am flabbergasted by the impression you are under," Loie protested when Rodin balked at doing business with her again. "... With my help, she (Alma) can perhaps obtain for you and your work the justice they deserve. No personal consideration has entered my head."

Rodin tentatively gave in, and Loie headed for San Francisco with some drawings and plaster molds by the artist, designed to whet Alma's appetite for more. She was greeted warmly by Alma, far less so by Adolph, who took an instant dislike to this badly dressed, goggle-wearing chatterbox. As an American proud of his German ancestry, he was further put off by Loie's unabashed ardor for France and her efforts to enlist Alma in raising war relief funds for France and Belgium.

Nonetheless, Adolph didn't interfere in the two women's plans. The rapidly expanding war in Europe, however, did. After leaving San Francisco with Alma's order for more Rodin works, Loie reached New York after a three-day train trip, only to find it was deemed too dangerous to return to Paris with the seemingly unstoppable German army at its doorstep. So back to San Francisco she went. It turned out to be a fortuitous delay. This time she left with not only a lucrative contract to appear at the Expo, but with $7,500 of Alma's money for additional Rodin pieces.

Once the German army's march toward Paris was halted (in part by moving 3,000 soldiers to the front using taxi cabs), Loie returned to France in late 1914. This time she had better luck with Rodin in inducing him to sell. She bought six pieces for Alma outright, including a full-size bronze cast of his immortal *The Thinker*. Loie also made down payments on eight more pieces still to be cast.

Loie's efforts were aided by the French government, which not only endorsed the sale of Rodin's works to Alma but reversed its earlier decision not to participate in the 1915 Pan-Pacific Exposition because of the war. To boost the country's morale, French officials decided to erect in San Francisco a ¾-scale replica of Paris' Palace of the Legion of Honor. The decision appealed to Rodin's patriotism, and reassured him his works wouldn't just disappear.

France was one of 22 foreign nations at the exposition, which was designed to celebrate the opening of the Panama Canal as well as the triumphant comeback of San Francisco from the 1906 earthquake that had nearly destroyed it. Built on a marsh filled in largely with debris from the earthquake, the 635-acre fair featured a 432-foot-high "Tower of Jewels;" a seven-block-long amusement center; 25 theaters, and a working auto assembly plant where viewers could watch Henry Ford's workers turn out 14 cars a day. Especially courageous—and well-heeled—fair-goers could fork over a hefty $10 for a 10-minute ride over the fairgrounds in an aeroplane.

The expo couldn't have come at a better time for Alma and Loie. For the former, it offered the perfect place to display *The Thinker*, which she and Adolph announced they would give to the city of San Francisco when the fair ended. Seeing their sculpture on view at the French Pavilion so moved Adolph that he agreed to Alma's desire for a full-scale, Spreckels-funded public art museum in the future.

For Loie, the expo gave her a badly needed source of income. Her dance troupe of 20 English girls, ranging in age from 12 to 16, performed once a week to sold-out crowds of 3,500. In essence, their performances were the equivalent of 20 young versions of Loie, dancing to lighting effects supplied by 10 electricians. "Rainbows, soap bubbles, wings of butterflies and silvered moths, sunset skies and midnight's purple have loaned up their colors to La Loie Fuller," a critic wrote in praise of opening night. "... Her pictures are music; her music is color…".

Best of all, as far as Loie's pocketbook was concerned, the girls were eating and sleeping for free, as guests of Alma at the Spreckels' bayside estate in nearby Sausalito. Alma's generosity was reciprocated by Loie's diligent efforts to support her friend's artistic and altruistic ambitions, both of which were driven by Alma's quest to be accepted by the city's social elite. Loie had not only encouraged Alma's interest in the arts, but had come through with the Rodin deals. She had also persuaded Alma to throw herself into raising funds for the war-torn countries of France and Belgium.

"I have received your message," Alma wrote after Loie had returned to France in late 1914. "It has sunk deep down into my heart...Come, and we will carry out the great relief work for France, which we both love so much, France, the country of my forefathers! And we shall, as you say, include that great little country, Belgium!"

Rather than simply seek donations directly from the Bay Area's upper crust—many of whom despised her and whom she loathed—Alma took a different tack. She set up what amounted to a raffle, which she called her "Tombola," after a popular lottery game in Europe, but on a grand scale. First, she and Loie solicited raffle-worthy items from friends, acquaintances, and famous people they didn't know at all.

The objects included a thoroughbred race horse from Adolph; a new Model T car from Henry Ford; autographed books from Theodore Roosevelt and Marie Curie; autographed photos from the presidents of France and the United States; an Australian opal; and a California heifer. Then they sold tickets at $1 apiece. In all, they raised $18,000 (about $292,000 in 2017 dollars). By the end of the war, ancillary efforts, such as selling postcards autographed by various celebrities and placing milk bottles in stores for people to put their spare change in, saw Alma raise a staggering $130,000-plus ($2.1 million in 2017) for relief efforts in France, Belgium and Romania.

While the proceeds from the raffle and other projects purchased ambulances and fed orphans in war-torn Europe, Alma remained a social outcast. She had ignored the city's civic and social leaders in her fundraising, and they froze her out of their own, more genteel, efforts. Rather than show gratitude, the Belgian counsel in San Francisco let it be known he thought the raffle was vulgar. But Alma did get the thanks of one group. The all-male Indoor

Yacht Club, a tongue-in-cheek civic booster group, made her an honorary life member.

"There is a great career in store for this estimable lady," the club's newsletter declared, "and the time is not far off when public appreciation will dedicate to her the love she deserves."

On a seasonably balmy evening in mid-September, 1915, Alma threw another party. This one was at her "studio," which was a former Spreckels residence set up as "the chief theater of Mrs. Spreckels' philanthropic activities." In essence, it was a fancy warehouse for her raffle items. The walls were covered with autographed photos and Rodin drawings; the shelves with autographed books; and her Rodin sculpture, *The Genius of War,* occupied the foyer. There was a room devoted to Asian art, and one to the small animal sculptures of the brilliant-but-broke local artist George Putnam.

The guests at this party were delegates to a just-concluded convention of the Pan-American Road Congress. The international group was dedicated to the construction of a highway that would stretch from Canada, along the U.S. West Coast, and ultimately to South America. One of its most outspoken leaders was Sam Hill.

"A feature of the evening's entertainment was the staging of a dancing fete by Loie Fuller and her girls," the papers said the next day. "Pretty lighting effects were used in the entertainment, which was held in the gardens surrounding the Spreckels place."

Alma introduced her dancer friend to her road-building friend, and the two hit it off. Sam was particularly appreciative of Loie's efforts to aid Belgium, because the Belgian king was a personal friend of Sam's. Loie mentioned she was close to the queen of Romania. They should introduce each other next time Sam was in Europe—if and when the war allowed it.

After the party and for the rest of 1915, Loie stayed in the Bay Area, giving occasional lectures about Rodin or the plight of France and Belgium, and working with Alma on war relief projects.

Sam went back to Portland, and pondered plans for the big house he was building on the banks of the Columbia River. His Washington D.C.-based architect had sent him at least three different designs, mostly because Sam couldn't make up his mind as to exactly what he wanted: Maybe a massive pipe organ. Perhaps a frieze around the main hall that featured the likenesses of Sam's father and a Native American chief who had made Sam a member of the tribe. What about a big copper box holding various papers, to be installed in a cornerstone?

If Sam didn't know what he wanted his new home to have in it, however, he had definite plans for what it would be.

"I have planned it for a good, comfortable farmhouse," he told a well-known Oregon journalist named Fred Lockley, who was Sam's friend, confidant, and periodic biographer. "Here I can let the world wag as it will. I expect this house to be here for a thousand years after I am gone."

NOTES FOR CHAPTER 3

She was rich, attractive The only extensive biography of Alma Spreckels to date is *Big Alma: San Francisco's Alma Spreckels*, by Bernice Sharlach (rev. ed., 2016).

"There they stood" Current and Current, op. cit., p. 224.

Loie talked Alma's Scharlach, op. cit., p. 79.

It wasn't easy. Ibid., p. 81.

It had been a rocky *Charlotte (N.C.) Evening Chronicle*, Jan. 5, 1914, p. 4., *New York Sun*, Jan. 24, 1914, p. 3., *New York Tribune*, Jan 4., 1914, p. 9.

The artist was Scharlach, op. cit., p. 81.

Viggo did provide Alma Fiona E.W. Colburn, "Alma De Bretteville Spreckels," *Overland Monthly and Out West Magazine,* March, 1924, pp. 102-106.

The ensuing jury trial *San Francisco Examiner*, Feb. 20, 1902, p. 1.

On the witness stand *San Francisco Chronicle*, Feb. 21, 1902, p. 12.

Anderson, who seemed Scharlach, op. cit., p. 57.

Adolph B. Spreckels was *Oakland Tribune*, June 13, 1908, p. 7; June 21, 1908, p. 19.

By 1886, Spreckels Jacob Adler, *Claus Spreckels: The Sugar King in Hawaii* (1966), p. 26.

De Young was slightly Stephen Birmingham, *California's Rich: The Life and Times and Scandals and Fortunes of the Men and Women Who Made and Kept California's Wealth* (1980), pp. 76-77.

That was okay with Scharlach, op.cit., p. 55.

San Franciscans were therefore *San Francisco Examiner,* June 7, 1908, p. 1.

"The de Brettevilles were" *Oakland Tribune*, July 11, 1908, p. 5.

The most noteworthy thing *San Francisco Chronicle*, Aug. 26, 1909, p. 7; Scharlach, op. cit., pp. 64-65.

"The new Spreckels home" *San Francisco Call*, May 25, 1913, p. 59.

The home, which was In 1990, the Spreckels mansion was designated an historical landmark by the city and county of San Francisco, not only for its architecture but also "its colorful occupants." It was purchased from the Spreckels estate by best-selling novelist Danielle Steel, who planted a controversial 30-foot "privacy hedge" around the property.

"Quite unheralded to" *Oakland Tribune,* Aug. 23, 1914, p. 11.

"I am flabbergasted" Current and Current, op. cit., pp. 225-226.

Once the German army's Rodin's original *The Thinker* was part of a door-surround panel called *The Gates of Hell* and was only 27.5 inches high. Before his death in 1917, Rodin oversaw the casting of 18 full-sized versions, including the one he sold Alma.

For Loie, the expo gave *San Francisco Chronicle*, June 2, 1915, p. 10.

"I have received your" Alma to Loie, Dec. 12, 1914, MMA.

"There is a great career" Scharlach, op. cit., p. 109.

On a seasonably balmy *Oakland Tribune*, May 9, 1915, p. 37.

"A feature of the" *Oakland Tribune,* Sept. 17, 1915, p. 4.

"I have planned it" *Oregon Daily Journal,* Feb. 28, 1915, p. 11.

CHAPTER FOUR

"We have found the Garden of Eden"

JULY 1917

Sam Hill wasn't sure what to do with it. After a bit more than three years, it wasn't even half-finished, and there wasn't enough ready cash to do more than nibble at the long to-do list. His hopes for making it a home for his daughter were all but destroyed by her deepening descent into madness. And at 60, Sam was reluctantly coming to grips with the realization that he was just too restless a spirit to ever settle down in one place.

So, walking around the grounds of the house on a warm clear mid-summer morning, accompanied by a round little woman wearing the uniform of a Romanian Red Cross nurse, Sam was wide-open to suggestions. Only Loie Fuller never just suggested: She advocated, enthused, exclaimed!

Sam should give his house to the people of the world! It could be nurtured by governments, but stand as "neutral ground," a gathering place for artists, where "various nations could bring to it fine arts to place in the rooms dedicated to their countries!" "This glorious country made me think about the building," Loie recalled nine years later. "The isolation, the loneliness of this monument was so wonderful to me that I wondered why it could not be organized into a museum for good will."

A museum wasn't close to what Sam had in mind when he started the project. At first it was to be a simple rustic farmhouse, a getaway spot for Sam, his friends, and especially his daughter Mary, who was fighting what would be a losing battle with depression and schizophrenia.

Perched on a ledge above the north shore of the Columbia River, at the western end of Sam's sprawling 5,200-acre spread, the site afforded spectacular views—and little else. There was no electricity, no roads beyond those Sam had built himself, and little realistic chance much would change anytime soon in the way of easy access to the outside world. Even so, by 1915, Sam's original plans had already metamorphosed far beyond "the good comfortable farmhouse" he had described to his friend Lockley. Now his plans envisioned a full-scale mansion.

It was to be a three-story Beaux-Arts concrete chateau, reinforced with steel. No wood was to be used in the structure's bones. The first floor was for the kitchen, laundry, furnace, storage area and five bedrooms for servants. The second floor was where Sam's library, den and bedroom would be, along with a dining room large enough to seat 250, and a huge reception hall with windows overlooking the river. On the third floor would be eight bedrooms, each with its own bathroom. A warming oven would be located in the hall, to which a servant might deliver food so guests could eat breakfast in their rooms.

But Sam was just getting started. On the roof, there would be a garden, where summertime guests could sleep under the stars if they chose. On each side of the house would be long ramps on which cars could be driven directly into the main floor, deposit their passengers, and drive out the other side. Under the ramps there would be parking garages for 48 vehicles. The house would be wired for electricity, even though the closest source was still three miles away (and would remain so until 1936). Coal, oil or wood could be burned in the furnace, and the entire house was set up for gas heating and lighting. An estimated five miles of plumbing pipe would run through the walls.

"Half a century hence," Sam's journalist friend Fred Lockley boldly and wholly inaccurately predicted in the *Oregon Journal*, "the Columbia will be lined with houses of this character, just as are the Hudson and the St. Lawrence today."

All in all, it was an outrageously expensive undertaking, at a time when the often-wealthy capitalist was sometimes running his enterprises on very little financial fuel. Adding up the costs of buying the land, building a comfortable cottage, a modest hotel, a reservoir and irrigation dam, a 10-mile paved "demonstration road," and the house's planning and construction, Sam had already spent more than $600,000 ($11.5 million in 2017 dollars.) On top of that, the Portland telephone company he controlled had just gone into receivership, with Sam as its chief creditor. And the stock market, in which Sam was heavily invested, was halfway through one of the worst crashes in its history.

"I have not much money to spend," Sam deadpanned to his architect,

James Marshall, in mid-June, about two months after America entered the world war. "My idea is to keep the house going slowly until I can get some money to push it faster. Of course, if the Germans take it, they can finish it."

Sam had as little time to spend on the house as he did cash. In the first six months of the year, he had been up and down the West Coast a half-dozen times making speeches on the need for better roads. He had also crossed the country twice to Washington D.C. Once it was to serve on a committee charged with finding ways the United States could aid Russia from the West Coast, via the Trans-Siberian Railroad. The second trip was to lobby President Woodrow Wilson and Congress on the need for a highway down the Pacific Coast from Canada to Mexico. Sam was considered an expert on both subjects.

Added to the strain of traveling and the financial stress was the fact that Sam had been ill. After returning from his first trip to Washington, he underwent a "minor operation" for an undisclosed problem. He returned from the second trip suffering from neuritis so bad he could barely lift his arms.

Loie, meanwhile, had been doing some traveling as well. Accompanied by a Romanian army officer, she arrived in New York in early June from a war-ravaged Europe as "an ambassador out-of-the-ordinary for Queen Marie of Rumania, most beautiful queen in Europe." Loie's lurid tales of German atrocities, such as dropping typhus-laden candy to Romanian children from airplanes, made front-page news across the country and doubtless helped in her quest to raise $500,000 for Romanian relief efforts.

In San Francisco, Loie visited Alma Spreckels and gave her an autographed photo from Queen Marie, in appreciation of Alma's efforts on behalf of Romania. Then Loie set her sights on Sam. "I fear you are very ill, am much worried about you have much to tell you have wonderful things to tell you," she telegrammed before leaving to meet him in Portland.

How wonderful Sam thought Loie's "wonderful things" were is uncertain. First, she wanted him to sign on as an official for a new Romanian relief committee she was forming. Second, she wanted him to finance a trip to Romania for her, via Russia. Third, she wanted him to pay off a $9,000 note she owed to a San Francisco bank, which was holding some of her Rodin collection as collateral. And fourth, she wanted his hulk of a house on the banks of the Columbia.

She got three of the four. Sam didn't have the money to pay off Loie's loan. But he did agree to serve on her Romanian relief committee. He did give her enough to get to Romania (although she didn't go). And—feeling under the weather both physically and financially—he decided a museum was as good an idea for the house as anything else he could think of at the time.

"My dear Loie Fuller," he wrote her later that July day, "after the eloquent pleading of today, I have decided to dedicate my new chateau at Maryhill, Washington, to a museum for the public good your hopes and ideals shall be fulfilled, my dear little artist woman."

If turning his mansion into an art museum was a Plan B or Plan C, so the mansion itself was something of an afterthought for a much grander scheme: creating an entire community.

The idea began to germinate in late 1905. Sam's bankbook was bulging. He had made a handsome profit on the sale of a Seattle utility company the year before. Thanks to an adroit stock maneuver by his railroad tycoon father-in-law—and a favorable U.S. Supreme Court ruling—Sam's shares in railroad securities had jumped almost overnight by $1.1 million ($29 million in 2017 dollars).

Looking for investment opportunities, Sam pondered building a particle board factory where the Klickitat River poured into the Columbia River, the latter of which separates the states of Oregon and Washington. The site had hydro power, and ample straw from the surrounding vast wheat fields for making boards. He engaged a prominent local attorney, Nelson B. Brooks, to begin making inquiries into buying land at the site.

Meanwhile, apparently hit by one of his periodic waves of nostalgia, Sam went "home" in early 1906 to his birthplace of Deep River, North Carolina, to visit relatives. Although he could lapse easily into the "thees" and "thous" of his Society of Friends upbringing when it suited him, Sam had not been more than a nominal Quaker since his youth. Surrounded by his religious relatives, however, he was inspired: He would create a Quaker community on land along the Columbia River Gorge, similar to the one started in the 1880s in Whittier, California (which would one day spawn another nominal Quaker named Richard M. Nixon).

If Sam's idea of trying to plant a bit of heaven on the Columbia was probably not divinely stirred, neither was it financially motivated. Making money was rarely the primary consideration in his quests. He seldom whined when he was broke, nor crowed when he was flush. "I have come to the conclusion that valuable as money is, the most precious commodity we have is time," he told a friend. "Money is only a means to the end." Sam's "end" was a fervent and sincere wish to do good in the world—and be fondly remembered for it.

"Lots of people laugh at me, and refer to me as a visionary and a dreamer," he defiantly told an interviewer, "(but) when I am drifting dust, people will realize that I had a true vision of the future...the longer you live, the more fully you will appreciate that the only permanent satisfaction you will get out of life is in making the world a better place in which to live."

Nature had certainly made the Columbia River Gorge one of the world's most scenic places in which to live. It was carved by a series of torrential floods that followed the end of the Ice Ages. Billions of gallons of water, moving at freeway speeds from North America's giant inland seas, had worn a channel hundreds of feet deep, running perpendicular to the spine of the Cascade Mountains. In its wake, the water left a marvelous mix of wetlands and waterfalls, basalt cliffs and rainforests, from the urban jungle of the Portland-Vancouver metroplex to the arid steppes of the Columbia Hills.

"The mind can only wonder at this mighty work of God, done in his own way, on a scale so great that man's best efforts appear but as the work of pygmies," wrote engineer Samuel Lancaster. One day, Lancaster, with Sam Hill, would build a highway through the gorge that would do honor to "this mighty work of God."

Sam, who fancied himself something of an expert in a number of natural sciences, was convinced he had found the ideal spot for a community within the gorge. It was about 100 miles east of Vancouver, Washington. He was positive it was precisely where the cool wet climate of the western part of the gorge met the warm dry climate of the east. His calculations were buttressed in part by a description of the area by the famous "Pathfinder," John C. Fremont, in 1843.

"Though we made but a few miles, the weather improved immediately,"

Fremont wrote, "and though the rainy country and the cloudy mountains were close behind, before us was the bright sky; so distinctly is climate marked here by a mountain boundary."

The site was a few hundred feet above the north bank of the river, which was reachable by a steep mile-long dirt road that in rainy weather could bury wagon wheels hub-deep in mud. Sam left out the mud when he described the area to his brother Richard in the fall of 1907.

"We have found the Garden of Eden," Sam wrote. "It is the garden spot of the world—the most beautiful country I have ever seen. I am going to incorporate a company called 'the Promised Land Company.' The only trouble is I would like to buy it all."

Restraining himself for the moment, Sam instead made investment pitches to his wealthy friends and acquaintances, including his father-in-law. "I personally made an examination of the country," he wrote Jim Hill, "and was convinced that land more productive than I had ever seen before was there. On one farm, I found nineteen varieties of grapes as good as any I have ever seen; peaches, plums, prunes, pears, apples, watermelons, quinces, apricots, almonds, walnuts, Indian corn of excellent quality, alfalfa growing without irrigation, etc."

Sam's enthusiasm notwithstanding, he attracted no heavy-hitter investors, nor anyone else outside of a very few close friends. Undaunted, Sam himself began buying all the land the locals were willing to sell. Using an agent so his name wouldn't drive up prices, Sam acquired 17 farms and ranches totaling about 5,300 acres in 1908 and 1909. He paid an average of about $29 an acre, and with ancillary expenses spent about $210,000 (about $5.5 million in 2017 dollars).

Contemporaneously with acquiring land, Sam went looking for people to live on it. Despite sending out a nationwide invitation to the Society of Friends, he found no takers among the Quakers. A Quaker meeting hall was the first structure built, but only one meeting was ever held there, and it attracted more curious locals than members of the faith.

So, Sam's promotions became more secular. When a Great Northern Railway official asked for information on the "town" for a railroad newsletter, Sam's cousin, who was working for him at the site, wrote back that the community was "situated in the center of the best fruit-growing district in the

Northwest;" that it already had a good hotel, "and there will be openings in the spring for all other businesses found in a good town, except a saloon, for which there is no opening" (and never would be).

A slick brochure for the town waxed even more poetic: "Expert geologists and chemists have pronounced the soil, water and climatic conditions of the best. This spot, though small in area, is, all things considered, UNRIVALLED, and is aptly called Nature's Sanitarium."

While waiting for the settlers to begin checking in to "Nature's Sanitarium," Sam started work on the town. He first called it Maryland, after his wife, daughter and mother-in-law, all of whom conveniently bore the same name. But when postal officials nixed the idea because it conflicted with the identically named state, Sam changed it to Maryhill. By 1909, a workforce of 100 men was laying out 426 lots along 15 streets named after fruit and shade trees. Service roads were put in; a general store and hotel built, a sewer system and fire hydrants installed. Sam also built a handsome eight-room "cottage" for his daughter to use when she visited.

At the same time he was creating one town, he was suffocating another. Columbus was a hamlet of about 100 residents on the bank of the river and about a mile downhill from Sam's nascent community. Established in 1860 as a site for riverboats to put in for wood to fire their boilers, Columbus by 1909 had three stores, two saloons, a brothel, railroad station and post office. Sam used his political clout to get the post office moved up to Maryhill, and his influence with his father-in-law's railroad to get the train depot designated the "Maryhill Station." Sam would have one of his automobiles at the station ready to quickly whisk detraining passengers out of Columbus and up the hill to his hotel at Maryhill. In essence, Columbus became an adjunct of a town that had yet to be unwrapped. Eventually it lost its identity altogether and became known as Maryhill.

"We didn't like the idea," recalled a Columbus resident in a 1978 self-published memoir, "but with his influence, of course he had his way." Another local was less diplomatic: "Samuel Hill was huge in physical stature, a braggart, an exhibitionist and ruthless in fulfilling his ambitions. He surrounded himself with doting followers, hypnotized the natives, and controlled neighbors and county officials because of his financial strength."

His bullying extended beyond Columbus. In September 1910, he indignantly announced he was halting all work at Maryhill because Klickitat County officials had refused to appropriate $10,000 to help pay for a road linking his new town to another part of the property. Fearful of losing the $12,000-plus Sam was reportedly spending locally each month on payroll and other items, county voters hastily approved a tax levy to raise the money.

Much of the money Sam was spending locally was on a daring experiment. For years, he had been one of the nation's most vocal proponents for building good roads. In 1909, he put his money—an estimated $100,000—where his mouth was.

Over the next four years, Sam built the first asphalt-covered macadam roads (basically crushed rock covered with asphalt to keep down the dust) in the Pacific Northwest, on a portion of his Maryhill domain. Designed by engineer Samuel Lancaster, the 10-mile loop used seven different construction methods to link Maryhill with a road leading to the nearby town of Goldendale. It included 25 curves and eight hairpin turns, at one point climbing 850 feet in 3.6 miles.

Living in tent camps on-site and working year-round, crews used eight-foot-wide scrapers pulled by four-horse teams to cut the route, followed by dynamiters and plows. Crushed rock was flattened by steam rollers, then covered with asphalt imported from California that was mixed with rock. Two specially built wagons with wheels six feet in diameter were used to move as much as four cubic yards of material at a time up the hill from the railroad depot.

In February, 1913, Sam (who two days before had been elected president of the American Road Builders Association), loaded a luxurious special train in Portland with food, liquor and 88 legislators and other officials, and brought them to see his road. Sam's neighbors, many of whom had decidedly mixed feelings about him, told the lawmakers his road was saving them at least $10,000 a year in the costs of moving their wheat.

The officials were impressed: "On Samuel Hill we look with pride/He'll ever find us at his side," they sang on the return trip. "Your famous highways hit us right/We'll start to build good roads tonight!"

They were a little premature. Actually, it would be another six months before work started on a highway on the Oregon side of the river, which would mark the pinnacle of Sam's road-building efforts. (As for his "demonstration road, about 90 years later "gravity sports" enthusiasts would be singing its praises as "the most famous road in the world for skateboarding.")

While his road was an expensive—albeit mostly symbolic—success, other parts of the Maryhill quest were expensive failures. To address the budding town's water needs, Sam began construction on two dams. But a spring-fed reservoir with a capacity of 250,000 gallons was built on porous clay and rock. As a result, it leaked continuously and never filled. The second dam, designed to store irrigation water, did fill—only it filled with silt.

Worse, Sam had been sadly misinformed on the region's climate and hydraulic features, or chose to ignore them. It could be foggy, cold and nasty in the winter, and extremely windy at any time of year. Wildfires were a constant danger in the summer and fall. While the soil and water table near the river was great for growing fruit, the hillside land was too dry to grow much beyond cattle feed. And despite his wealth and influence, Sam had been unable to persuade the farmers near the river to part with their acreage—and hardly anyone else to settle on the land he had bought.

"We are all very busy here," he wrote to a friend in Virginia, "(but) not very prosperous. The grasshoppers have eaten us up for three years. I am building a house at Maryhill and am doing the best I can to keep the threads together."

In May 1913, Sam's "Promised Land" became Sam's cattle ranch. He imported 70 beef cattle and two Hereford bulls, all but abandoned the idea of a utopian community, and turned his scatter-shot attention to building "a good comfortable farmhouse" in a corner of his Maryhill kingdom. Much of Sam's efforts on the house seemed to involve trying to drive Jim Marshall crazy.

James Rush Marshall was a slender, serious man with a receding hairline and a full, dark beard. He was, by most accounts, exceedingly modest and self-effacing, and a very good golfer. He was also one of the most successful architects in the country. As a partner in the Washington, D.C. firm of Hornblower and Marshall, he had designed such public buildings as the Army and Navy Club in Washington; the U.S. Customs House in Baltimore, and the Natural History Museum and other buildings in the Smithsonian Institution complex. But the firm's specialty was private residences.

Their trademark style was called "Romanesque Revival." It was a clean, austere design, eschewing the gingerbread detail of Victorian houses and using molded brick for classical detail. The firm's homes often featured short columns, rounded arches, rough textures and massive proportions.

Marshall had worked on an estate Sam had purchased in Massachusetts and designed an eccentrically eclectic house for Sam in Seattle. So when Sam enlisted him to build the home at Maryhill, Marshall must have known what he was getting into. Work on the Maryhill home's foundation began in April 1914. But Sam had already started working on Marshall's nerves. In March, for example, Sam decided to add a massive pipe organ to the premises.

"Where is it you expect to put it?" Marshall exasperatedly asked. "… If you really mean a full-fledged pipe organ, I should say you would require the whole space marked 'den' to accommodate it, or else put your pipes somewhere in the cellar and bring the opening for the sound up through the walls."

Sam dropped the organ idea. But over the next 18 months, the changes—and expenses—added up: solid metal doors and window frames; two dozen ornamental grates for basement windows; 9,300 feet of metal lath, 10,000 yards of furring. By the time Marshall had sent his third "design scheme" in the fall of 1915, the architect and owner decided to meet in person at Maryhill. "The work is going slowly at the house," Sam wrote, "and when you are here you will see what condition things are in."

The meeting produced more design changes, and more delays. By early 1917, the inside walls had yet to be plastered, a 10-foot crack in the roof had to be repaired, and prices for many of the windows were "out of reason" and therefore had not even been ordered. By the time Loie Fuller arrived in July, it seemed Sam had all but lost interest in the place.

Shortly after she left, he began to have doubts about turning it into a museum. There was still no highway on the Washington side of the river connecting Maryhill to the populous areas to the west. To finish the building would cost a bundle. Loie hadn't lined up commitments of support from European artists and governments. Worse, her most important artist connection, Rodin, had died and left all his works to France.

"I have closed down the work here until I hear from you," Sam wrote Loie in November, 1917, "as I do not wish to put in any steel partitions which will have to be taken down. I hope our (artist) friends will not think me unduly insistent when I say I should like to hear from them by the first of February definitely as what they want to do. I hope by that time to open up the work again and finish the house for occupancy in case it is decided not to use it for the purpose indicated to you in my letter of July 24, 1917."

Loie hastily sought to reassure him. "Everyone here is simply crazy about your Museum," she wrote him from Paris in early 1918, "and the most wonderful ideas are being evolved for it."

Whether Sam was mollified or not, work on the Maryhill house-museum remained on hold. Besides, Sam was soon off on other quests.

NOTES FOR CHAPTER 4

Sam should give his *Portland Oregonian,* Nov. 4, 1926, p.11.

"Half a century hence" Oregon Daily Journal, Feb. 28, 1915, p. 11.

"I have not much money" Sam to James Marshall, June 17, 1917, MMA

Loie, meanwhile, had been *Richmond (Ind.) Item*, June 5, 1917, p. 1.

In San Francisco, Loie Loie to Sam, July 17, 1917 and July 19, 1917, MMA

"My dear Loie Fuller" Sam to Loie, July 24, 1917, MMA.

The idea began to *New York Sun*, May 31, 1905, p. 6; *Wilkes-Barre (Pa.) Record*, May 31, 1905, p. 3.

If Sam's idea of *Oregon Daily Journal*, May 18, 1913, p. 5.

"Lots of people" *Oregon Daily Journal*, Feb. 27, 1931, p. 1.

"The mind can only" Kathie Durbin, *Bridging a Great Divide: The Battle for the Columbia River Gorge,* (2013), p. 22.

"Though we made but" John C. Fremont, *Memoirs of My Life,* (1887), p. 284.

"We have found" Sam to Richard Hill, Oct. 18, 1907, MMA

"I personally made" Sam to James J. Hill, Nov. 23, 1907, MMA

So Sam's promotions became Daniel B. Hill to S.J. Ellison, Dec. 10, 1909, MMA

A slick brochure for *"Maryhill: The Land Where the Rain and Sunshine Meet,"* 1908 brochure, MMA.

"We didn't like the idea" Lois Davis Plotts, *Maryhill, Sam Hill and Me*, (1983); Ruth Jordan Peterson, *This Land of Gold and Toil,* (1982), p. 99.

The officials were impressed *Oregon Daily Journal*, Feb. 10, 1913, p. 1.

They were a little *New York Times,* July 20, 2010.

"We are all very" Sam to D.T. O'Connell, Dec. 12, 1914, MMA.

James Rush Marshall was "Hornblower and Marshall, Architects," National Trust for Historic Preservation, 1978.

"Where is it you" James Marshall to Sam, March 14, 1914, MMA.

Sam dropped the organ Sam to James Marshall, Oct. 25, 1915, MMA.

"I have closed down" Sam to Loie, Nov. 18. 1917, MMA.

Loie hastily sought Current and Current, op. cit., p. 257.

CHAPTER FIVE

"Young, handsome, talented and rich"

Sam's Story

JULY 1918

Sam Hill, a friend once drolly noted, "will fight at the drop of a hat for his convictions. He is for peace, and if you don't want a black eye and broken head, you will be for peace also."

Peace loomed large in the minds of most Americans in the summer of 1918. The country had been engaged in the four-year-old world war for 16 months. More than 300,000 U.S. troops were in Europe, with another million on the way. Even Sam, at the age of 60, had been "over there."

Just what he did in his trips to Europe during the war isn't entirely clear. In 1915, he visited the front lines. It was at the invitation of his friend King Albert of Belgium, whom he had met when the then-crown prince visited the United States in 1898. Sam wrote later that he spent four hours on the body-strewn battlefield, which was "three hours and fifty-nine minutes too long. One minute was all I needed." Both before and after his trip, Sam was a generous contributor and fundraiser to Belgian relief causes.

In 1916, on the recommendation of King Albert and the request of the Russian government, Sam traversed the length of the Trans-Siberian Railway, looking for ways to alleviate the traffic jams that were plaguing delivery of war supplies. That in itself was a dangerous undertaking. Less clear is whether he also threw in a bit of spying for the Allied cause.

It was at least plausible. Sam spoke fluent German and passable French, and traveled under a Russian, rather than a U.S., passport. Sam himself broadly hinted that he was looking at more than railroad schedules. At one point, he claimed in a 1921 interview, he encountered a would-be assassin who failed to recognize him but told him the Germans had put a £40,000 price on Sam Hill's head. Sam said he would help track down "this American" for a share of the bounty, then slipped quietly away.

However much James Bond there was in Sam Hill, his first-hand views of the war's horrors spurred him to action when he returned home. True to form, it was an act heavy on inspiration and symbolism, and light on planning and execution. In April, 1918, the *Goldendale Sentinel* reported Sam would dedicate land on his Maryhill estate as a cemetery for the fallen soldiers and sailors of Klickitat County. Within a month, however, he changed his mind, possibly spurred by the fact the county's war death toll stood at only three.

Instead of a cemetery, Sam announced he would build a full-sized replica of the ancient British monument Stonehenge. He had toured the real thing in 1916 and been told (erroneously) it was a site where the Druids had made human sacrifices to the god of war. "It seems fitting that this sacrifice which we (Americans) have been called on to make to the war god of the heathen should be fittingly remembered in some permanent way," he said. "I thought this would be a good way."

Coincidentally, the esteemed astronomer William W. Campbell of the University of California's Lick Observatory was in the Maryhill area at the time because the region was directly in the path of an upcoming solar eclipse. Sam promptly enlisted Campbell to help site the planned monument so the altar stone would line up as closely as possible to the path of the sun on the Summer Solstice, ala the real Stonehenge. When the best spot happened to be where Sam's hotel was located, Sam had the hotel taken down and moved.

On a scorching Fourth of July, before a crowd of about 500 locals and various dignitaries from Oregon and Washington, the monument's altar site was dedicated. (The two-hour ceremony and subsequent picnic shared the front page of the *Goldendale Sentinel* with a story of a shootout between cattle rustlers and county lawmen that left one of the bad guys dead and a deputy wounded.)

Wearing his customary frock coat and large cravat, in spite of the heat, Sam declared that "on our country's natal day, it is right and fitting that we should pledge ourselves anew to support those principles which our government was formed to maintain. Our forefathers gave us the liberty we enjoy; that heritage now incites us to aid in conferring the same on others."

But the war ended four months later, and Klickitat County suffered only 13 war-related deaths. Coupled with the fact that Sam sometimes had the attention span of a gnat, the result was it would take 11 years to finish the monument, and then only because grieving members of the dead soldiers' families and local officials periodically badgered Sam to complete what he started.

When it was finished, it would consist of two million pounds of steel-reinforced concrete, constructed to resemble what the real Stonehenge had looked like when it was new: circle 108 feet in diameter, with 30 massive stones 16 feet high and two ovals of five pairs of trilithons (two vertical stones topped with a horizontal stone), each 28 feet high. It would surround an altar 18 feet long. The pillars would bear bronze plaques with the names and dates of birth and death for the fallen of Klickitat County.

And it would turn out to be not only a war memorial, but Sam's final resting place, an annual gathering place for biker gangs, the scene of a murder—and a monument to Sam's lifelong quest to permanently remind the world that he had been there.

Sam Hill was born in the tiny settlement of Deep River, North Carolina, on May 13, 1857. His parents had deep roots in the region. His father was a fifth-generation American whose family had come to central North Carolina in the 1760s. His mother had forebears who had explored the frontier with Daniel Boone. Both parents were Quakers. Nathan Branson Hill, Sam's father, was a doctor. Nathan married Eliza Mendenhall in 1845, and in 1850 began a fairly prosperous practice in Randolph County. Eliza would have six children. Sam was the fourth.

In large part because of its sizeable anti-slavery Quaker community, Randolph County was an anomaly in pre-Civil War North Carolina. Relatively few families owned slaves, and the county voted against secession when it was proposed. Even so, the Hills' apparently well-earned reputation for helping runaway slaves sparked hostility from their non-Quaker neighbors. When North Carolina left the Union in May 1861, the Hills left North Carolina. They settled in Minneapolis. Although Sam's later self-narratives sometimes portrayed the family as struggling to make ends meet, the Hills actually fared well financially. Sam's father became chief surgeon for the region's railroads and president of the Minnesota Medical Association.

While economically secure, the family was repeatedly struck by personal tragedy. Sam's oldest sister died shortly after the Hills reached Minneapolis.

His mother died when he was 11, and another brother and sister soon after. In 1875, his father was watching a Senate debate at the state Capitol when he suffered a fatal stroke. Sam often contended that after his father died, he was forced to quit school. "It was a case of having to work if we wanted to eat," he told an interviewer in 1928. "I got a job piling mill wood at ten cents a load I had to work hard all day to earn as much as a dollar."

In fact, he not only graduated from high school, but in later years served as president of its alumni association. And whatever work he actually did, it wasn't in order to eat. Dr. Hill left an estate estimated to be worth at least $62,500 (about $1.3 million in 2017 dollars.) The estate was divided among Sam; his younger sister Anna, who was a semi-invalid in the early stages of tuberculosis, and his older brother Richard, who was in his last year of medical school in Philadelphia and about to start a three-year hitch as a surgeon with the U.S. Army on the Arizona frontier.

As for Sam, he set off for a few years of higher education. His first choice for college was at Cornell, in upstate New York. After a short stay, however, he contracted pneumonia and had to return home. Once recovered, Sam changed course, and entered Haverford College, a small Quaker-founded school a few miles from Philadelphia. He excelled. He earned a degree from Haverford in just three years. His appetite for education whetted, Sam enrolled at Harvard University in the fall of 1878, entering as a senior because of his time at Haverford.

In a class of 189 at America's foremost college, Sam stood out only because, according to the class secretary, at six feet tall he was three inches taller than the average senior. He finished 62nd in his class, played on no sports teams, and was a member of only two clubs. Tellingly, given his later dual career as cold-hearted businessman and starry-eyed philanthropist, they were the Finance Club and the Philosophical Society. His vocational goals were also not unique: Like 67 of his classmates, he thought he would become a lawyer.

However undistinguished his time as a student was, Sam relished being a "Harvard Man" for the rest of his life. As his fortune grew, he gave generously to the university. In 1900, Sam was elected to a five-year term on the university's Board of Overseers, only the second board member from west of the Mississippi River. "You ask, does anything interest me," he wrote to his class secretary in 1905. "I answer 'yes, Harvard.'"

Sam returned to Minneapolis in July, 1879. His Harvard degree, and the community's fond memories of his father, helped him land a clerkship at the city's most prestigious law firm. In December, 1880, Sam became a full-fledged attorney. His courtroom style was a mix of hard work and showmanship. He memorized legal precedent rather than referring to law books in the courtroom, and rarely used his preemptory challenges of prospective jurors: "I would look at the jury and say 'I do not have to challenge any of the jurors, because I know they want to see justice done …' the result was I had mighty good luck with my cases."

Along with his law practice, Sam plunged into the red-hot Minneapolis real estate market. He bought and sold vacant lots, rented out existing buildings, and in one case, demolished a row of houses and replaced them with new homes "provided with complete kitchens." In 1883, Sam formed a partnership with a well-known lawyer named John B. Atwater. The two became not only law partners, but business partners. Together with Atwater and on his own, Sam invested in a panoply of enterprises throughout the state: a printing company in Fergus Falls; a street railway company in Duluth, a natural gas company in Minneapolis. He was on the board of a company that floated logs down the Mississippi to the sawmills, and the board of another company that sorted out the logs when they got to the sawmills.

In May 1886, the *St. Paul Globe* ran a full-page story under a headline of three large dollar signs. The article consisted of sketches of the 100 wealthiest individuals and families in the Twin Cities. Sam was No. 100: "Samuel Hill inherited a little, speculated some and made plenty more. Young, handsome, talented and rich, he is currently spending a portion of his half-million in Europe."

It was one of four trips he would make to Europe in the decade, and more than 50 in his lifetime. But even when he was in Minneapolis, Sam seemingly never stayed home. Nearly every list of "notables" in attendance at charity balls, weddings, holiday parties and celebrity receptions included "Samuel Hill."

So did the membership roster for dozens of social, charitable and recreational organizations. He was president of the Athenaeum, a nonprofit group that served as the city's library. He gave speeches in German to the Harmonia Society and read the annual poem at the Bachelors Club. And he created a men's social organization known as the Nicollet Club, which became the elite group of its kind in the Twin Cities.

He also displayed a knack for politics. "Mr. Hill is winning the reputation of being so much of a politician that he is an expert judge of human nature and a keen handler of men," the *Globe* reported, "an ability seldom displayed in one so young." While he professed little interest in running for office himself, he delighted in the back-room maneuverings that got other people elected.

Even staying in the back rooms, Sam's dashing good looks and personality made him stand out in a crowd. A thick shock of wavy black hair added to the height of his trim six-foot frame. He was stylishly dressed and gregarious, with a disconcerting habit of leaning into the person he was talking to, as if taking them into his confidence. "He was charming, filled with enthusiasm, the complete extrovert," a friend described him. "He was blessed with a vanity that was captivating."

Given all he had going for him, it may not have surprised Twin Cities residents too much when they picked up their papers on May 6, 1888 and read that the most eligible bachelor in Minneapolis was engaged to the daughter of the richest man in St. Paul.

Near the end of F. Scott Fitzgerald's *The Great Gatsby,* the father of the title character is lamenting the death of his young, handsome, rich and talented son. "If he'd of lived, he'd of been a great man," the father says. "A man like James J. Hill. He'd of helped build up the country." Sam was already Gatsby. He wanted to be James J. Hill.

So did a lot of people. Jim Hill (who despite the identical surname was in no way related to Sam's family) was very rich: The newspaper story listing the 100 wealthiest people in the Twin Cities, which had ranked Sam at No. 100, listed Jim Hill at No. 1. "Today he is regarded as one of the most successful and wealthiest railroad men in the world," the article said.

By many measurements, Jim Hill was a great man: Before his death, he would control the transportation and commerce for a huge section of the United States, and be internationally known as "the Empire Builder." Born in Canada in 1838, James Jerome Hill came to St. Paul at the age of 18 and worked at every job he could find. In 1878, he formed a partnership with four other men, and took over a bankrupt Midwest railroad. Hill methodically expanded the railroad, building into other areas: wheat in Minnesota and the Dakotas; coal and other minerals in Montana, and lumber in the Far West.

By the time of his death in 1916, the Great Northern Railway and its auxiliaries spanned an empire of more than 6,000 miles of track in six states, and had massive holdings in iron ore, coal and real estate. Jim's personal estate was valued at $75 million—about $1.8 billion in 2017 dollars.

Before tying the knot with Jim Hill's oldest daughter, Mary Frances, Sam had already tied himself professionally to Jim as an assistant counsel to the railroad company. Just how that came about is unclear. Sam's version was that it was because of his legal skills. It's more likely Jim Hill admired Sam's political and people skills more than his courtroom prowess, particularly since those were among the few skills that Jim Hill lacked. "Hill was a wonderful discoverer of men," Sam told an interviewer, "but he always sent me to make the arrangements and hire them."

The two men were vastly dissimilar. Sam was tall, handsome and had a full head of dark wavy hair. Jim "was somewhat below the average height, built like a buffalo, with a prodigious chest and neck and head," and balding by his 30s. Although his vanity could make him a bit prickly at times, Sam was a pussycat compared to Jim, whom a biographer suggested "was not a man to disappoint, anger or cross." Then there was their work ethics. Sam took two long European vacations during the first two years of his association with Jim. Jim routinely worked 18-hour days, six days a week. But sometimes opposites attract, and Jim Hill apparently had no strong objections when Sam Hill began courting his daughter.

If Sam seemingly had little in common with Jim Hill, he may have had even less with Mary Frances Hill, known by family and friends as "Mamie." She was 18 when they met, he was 29. She was a practicing Catholic, he was a casual Quaker. He was a Harvard man, she was educated at a local convent academy. He was friendly and outgoing, she was, according to various descriptions, "pouty," "melancholy," and "hypochondriacal." He was big and strikingly good-looking, she was slender and darkly pretty, but not beautiful. And while Sam was chatty to the point of being annoying, Mamie, like her family, was taciturn to a fault. "There is a singular streak in the (J.J.) Hill family," Sam told the Wall Street journalist Clarence Barron. "Hill would not speak to his wife for sometimes a whole week. My wife would not speak to her mother for a year."

However unlikely, the courtship began sometime in 1886. The wedding took place on Sept. 6, 1888, at Jim Hill's mansion in St. Paul. About 100 people were invited to the ceremony itself, and 1,000 to the reception. The bride wore a heavy white silk gown "cut high and trimmed with heavy folds of old point lace." The groom wore bruises.

The morning of the wedding, Sam and John Atwater, his law partner and best man, were riding in a light buggy when the horse spooked "and dashed down the street at break-neck speed." Both men were thrown out. Atwater broke a leg, but Sam escaped without serious injury. "The buggy," *The New York Times* solemnly reported at the end of its wedding story, "was wrecked."

The couple, who had to postpone the honeymoon because of Sam's accident, could take considerable consolation from their wedding gifts. These included a rope of pearls, $3,000 worth of cut glass, "and some of the most useful and ornamental gifts that a St. Paul bride has ever received." While not particularly ornamental, Jim Hill's gift was spectacularly useful: $100,000 worth of bonds and $100,000 worth of railroad stock.

The gift ensured the weddings' coverage by newspapers around the country, and dominated the headlines: "A Nice Little Present;" "He Makes Sure of Heiress;" "The Bridegroom Certifies His Courage and the Father a Large Check." Even on his wedding day, Sam had been overshadowed by his father-in-law.

By marrying Jim Hill's daughter, Sam became inextricably linked to the Empire Builder. For the rest of his life—and even beyond—Sam would constantly be identified not by his own accomplishments, but by his relationship to James J. Hill. When Sam announced plans to build a museum at Maryhill, Washington, nine years after Jim Hill's death, *The New York Times* headline identified him as "Samuel Hill, James. J. Hill's son-in-law." When Sam himself died, the *Times'* secondary headline on his obituary was "helped the 'Empire Builder,' James J. Hill, to develop the Northwest."

Sam was painfully aware of the huge shadow his father-in-law cast over his life. "I sometimes think you do not know how difficult it is for me to speak or act, lest such word or act should be thought coming from you," Sam wrote Jim in August, 1893, "or as an indication of your views."

For twelve years, Sam Hill tried to get comfortable in his new life. While he stayed active in civic affairs, the clubs and parties were out. He and Mamie settled into a comfortable but hardly grand house that Jim Hill had given them. Vacations became less frequent, closer to home, and often in the company of his wife's mother, sisters and other relatives.

Ten months after their wedding, Mamie gave birth to a daughter. "Mary sends her love to you and asks that you find a name to go with the rattle you are to get for the baby in New York," Sam telegraphed Jim a few days after the baby arrived. "I think she likes your mother's name (Anne)." Instead, they decided on Mary, after both the baby's mother and Sam's mother-in-law. Four years after giving the Empire Builder his first granddaughter, Sam and Mamie gave Jim his first grandson, naming him James Nathan, after the baby's grandfathers.

On the surface, the couple seemed to adjust to married life. But even before the birth of James Nathan, Sam and Mamie found that they functioned quite nicely without each other. Mamie often went off with her mother to see specialists when one or both them had some real or imagined malady. In 1894, Mamie and the children began a practice of escaping the brutal Minnesota winters by relocating to Washington D.C.

Jim Hill heaped titles and responsibilities on his son-in-law. From 1890 to 1900, Sam was president, or on the board of directors, of 21 companies, almost all of them subsidiaries of the Great Northern Railway. One that wasn't directly connected to the railroad, the Minneapolis Trust Co., had been formed in November 1888, with Sam as president. But Jim Hill's presence was heavy even there: Of the $500,000 in capital the trust began with, $25,000 was Sam's and $100,000 was Jim's.

Not all Sam's duties were at the executive level. He functioned as Jim's chief lobbyist in St. Paul and Washington, pulling strings and rounding up votes for issues that concerned the Great Northern's far-flung interests. J.J. Hill's "most active agent," a Chicago newspaper noted, "is his son-in-law, Samuel Hill, a young man who has a million or two in his own name and quite a political pull."

No matter how hard he worked, however, Sam remained a son-in-law and not a son. Although Sam would later claim he had been groomed to take Jim Hill's place at the head of the railroad empire, but chose not to, the reality was Jim clearly intended for his youngest son Louis to take over. Fifteen years younger than Sam, Louis Hill was thoughtful, conscientious and an astute judge of public tastes. He was also not particularly fond of Sam. An acquaintance of both men observed that "Louis was often bemused, possibly often annoyed, by the performance of his handsome, virile and volatile brother-in-law, with (Sam's) tremendous flair for the dramatic and the spectacular."

Jim was not only more comfortable with the thought of Louis succeeding him, but more and more troubled with the growing marital problems between Sam and Mamie. Jim Hill and his wife were severely straight-laced, even by Victorian standards. When their eldest son married a divorcee, he was ostracized by the family. When Sam and Mamie's disaffection became increasingly obvious, Sam received much of the blame. They were also concerned about the effect the estrangement was having on their eldest grandchild, who was beginning to exhibit signs of the mental illness that would plague her life.

The relationship between Jim and Sam was strained further by a criminal libel suit Sam filed against the editor of the *Minneapolis Times* in 1898. The *Times* had charged that the trust company Sam ran had short-changed creditors in a bankruptcy proceeding. The charges were groundless. But Sam's thirst for revenge against the paper resulted in a highly publicized six-week trial that dwelled in detail on Sam's relations with Jim Hill and prominent politicians. In the end, a jury decided the editor had lied, but acquitted him anyway.

The publicity apparently greatly disturbed Jim. A rumor spread that Jim had told Sam "that if he lost this case, he had better go to the Klondike or some distant country, as his usefulness where he was now known would be gone." However much truth there was behind the speculation, the incident shook Sam considerably.

"Sometimes the longing comes back," Sam wrote to a former law partner, "to see those kindred spirits whom I knew when I was Sam Hill, and before I went to work for the railroads, and before I lost, in a measure, my identity."

Gradually, he began winding down his role in the Great Northern empire, and spent more time on his own growing business interests in Seattle. Although he continued to do some lobbying for Jim, and stayed on as trust president until 1903, Sam relinquished his active management role in the railroad. The shift was duly noted in newspapers in both the Twin Cities and Seattle. "While he was in Seattle, Mr. Hill was interviewed and quoted as saying that he intended to remove his family to that city and reside there permanently," the *Minneapolis Journal* reported in September, 1901. "Today he declined either to deny or affirm the story."

But Sam had already made the break with his father-in-law. In July, he sent Jim a letter, returning several checks from various Hill companies "to which I do not think myself entitled. In returning the checks I wish to thank you for the great generosity shown me while connected with your service, and to assure you that no one regrets more than I my inability to meet your expectations. While it is no defense to my shortcomings, I believe no one has ever had for you a more affectionate regard than I. That I have often been an embarrassment to you I am sorry for…". Apologies made, Sam set off to build his own empire.

Even before he left Minneapolis, Sam had bought controlling interest in Seattle's only utility firm, the Seattle Gas & Electric Co. Despite his almost complete lack of experience or understanding of the business, Sam was supremely confident he could develop a utility kingdom in the Pacific Northwest.

"I like the work more than any work I have undertaken in a long time," he wrote one of his brothers-in-law in May 1902. "… I have come to like the place (Seattle) and enjoy myself, and am beginning to feel young again. I shall feel that I have wasted my time this year if the company is not better off by $100,000 than it was the year before."

His good feelings soon faded. Sam's company lost its exclusive franchise within the city, in large part because it was charging double the rates of those in other big cities. A "Gas War" soon developed with a new, rival firm, started by a New York man named Lyman Smith, who had made a fortune in typewriters and knew as little about gas companies as Sam.

Sam professed to relish the fight. "I do not care so much about making money as I do about having my own way," he wrote his brother-in-law. "I have put the price of gas down and mean to keep it down so that Smith cannot make any money during the lifetime of his franchise...knock him out I must and will."

The war, however, soon took on comic-opera overtones. Sam bought gas from his own company, then sold it privately at a loss to some favored customers to get around a law requiring a single fixed rate. Smith's company built gas lines under streets where there were no houses, then had to pay to tear up the streets so the lines could be connected to houses when they were built. There were labor troubles, legal and political skirmishes, and equipment failures. "Our gasworks looks like a barnyard of chickens," Sam fumed to a friend, "all running in different directions."

After heated and protracted negotiations, both companies sold out in the spring of 1904, to a third party that consolidated the firms. Sam walked away claiming a dubious victory, and with a few hundred thousand dollars in profits. In the meantime, his wife walked away from him.

Mamie Hill hated Seattle. She hated the rain, she hated the distance from family and friends, she hated what she deemed its provincialism—and she wasn't real fond of Sam for bringing her there. So, in mid-1903 she took daughter Mary and son James and moved to a palatial home in Washington, D.C. Her deep Catholic roots meant there would be no divorce, but for all intents and purposes, the marriage was over. Sam was disconsolate, although from the tone of his correspondence it was as much from having failed at marriage as from missing his wife. "I sometimes feel if I had my family here and was in a comfortable home and hard at work, I would be a contented man," he wrote to friend, the key word being "sometimes."

Sam hated Washington D.C. as much as Mary hated Washington state. "I have gone there year after year with a thorough and profound contempt for the entire city," he wrote his son "… I regard Washington as a town containing but three classes of people: Negroes, clerks and grafters."

In hopes of finding neutral ground where the family could be together at least part of the year, Sam bought a rambling estate near Stockbridge, Massachusetts in 1905, putting the deed in his wife's name. Mamie, however, insisted that Sam deal long-distance with every problem that arose, from installing a telephone and ordering sawdust to cover the ice in the icehouse, to firing a chauffeur who wrecked the family car, was arrested for drunk driving—and then demanded a letter of reference.

Unsurprisingly, Sam developed an intense dislike for the place, and visited infrequently. "After spending a summer in Massachusetts, I am more convinced that some effort should be made to teach the principles of common honesty in New England," he wrote a friend. His dislike of the East, cold relations with his wife and egocentric obsessions with business and travel all contributed to Sam's troubled relationships with his children.

By the time she was in her mid-teens, it was clear there was something very wrong with Mary Mendenhall Hill. "She was somewhat plump but nice enough looking," an acquaintance recalled, "with a wealth of black hair, only her dark eyes seemed unnaturally bright, and she wouldn't talk."

She was also prone to fits of hysteria and deep depression, and may have been mentally disabled. Worse, her father was almost always thousands of miles away and her mother had her own deep-seated emotional and mental problems. In 1910, when Mary was 21, her maternal grandparents decided the best course was for them to take custody of her, and reluctantly started legal proceedings. Sam solved the problem, albeit only temporarily, by in effect kidnapping his daughter. Accompanied by a female doctor and a nurse, Sam brought Mary to Washington state in mid-1910.

"I have had a great deal of trouble and sorrow," he wrote to a former Harvard classmate, "but have decided to act hereafter on my own responsibility. Mary seems very delighted with Seattle and with the place here at Maryhill."

She was too—as long as Sam was around. She diligently practiced her piano, made jam, and became an adept horsewoman. Sam was a doting father, when it suited his schedule, from letting her win at games of dominoes to building her a handsome eight-room residence at Maryhill, complete with rich wood paneling and a wide wrap-around porch. In one letter, Mary wrote that a 1911 auto trip with her father to California had been "the grandest time" of her life.

For the next few years, she spent most of her time in Washington state, visiting her mother and grandparents occasionally. But Sam was often away, leaving her in the care of his servants and a live-in nurse. In 1916, while he was on his wartime Russian adventure, Mary had a serious breakdown and had to be hospitalized in Portland for three months.

A local physician proposed exploratory surgery in her digestive system, theorizing that her mental problems might be the result of "a large amount of feces being held for long periods in the large intestine." Sam's physician brother vigorously demurred, as did the famed Mayo brothers, who were Hill family friends. His surgical suggestion thwarted, the Portland doctor succeeded with his alternative idea—institutionalizing her. "Your daughter cannot take care of herself," he warned Sam in a letter. "She will have to be guarded for a long time to come."

"A long time" turned out to be the rest of Mary's life. It's unclear where she was committed, although there is some evidence it was first in California, then the Midwest. She died in 1941, at the age of 51. After her commitment, Sam rarely, if ever, mentioned her in letters or conversation again.

Sam's relationship with his son, James Nathan Branson Hill, was more deplorable than tragic. Like Sam, "Jimmy" was tall. Unlike Sam, he was thin, stooped-shouldered and suffered from persistent bronchitis. He was also lazy, spoiled, and either not very bright or totally disinterested in academics. Or both. The Hill family joke was that Jimmy's middle initials, N.B., stood for "no brains." He was also well aware of his family's wealth.

"He (Jimmy) has gone on with the same attitude of cynical indifference," the headmaster of an Eastern prep school wrote Sam, just before Jimmy was expelled. "… His indifference seems to repulse every effort we make. He is averaging 45 out of 100 in all his classes."

In letters to friends and relatives, Sam alternately berated himself for spoiling the boy and made excuses for him. He acknowledged indulging his son with money whenever he wanted something, failing to find areas of mutual interest, and being absent too much from the boy's life. In letters to Jimmy, however, Sam alternated between talking about himself and his own troubles and harshly criticizing the boy for failing to live up to Sam's expectations.

"I cannot tell you how deeply humiliated I am; how chagrinned I am," Sam wrote in one such letter. "… If you do not change, and change at once, you will have disgraced yourself, your mother and me, and will have proved untrue to the traditions which have been handed down in my family from father to son."

But Jimmy didn't change, at least not enough to suit Sam. Sometime near the end of 1913, while Jimmy was meandering through Harvard, father and son had a final showdown over Jimmy's constant requests for more money. Correspondence between the two seems to have ceased. After finally graduating, Jimmy Hill dabbled at several business ventures and until his death in 1975 lived mostly off trusts established by his father and grandparents, and a sizeable inheritance from his mother. He never married, and resurfaced in the Maryhill story only after the death of Sam—and then in a most unpleasant way.

Despite lacking a family to live in it—and with no real desire to live it in himself—Sam decided in 1906 to build a house in Seattle. It was to be on land in the city's Capitol Hill district, with impressive views of Lake Union and distant Mt. Baker and Mt. Rainier. And as usual with Sam, it was to be unusual.

Designed by James Marshall, the Washington D.C. architect who would later draw up plans for the mansion at Maryhill, the 8,000-sq.-ft., two-story building was basically a steel-reinforced concrete cube. It was 52 feet by 52 feet, with six bedrooms and six bathrooms, a sub-basement, basement, garage and an elevator to the rooftop garden, complete with two feet of soil and a lush lawn.

Sam was intimately involved in the construction details, from the six-inch steel cable he salvaged from an abandoned coal mine to wrap around the foundation, to the wall niches that allowed mounted photographs to be illuminated from behind. "In the whole house, you will not find a crack, a knot or a blemish in any of the beam ceilings of woodwork," he bragged. There was a steel vault for valuables, and an elaborate intercom system. There was even a garden sundial so painstakingly designed and located it was said to be accurate within one minute.

Sam estimated construction costs came to precisely $37,828. The house, which in 1976 was placed on the National Register of Historic Places (as was the sundial separately), was listed for sale in 2017 at $15 million, making it one of the most expensive residences in Seattle.

But even with all the effort he put into it, Sam seldom lived there. Some years he occupied it for no more than total of a few weeks. Once, when he mentioned his "house" in Seattle to a young girl, she asked him why he didn't refer to it as his "home." "Ah," Sam replied, "when you are older, you will know the difference."

When he wasn't in Seattle or Maryhill, Sam was, well, everywhere else. By his own count late in his lifetime, he had made 51 trips to Europe; three to Russia; nine to Japan, and five around the world. He kept cases at various hotels and private clubs all over the United States and Europe, containing suits, formal wear, shoes, ties and toiletries. That enabled him to travel at a moment's notice with only a small black bag. On one trip to Europe, Sam took along his road-building engineer buddy Samuel Lancaster. "To my surprise, he knew the porters, the bellboys and the proprietors of most of the hotels at which we stopped," Lancaster recalled. "Inasmuch as he spoke German, French and Italian fluently, we had no difficulty in getting along."

Sam's 1909 trip with Lancaster combined two of his greatest pleasures: being on the road, and roads, period. A 19th century railroad man, he foresaw the 20th century would belong to the motor vehicle, and took it upon himself to prepare America for the shift. "Good roads are more than my hobby, he said, "they are my religion. The safety of the Republic is involved in the building of better highways."

He practiced his religion religiously. He lobbied presidents, governors, congresses and legislatures. He helped organize and lead international road conferences. He helped establish and finance a highway engineering department at the University of Washington, with Lancaster as its chair. He lectured to anyone who would listen: business groups, women's clubs, school children, using colored slides that cost up to $500 each and speaking up to four hours per day for weeks on end at various venues. A story was told that when a Portland elementary school class was asked "What was the Colossus of Rhodes," many of the students shouted "Sam Hill!"

School kids weren't the only ones to extend Sam the recognition for his road work that he had sought in other endeavors. *The New York Times* devoted a full page to him in August, 1913—complete with a three-column portrait.

The story lionized him as "the great prophet of a new era," and "the head of an extraordinary movement." The *Times'* praise was centered on Sam's efforts to build a highway linking the U.S. West Coast from Canada to Mexico. But his greatest success in road building came about, at least indirectly, as a result of his greatest disappointment, and perhaps the single biggest hurdle in realizing his Maryhill dreams.

As founder and first president of the Washington Good Roads Association, Sam had generally been successful in convincing the state's political leaders to see things his way when it came to building a road system. His successes ranged from using prison inmates as paid road builders (and allowing them access to axes and explosives, without incident) to picking construction methods and materials.

But he repeatedly failed to convince elected officials to build a road along the Columbia River that would link the urban areas of Portland and Vancouver Washington in the west to the rural areas—including Maryhill—in the east. Legislators, as well as a governor whose election campaign Sam had worked hard for and heavily contributed to, balked at a grossly overestimated cost of $35,000 per mile. Worse, the newly elected governor nixed the further use of convict labor on roads.

Furious, Sam took his crusade across the river. He began courting Oregon politicians and business leaders, bringing them to Maryhill to show them his 10 miles of "demonstration roads." With Lancaster, he argued that the formidable natural obstacles the gorge presented to building a road through it would turn out to be the road's greatest asset, attracting thousands of cash-spending tourists to marvel at its waterfalls and rock formations. "We will cash in, year after year, on our crop of scenic beauty, without depleting it in any way," Sam said.

The Oregonians proved receptive listeners. With public and private financial support, construction on the Columbia River Highway was begun in 1913 and finished in 1922. Principally engineered by Lancaster and promoted by Sam, it was a stunning technical and civic achievement. Lancaster employed new and innovative engineering methods while Sam kept up a constant drumbeat of public enthusiasm.

The highway was effusively lauded. Former President Theodore Roosevelt proclaimed it "the most remarkable road engineering in the United

States, which for scenic grandeur is not equaled anywhere." Major General George Goethals, who oversaw the building of the Panama Canal, called it "splendid engineering, and absolutely without equal in a America for scenic interest."

Sam basked in the praise, but fumed that as far as Maryhill was concerned, the beautiful new highway was on the wrong side of the river. A decidedly more modest paved road on the Washington side of the river would not be completed all the way to Maryhill until 1937. And a bridge connecting the Oregon highway to Maryhill and replacing a harrowing ferry ride across the river would not be completed until 1962. It would be named the Sam Hill Memorial Bridge.

As the Great War ended, Sam Hill drifted. His quixotic eight-year struggle to become a force in the still-young telephone business had ended in defeat. It began in March 1909, when he took control of the Home Telephone Co. in Portland. The company had been badly run, was $225,000 in debt and was crippled by an onerous operating agreement with the city. Worse, it was competing with the Pacific Telephone and Telegraph Co., part of the giant Bell System.

Through automation, adroit marketing and dogged litigation, Sam managed to turn the company around and fight Ma Bell to a draw, for a while. But the firm's profits were consumed by improvements and expansion needed to stay competitive, and stockholders, including Sam, received no dividends. By 1917, the company was insolvent, and Sam was once again out of the utility business.

While he was still as enthusiastic as ever about good roads, the movement had gained so much momentum his efforts were no longer so vital to the cause as they had been. He had cooled off considerably on his promise to Loie Fuller to turn his unfinished Maryhill mansion into an oasis of art. At one point, he even dabbled with the idea of turning much of the ranch into a colony for Belgian war refugees.

A month or so after an armistice was proclaimed, and World War I effectively ended, Sam took a trip to Japan, returning to Seattle in January, 1919.

Two months later, he was off to Europe. He hoped to be there in time for the April 8 birthday of his pal King Albert of Belgium.

With other world leaders, the king was scheduled to attend what would turn out to be epochal post-war peace talks in Paris. Loie would be in Paris too. So would a woman Sam had never met, but in his old-fashioned, courtly way, had already promised his eternal loyalty. She was the queen of Romania.

NOTES FOR CHAPTER 5

Sam Hill, a friend *Oregon Daily Journal*, Aug. 13, 1922, p. 14.

Just what he did *Records of the Harvard Class of 1879*, 1927, p. 239.

It was at least Clarence A. Barron, *They Told Barron: Conversations of an American Pepys in Wall Street*, 1930, pp. 65-66.

Instead of a cemetery *Goldendale Sentinel*, May 2, 1918, p. 1.

Wearing his customary *Oregon Daily Journal,* July 7, 1918, p. 13.

Sam Hill was born Anne McCarthy, *The Hill Family of Chowan County*, North Carolina, 1990.

In large part because Randolph County Historical Society, *Randolph County, 1779-1979*, pp. 71-73.

While economically secure *Oregon Daily Journal*, Feb. 14, 1928, p. 13.

In fact, he not only *Minneapolis Tribune*, Feb. 9, 1875, p. 3; *Minneapolis Tribune*, Feb. 19, 1875, p. 4.

In a class of Harvard Class of 1879 *Secretary's Report #1*, 1879.

However undistinguished Harvard Class of 1879, *Secretary's Report #26,* 1905.

Sam returned to Minneapolis *Oregon Daily Journal*, Feb. 14, 1928, p. 13.

In May, 1886 *St. Paul Globe*, May 16, 1886, p. 12.

He also displayed a *St. Paul Globe*, Sept. 26, 1886, p. 11.

Even staying in the Stewart H. Holbrook, *Rivers of America: The Columbia*, 1957, pp. 264-65.

So did a lot of *St. Paul Globe*, May 16, 1886, p. 12.

Before tying the knot Barron, op. cit., p. 66.

The two men were *New York Times*, May 30, 1916, p. 1; Michael J, Malone, *James J. Hill: Empire Builder of the Northwest,* 1996, p. 208.

If Sam seemingly Barron, op. cit., p. 67

However unlikely, the courtship *Chicago Daily Tribune*, Sept. 7, 1888, p. 1.

The morning of the wedding *New York Times*, Sept. 7, 1888, p. 7.

The couple, who had Ibid.

By marrying Jim Hill's daughter *New York Times*, Jan. 31, 1925, p. 7; *New York Times*, Feb. 27, 1931, p. 21.

Sam was painfully aware Sam to J.J. Hill, Aug. 25, 1893, Minnesota Historical Society Archives.

Ten months after their Sam to J.J. Hill, July 8, 1889, Minnesota Historical Society Archives.

Not all Sam's duties *Chicago Daily Tribune*, Nov. 20, 1888, p. 2.

No matter how hard Holbrook, op. cit., p. 265.

The publicity apparently *Great Falls (Mt.) Leader*, Feb. 12, 1898, p. 4.

"Sometimes the longing" Sam to J.B. Atwater, July 7, 1899, MMA.

Gradually he began Minneapolis Journal, Sept. 5, 1901, p. 6.

But Sam had already Sam to J.J. Hill, July 30, 1901, Minnesota Historical Society Archives.

"I like the work" Sam to Anson Beard, May 24, 1902, MMA.

Sam professed to relish Sam to Anson Beard, Dec. 29, 1902, MMA.

The war, however, Sam to F.C. Shephard, Dec. 5, 1902, MMA.

Mamie Hill hated Sam to J.D. Farrell, Dec. 18, 1905, MMA.

Sam hated Washington Sam to James N.B. Hill, Nov. 25, 1912, MMA.

Unsurprisingly, Sam developed Sam to Anistice Abbot, Dec. 2, 1905, MMA.

By the time she Plotts, op. cit., p. 14.

"I have had a" Sam to Francis McLennan, June 13, 1910, MMA

A local physician Dr. Kenneth Mackenzie to Sam, Aug. 18, 1916, MMA.

Sam's relationship with Letter from James J. Hill biographer Albro Martin to Lois Plotts, March 10, 1980, MMA.

"He (Jimmy) has gone" Alfred E. Ellis to Sam, Oct. 28, 1907, MMA.

"I cannot tell you" Sam to James N.B. Hill, Nov. 5, 1907, MMA.

Sam was intimately *Oregon Daily Journal*, Jan. 20, 1930, p. 4.

But even with Tuhy, op. cit., p. 109.

When he wasn't in *Oregon Daily Journal*, Sept. 6, 1919, p. 6.

Sam's 1909 trip *Oregon Daily Journal,* Aug. 12, 1922, Sec. 2, p. 6.

School kids weren't *New York Times,* Aug. 17, 1913, p. 10.

Furious, Sam took Samuel Lancaster, *The Columbia: America's Great Highway from the Cascades to the Sea,* (3rd ed., 1926), p. 116.

The highway was effusively lauded In the National Park Service's *Columbia River Highway NRHP Registration Form,* Aug. 1986, p. 46.

CHAPTER SIX

"Very naughty, but a very clever woman"
Marie's Story
APRIL 1919

If she wanted Transylvania, the queen of Romania would have to go shopping. And Marie Alexandra Victoria wanted Transylvania.

After all, the large and mountainous region, which was currently part of Hungary, was populated in large part by people who considered themselves Romanians. Hungary had been on the losing side of the recently concluded world war. Romania had, sort of, been on the winning side. It seemed fair and natural that the territory switch hands.

But to convince the leaders of the major nations—France, England and the United States—who were dividing up post-war Europe at the "peace talks" in Paris, Marie had to play up her assets. These were her charm, wit and mesmerizing good looks. She had to look as queenly as possible.

The war's privations, however, had taken their toll. Her daughters, who had accompanied her to the French capital, were wearing dresses made from Marie's old coats. Marie's own wardrobe was five years out of date. Her jewelry was fake. The real stuff, which had been shipped to Russia for safekeeping from the Germans, had been stolen by the Bolsheviks after the Russian Revolution. So, from her 22-room suite at the Hotel Ritz, the queen went shopping. Sixty gowns, 31 coats, 22 fur pieces, 29 hats and 83 pairs of shoes later, she was ready to meet the world's leaders.

"Perhaps it does seem a good many," Marie acknowledged to her friend Mabel Potter Daggett, an American writer and women's rights leader. "Still, I feel this is no time to economize. You see, Romania simply has to have Transylvania and what if for lack of a gown, a concession should be lost?"

To ensure that didn't happen, Marie planned precisely which ensemble she would wear in each meeting with the various countries' leaders. "The gown of cloth and gold with heavy gold embroidery I specially selected for the luncheon with your American president," she told Daggett.

However precise her plans, Marie's diplomatic efforts at the peace talks were at least technically unofficial. Romania's formal lead representative was the prime minister, Ion Bratianu II. Very rich and unquestionably smart, Bratianu was also arrogant, pretentious, and in the words of one diplomat, "a most unpleasing man." Marie thought he was "a tiresome, sticky and tedious individual."

He had also largely been a failure insofar as Romania's hopes for securing some of the post-war spoils. So, despite some misgivings, Marie's husband King Ferdinand asked if she would go to Paris and see what she could do. "A shiver of pride shuddered through me," Marie recalled. "I? Yes, of course Yes, I think I felt capable of holding my own, even with 'the Great Three,'" referring to the leaders of Britain, France and the United States.

Romania needed all the help it could get. It hadn't entered the war on the side of the Allied Nations until August, 1916, two years after the fighting began. Its entry came only after Britain, France and their allies secretly agreed that Romania would get all the territory it coveted—Hungary-controlled Transylvania, as well as slices of Austria, Russia and what would become Yugoslavia—after the war.

But Romania fared very badly on the battlefield. After some heady initial success, its army was steadily pummeled by German and Austro-Hungarian forces, and steadily rolled back until it was forced to drop out of the fighting in May 1918. Its forced separate peace deal with Germany angered Romania's allies, who were thus in no mood to honor the 1916 deal. In fact, Romania was not initially even invited to the peace talks, and admitted only grudgingly.

Then came Marie. While the Romanian war effort had floundered, the queen had emerged as a hero in Western Europe and America. Her life-risking efforts as a frequent visitor to wounded soldiers, her defiant public denunciations of German atrocities and her eloquent appeals for humanitarian aid were frequently and glowingly reported in U.S., English and French newspapers.

Her wartime acclaim followed her to Paris. She was mobbed at every public appearance. She was asked to formally review French troops on parade, a rare honor for a foreign leader. The prestigious Académie des Beaux-Arts, a French intellectual society, admitted her as its first female member, mainly for her inspirational writing during the war.

"I have met several kings, queens and princes of the blood, but none ever quite like Marie," wrote the distinguished American journalist Herbert

Bayard Swope, after the queen had held her first press conference. "She has beauty, charm, character, decision and intelligence, and the combination makes a greatly favorable impression."

Even Marie was impressed by Marie. "It is lucky I am 43," she wrote in her journal, "or I might really imagine I am irresistible. As it is, I feel what a degree of natural magnetism I have."

The "Great Three" felt it too—or at least two of them did. The British Prime Minister David Lloyd George, himself a notorious flirt, found her "very naughty, but a very clever woman." French Prime Minister Georges Clemenceau, a crusty old politician known as "The Tiger," was equally charmed. As Marie rose to leave at the scheduled end of their first meeting, Clemenceau waved her back to her seat. "I have plenty of time for you," he said. "You speak up, I like that!"

If the French leader liked the Romanian queen, however, the American leader did not. President Woodrow Wilson first tried to dodge Marie altogether, saying he was much too busy to meet her after 9 a.m. Marie countered that she was an early riser. After a brief early-morning meeting, Marie invited herself to lunch with Wilson a few days later. She showed up 30 minutes late, and with a retinue of 10 people instead of the agreed-upon five. Then the queen and president clashed over whether Romania's harsh treatment of its Jewish population was worse than America's treatment of its black and Japanese residents.

Noting that Marie had "the tact of a badger," Wilson's wife later wrote that she looked at her husband "and seeing his jaw set, I knew this very beautiful woman had met one man whom she failed to charm."

Notwithstanding her failure to charm Wilson, (whom Marie thought was pompous and preachy), the peace council eventually gave Romania most of what it wanted. The country nearly doubled in area, while its population soared from eight million to 18 million. What had been a tiny, defeated afterthought of a nation had become the fifth-largest country in Europe and the most important power in the Balkans.

While Marie's coquettish diplomacy was influential, it was almost certainly outweighed in the council's decision by Western Europe's hope that a strong Romania would stop the spread of Russian Bolshevism. "This is what I tell you," French General Ferdinand Foch, the Allies' supreme commander during the war, advised the peace council's leaders, "build upon Roumania, because then you have not only an army (to stop the Bolsheviks), but a government, a people."

Regardless of the reason, Marie was thrilled. "In all fairness, I have to admit that we had come away with the lion's share," she wrote, "and I was humbly, almost tremblingly grateful before the magnanimity of fate, which had assured us to be among the winners." If she was "humbly" grateful at the results, however, Marie wasn't at all humble about her role in achieving them. "Nando," she told her husband on her return to Romania, "it's a good thing God gave me a personality that pleases people."

Marie Alexandra Victoria was born on a stately English estate on Oct. 29, 1875. And if ever a woman was born to be a queen, it was Marie Alexandra Victoria. Her extended family was a veritable manufacturer of European monarchs. Her paternal grandmother was Queen Victoria, ruler of the vast British Empire. Her maternal grandfather was Emperor Alexander II of Russia. During Marie's lifetime, her various sons, daughters, sisters, aunts, uncles and cousins occupied the thrones of Great Britain, Russia, Denmark, Norway, Greece, Yugoslavia, Spain, Germany and, of course, Romania.

While there were certainly distinct advantages to being born into 19th century royalty, however, there were also drawbacks. One was that it was an unwritten rule—and often a written one—that those royals who were in line for a throne could only marry other royals. This drastically limited the field of eligible spouses. It also explained why Marie's mother and father married, even though they had nothing in common and probably never even liked each other.

Marie's father was Alfred, Duke of Edinburgh, known as "Affie" in family circles. (European royalty, it should be noted, often had family nicknames in order to tell each other apart, because so many had the same first names.) He was the second son of Queen Victoria. As such, he was also second in line to the throne, behind his brother Edward. He dropped to fourth after Edward had two sons. Alfred's consolation prize was that he eventually became duke of the German duchy of Saxe-Coburg-Gotha (the modern-day states of Bavaria and Thuringia), as the result of an inheritance from an uncle.

Tall, dark and handsome, bad-tempered and with an over-fondness for liquor, the duke was known mainly for a long career in the British navy (during which he was wounded in an assassination attempt while becoming the first member of the British royal family to visit Australia); owning an impressive collection of ceramics and glassware, and being an enthusiastic but mediocre violinist.

Marie's mother was the Grand Duchess Marie Alexandrovna. She was the only surviving daughter—and favorite child—of Emperor Alexander II of Russia. Nine years younger than her husband, the duchess was short, vaguely pretty and prone to plumpness. She was extremely intelligent, speaking four languages fluently. She was also extremely arrogant. People who turned their backs to her when they left the room were certain to incur her wrath. She fumed when addressed as "royal highness" rather than "imperial highness," since she was the daughter of an emperor and not a mere king or queen. And she generally despised England.

The two were married after a long and lukewarm courtship, which seems to have been based on the facts that she was very rich and he was from the most powerful family on earth, and with the hope that the marriage might help thaw the frosty relations between Great Britain and Russia.

Alfred was an indifferent father, often being away from home for long periods, and being aloof when he was there. "He was a little bit of a stranger to us," Marie recalled in her memoirs. "… The days when he paid attention to us were red-letter days." The duchess, however, got high marks, at least from Marie. "It was Mamma who settled things, Mamma who we turned to, Mamma who came to kiss us goodnight," Marie wrote. "… Mamma loved us passionately."

Known as "Missy," Marie was the second of five children. And despite her parents' dissonance, Marie's early years were blissful. "Our childhood was a happy carefree one," she recalled, "the childhood of rich, healthy children protected from the buffets and hard realities of life." Things only got better, as far as Marie was concerned, when the family moved to the Mediterranean island of Malta when she was 11. Her father had been named commander of the British Mediterranean Fleet, and the island became a wondrous playground for Marie and her siblings. It was there she became an expert and fearless horsewoman. It was also where she developed a deep crush on a first cousin who was 10 years older and an officer under her father's command—and who would eventually wind up as George V, king of England.

The feelings were mutual: "I am so longing to see you my darling Missy you are always in my thoughts," he wrote her while he was at sea. There was serious talk among the royal family's members—including Queen Victoria—of the two becoming betrothed. But Marie was only 15 at the time, and George was in no hurry to wed. Moreover, George's mother had an intense dislike for Marie's mother, and Marie's mother was horrified at the thought of her daughter marrying an Englishman. The discussion gradually ended. Instead, Marie began slowly drifting toward marriage in a very strange country, to a man who loved someone else.

Marie was 10 years younger than the man she would marry—and three years older than the kingdom they would rule. Despite its ancient and remarkably varied culture, Romania didn't formally exist as an independent nation until 1878, and only then after a series of events that were a bit bizarre even by Eastern European standards.

Romania's roots were in a kingdom of Thracian tribes known to the Romans as Dacia, which existed for about a century before being conquered by the Roman emperor Trajan in 106 A.D. The region eventually and generally became known, somewhat unimaginatively, as "Roumania." After the Roman Empire collapsed, the region was periodically rolled over by Goths, Huns, Bulgurs, Avars, and other "barbarian" groups.

In the mid-15th century, the Ottoman Turks took over much of the region, despite the efforts of local leaders such as Vlad III, better known to history buffs and horror fans as "Vlad the Impaler," or "Vlad Dracula." (There was also the lesser-known-but-more-important "Michael the Brave," about whom no one would make a seemingly endless series of movies.) In the late 17th century, the Habsburgs moved east from what is now Austria and Hungary and took Transylvania away from the Turks.

That, in turn, was followed by more than a century of more-or-less continual fighting over the region. "Roumania, lying between Russia, Austria and Turkey, was ever a pawn in their envious designs," wrote the American travel writer Winifred Gordon, a confidant of Marie's, "and was looked upon by each as a buffer acquisition, or as a hostage to bargain with."

At the end of the Crimean War, in 1862, the winning countries established the principalities of Moldavia and Wallachia as a semi-independent nation. A few years later, the Romanian aristocrats decided to import a ruler, since none of them trusted each other. A German prince named Karl of Hohenzollern-Sigmaringen was brought in. After yet another war, Romania became a bonafide country in 1878, and three years after that, Prince Karl became King Carol I, the first regent of Romania.

Just to complicate things further, Carol's only child died in infancy. After his brother and his eldest nephew turned him down, Carol settled on another nephew to be his designated successor to the throne. His name was Ferdinand Victor Albert Meinrad, but family members called him "Nando."

If there was one word to describe the king-to-be, it was "awkward." As an infant, his ears protruded so much that his family had them bandaged to the sides of his head. It didn't work. He had short legs and a long torso, so it sometimes appeared as if he were about to topple over. He was also painfully shy, which triggered nervous giggling and speech impediments, and he preferred stamp collecting and studying plants to the more princely pursuits of riding horses and politics. "He never came into a salon," noted a Romanian noble, "except sideways, as if his left shoulder was making excuses for what his right shoulder was obliged to do."

Early on in his time in Romania, Ferdinand fell in love with a Romanian woman who was part of his aunt's royal retinue. But the country's constitution explicitly required that the crown prince marry a foreign princess. The lady-in-waiting was exiled. Resigned to his fate, Ferdinand then went foreign princess hunting, and set his sights on the young and exceedingly beautiful Marie of Edinburgh. "Quick action has to take place," he wrote his parents, "before someone else engages her, better today than tomorrow."

Marie rather liked her suitor. She saw that beneath his awkwardness, he was extremely intelligent, thoughtful, and generally pleasant to be around. Marie's mother liked him because he was German and not English—and was also going to be a king. Other relatives were less pleased. "The country (Romania) is very insecure and the society dreadful," Queen Victoria wrote one of her daughters. "And she (Marie) is a mere child and quite inexperienced."

Despite such reservations, and after a seven-month engagement, the two were wed in early 1893, in a centuries-old castle above the Danube River in Germany. It took three ceremonies: a Catholic service to satisfy the Romanian constitution; a Protestant service to satisfy Marie's Anglican relations, and a civil ceremony, to mollify the German bureaucrats. Marie was 17.

It would have been difficult for any girl to be less prepared for marriage, and not just because no one had ever bothered to explain sex to her. Marie had never been to Romania, and did not speak the language. Her new uncle-in-law, King Carol I, had made it clear he would run the newlyweds' lives, down to allowing them only one day for a honeymoon. He forbade Marie from dancing with any young men at the interminable series of welcome parties thrown for the couple, but required her to dance with the old men.

The king also dictated what she could or couldn't do on a daily basis, and the "couldn't" list was the much longer of the two: No hiring her own servants; no contact with people her own age, especially males; little activity outside the castle grounds except for formal occasions; restricted travel outside the country, even very few meals without the king being present.

Her husband, whose extreme shyness led most people to conclude he was something of a fool, would not stand up to his uncle, which infuriated Marie. Worse, Ferdinand proved to be as awkward in the bedroom as he was elsewhere. "All intimate life with a man is difficult for me," Marie confided in a letter to her mother. "My husband sees me cry. He is awfully sorry, he wants to console me, he has every intention to do so. He begins to kiss me, and then he forgets that, and tries to console me by giving way to just that, that I dread most on earth."

If he was an awkward lover, however, the crown prince was at least efficient. Marie was pregnant within two weeks of their wedding. She was so naïve, she was shocked when the cause of her morning sickness was explained to her. Within a few months of giving birth to a son, dutifully named after Uncle/King Carol, Marie was pregnant again. She was 18.

Over the next 20 years as crown princess, Marie grew up. From a pretty palace ornament who spent extravagantly and constantly chafed at all the restrictions on her life, she became a trusted advisor to her uncle-in-law the king, and a well-loved figure among everyday Romanians.

It was a bumpy transition. Marie had six children, although how many of them were also Ferdinand's was a source of widespread, salacious—and possibly inaccurate—speculation. Her youngest son would die as a toddler, of typhus. Her youngest daughter would become abbess of a convent in Pennsylvania. One daughter would be queen of Greece, another queen of Yugoslavia. Her second son would spend most of his life in exile. Her oldest son would become the bane of her existence—and of Romania's.

Marie was not a model parent. While she dearly loved her children, in later years she readily acknowledged she viewed motherhood primarily as a royal duty. As a teenaged bride wholly unready for maternal duties, she too readily acquiesced to interference from her in-laws, and the nurses and nannies they hired. She was also a lousy disciplinarian. "I had an insurmountable aversion to scolding," she wrote. "I confess that many of the failures, even the disasters, of my life can be brought back to the fundamental inability to scold or reprove."

While she may not have been mother-of-the-year material, Marie was also not nearly as faithless a wife as her reputation suggested. It was a reputation that dogged her throughout her entire adult life, and so often repeated it became routinely accepted as fact. "She flitted from court to court, and frequented the gayest spas and casinos," reported one U.S. newspaper in 1919, in an article that otherwise hailed her as a heroic war figure. "She took delight in amorous conquests. Every handsome man she considered fair game. Titled or untitled, it made no difference to her."

Marie's list of alleged lovers was as varied as it was lengthy. It included the fabulously wealthy young American William Waldorf Astor and the crusty old Canadian soldier of fortune Col. Joseph Boyle. Even Sam Hill occasionally made the list. Several factors contributed to her sexy notoriety.

One was that she was magnetically beautiful, which by itself made men hopeful and women suspicious. Another was that her husband Ferdinand was openly a serial philanderer, and it was assumed she didn't object because of her own escapades. The truth was that she and Ferdinand had made peace with the fact they weren't in love anymore. "At least Nando and I are very good friends now," Marie wrote her mother in 1906, "and I hope that we may work together in spite of what is missing."

Most reputation-damaging of all, however, was the fact that Marie was an incorrigible flirt. An aunt compared Marie to a butterfly, noting that "instead of hovering over the flowers (she) burns her pretty wings by going rather near the flame." Even Marie admitted that "prudence was not my specialty." Early in her marriage, after a dalliance with the Romanian officer assigned to be her aide-de-camp, which Marie swore was never physical, King Carol I sent her out of the country for more than a year until the rumors died down.

Marie seemed to view her round-heeled-woman reputation more with bemused sorrow than anger. "Because I am animated, alive, keen they imagine that the 'animal' in me must play a big part," she wrote. "They cannot understand 'high spirits' without an underground of something more lurid."

Years after her mother's death, Marie's youngest daughter Ileana offered a more direct disputation of her mother's reputation. "At heart she was a puritan," Ileana said. "With all her glamour and men falling at her feet, she really hated any physical contact. She had a horror of it, quite simply because of the initial shock of her marriage." Ileana's frank defense of her mother's virtue may have been spurred in part by the widespread speculation that she and her youngest brother Mircea had a different father from the rest of Marie's children.

His name was Barbo Stirbey. Tall, athletic and possessing both great wisdom and sharp wit, Stirbey was from one of the most respected families in Romania. Having amassed a fortune by building a business empire, and very influential in European financial circles, Stirbey became a close political and economic adviser to both King Carol I and Marie's husband Prince Ferdinand. For more than 20 years, Stirbey was by the Romanian royal family's side. That he and Marie loved each other is probable, based on their correspondence and other writings. That they were actual physical lovers, however, is unclear.

What is clear is that Stirbey was instrumental in getting Marie to think of herself as a gifted leader—and getting others to see her as more than just a pretty face. "It's essential not to break her will," he advised King Carol. "But if we can persuade her to take herself and her duties more seriously, her natural intelligence will do the rest." Carol took the advice. He began to talk to Marie about politics and Romania's future.

Marie, who never considered herself anything but an Englishwoman, nonetheless developed a passion for Romania. "My love for this country that I have made mine through sighs and tears has become as a religion to me," she wrote. She quickly embraced the dream of a "Romania Mare," or "Greater Romania." This referred to the reunification of Transylvania, Moldavia and Wallachia, which had last occurred under Michael the Brave in 1601, and lasted only briefly. "My eyes were opened to several truths, and when I began to go more deeply into the interests of my country, my horizons widened," Marie wrote. "Now I had definitely grown up. I was no more a stranger in a strange land."

Her eyes were opened further in 1907, when Romanian peasants staged a widespread revolt against a property ownership system that hearkened back to the Middle Ages. While the crown princess and her children fled to the relative safety of a castle in the Carpathian Mountains, the army crushed the rebellion, killing thousands in the process. "Order had been re-established," Marie noted, "but certain lessons, never again to be so easily forgotten, had been learnt."

New laws were passed to redistribute some land and to make it easier for peasants to buy property, and even more reforms followed when Ferdinand succeeded his uncle as king. Marie whole-heartedly approved of and encouraged the reforms, and sympathized with the peasants' plight. Her empathy, however, went only so far. "I do not believe in equality," she told an interviewer. "God makes one class higher than another. Mine happens to be the highest of all."

In addition to her political awakening, Marie's greater freedom and subsequent maturity spurred an interest in the arts. When she and Ferdinand were finally allowed to move into their own home, she began designing and decorating furniture, interiors, courtyards, and gardens. She promoted a distinctly Romanian form of Art Nouveau, which mixed the influences of the various cultures that had dominated the country, from the Byzantine of the Turks to the Baroque of the Austro-Hungarians—plus her own fondness for lilies and Celtic crosses. She also began to write. Her first efforts were versions of the bedtime stories she told her children.

"They were not wonderful literature," she recalled in her memoirs. "I knew nothing about writing, about style or composition, or about the 'rules of the game.' But I did know how to conjure up beauty, and at times, emotion. I also had a vast store of words."

Her "vast store of words" would prove useful to Marie in efforts that ranged from appeals for international aid for her country to an internationally best-selling and critically acclaimed autobiography toward the end of her life. They would also become forever colored by the horrors of war, of which Marie would have plenty of personal experience.

In October, 1912, several Balkan nations began a seven-month war with the Ottoman Empire in an effort to finally break free of Turkish influence. An already-independent Romania stayed out of it. But when hostilities renewed the following year, Romania went to war with neighboring Bulgaria. The Romanian army beat the Bulgarians decisively, only to be devastated by a cholera epidemic as the fighting ended.

Visiting a military hospital at the front, Marie was appalled at what she saw. Soldiers lay on straw pallets in the mud, under leaky makeshift tents that steamed under scorching summer temperatures combined with occasional torrential rains. "Something never before felt rose from the very core of my being," she recalled, "an immense urge toward service, a great wish to be of use, even to sacrifice myself if necessary."

After successfully pleading her case with King Carol, Marie took over operation of a cholera camp, raising funds for supplies and enlisting doctors and nurses. She put on heavy riding boots and day after day moved from soldier to soldier, handing out candy, cigarettes, flowers and words of encouragement, "gritting my teeth so as to stand the sights and smells." At the end of each shift, she stood in a tub while scalding water was poured over her boots to help prevent the spread of the disease. The work made Marie a national hero, and an international celebrity. It also provided some grimly useful practice for what was to come.

With the outbreak of World War I in August, 1914, Romania found itself squarely between the horns of a dilemma, and from both horns dangled sticks and carrots. On the one horn was the Central Powers, led by Germany and including Austria-Hungary, Turkey and eventually Bulgaria. There were more than a few compelling reasons for Romania to join the group.

For one thing, Romania had signed a secret treaty in 1883, allying itself with Germany, Italy and Austria-Hungary, and King Carol had, secretly, renewed it several times since. For another, both Carol and Marie's husband Ferdinand were German by both birth and sentiment, a fact that agonized the English-born crown princess, who generally disliked Germany. In addition, it was probable that as a prize of a war won by Germany, Romania would regain control of the region of Bessarabia that it had lost to Russia in an earlier war.

There were even more pragmatic reasons. Romania was nearly surrounded by Central Powers countries. The only bordering country belonging to the other side was Russia, and hardly anyone in Romania trusted Russia as a reliable ally. Romania's main pre-war source of armaments was Germany. And finally, both Carol and Ferdinand firmly believed Germany was invincible, particularly if, as expected, America stayed out of the war.

On the other horn was the Entente, consisting of France, England, Russia, Greece and eventually Italy and the United States. Most Romanians favored this side, for two reasons. One was that Romanian culture—language, artistic and literary tastes, even the cuisine—had more in common with Western Europe than its Balkan neighbors. "We are a Latin island in a sea of Slavs," was a popular Romanian saying. Romanians also warmly recalled that France had been an early and ardent supporter of their independence from the Ottoman Turks.

But there was an even bigger reason for joining the Entente, and the reason the king had kept the decades-old secret alliance with Germany and Austria-Hungary secret: Transylvania. Although a majority of Transylvania's populace was Romanian in origin, the region had been controlled by Austria-Hungary since the late 17th century. The Transylvanian Romanians had been routinely persecuted and treated as second-class citizens. Most Romanians thus hated Austria-Hungary, and would have been furious to learn of Carol's alliance. They wanted Transylvania back. That would be impossible if Romania sided with the Central Powers, which included Austria-Hungary.

Still, King Carol went with his heart. In early August, he asked his Crown Council to ally Romania with the Central Powers and his beloved Germany. The council, however, rejected the request, opting to keep the country neutral. Two months later, the 75-year-old Carol was dead. The indecisive and easily swayed Ferdinand was king—and Marie was in the driver's seat.

She wasn't the only pro-Entente person to have the king's ear. Both Barbo Stirbey, Marie's presumed lover and royal family adviser, and Prime Minister Ion Bratianu also favored joining the English-French-et. al. side. But Marie was uniquely positioned. After all, her first cousin George was king of England and her first cousin Nicholas was tsar of Russia. Even her first cousin "Willy"—better known to the world as Kaiser Wilhelm of Germany—was head of a major wartime power. (He thought of her as "that meddlesome little flirt;" she thought of him as "large, showy and loud.")

Both sides wanted to enlist Romania for its strategic location and its vast oil and grain resources as much as for its army. And Marie's influence was not lost on those courting the country. "In the near future, Roumanian policy might come to depend not so much upon Ferdinand as upon his versatile wife," an Austrian diplomat observed. "Her character and mentality is one of the most important reasons for putting relations with Roumania on another basis." In fact, the Central Powers were wasting their time. "I am an English woman," Marie wrote a friend. "When Roumania comes into this war, there is but one side to choose."

For the next two years, Romania ostensibly stayed neutral, selling vast quantities of grain to, and entertaining diplomatic missions from, both sides. Secretly, however, Marie—coached by Stirbey and Bratianu—was negotiating the best deal Romania could get from the Entente. In long letters to "My Dear George" and "My Dear Nicky," Marie listed to the English king and Russian tsar Romania's requirements for coming in on their side: all of Transylvania, as well as other parts of the Austro-Hungarian Empire, Russia and what would become Yugoslavia. After months of negotiation, the Entente reluctantly agreed. In late August, 1916, Romania entered the war.

In a nutshell, Romania's war was a disaster. Its army of 600,000 was poorly led, badly equipped and over-confident. The country's military strategy relied heavily on considerable support from its Russian ally, which soon turned out to be a very bad idea.Within hours of the declaration of war, Romanian troops were pouring into Transylvania. Within days, they were retreating. Within weeks, they were waging a desperate fight to hold onto Romanian soil. Within months, three-fourths of the country was in enemy hands and the capital of Bucharest had fallen to the Germans. The government and royal family had fled to the town of Jassy, in the northeastern corner of the country. Not all of the family made it.

On the evening of Oct. 7, Marie wrote in her journal that she was taking comfort from the war's reversals by watching her two youngest children, Ileana and Mircea, play. "It did me good to hear their happy, innocent voices, to watch their games." Less than three weeks later, the happy, innocent voice of three-year-old Mircea had turned to screams. He had contracted typhoid fever. On Nov. 2, three days after her 41st birthday, Marie wrote that her son "screams no more, but for two days he has had an incessant movement of the jaw, clacking and grinding his teeth." He died later that night, "his hand in mine."

The toddler prince's death demonstrated how democratic the war's horrors were. The winter of 1916-17 was Romania's coldest in 50 years, with temperatures dropping to 30 degrees below zero. The entire country had one functioning railroad to bring in medical and food supplies, which were exceedingly rare anyway. An estimated 300,000 people—about 5 percent of the entire population—died of disease and starvation that winter. Even the royal family subsisted on a diet that often featured horsemeat and beans, and was grateful to get a hot Thanksgiving meal at the American consulate.

"We are facing invasion, famine, pestilence—we are looking them in the face," a grimly defiant Marie wrote Loie Fuller, "but hand in hand, jaws set—until the end we shall stand, and if we fall, it shall be face to the enemy, when our last ball has been fired."

In the spring and summer of 1917, the remnants of the Romanian army rallied briefly, and fought German and Austro-Hungarian troops to a draw in a major battle. But the end was in sight. The Russian Revolution eliminated any substantial help from the Entente. In the spring of 1918, King Ferdinand and his government accepted a peace treaty from Germany that stripped Romania of territory, imposed financial reparations and demobilized its army.

Marie was furious, ignoring the fact that two-thirds of the army was already dead, wounded, sick or captured. "I shall never be reconciled to a humiliating peace with Germany—never!" she declared in a statement to the American press. "And I hope, indeed I know, that I shall have the support of Americans as well as Roumanians in continuing the fight against the invaders." Her bravado, while melodramatic and ineffectual, nonetheless enhanced her reputation. "There is only one man in Roumania," quipped the French ambassador to the country, "and that is the queen."

Marie cemented her hold on an enviable international reputation through her fearless work with sick and wounded soldiers. She directly oversaw four field hospitals and three mobile medical units, and made visits to virtually all of the country not controlled by the Germans. The conditions were horrendous. Most of the men occupied either pallets on the floor, or the floor itself. Lucky ones had a sheet or blanket; most did not. At one railroad station triage center, Marie at first thought the wounded were sprinkled with some sort of sand. She was wrong. The grains of "sand" were actually lice.

"I have myself seen with my own eyes men virtually dying of starvation and disease," wrote a British diplomat in Jassy. "There was nothing but paper scraps or sawdust to address their wounds. And when the men had already been without food for days (there was) nothing to build them up in the shape of nourishment."

On her visits, which often stretched out for hours, Marie handed out cigarettes, religious icons—and hope. Asked to wear gloves to protect herself from typhus, Marie retorted "the soldiers want to kiss my hand; how can I offer them a hand of rubber?" An American reporter accompanying her on one visit noted "to the very last man in the hospital each one received personal attention, a heavier morning's work than most women know."

Rumors began to spread that Marie's touch could heal wounds. She became known as "Mamma Regina," a term that was scrawled everywhere on hospital walls. "Her presence immunizes us better than all the vaccines," a nurse told the French ambassador.

On Nov. 9, 1918, Marie saw her dream of Romania re-entering the war come to pass when it re-declared war on Germany and Austria-Hungary. It was wholly symbolic, since the Central Powers had all but quit by then, and all the fighting officially stopped two days later. Still, the morale boost to Romania was significant. When Marie finally returned to Bucharest after a two-year absence from the capital city, she was hailed by massive crowds as "Empress of all the Roumanians."

"Before the war, the world had known Queen Marie as a brilliant, beautiful woman, somewhat addicted to extravagance and romance," commented the *Washington Post.* "Now she is revered as a heroine not surpassed by any woman in the war. No queen has shown such friendship with her people in modern times."

Now all she had to do was go to Paris, double the pre-war size of her country, and gather all the food, clothing, medical supplies, train engines and everything else she could get.

Between her diplomatic forays at the Paris peace talks, Marie made time for an old friend—and met a new one. Throughout most of the spring of 1919, Loie Fuller had been bedridden in her modest suite at the Hotel Plaza-Athénée with colds and bronchitis. So, Marie managed from time to time to escape her constant retinue of reporters and well-wishers, and visit the ailing dancer, when Loie could not come to the queen's spacious digs at the Ritz. They had remained faithful pen pals, but the two had not seen each other since before the war.

"Although she (Loie) had countless friends and patrons," Marie wrote in her journal with her usual guileless narcissism, "I was the chosen one of her heart. I was the culminating experience of her life." In gratitude for Loie's work on behalf of Romania during the war, the queen gave her full authority to produce on the stage and on film the fairy stories Marie had written over the years. In return, Loie introduced Marie to an ardent admirer from America who was visiting Paris.

"The great big man had a strangely soft voice, little in keeping with his immense stature," Marie wrote of her first meeting with Sam Hill. "And though he was certainly no drawing-room hero, he was politely ceremonious in a quaintly old-fashioned way." Marie also noted Sam "was a visionary.

He saw everything over life-size, was always ruminating over some gigantic project, but especially he dreamed. Some of his dreams occasionally came true, but some were so fantastic they had to remain dreams."

For his part, Sam had been smitten with Marie for at least two years before he ever met her. While visiting Maryhill in mid-1917, Loie had filled Sam's head with stories of Marie's beauty, charm, and courage. Enthralled, Sam had dashed off a letter to the queen. "Our friend, Miss Loie Fuller, has told us something of the (Romanians') sufferings, which seem almost beyond comprehension, and it has touched our hearts with the feeling which we find hard to express 'you have fought the good fight; you have kept the faith.' With admiration and respect, I beg to sign myself your most obedient servant, Samuel Hill."

Sam had come to Europe in part to see Loie and in part to attend the birthday celebration of his friend King Albert of Belgium. He had been accompanied by Hervey Lindley, a prominent Seattle businessman who had been a high school classmate of Sam's in Minneapolis and was a longtime pal. Lindley was also head of the Red Cross in the Pacific Northwest, and was part of a sizeable delegation the organization had in Europe to assess the various needs of the devastated countries.

Marie saw an opportunity. "Dear Mr. Hill," she wrote Sam while he was in Belgium, "will you and your friend not come to Bucharest to see our sad situation and see what you can do to help? You can help and we need you. I shall bless you always, Marie."

The plea proved profitable, at least in part. Sam and Lindley traveled on to Bucharest and then to Transylvania with King Ferdinand and Marie. Nearly 20,000 tons of U.S. flour, as well as clothes and other supplies were distributed in Romania by the Red Cross. In gratitude for his part in providing the aid, Lindley was named honorary counsel of Romania for the Northwest, just as Sam had been for Belgium.

But Marie had another favor to ask Sam. Carol, Marie's oldest son was good-looking and intelligent, and also self-indulgent and arrogant. The heir-apparent to the Romanian crown, was embarrassing himself and the country by consorting with a fortune-hunting woman who was not of royal blood. During the war, the crown prince had deserted his army post, and eloped to Russia with the woman. It was an offense grave enough that King Ferdinand briefly considered having him executed for treason. Instead, he got two and one-half months imprisonment in a monastery.

"God! What a mess he has got himself and us and the country into," Marie wrote in her journal. "But I must try and save him if I can, I and those who love us." The marriage was annulled. But Carol continued to periodically threaten to abdicate. With the war over, he decided to defy Romanian law and remarry the commoner, especially because she was now pregnant.

Desperate to keep the couple apart and preserve the succession to the throne, the king and queen vainly tried various ploys. When they asked Carol to go on a mission to the Far East, he shot himself in the leg to get out of the trip. They also schemed to send the prince to America for a tour with Sam, a plan to which Sam readily assented. This time Carol's refusal stopped short of gunplay, but was a refusal nonetheless.

"I suffered every degree of humiliation and torture, which would have been unendurable had not Mr. Hill been the angel that he is," Marie wrote Loie. "We sat hand-in-hand, I poured out my mother's agony, and he understood."

The petulant prince eventually dropped his threats, and agreed to a seven-month cooling-off trip around the world. Sam met him in San Francisco and escorted him to Portland and a tour of Sam's beloved Columbia River Highway. Marie felt she owed this big American a big favor in return for his generosity, and she intended to someday repay her debt.

NOTES FOR CHAPTER 6

"Perhaps it seems" Mabel Potter Daggett, *Marie of Roumania: The Intimate Story of the Radiant Queen,* 1926, pp. 268-69.

To ensure that Ibid, p. 275.

However precise her Margaret MacMillan, *Paris, 1919: Six Months that Changed the World,* 2003, pp. 126-127.

He had also Diane Mandache (ed.), *Later Chapters of My Life: The Lost Memoirs of Queen Marie of Romania,* 2004, pp. 18-19.

"I have met" *Baltimore Sun*, March 9, 1919, p. 1.

Even Marie was Mandache, op. cit., p. 31.

The "Great Three" MacMillan, op. cit., p. 134; Mandache, op. cit., p. 31.

Noting that Marie Edith Bolling Wilson, *My Memoir*, 1939, p. 258.

While Marie's coquettish MacMillan, op. cit., p. 263.

Regardless of the Mandache, op cit., pp. 105-106; Daggett, op. cit., p. 275.

Marie Alexandra Victoria In addition to a three-volume autobiography published in the 1930s, followed by a fourth volume published posthumously in 2004, Marie has been the subject of two biographies: *Marie of Romania*, by Terence Elsberry (1972), and the excellent *The Last Romantic*, by Hannah Pakula (1984).

Alfred was an Marie, Queen of Roumania, *The Story of My Life,* 1934, p. 4.

Known as "Missy," Ibid.

The feelings were mutual Pakula, Op. Cit., p. 47.

That, in turn, was Winifred Gordon, *Roumania, Yesterday and Today,* 1918, p. 61.

If there was one Elsberry, Op. Cit., p. 37.

Early on in his Pakula, Op. Cit., p. 57.

Marie rather liked Ibid., p. 59.

Her husband, whose extreme Julia P. Gelardi, *Born to Rule: Five Reigning Consorts, the Granddaughters of Queen Victoria,* 2005, p. 87.

Marie was not an Marie, Queen of Roumania, Op. Cit., p. 516.

While she may not *Oregon Daily Journal*, July 27, 1919, p. 5.

Marie's list of Pakula, Op. Cit., p. 145.

Most reputation-damaging of" Elsberry, Op. Cit., p. 67.

Marie seemed to view Marie, Queen of Roumania, Op. Cit., p. 458.

Years after her mother's Elsberry, Op. Cit., p. 89.

What is clear is Ibid, p. 86.

Marie, who never Marie, Queen of Roumania, Op. Cit., p. 589; ibid., p. 530.

Her eyes were opened Ibid., p. 531

New laws were Daggett, Op. Cit., p. 212.

"They were not wonderful" Marie, Queen of Roumania, Op. Cit., p. 578.

Visiting a military Ibid., pp. 551-552.

Both sides wanted to Gelardi, Op. Cit., p. 155; ibid., p. 213.

On the evening of Elsberry, op. cit., pp. 127-129.

"We are facing invasion" Marie to Loie, Feb. 14, 1917, MMA.

Marie was furious *Salt Lake (Ut.) Tribune*, May 12, 1918, p. 43; Pakula, Op. Cit., p. 227.

"I have myself seen" Gordon, Op. Cit., pp. 221-222.

On her visits, which William T. Ellis, "Rumania's Soldier Queen," *Century Magazine*, Vol. 96, No. 1., May 1918, p. 330.

Rumors began to spread Gelardi, Op. Cit., p. 224.

"Before the war," *Washington Post*, Nov. 3, 1918, p, 6.

"Although she had countless" Mandache, Op Cit., p. 80.

"The great big man" Ibid, pp. 80-81.

For his part, Sam Sam to Marie, July 24, 1917, MMA.

Marie saw an *Oregon Daily Journal*, July 27, 1919, p. 5.

"God! What a mess" Pakula, Op. Cit., p. 254.

"I suffered every degree" Marie to Loie, June 6, 1919, MMA.

CHAPTER SEVEN

The best laid plans...
OCTOBER 1926

The queen forgot her seasickness pills. "Since her forthcoming voyage to the U.S. looms as the queen's first long sea journey," *Time* magazine waggishly reported, "she had attached great importance to that particular vial of pills." Fortunately, a plane was quickly dispatched from Romania with the medicine, and arrived before the *SS Leviathan* sailed from Cherbourg for New York. Sometimes it's good to be the queen.

Since the end of the war, it had been mostly good to be queen of Romania. The country had fended off the twin threats of communism and democracy that had toppled or greatly weakened a dozen other European monarchies. The newly acquired state of Transylvania had been successfully absorbed, although only after a brief and bloody communist-led uprising was quelled. And King Ferdinand had made good on the economic reforms he had promised during the war. "The royal family was exceedingly popular," Marie wrote in her memoirs. "Our people were staunchly loyal towards their dynasty, which had shared with them both good and evil days."

Marie's popularity was reflected by, and in large part due to, her tireless work with post-war relief efforts. While she did little of the actual hands-on work, as she acknowledged with frank immodesty, "nothing stood firmly on its feet without my patronage. (The) many appeals to different public authorities never received proper attention unless my voice or pen gave the alarm signal."

Transylvanians were so grateful to the queen, they gave her a 14th century fortress near the town of Bran. The structure was widely, but erroneously, believed to have once housed Vlad III, the 15th century prince revered by Romanians for having fought the invading Turks, and who served as inspiration for Bram Stoker's immortal literary figure "Dracula." The castle quickly became Marie's favorite residence, and she filled it with Renaissance and Baroque furniture, Persian pottery, and German silver.

When not overseeing charities and redecorating medieval castles, Marie stayed busy marrying off her children. In February 1921, eldest daughter Elizabetha married Crown Prince George of Greece, which prompted eldest son Carol to marry George's sister, Helen. The following year, second daughter Mignon married Alexander, king of Serbia, Croatia, and Slovenia, which was shorthanded to "Yugoslavia" a few years later. The matrimonial flurry earned Marie a media sobriquet of "Mother-In-Law of the Balkans," and also speculation that she was scheming to build a new post-war empire in Eastern Europe.

Marie was both offended and pleased by the speculation. "I know I have been considered an ambitious, intriguing woman. I read those descriptions of myself with astonishment, because they certainly do not correspond with the truth," she told her friend Mabel Potter Daggett. But, she added, "I am a winner in life. Somebody has to lose. But I am a winner in life."

Her crowning moment came in October 1922, when she and Ferdinand were re-coronated as rulers of the "new and reunified" Romania. At an elaborate ceremony in the Transylvanian town of Alba Iulia, Marie received a crown of gold, weighing four pounds and set with rubies, emeralds, turquoise and moonstones. Ferdinand settled for an iron crown fashioned from an artillery shell used in a 19th century battle against the Turks. Marie's crown was worth an estimated $5,000 ($70,000 in 2017 dollars,) and the entire ceremony cost about $1 million ($14.6 million.) It was sometimes definitely good to be the queen.

But not always. After a brief period of good behavior, Crown Prince Carol once again became a royal pain. Within a year of siring a son with his new wife, the heir-apparent began a widely known affair with a seductive red-headed divorcee. By December 1925, Carol had again renounced his birthright, abandoned his wife and child, and moved to Paris with his mistress. His four-year-old son Michael became next in line to be king. Meanwhile, the health of the current king, Ferdinand, began to fail. And Marie's daughter Elizabetha and her husband were forced from the Greek throne by a revolution and fled to Romania. "I feel like a deer when the hounds with flashing fangs gloat over what they consider his fall, perhaps even his end," Marie wrote to several friends about her troubles.

What she wanted was a change of scenery—and America had plenty of it. The queen had wanted to visit the United States even before the war. In particular she longed to see the Wild West that she had read about in novels by Zane Grey and largely fanciful stories about her American hero (and former Loie Fuller employer) Buffalo Bill Cody. But something always seemed to get in the way.

Plans for a 1921 trip were cancelled when rumors spread Marie was really coming to star in a movie. The queen was insulted. "It certainly has cooled me down about visiting a country where such a point of view can even be admitted," she complained to Loie. The following year, a trip to Detroit to promote U.S. business investment in Romania was abandoned because of plans for the re-coronation.

But Loie, who had been pushing for years for Marie to cross the Atlantic, kept pushing. The aging dancer's motives were partially idealistic—to better relations between the two countries and help Romania recover from its war wounds—and partially financial—a highly publicized royal tour planned and led by Loie wouldn't hurt her dance company's prospects at U.S. box offices.

Much of America was enthused by the prospect of Marie coming. She was widely known and admired for her heroics during the war. Her son Carol's soap-opera marital escapades had been avidly reported by the U.S. press. And in 1925, Marie had titillated, amused and even shocked American readers with a highly popular series of 16 articles under the group title of *A Queen Looks at Life.* Syndicated by the North American Newspaper Alliance, the articles included "My Experience with Men;" "Changing Ideas of Marriage," and "Facing Fifty." All Marie needed was an official excuse to cross the Atlantic. She settled on a two-year-old, somewhat nebulous invitation from Sam, engineered by Loie, to dedicate the Maryhill Museum.

"Whenever a queen is invited to come to a country she cannot come just for no reason at all," Marie explained to reporters. "She must have some reason to put up to her government as justifying her departure. I told my friends that they must invite me for some special definite time and some special definite function, with some significance, and the dedication of the Rumanian Room in the Maryhill Museum was such a function."

Marie's government had mixed feelings about the trip. The minority Liberal Party fretted about the cost and the fact that diplomatically, Marie was something of a loose cannon. But the ruling Conservative Party prevailed, reasoning that if she could do for Romania in America what she had done for it at the Paris Peace Talks, the country should let her go. So, with son Nicholas and daughter Ileana in tow, along with 21 packing cases of bronzes, marbles, statuary, costumes and furniture for Maryhill, and 30 trunks of newly purchased Paris fashion for her– and also the queen's seasick pills—Marie Alexandra set off to dedicate a museum that didn't exist.

Bringing the museum into existence wasn't particularly high on Sam Hill's agenda during the years following the war's end, assuming he had an agenda. Mostly he wandered around the world, bouncing from project to project, few of which seemed to be completely thought through before they were begun.

One of his projects during this time was quintessentially Sam. It involved lofty symbolism, headline-grabbing ballyhoo—and 3,500 bags of concrete. It was unique, however, in that he actually completed it. The Peace Portal wasn't all Sam's idea. It was first proposed in 1913 by the Pacific Highway Association, of which Sam was a founding member, as a way of promoting construction of a road stretching continuously along the Pacific Coast from Canada to Mexico. The idea was to erect a monument commemorating a century of peace between the United States and Canada. But when no one stepped up to get the proposal off the ground, Sam took over.

He bought five acres of swampy land on the U.S.-Canada boundary, and paid for most of the costs of building a 70-foot-high Doric arch straddling the border. The arch stood on 76 pilings, driven to a depth of 30 feet, covered with two layers of concrete and reinforced with 50 tons of steel. Sam later estimated it cost him $100,000 ($1.6 million in 2017 dollars). With construction beginning on July 4, 1920, and Sam not there to supervise, the arch was finished in eight months. But various problems pushed its formal dedication back until September 1921. In the meantime, Sam hunted for a sure-fire way to generate international publicity for his structure. He found it in a rural English barn.

In the barn, which belonged to a Quaker community, were the remains of a ship said to be the *Mayflower*, the iconic vessel that had brought the English Puritans known as the Pilgrims to the New World in 1620. Alerted to the hulk's existence by a friend, Sam went to England and consulted Scotland Yard. There, a detective acquaintance told him the story had been reported by the *Manchester Guardian* and the *London Times*, and they were reliable newspapers. That was good enough for Sam, who persuaded his Quaker brethren to part with a chunk of wood from the ship. Then, with Loie's help, Sam filmed the presentation, as part of a movie he produced about the long peace between the two neighboring countries.

However far-fetched the whole thing sounded, it worked. Newspapers from the East Coast to the Far East dutifully reported Sam's plan to install the wood piece in the Peace Portal, along with a piece from a venerable Canadian ship, the *Beaver,* which had been the first steamship to cross the Pacific.

At the two-hour dedication ceremony, which drew a crowd estimated at 10,000, Sam read congratulatory telegrams from various world leaders, including Belgium's King Albert, the French prime minister and U.S. President Warren G. Harding. "Dedication of this portal marks the recognition of the oneness of the English-speaking race," Sam declared in laying the cornerstone, "and its earnest desire to be at peace with all the world."

With the Peace Portal completed (and still visited by an estimated 500,000 people each year), Sam soon took off to see "all the world" again, or at least a good part of it. Struck by one of his periodic fits of startling generosity, he had offered to pay for an around-the-world tour by a French war hero, General Joseph Joffre. In December 1921, Sam sailed for Japan, where he met with Joffre's party of eight and traveled with them to China and Korea and then across the United States and back to Europe. The trip, which Sam said cost him another $100,000, included a visit to Alma in San Francisco and a re-dedication of the Peace Portal—but not a trip to Maryhill.

By the beginning of 1923, in fact, Sam was in a deep quandary over Maryhill, and life in general. His beloved brother Richard had just died of tuberculosis. Sam had broken off a romance with a woman who had accompanied him on at least part of the trip with Joffre. He seldom visited Maryhill, and one of his few trips there was dedicated mostly to finding a suitable place for his future grave. In addition, the outsized expenses of the peace arch and the Joffre trip, combined with sagging railroad stock dividends, put a sizeable dent in his wallet.

"My plans for the future are uncertain," he wrote Loie in February, explaining he was opening his first mail in two months. "Just what my plans will be, or where I will go, or what I will do, I do not know," he wrote Alma's sister a few days later. To another friend, on the same day, he wrote "How would you like to have seven thousand acres around your neck, of which five thousand are rock…?"

For Sam, the cure for lassitude was travel, so he once again headed for Europe, first to a transportation conference in Spain, then to see his buddy the king in Belgium. And somewhere along the road, museum fever hit him. In Brussels, Sam told King Albert about plans for a "wholly modern" museum, "and asked if he would not help with making lasting friends for Belgium" by contributing to it. Albert and his wife agreed to pose for portraits for the museum. The king even threw in an artillery shell (still at Maryhill) said to be the first German ordnance fired at Belgium in World War I.

"I am thinking all the time about the museum," Sam wrote Loie on his return from Europe. He asked her to come up with a formal name for it, and said he planned to incorporate his almost-uninhabited acreage "so as to make it an organized town with a mayor."

Instead, Sam incorporated the "Maryhill Museum of Fine Arts" in August 1923: "The objects for which said corporation is formed are educational and scientific, with the right to make and establish a library and museum of fine arts, and a scientific society, and to perform other acts and things as may be necessary or convenient in connection therewith." The board of directors consisted of Sam; Loie; Charles Babcock, an attorney and longtime friend who had followed Sam from Minneapolis to Washington; Sam's cousin, Edgar Hill, an Indiana banker and businessman; and eventually Albert Tirman, a French government official who was a friend of Sam, Loie and Alma.

In October, Sam transferred ownership of 32 acres surrounding his unfinished Maryhill mansion to the nascent museum corporation. Then he and Loie began brainstorming on just what the museum would be. The result was a remarkably vague and convoluted 20-page document entitled "The Idea and Purpose of the Maryhill Museum of Fine Arts."

It was to be a "people's museum," with a distinctly international character. It would not only be a collection of objects, but a gathering place for artists to create, and exchange ideas. Visitors would thus see not only the finished works, but their production. Docents would lead tours, and the museum's directorship would rotate among experts from different countries, on a three-to-six-month schedule. Books would be commissioned to be written on the museum's various collections as well as patrons and personages associated with Maryhill. Admission would be charged, but 80 percent of the revenues would go to artists who created things for the museum. An art school would be established.

The envisioned collections sounded a bit like a vast artists' swap meet. There would be at least two dozen rooms dedicated to themes and subjects ranging from Rodin to American presidents to monuments of Paris to items that once belonged to the queen of Yugoslavia when she was a child, including a piece of ordinary string. Seriously.

Although not included in the original manifesto, Loie soon strained credulity further by proposing a 50-foot-high model of General Joffre's right hand to be located outside the museum. It would house a gift shop and attract the attention of train travelers along the river below. Finally, Sam and Loie expressed the hope the museum would at long last attract settlers to Sam's "town," so that "little by little, an intellectual colony of real workers could become the foundation of a future city."

By the beginning of 1925, newspapers from coast to coast were reporting the museum would be open within two years, and that Sam had already collected or been promised an impressive inventory of artistic and historical items. "He has devoted years of work and thought to the idea," the Portland *Oregonian* overstated, "and having the entrée, as he has, to European courts and the circles of international finance, he has been wonderfully equipped to get results."

But for all his prowess and well-earned reputation as a road-builder, Sam could not get results on one issue vital to the museum's future: construction of a road along the north bank of the Columbia, linking Maryhill to the populous Portland-Vancouver metroplex and the north-south Pacific highway corridor. He tried everything, from elaborate slide shows to weeks-long speaking tours. He invited Washington state lawmakers to Maryhill, as he had successfully done 13 years earlier with their Oregon counterparts. But bad weather scrubbed the trip, and Washington's economic and political powers, far at the other end of the state from Maryhill, were not much interested in its needs or its potential. Finally, Sam had had enough.

In a long and angry letter to the Klickitat Board of County Commissioners in April 1926, he spelled out his grievances. "I am only waiting to fill the museum when there is a chance to entertain the people who would travel east I will not wait another fifteen years to expedite the building of the North Bank Highway."

While Sam and Loie were planning a museum, Alma was building one. She had all the key ingredients: a ready design, a healthy starting supply of art, and her husband's money. Actually, Adolph Spreckels wasn't all that keen on keeping his five-year-old promise to Alma that he would finance an art museum for the city of San Francisco, especially one that would be filled with French art inimical to his German heritage and tastes. But Alma played to his American patriotism, arguing the museum would be a fitting and permanent memorial to U.S. veterans of the Great War. In January 1920, Adolph handed a $320,000 check ($4.8 million in 2017 currency) to the San Francisco Board of Park Commissioners as a down payment for building "a home of art and historical treasures to promoting the education and culture of our citizens, and especially the rising and coming generations."

Almost before the ink was dry on Adolph's check, Alma was off and running. The building would mirror the hallowed Palace of the Legion of Honor in Paris. She lined up Henri Guillaume, the French architect who had built his country's exhibit at the 1915 Pan Pacific Expo, to design the museum, while George Applegarth, who had designed the opulent Spreckels mansion in Pacific Heights, was hired to oversee the day-to-day, nuts-and-bolts operations. Alma buffaloed the city Parks Commission into dropping its first choice for museum director and hiring Cornelia Sage Quinton, the director of the Albright Art Gallery in Buffalo, who had been at the 1914 Paris dinner when Alma first met Loie.

And after deciding against her initial choice of locating the museum near her mansion, Alma got the city to donate five acres of a park overlooking the entrance to San Francisco Bay—the Golden Gate. To accommodate the new building, the city's only public golf course was reconfigured, and hundreds of bodies from a forgotten Gold Rush-era pauper's graveyard were moved. Adolph eventually forked over another $700,000 or so to pay for it all.

On the advice of Loie (who also advised her to bring $20,000), Alma left in May 1920 for the first of what would be several trips to Europe to buy, borrow and solicit the donation of items for her museum. On a six-month jaunt in 1922, she met up with Sam, who was saying goodbye to General Joffre after their around-the-world trip. Together, they met with French President Alexandre Millerand. The president thanked Sam for sponsoring the Joffre trip, and Alma for building her homage to French culture in California. Both said you're welcome by making sizeable contributions to a fund for safeguarding French art.

On the same trip, accompanied by Loie and two of Alma's friends, Alma visited Romania. She met Marie, for the first time, at the queen's summer palace near the town of Sinaia, and was enchanted by the beautiful and gracious monarch. The queen, in turn, was impressed by the outsized and outspoken American. Marie decorated Alma for her war relief efforts on Romania's behalf. Moreover, she promised Alma's museum a reproduction of the Sinaia castle's "Byzantine Gold Room," a model of her crown, a gold robe she had worn at the coronations of England's King Edward VII and Russia's Tsar Nicholas II, and a set of furniture to be crafted under Marie's direct supervision.

The two women also did a bit of business. Alma agreed to pay Marie $40,000 for a frescoed background for the Golden Room reproduction. The deal for the background, apparently brokered by Loie, called for Alma to write checks Marie couldn't cash until the background was done and delivered. Marie promised half the money to charity. Alma also paid $12,000 for a collection of religious icons and other artifacts.

The Romanian visit was truncated because Alma had received an unexpected request before leaving Paris: The U.S. Department of Labor wanted her to investigate working conditions among European women in several countries, and file a report. Alma, who had not held an actual job for two decades, readily accepted. In October 1922, Alma presented her report in person to Labor Secretary James J. Davis. The seven-page document said many European women had taken manual labor jobs due to the war-caused shortage of men, "and they show aptitude and ability which are astounding." Alma outlined women-related European labor laws that the United States might consider, ranging from guaranteed holidays to sexual harassment protections. Secretary Davis deemed the report "of valuable assistance," and her personal visit "no less profitable than interesting."

Her patriotic duty done, Alma returned to France in 1923. In June, she staged an exhibit of some of the objects she had collected and was storing in Paris while waiting for the San Francisco museum to be completed. They included 11 Rodin pieces, 79 pieces by the American sculptor George Putnam, a marble copy of the Louvre's "Winged Victory," and Sévres porcelain and Gobelin tapestries donated by the French government. The exhibit was a huge hit, as was Alma. "All the greatest of France were there," reported a San Francisco magazine. "Parisians present say they have never seen such marvelous homage paid to anyone as Mrs. Spreckels received."

Back on her home turf, however, Alma was still a social pariah in some circles. Undaunted, she poured it on, rubbing the upturned noses of the Bay Area bluebloods in her success. She launched a massive remodeling of a thoroughbred horse ranch Adolph owned near the town of Napa. The "remodel" included construction of a 57-room mansion she filled with antiques and art. She also posed for a bit of art herself. Unlike her youthful modeling, this time she kept her clothes on.

The seven-feet-by-five-feet portrait by the Finnish-born artist Richard Hall depicted Alma sitting on an elaborately carved wooden throne-chair, which was part of the furniture Marie had donated for the San Francisco museum. Alma wore a brocaded dress, a sable-lined red mantle, and a somber visage. When the portrait was done, she then invited 250 of her closest friends to a tea party to have a look at it. Many of them were impressed. A few weeks later, she was honored by a local literary society for her contribution to "advancing arts and letters on the Pacific Coast" in a ceremony that included five Army airplanes dropping flowers from the sky.

But Alma's rise to the top of San Francisco's social pile hit a painful bump on the evening of June 27, 1924. Adolph, who was recovering from a bout of pneumonia, played some cards and then went to sleep. He never woke up. The 67-year-old tycoon's death from an apparent cerebral hemorrhage devastated Alma. Her husband had been her mentor, her protector, her confidant and her best friend. "Everything I know, I learned from my husband,"

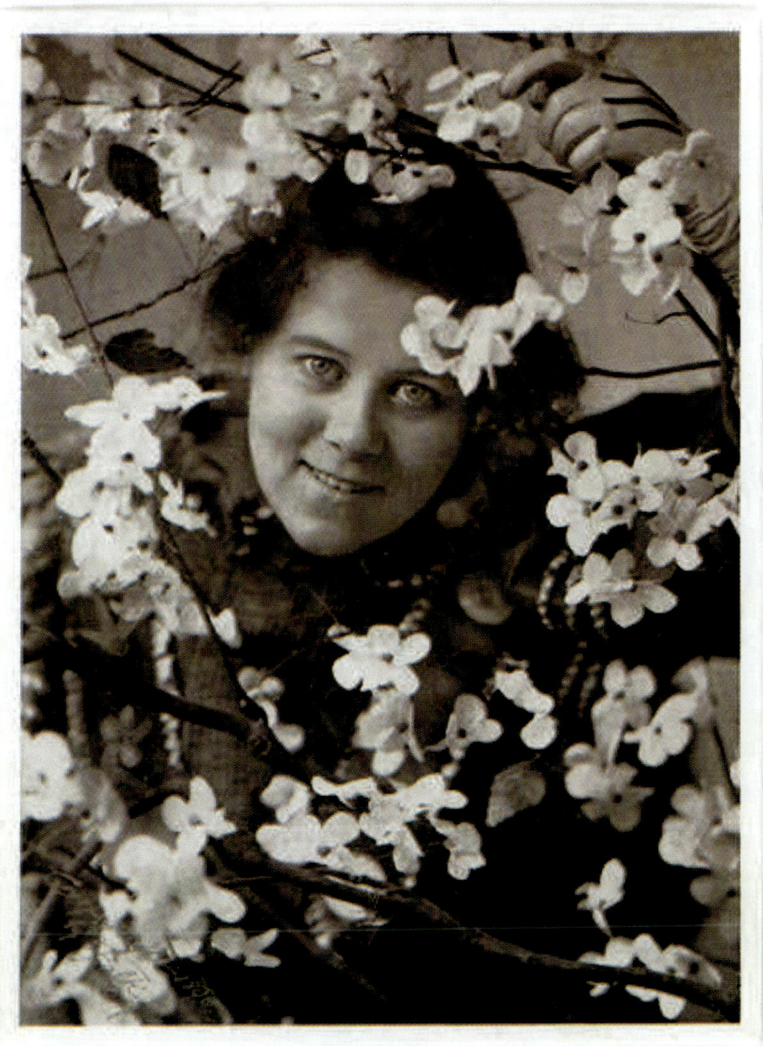

A young Loie Fuller, probably taken shortly after her smash debut at Paris' Foiles-Bergére in late 1892.
—Maryhill Museum of Art

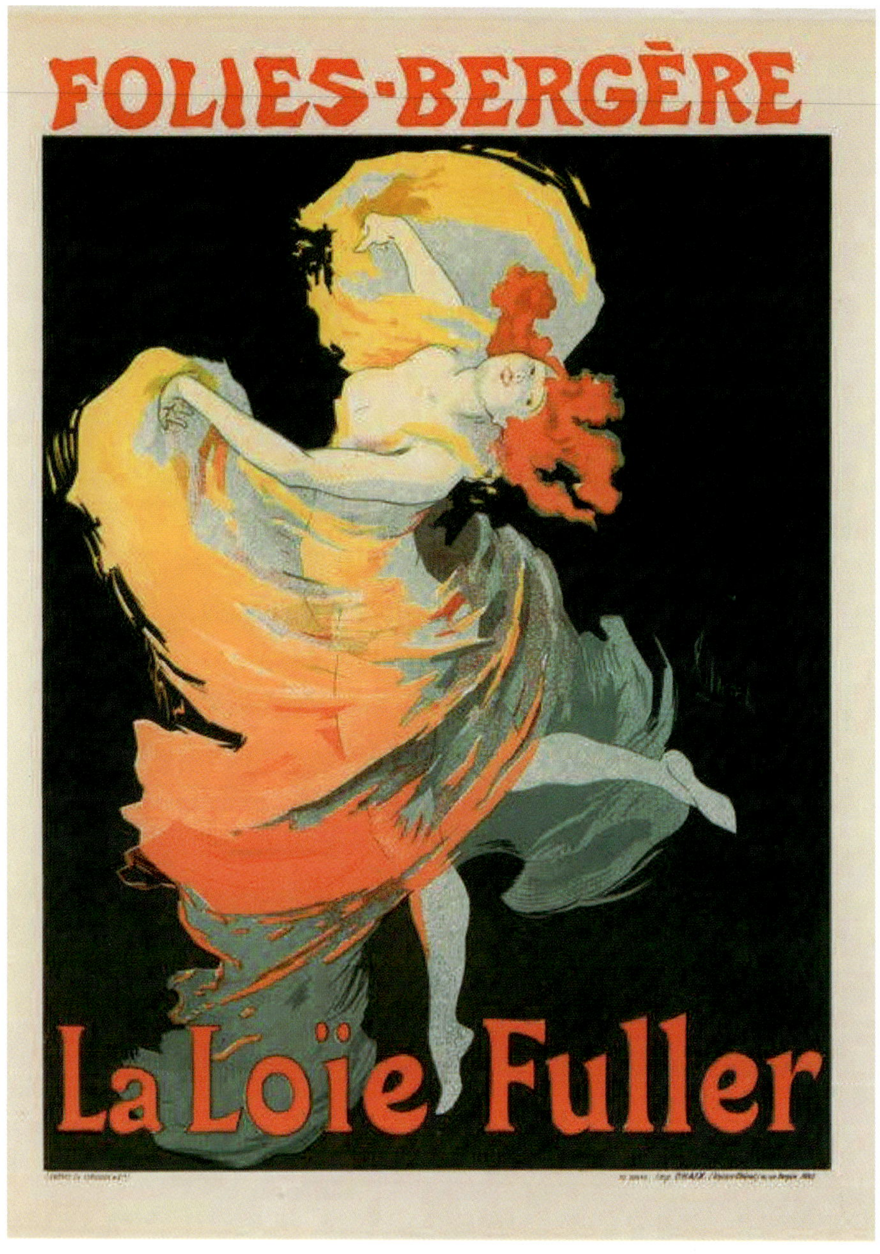

An 1897 poster of Loie, by the French artist Jules Chéret.
—*New York Public Library.*

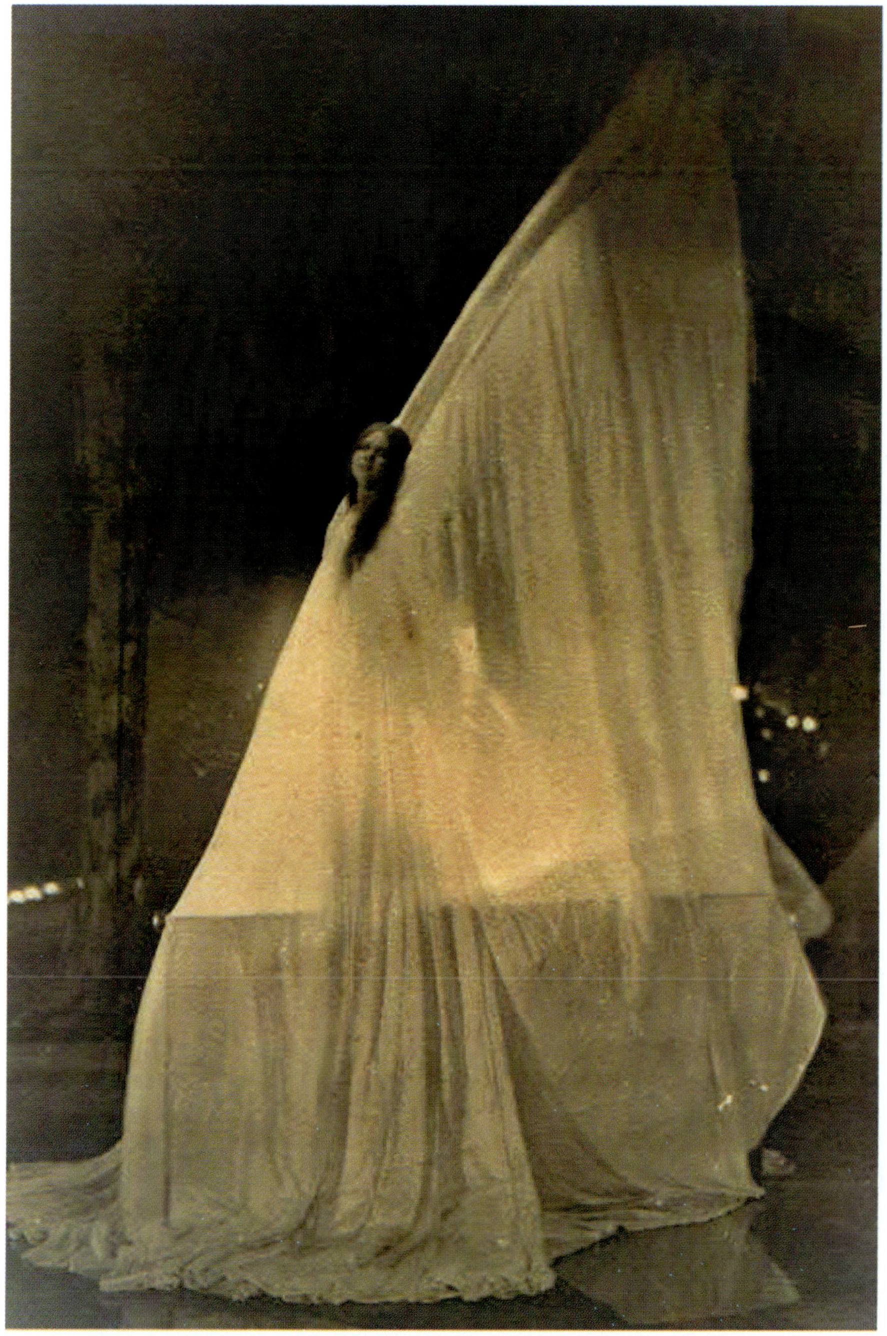

Loie in one of her elaborate dance costumes, which involved hundreds of yards of material, and concealed bamboo or metal rods to manipulate it.
—Maryhill Museum of Art

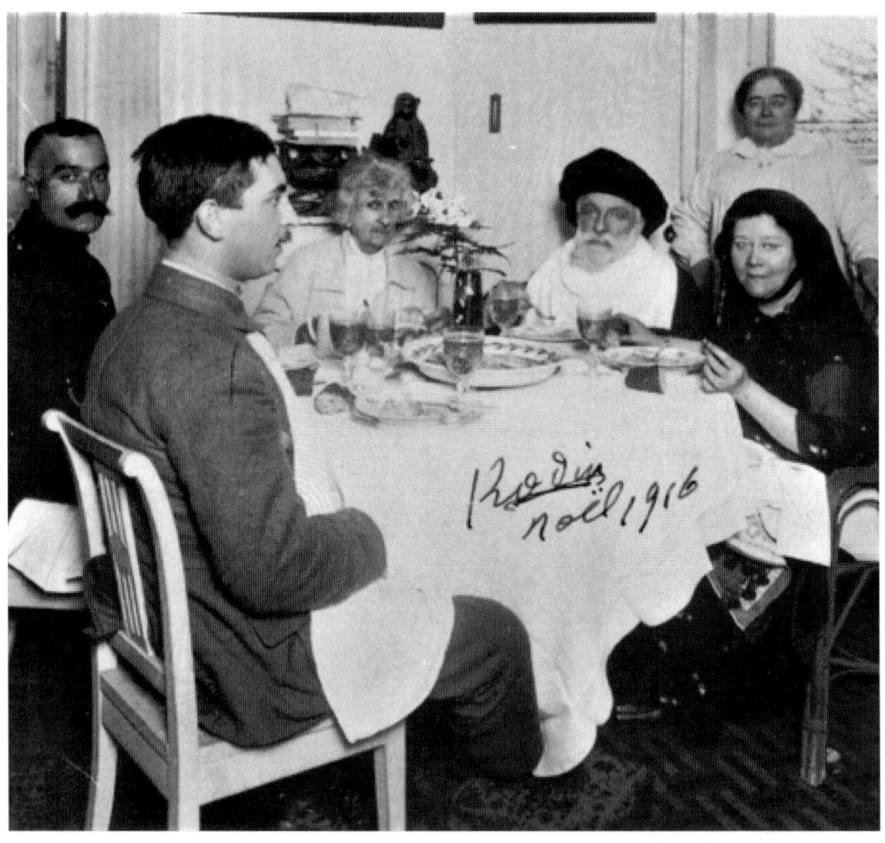

Loie, at far right, sitting next to her revered artist friend Auguste Rodin at Christmas dinner, 1916. The dancer and sculptor had a close, platonic—and sometimes stormy—relationship.
—*Maryhill Museum of Art*

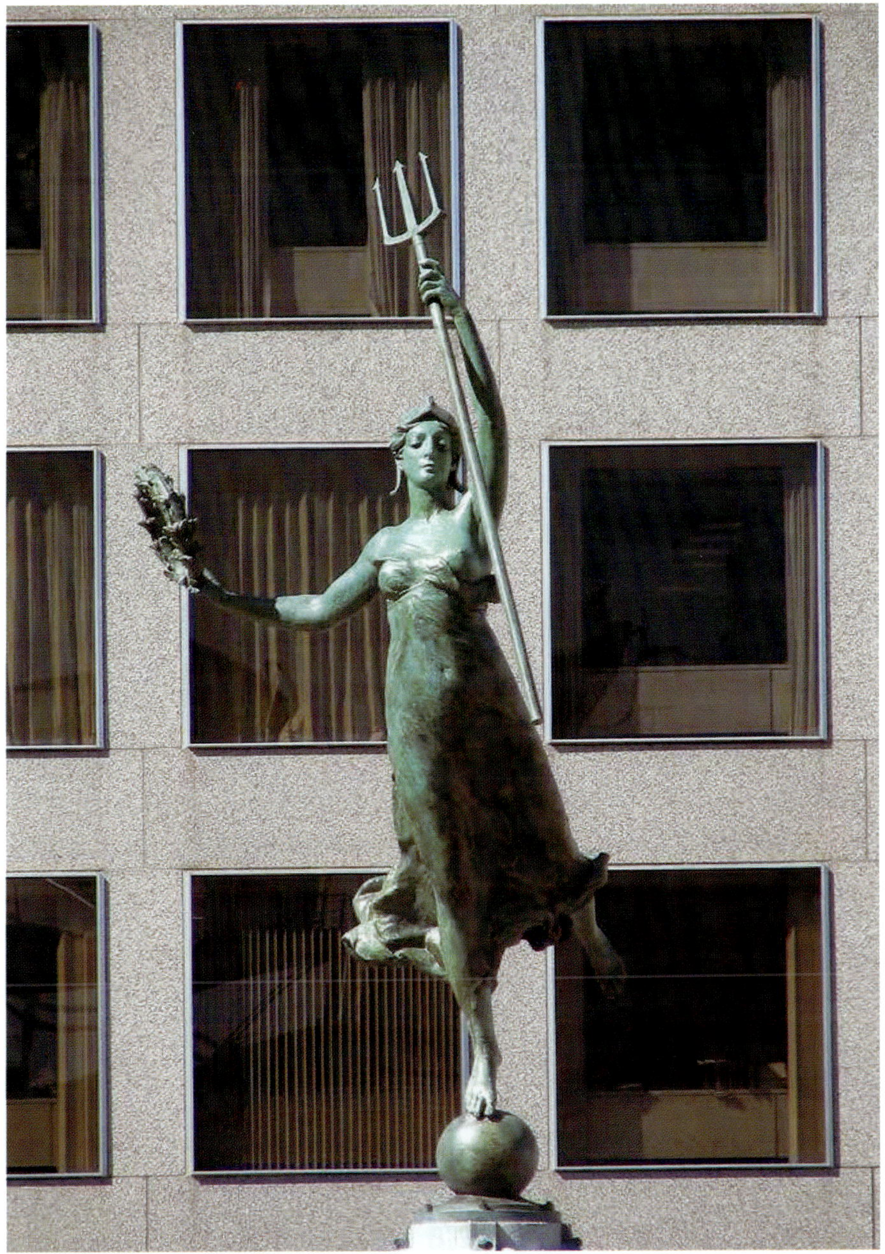

Alma de Bretteville posed in 1902 for this statue in San Francisco's Union Square. The monument, which still dominates the square, commemorated the U.S. victory in the Spanish-American War. It also brought the model to the attention of sugar baron Adolph Spreckels.
—Courtesy of Peter Kaminski

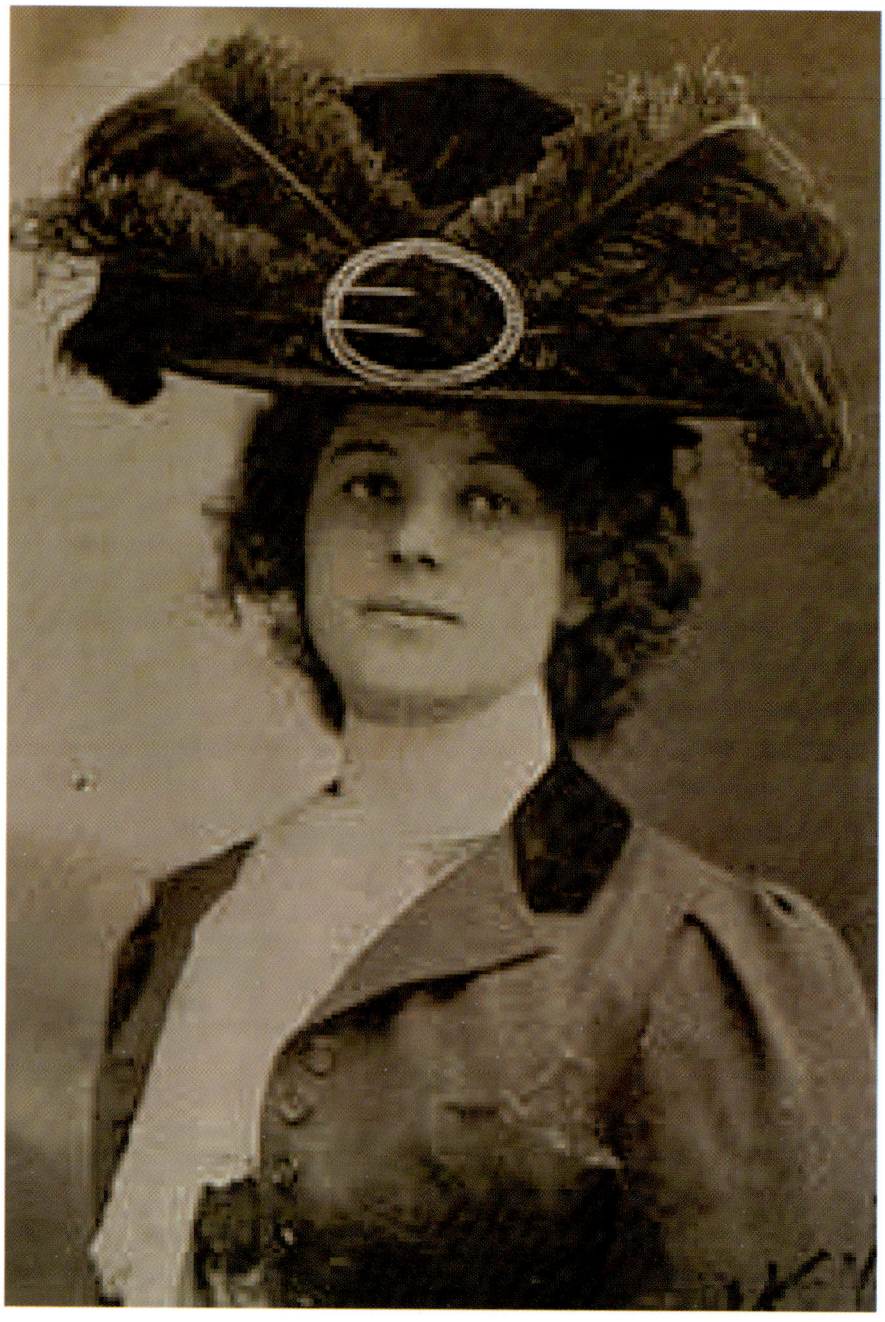

A 23-year-old Alma, sporting a new hat on a trip she and her family took to Denmark in 1904 to visit relatives. The trip – and probably the hat – were paid for by her "sugar daddy," Adolph Spreckels. The two were wed in 1908. —*San Francisco Public Library.*

A photo of a heavier, but still striking – and very rich—
Alma, probably taken in the late 1920s.
—*Maryhill Museum of Art*

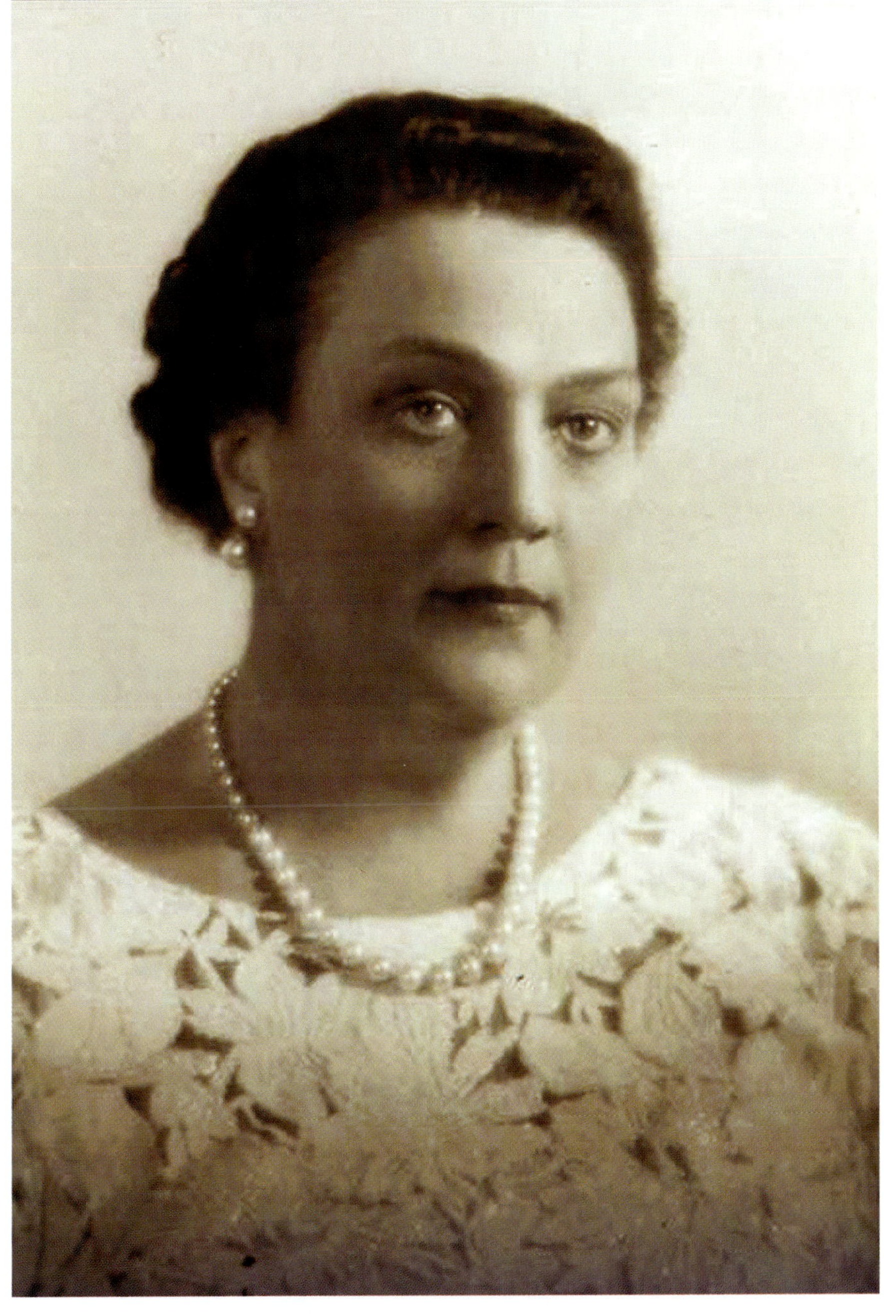

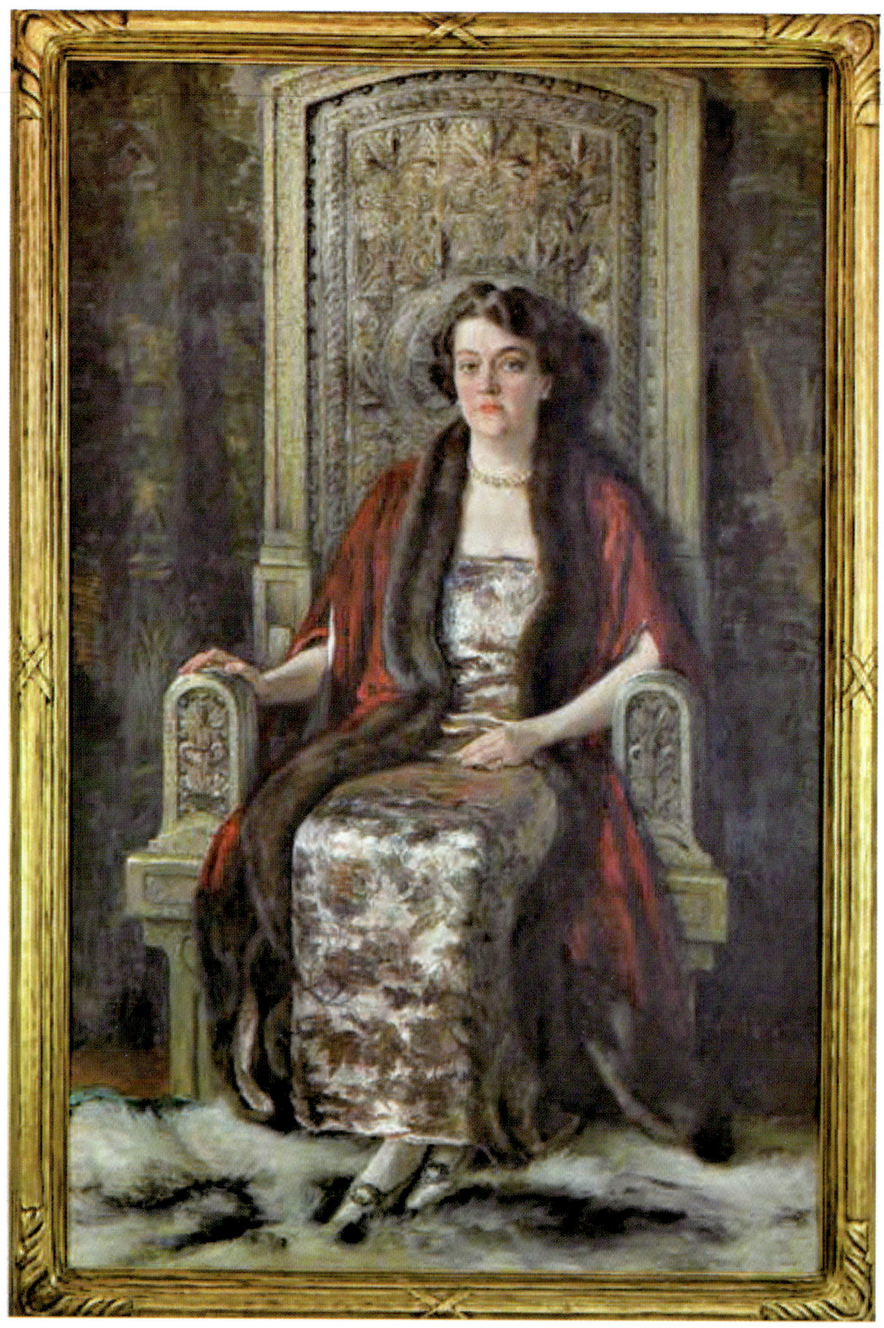

This 35-square-foot portrait of Alma, painted in 1923, depicts her sitting in a carved wooden "throne chair" given her by Queen Marie. Alma gave the painting to Maryhill on the condition it be permanently and prominently displayed. For many years, it was. *—Maryhill Museum of Art*

The young, handsome and dashing Sam Hill, as he looked about the time he graduated from Harvard in 1879.
—*Maryhill Museum of Art*

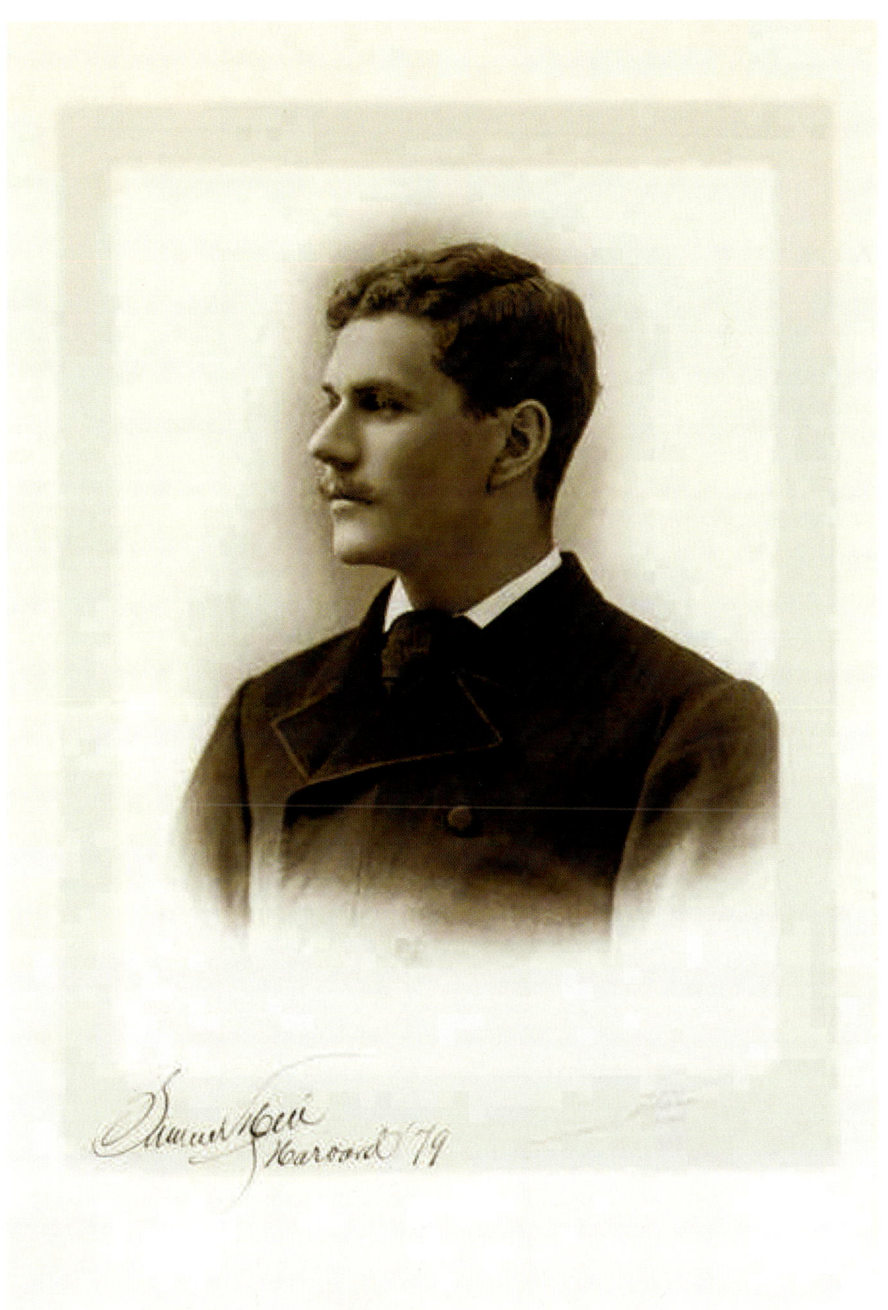

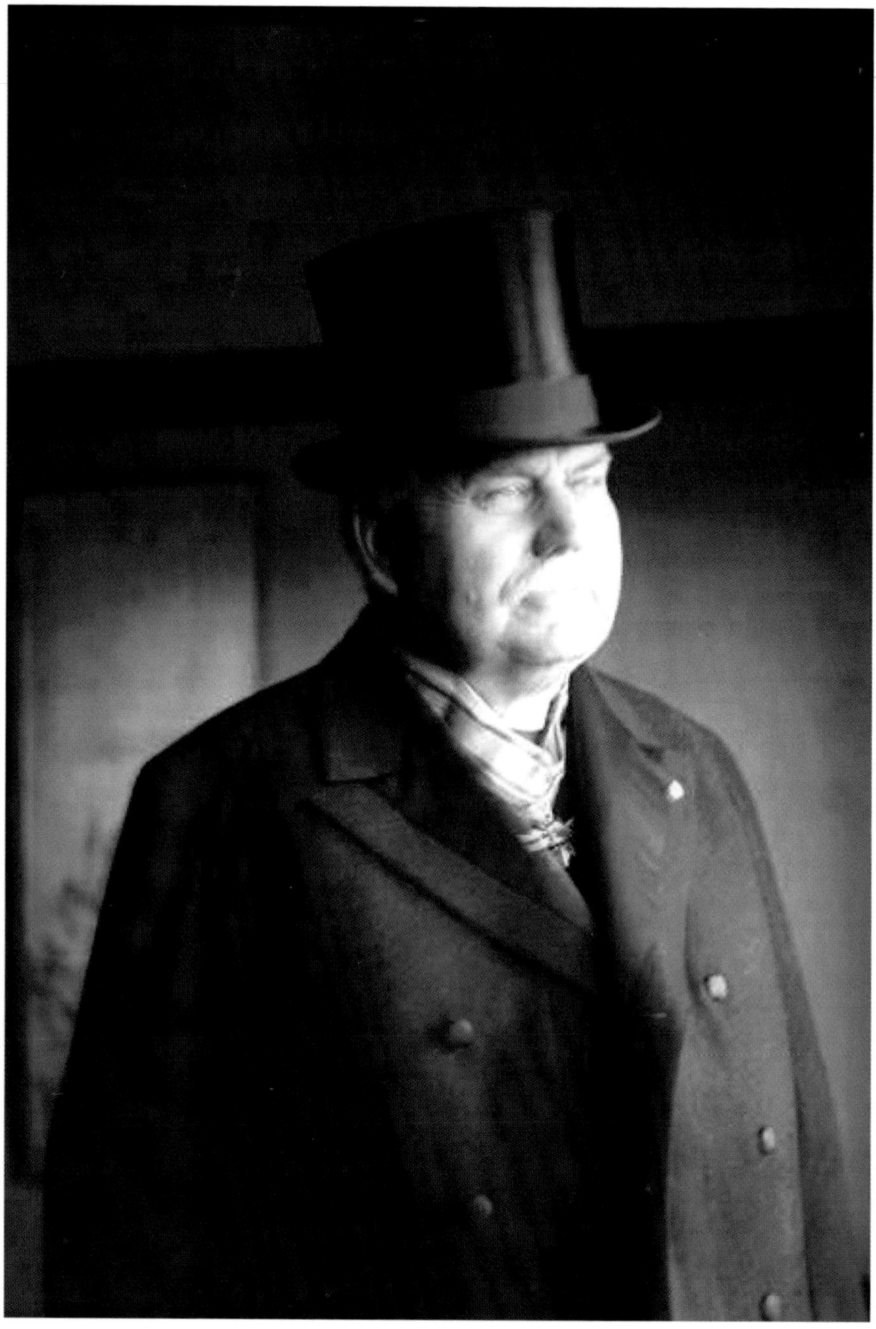

Sam in top hat. Around his neck is one of the numerous decorations he received from several foreign nations for his road-building leadership and humanitarian work. —*Maryhill Museum of Art*

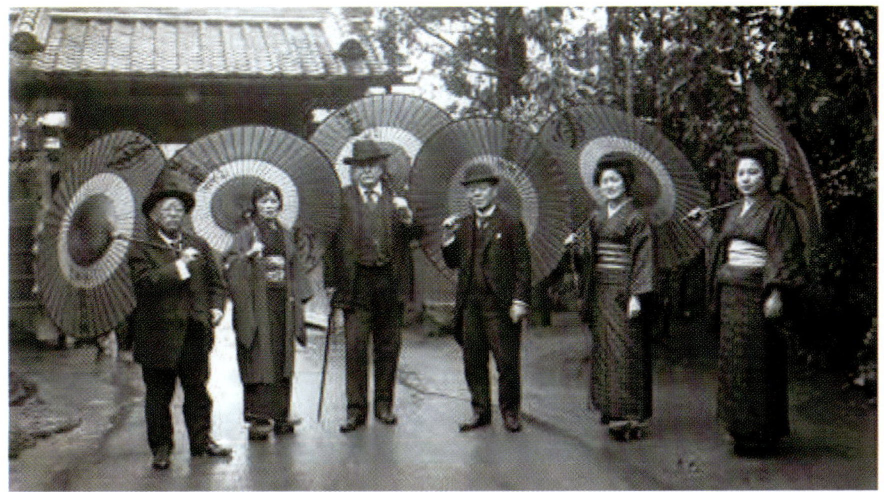

Sam posing on what was one of at least nine trips he made to Japan to promote the importance of good roads, as well as good relations between the U.S. and Japan. —*Maryhill Museum of Art*

An introspective Sam, gazing into his beloved Columbia River Gorge. —*Maryhill Museum of Art*

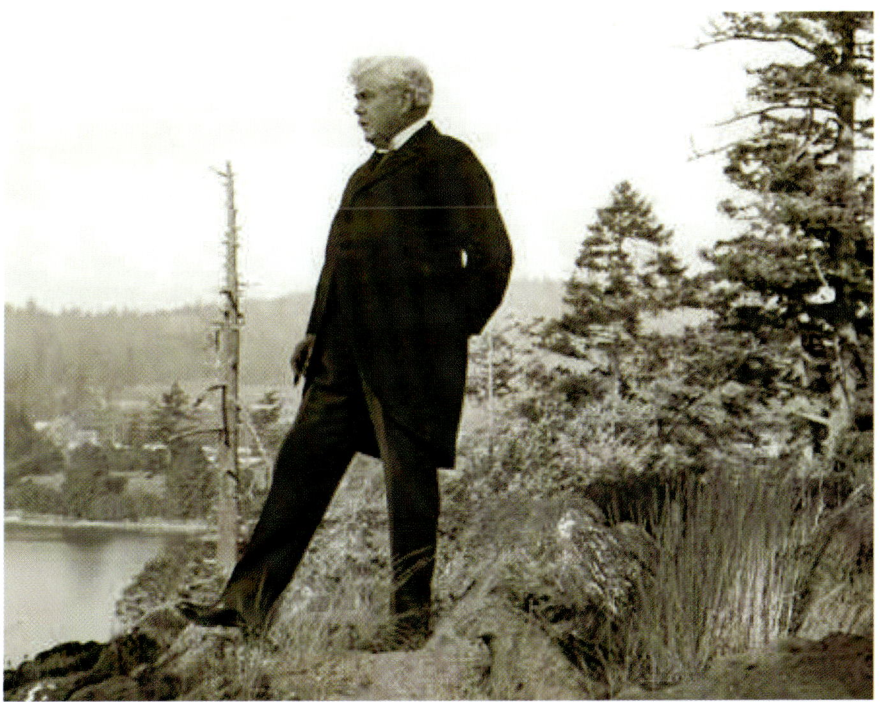

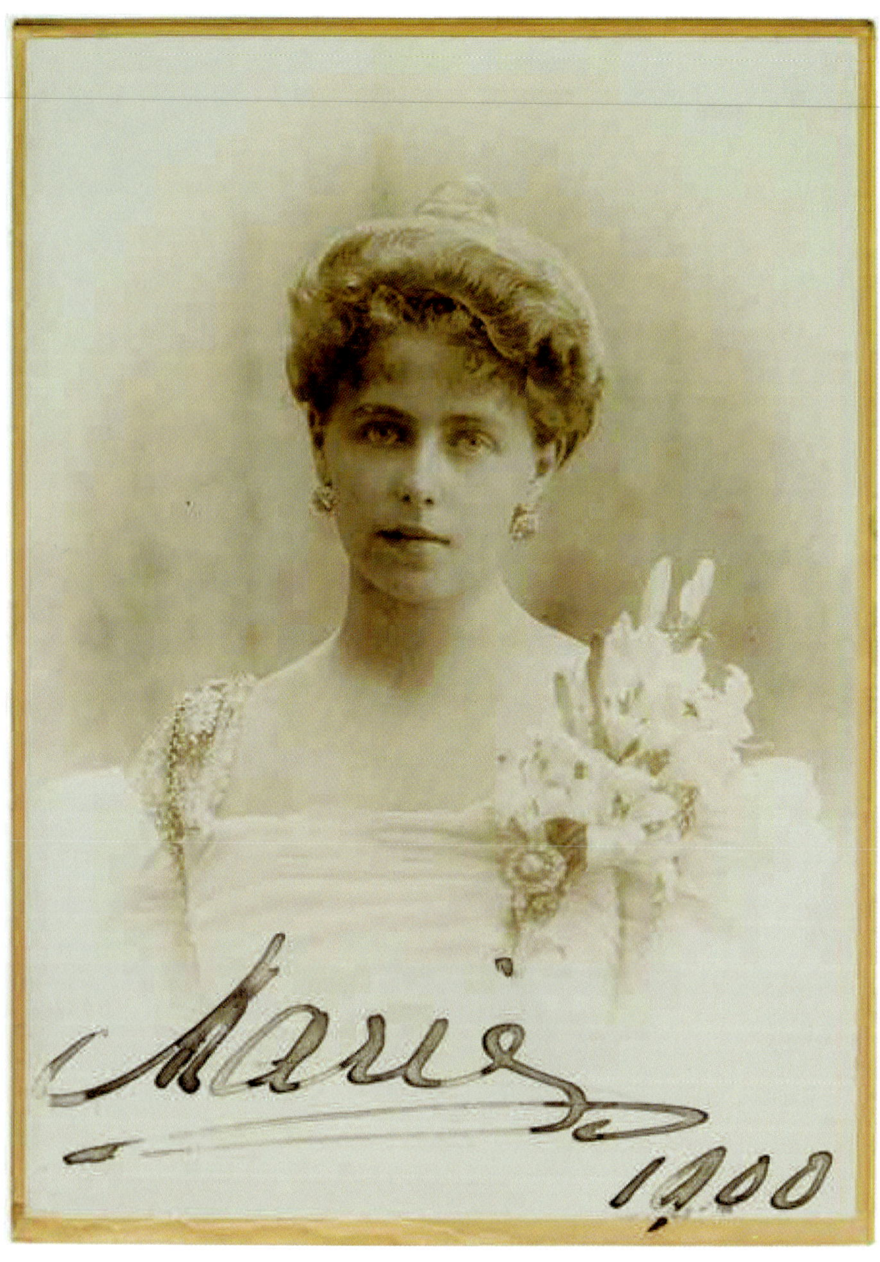

Marie of Romania, at the age of 25. The crown princess was widely considered the most beautiful royal in the world, despite having already borne four children.
—*Maryhill Museum of Art*

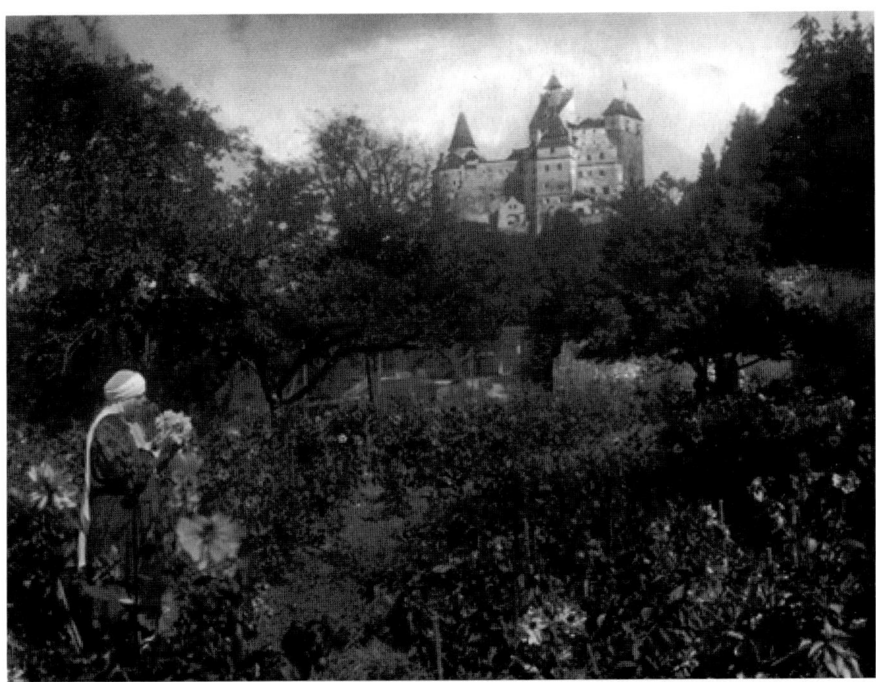

Marie in the garden at Bran Castle, which grateful Transylvanians gave her after World War I for helping free them from Hungarian rule. Popular legend declared the ancient castle had once belonged to Vlad III – better known to horror buffs as "Dracula." – *Maryhill Museum of Art*

Marie, dressed as a peasant, hands out clothing to World War I orphans. —*Library of Congress*

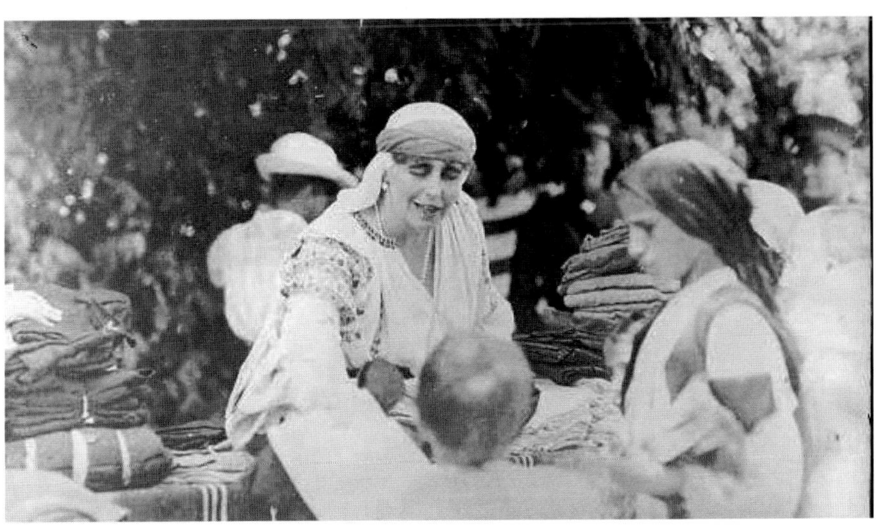

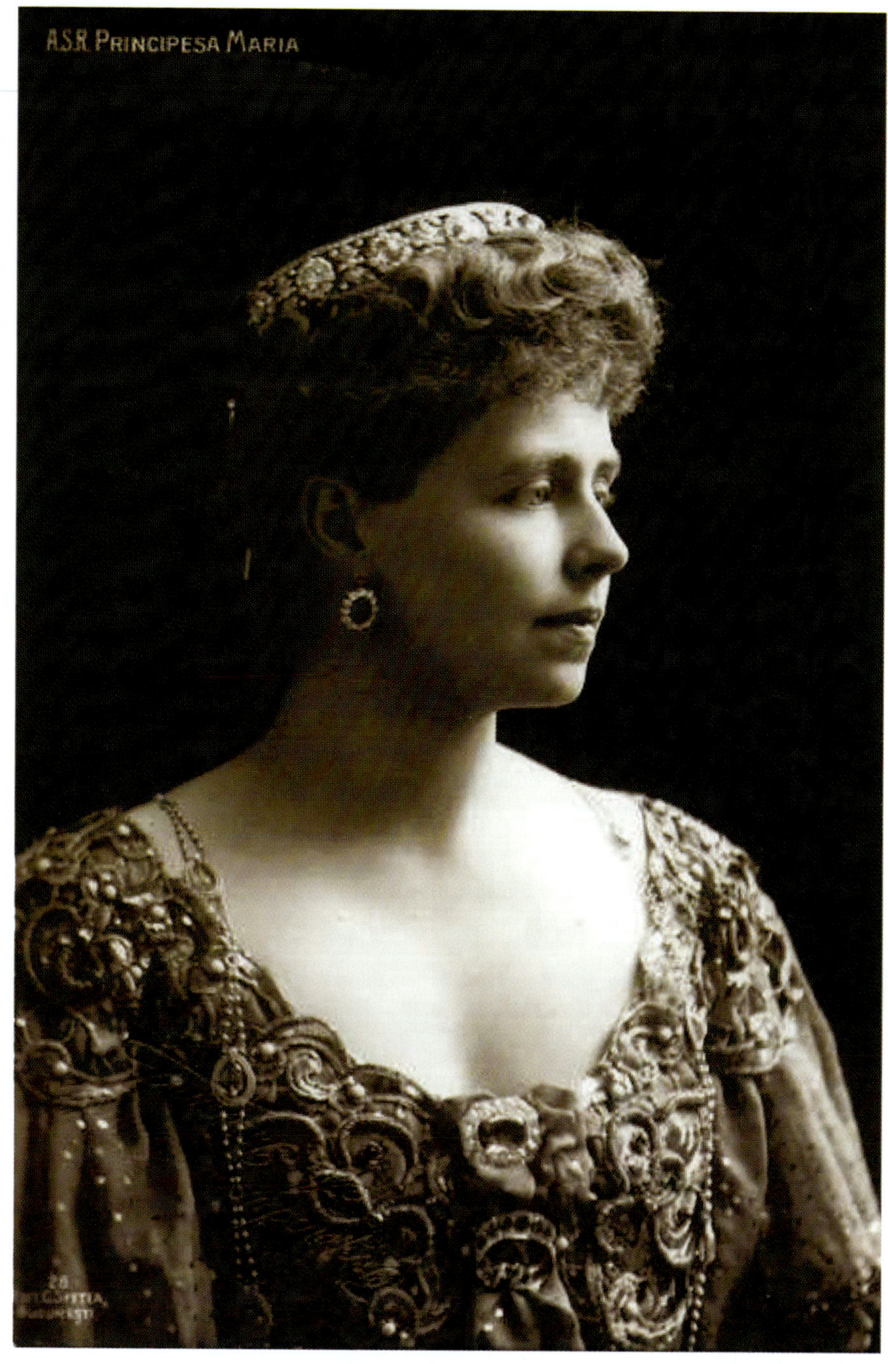

Marie at 40, taken in 1915, not long after the start of World War I.
—*Maryhill Museum of Art*

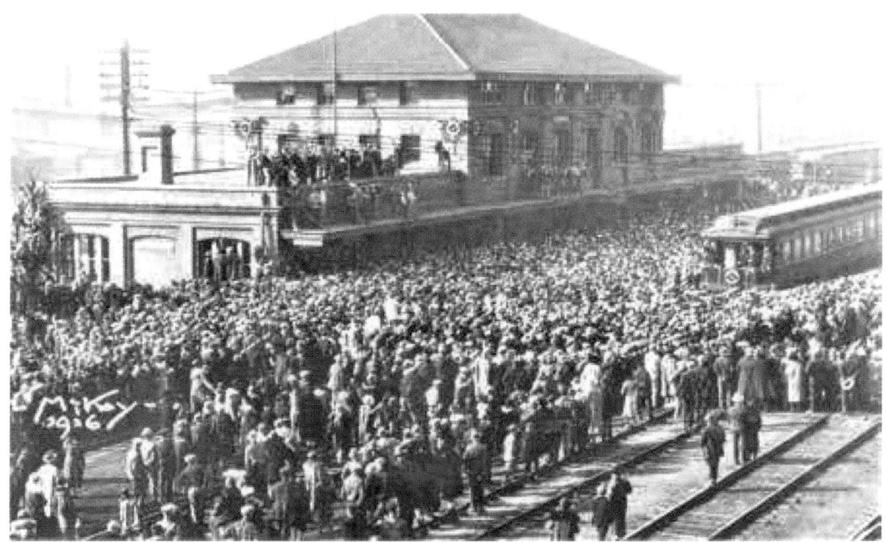

Huge crowds gathered at each stop of Marie's 1926 train ride across North America. Here, it looks like most of Missoula Montana has turned out for the queen's brief appearance at the back of her special train. —*Mansfield Library Collection, University of Montana.*

An audience of about 2,000 was on hand for Marie's dedication of the Maryhill museum on Nov. 3 1926. The museum would not open for another 14 years. —*Maryhill Museum of Art*

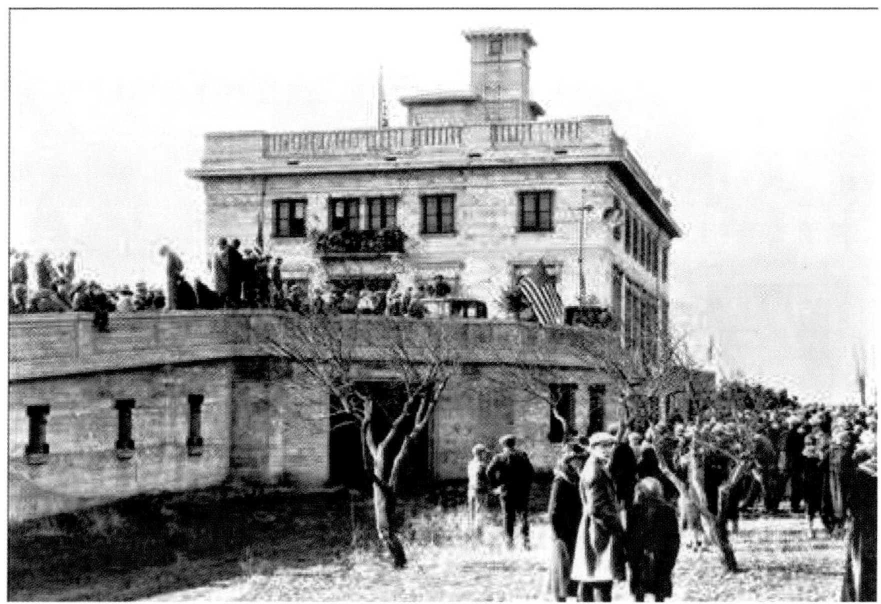

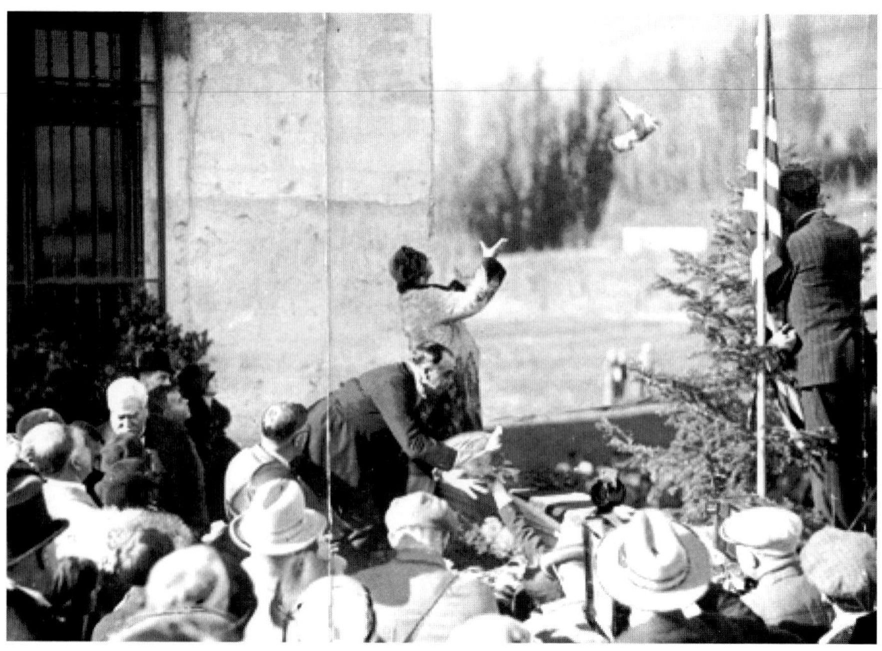

Queen Marie releases one of 10 carrier pigeons bearing goodwill messages to various Western U.S. cities during the museum's dedication ceremonies. The white-haired Sam is standing in the crowd behind her. *—Maryhill Museum of Art*

A somber Sam poses with Queen Marie to his left and Prince Nicholas and Princess Ileana to his right at the Maryhill dedication. Behind them is Portland Mayor George Baker. *—Maryhill Museum of Art*

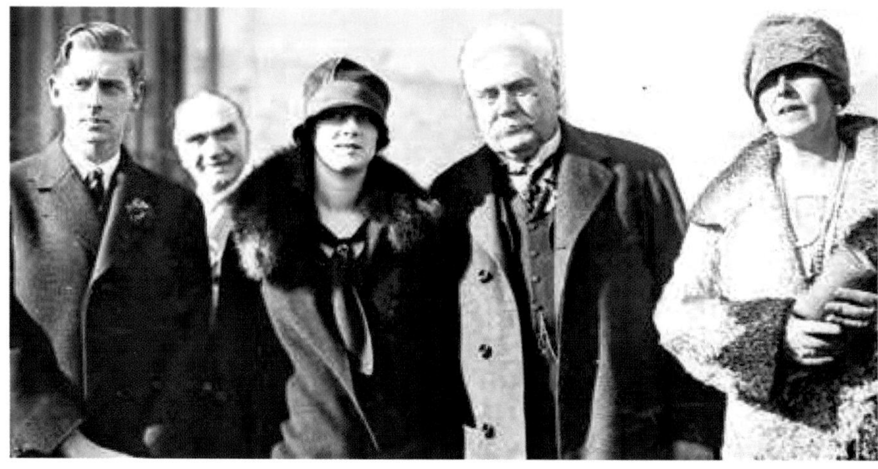

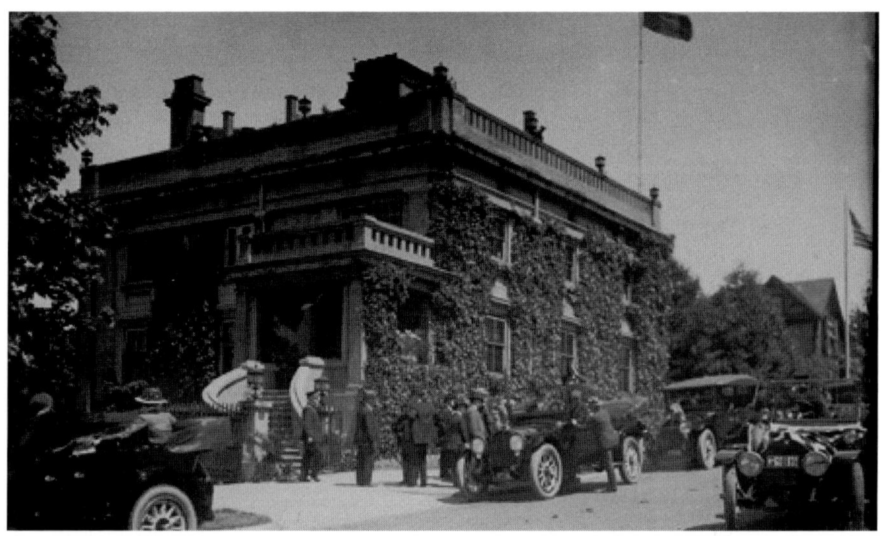

Sam greets a delegation of Belgian government officials at his Seattle mansion in 1918. The steel-reinforced home featured a rooftop garden and a sundial said to be accurate within one minute. *—Maryhill Museum of Art*

Part of the crowd gathered on July 4 1918 to dedicate the altar for Sam's Stonehenge Memorial to local World War I casualties. The monument would take a decade to complete, and required moving the hotel in this picture so the memorial could closely line up with the summer solstice, as does the actual Stonehenge. *—Klickitat County Historical Society*

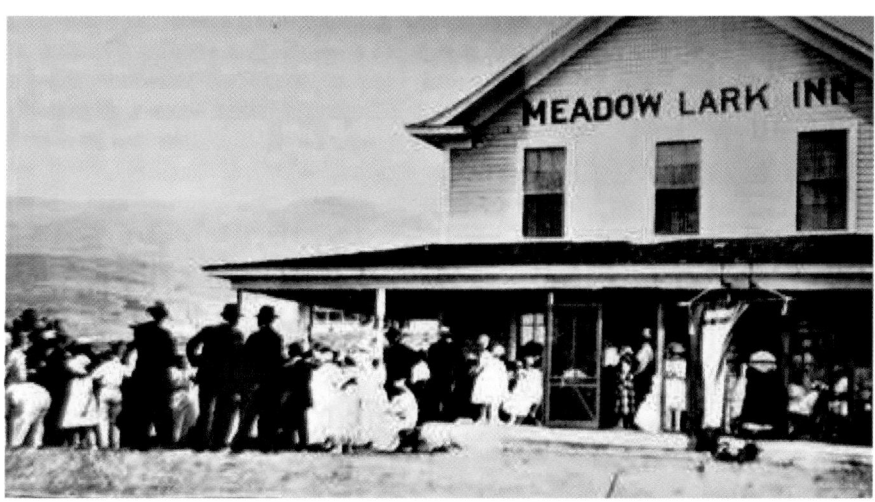

Sam Hill's Stonehenge in 2019. Located about three miles east of the museum and free to visit, the memorial has added to Maryhill's eclecticism, but has been costly and time-consuming to maintain.
—Ceil Dolan Wiegand

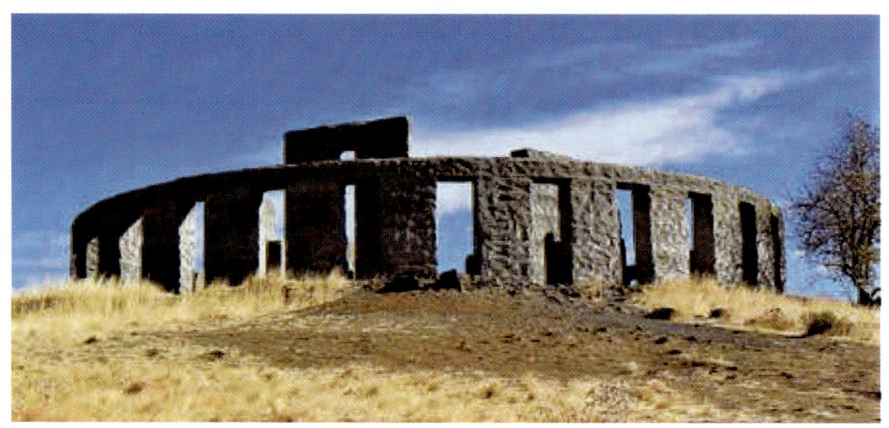

Sam's memorial, just below Stonehenge. His original crypt at the site was replaced with this monument after it was repeatedly vandalized. Sam wrote his own epitaph. *—Ceil Dolan Wiegand*

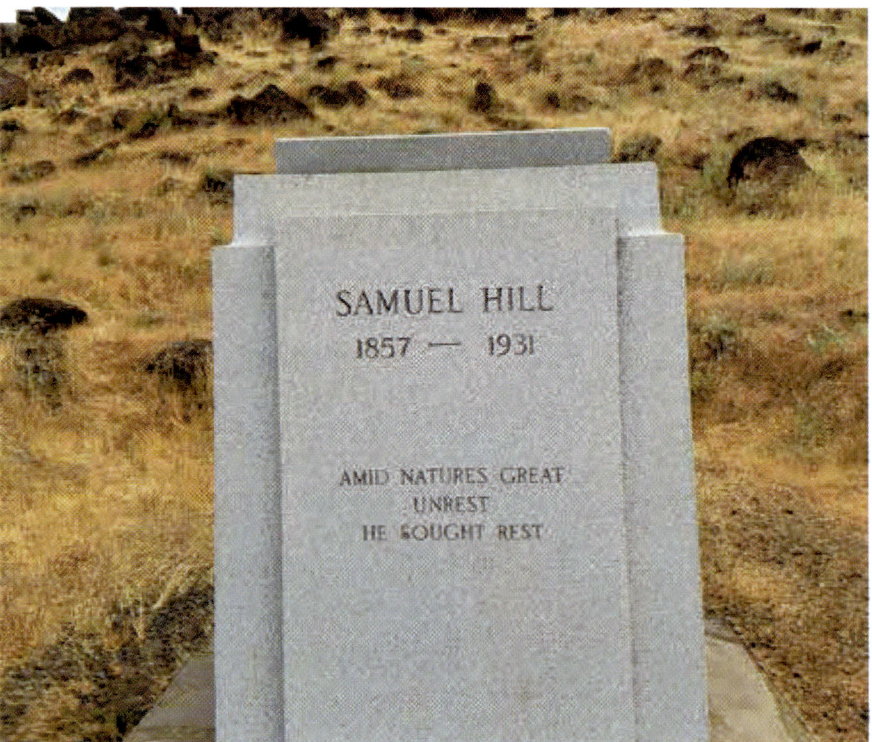

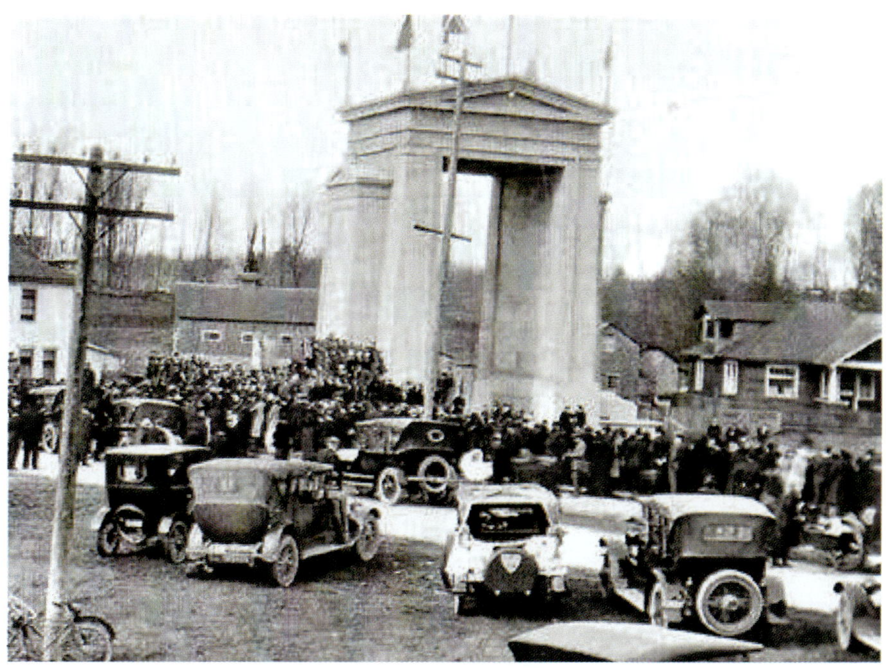

The 1921 dedication of Sam's Peace Arch, straddling the U.S.-Canada border at Blaine Washington. —*Maryhill Museum of Art*

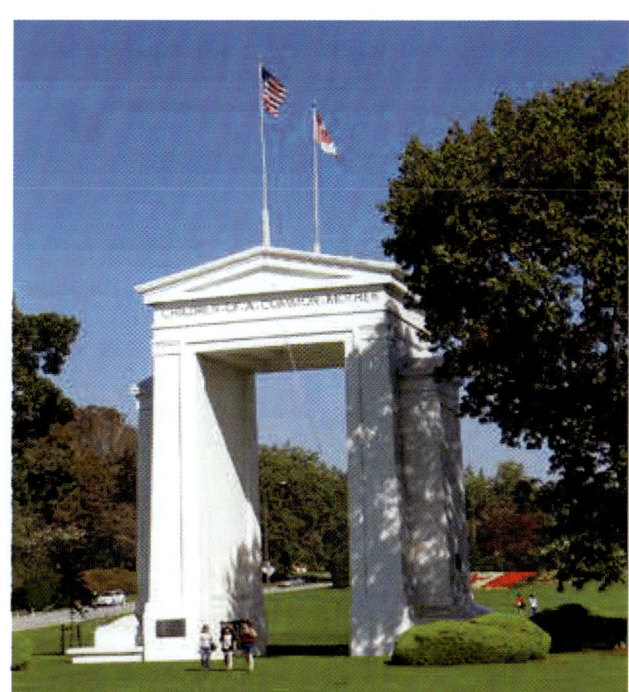

Three of the 500,000 or so annual visitors to Sam Hill's Peace Arch stroll onto U.S. soil from Canada. —*Ceil Dolan Wiegand*

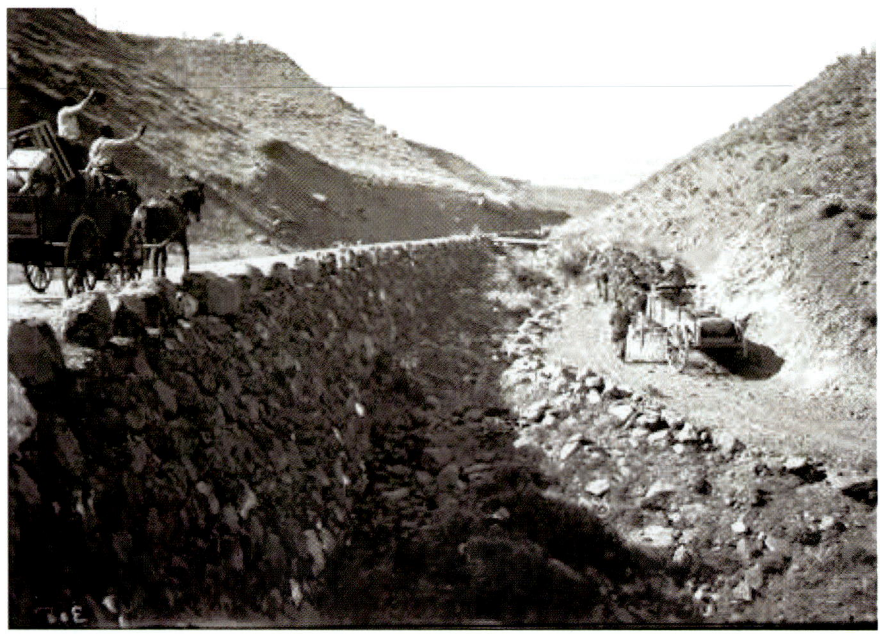

Grading Sam's 10-mile-long "demonstration road" in 1910 or 1911. The thoroughfare, which became known as the Loops Road, used seven different construction methods, had 25 curves and eight hairpin turns.
—Maryhill Museum of Art

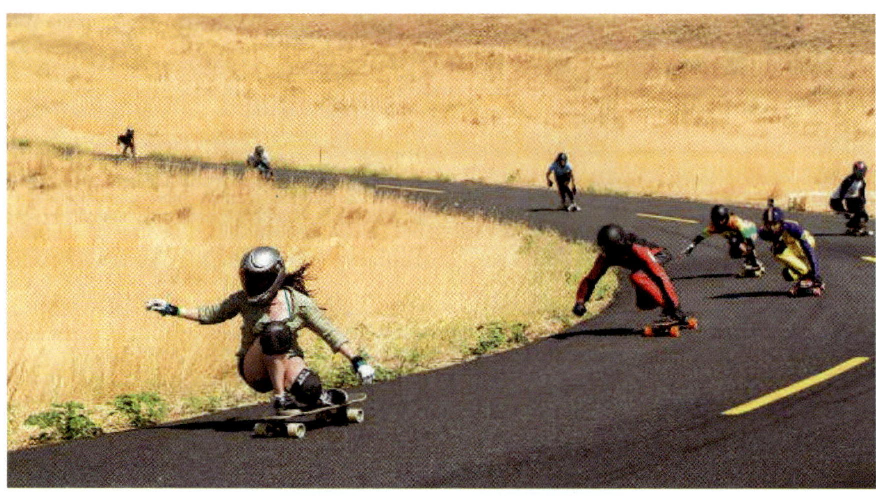

Sam's "demonstration road" today is a money-making vehicle for the Maryhill museum, which leases it for car commercials, vintage auto rallies and "gravity sports" events, such as this 2015 skateboard race.
—Ian Logan Photography

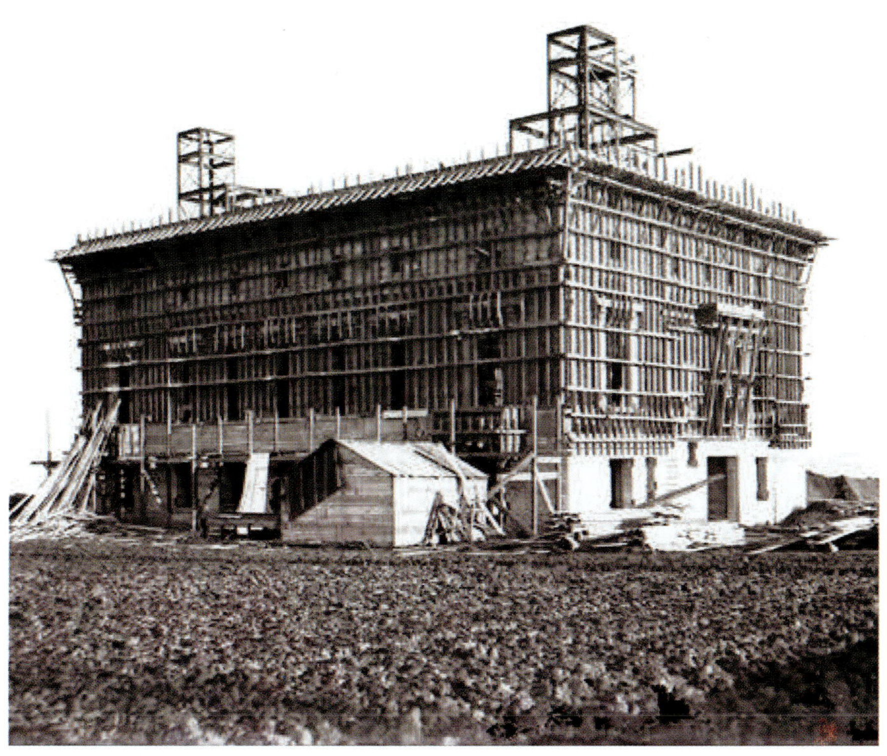

Maryhill under construction, probably around 1916.
—Maryhill Museum of Art

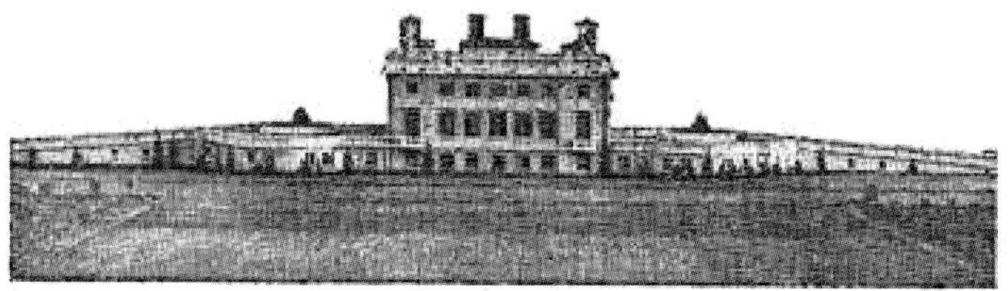

130

The official invitation to Maryhill's opening, May 13 1940. The 242 guests who showed up were outnumbered by the cattle grazing on the museum grounds. —*Maryhill Museum of Art*

THE BOARD OF TRUSTEES

of the

Maryhill Museum of Fine Arts

invites you to be present at the

INVITATIONAL OPENING OF THE MUSEUM

on Monday, May 13, 1940

at the hour of one fifteen o'clock p. m.

This opening date has been selected, as it is the anniversary of the birthday of the late Samuel Hill, it's founder

Please present this invitation, which will admit you and three guests of your choice

The Museum will be open to the public on May 14, and thereafter

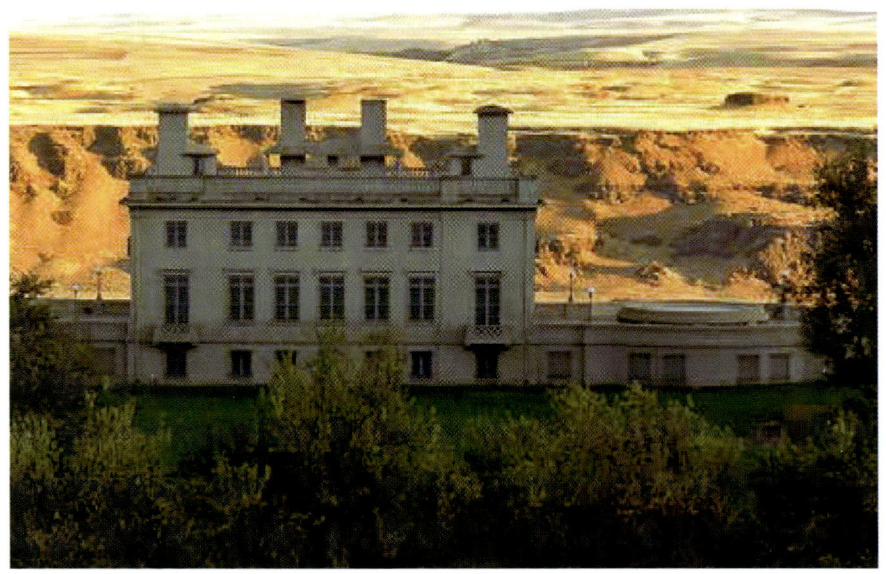

Maryhill trustees planted grapes around the museum, hoping to come up with another revenue source. The effort failed, but by 2019, the Columbia River Gorge was the home of many award-winning wineries.
—Maryhill Museum of Art

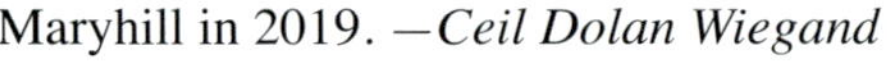

Maryhill in 2019. *—Ceil Dolan Wiegand*

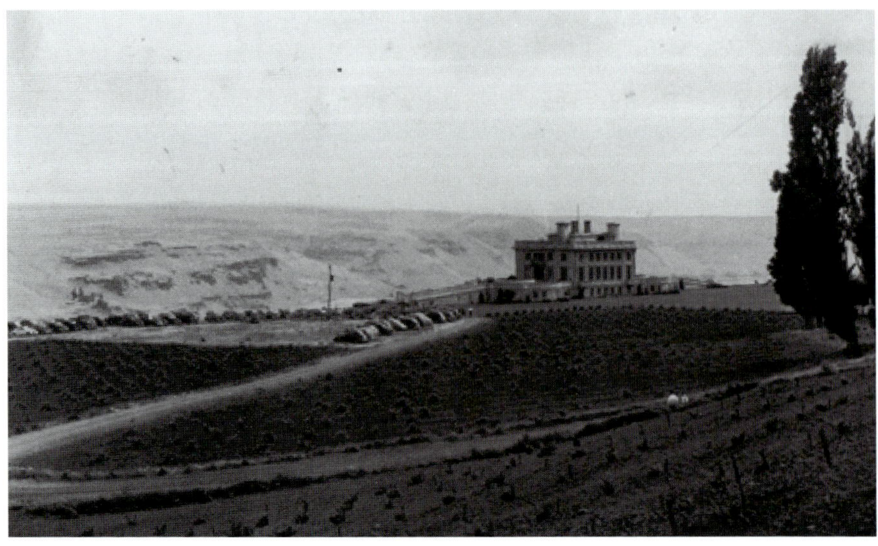

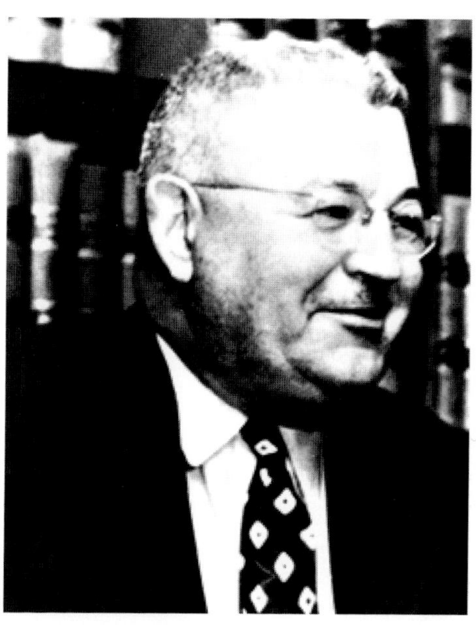

Zola Brooks in 1949. Brooks served as Sam Hill's lawyer and as a Maryhill trustee for more than 30 years. Often at odds with other trustees and museum director Cliff Dolph, Brooks nonetheless played a major role in Maryhill's survival. —*Klickitat County Historical Society.*

Clifford Dolph in 1962. Dolph began his career at Maryhill as a handyman, and ended up as the museum's director for more than 30 years. —*Maryhill Museum of Art*

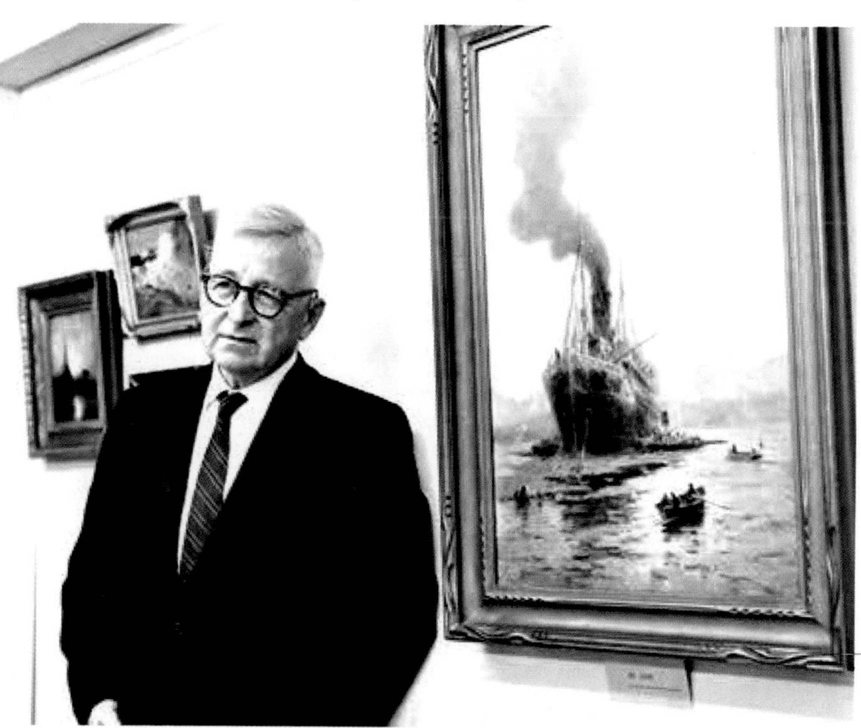

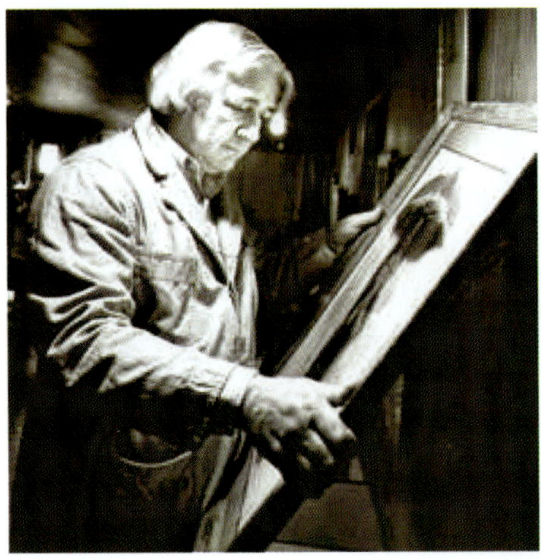

Robert Campbell, Maryhill's second director, in 1976. While innovative and enthusiastic, Campbell's 15-month stint as the museum's leader was dominated by controversies that ended in his dismissal, as well as multiple lawsuits. —*Maryhill Museum of Art*

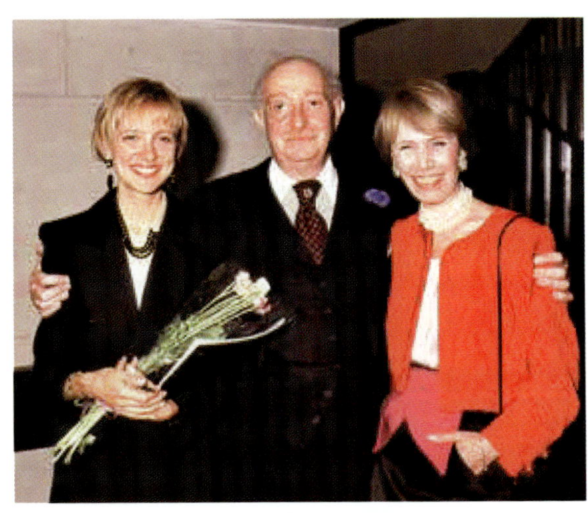

Maryhill director Linda Mountain, left, at the 1990 opening of the restored Théâtre de la Mode at the Louvre in Paris. Mountain, who later remarried and changed her last name to Tesner, was Maryhill's first professionally trained director, and a key factor in restoring the museum's credibility. —*Maryhill Museum of Art*

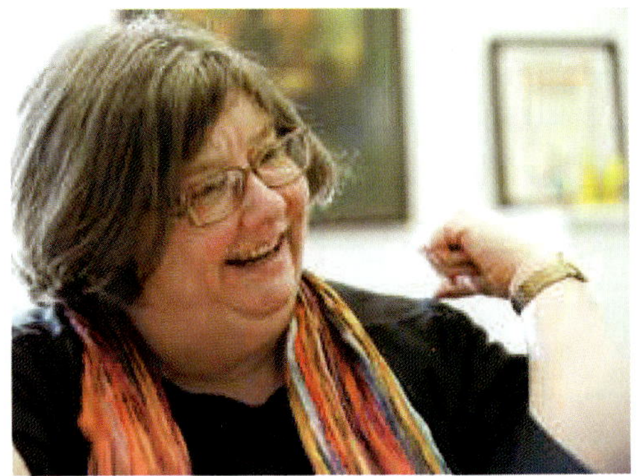

Colleen Schafroth began at Maryhill in 1986 as education curator, and became the museum's director in 2001. She oversaw Maryhill's bold expansion drive that more than doubled the museum's size. —*The Columbian (Vancouver Wa.)*

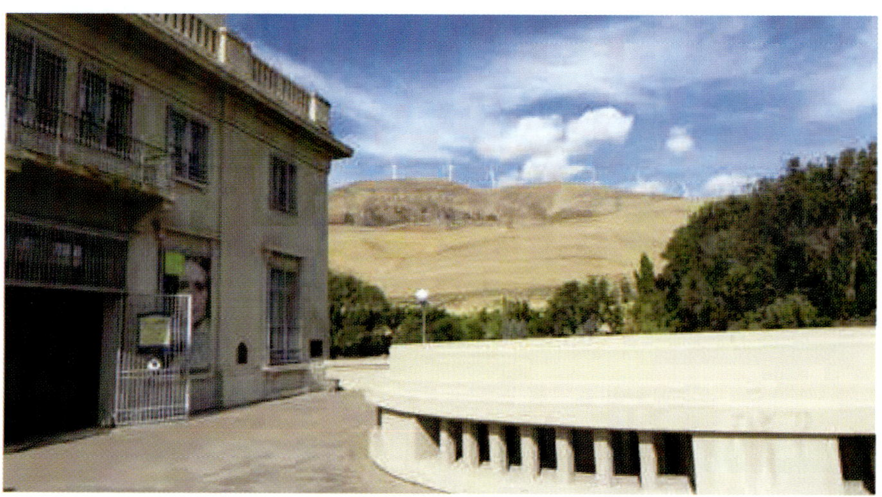

At Maryhill, the wind helps keep the doors open. On the hill behind the museum are some of the 40-story-tall wind power turbines on museum-owned land. Lease revenues from the wind farm can amount to as much as 20 percent of Maryhill's annual revenues. *—Ceil Dolan Wiegand*

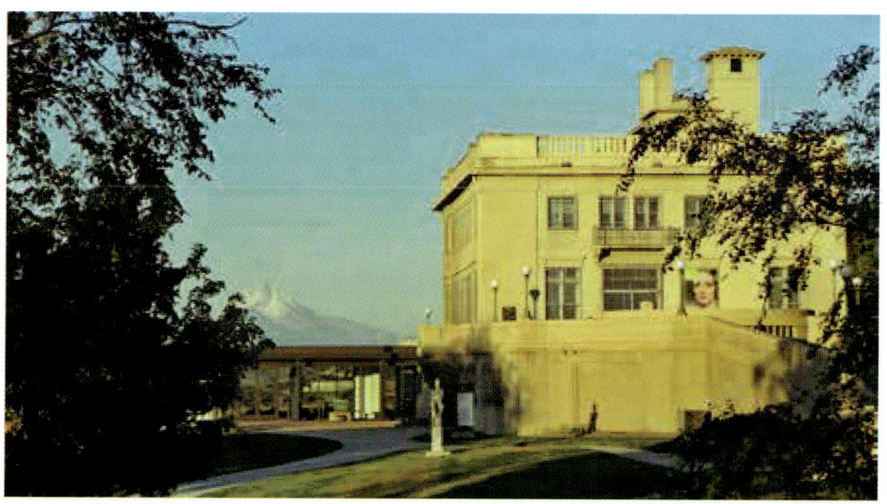

Old and new: To the left of the original building is the 22,000-square-foot *Mary and Bruce Stevenson Wing,* opened in 2012 and constructed mostly underground. Looming behind the wing is Oregon's towering Mt. Hood. *—Ceil Dolan Wiegand*

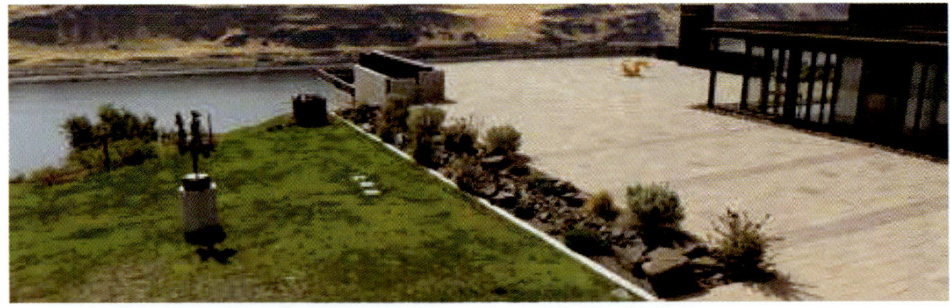

A view of the Columbia River from the museum's outdoor plaza. Permanent and temporary sculptures are displayed throughout the grounds surrounding the museum. *—Ceil Dolan Wiegand*

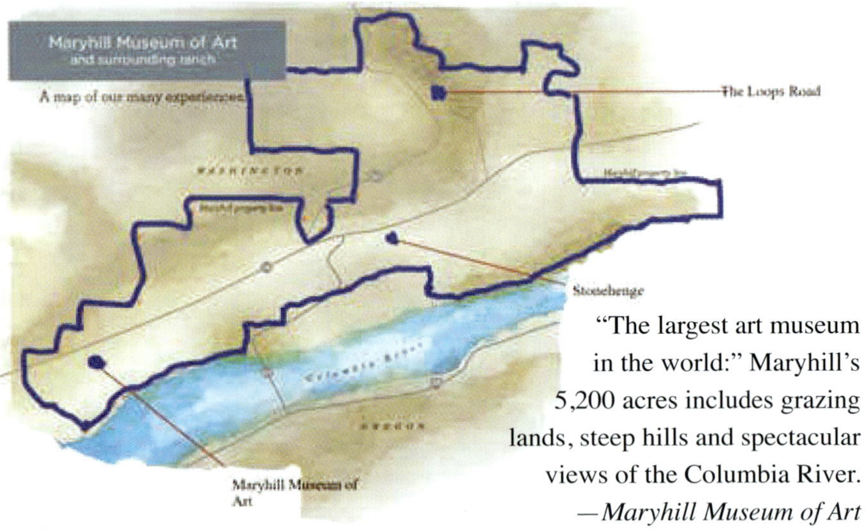

"The largest art museum in the world:" Maryhill's 5,200 acres includes grazing lands, steep hills and spectacular views of the Columbia River. *—Maryhill Museum of Art*

It may not exactly be in the middle of nowhere, but the Maryhill Museum of Art is a fair distance from any big city. It's 100 miles to Portland and 223 to Seattle. In fact, the nearest city with as many as 15,000 residents is 90 miles away.

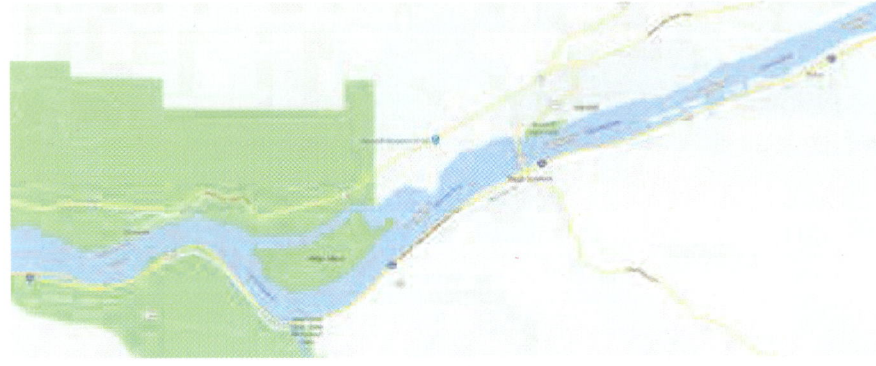

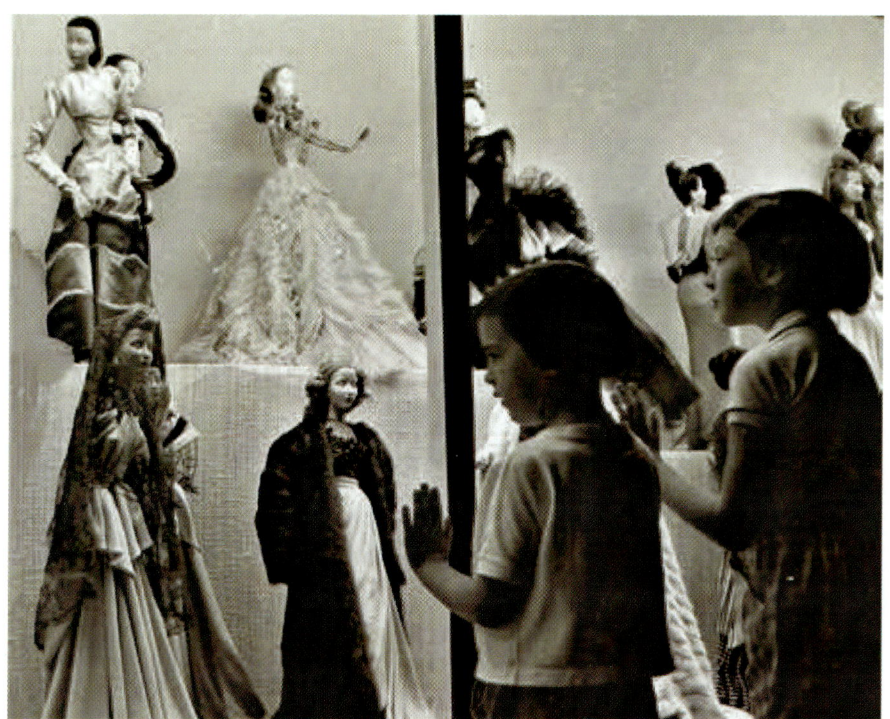

Two young girls admire Maryhill's Théâtre de la Mode fashion dolls in 1962. The mannequins were displayed in plain glass cases until the mid-1990s. *—Portland Oregonian*

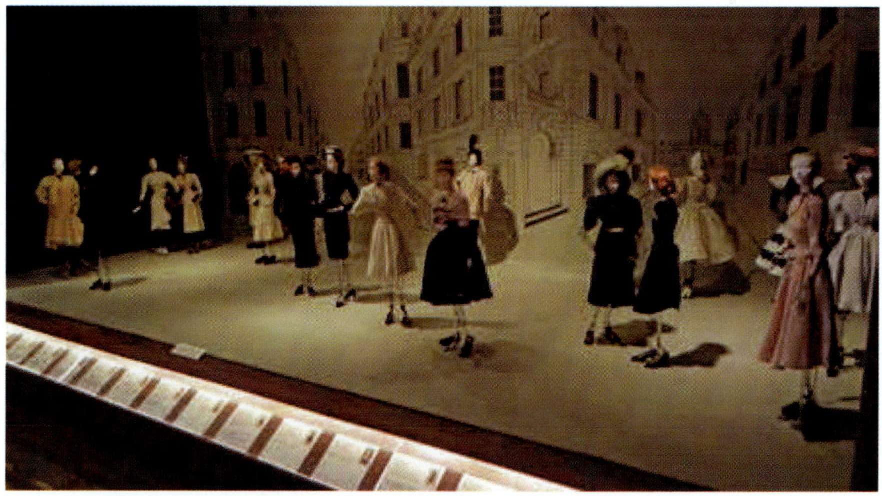

In 1996, Maryhill began displaying its Théâtre de la Mode figures on replicas of the original sets built in France in 1945. The sets are periodically rotated. *—Ceil Dolan Wiegand*

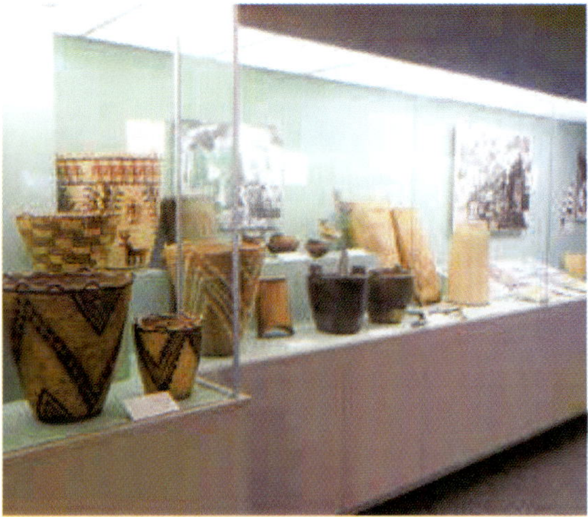

Part of the museum's vast and varied Native American collection, which began with more than 150 baskets collected by Sam Hill. The collection now ranges from Paleolithic rock sculptures to contemporary pieces.
—Ceil Dolan Wiegand

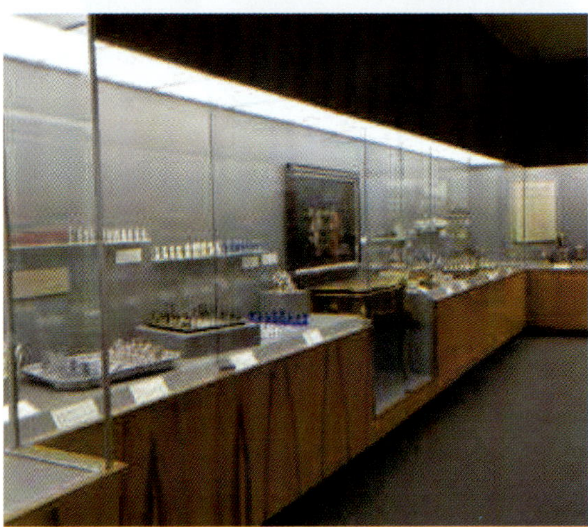

A gallery of some of the museum's more than 350 chess sets, which are periodically rotated for display. The sets, which Maryhill began gathering in 1957, represent one of the largest and most varied such collections in the world.
—Ceil Dolan Wiegand

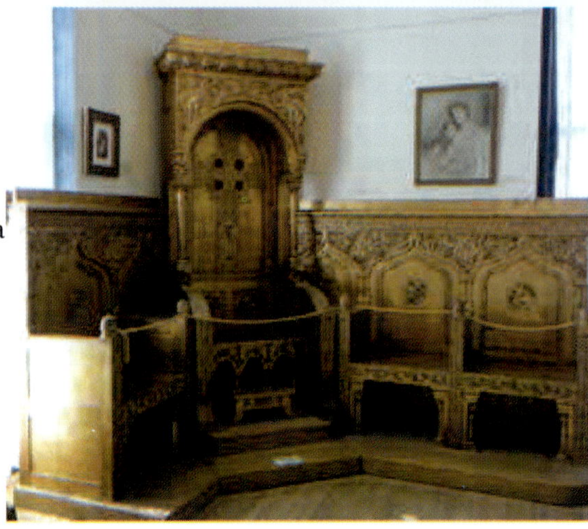

Some of the "Royal Romanian" furniture donated to the museum by Alma Spreckels. Above the furniture, much of which was designed by Queen Marie, is a drawing of the queen and her youngest daughter, Ileana.
—Ceil Dolan Wiegand

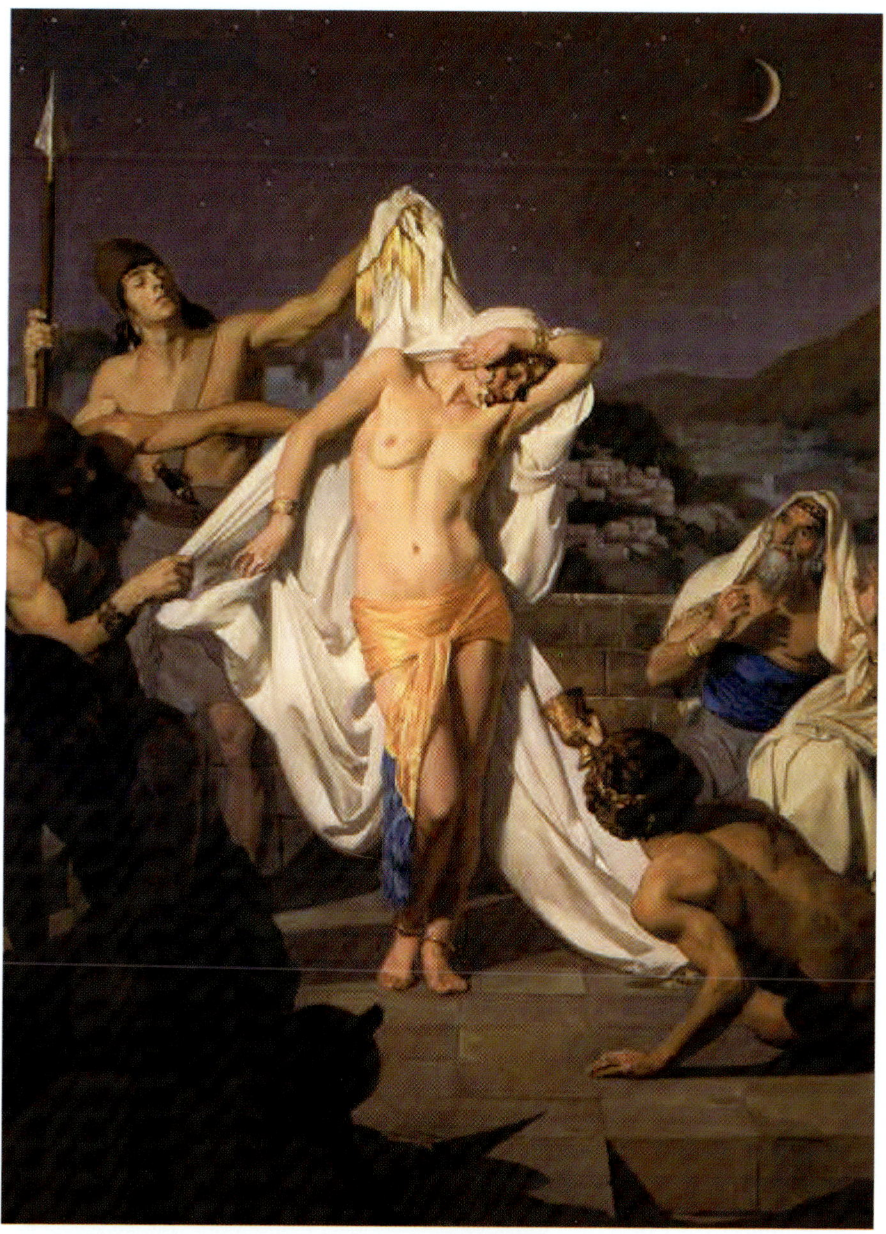

The Dream of the Shulamite Woman, painted by R.H. Ives Gammell in 1934, is representative of the "Classical Realism" school that was loved by longtime Maryhill director Cliff Dolph. The museum has more than 70 works by Gammell and other classical realist artists.
—Maryhill Museum of Art

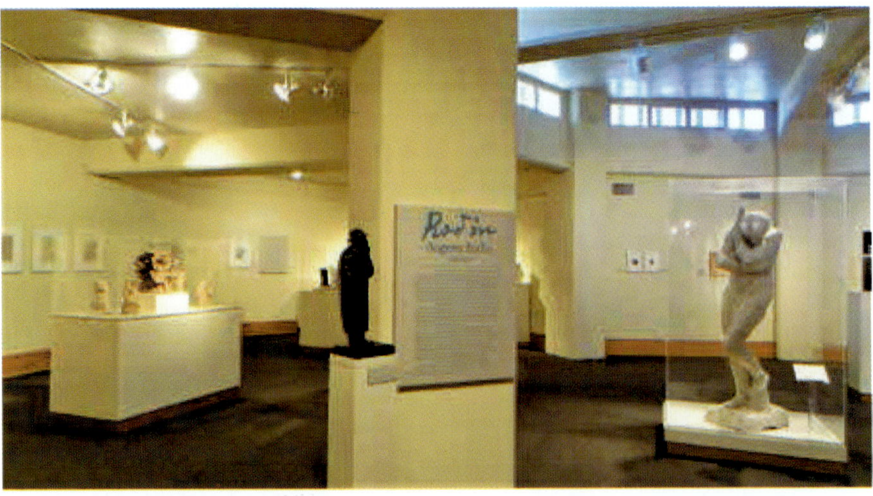

Maryhill's collection of more than 80 works by the master Auguste Rodin is one of the most impressive in the world in terms of its variety. Items range from rare line drawings to bronze and plaster sculptures created by the artist himself, rather than cast after his death. *—Ceil Dolan Wiegand*

Maryhill's Rodin collection includes a plaster version of The Thinker. The sculptor signed it "a Loie." Rodin deliberately removed the right foot, which he sometimes did to mimic the incomplete works of Greek antiquity, or simply because he regarded a limb as unnecessary or distracting. *—Ceil Dolan Wiegand*

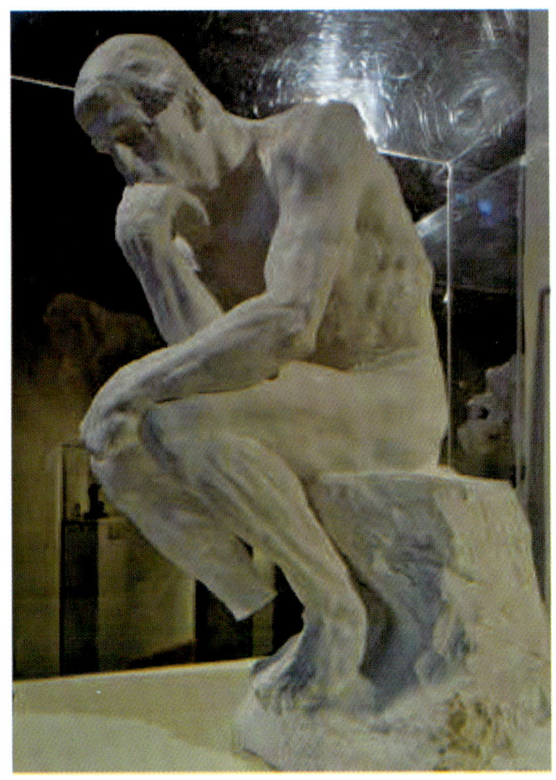

she told a friend.

In his will, Adolph divided his sizeable estate among Alma and the three children. Well aware of Alma's penchant for profligate spending, he left the money in trusts. His executors and Alma reached an agreement that a limit of $25,000 a month (about $356,500 in 2017 dollars) "would be a proper amount to support Mrs. Spreckels in the manner of life to which she is accustomed."

Despite her grief for the loss of Adolph, the redoubtable widow rebounded enough to reign—suitably attired in black dress and veil—over the opening of "her" museum, less than five months after his death. On Nov. 4, San Francisco voters approved a measure formally accepting the Palace of the Legion of Honor Fine Arts Museum. On Nov. 11, Armistice Day, "one of the stateliest edifices of the Western World" was "dedicated to the memory of the American men and women killed in the service of their country in the world war." Alma was specially honored when French Counsellor Albert Tirman—one of the directors of the unborn Maryhill Museum—presented her with the French Cross of the Legion of Honor, one of France's highest accolades.

The museum's opening collection of 19 galleries and 700-plus works of art included Alma's 31-piece Rodin collection; Arthur Putnam's bronze animal sculptures; paintings on loan from the Louvre by Paul Cézanne, Edgar Degas, Paul Gauguin and Vincent van Gogh; a Romanian Room with gifts from Queen Marie; a handsome 400-seat theater, and a collection of rare Egyptian art. In the rotunda was a huge pipe organ, valued at $250,000 and donated by Adolph's brother John. "A Louvre of the West has arisen to take its place among the famous art shrines of the world," enthused one wire service.

But the warm glow from the dedication ceremony was soon cooled by the harsh reality that the museum wasn't hers to do as she pleased. Although the museum's charter required a Spreckels to always be on the board of directors, the seat was initially given by the parks commission to her brother-in-law John, not her. To rub salt in the wound, Alma's plan to insert Adolph's ashes in a museum niche prepared for both him and her ran afoul of a city ordinance regarding the disposition of human remains. After an effort to sneak an exemption through the county's board of supervisors was exposed in the press, Alma dropped the idea.

By the beginning of 1926, Alma had learned to enjoy the life of a very wealthy middle-aged widow. She had a brief and public dalliance with Alexander P. Moore, a newspaper publisher and former U.S. ambassador to Spain who had once been married to the late legendary actress Lillian Russell. But it soon fizzled. "Mrs. Spreckels is most intelligent, most charming and very rich," Moore told reporters, "but I consider her too smart to desire to marry anyone, especially me."

Alma was also smart enough to know she could not run Adolph's business empire. She and other Spreckels family members agreed to liquidate many of the clan's holdings. Alma bought a chateau in a Paris suburb, with the soon-discarded idea of educating her children in French schools. In the spring, she left again for Europe. "The White Star (shipping company) is sending my Rolls Royce for me via the Panama Canal, and then on board the *Olympic* and then getting me a driver, and two days after we are in Paris, I will have my car," she wrote Loie. "Isn't that lovely?"

However lovely Loie thought it, she was busy preparing for Marie's visit to America—and Maryhill. It was an effort that didn't much interest Alma. Still, she thought, a side visit by the queen to California, under her auspices, could reap valuable publicity for the city's new museum, and lots of social points for her. In addition, Alma, like Marie, felt she owed a debt of gratitude to Sam Hill. "I will never forget the kindness of Sam Hill," she wrote years later. "He traveled thousands of miles after Adolph's death to ask if there was anything he could do for me." So Alma moved a couple of relatives into her new chateau, put her Rolls Royce back on the boat, and headed back to America to wait for the queen.

Unlike Marie, Sam and Alma, Loie Fuller had to work for a living. As she entered her sixties, this wasn't easy. Her never-all-that-great health was worsening. Bouts of bronchitis and other respiratory ailments sometimes kept her bedridden for weeks. That meant Gabrielle "Gab" Bloch, the French woman who for 30 years was Loie's best friend, sometime-roommate and probable lover, was left to travel with and oversee Loie's dance troupe. In addition, Loie's vision had been damaged by years of constant experimentation with lighting and chemicals. To shield her eyes from the painful glare of ordinary lights, she wore thick, dark goggle-like spectacles.

But neither lungs nor eyes affected her boundless, almost desperate, enthusiasm for new challenges. In the early 1920s, these ranged from inventing new art forms to serving as a travel agent for royalty. She began with a fairy tale. At the end of the war, Marie had given Loie permission to stage and/or film some of the queen's children's stories. On the evening of July 1, 1920, at Paris' Théâtre National de l' Opéra, Marie watched her *Lily of Life* story "turned into magic reality by the art of Mme. Loie Fuller and her pupils," the *New York Times* reported. "It was the most brilliant night that has been at the opera since before the war."

It was also a one-night-only show, with most of the proceeds going to Romania's war orphans. But the play's success helped push Loie back to the forefront of the European theater scene. Over the next few years, her dance troupe performed before standing-room-only crowds in England, Germany and Spain as well as France.

One production featured gigantic shadows of the dancers cast on large backlit screens. Another used a sea of silk and linen to create the illusion of ocean waves. A third used special effects "as to almost bewilder the audience," with lighting that made the dancers "burst into green and black flames." The *New York Herald* said Loie herself appeared "just as young, albeit a little stouter, than she did when she captured Parisian theatergoers more than twenty-five years ago by her Serpentine Dance."

She was easily the most celebrated American woman in France. There was a "Loie Fuller" line of cosmetics and perfumes. A popular night spot called the Monico offered a "Loie Fuller" cocktail featuring seven different-colored liqueurs poured in layers. The posh Tour d'Argent restaurant featured a fish dish entitled "Filet de Sole Loie Fuller." And "Loie Fuller" stockings, woven with a multitude of colored threads, were all the rage on Paris streets.

Even her artistic doodling was popular. "One day she stretched a double-bed sheet on the floor and went to work to express herself on it with tubes of paint," reported the noted Southern writer Helen Pitkin Schertz. Two dozen sheets later, Loie's laundry was being exhibited in the Louvre, and she eventually gave or sold them to Sam, Marie, the banker Baron Henri de Rothschild, and Mr. and Mrs. Rudolph Valentino, among others.

For the first time in years, Loie was flush enough to move out of hotels.

She took over a villa just outside Paris loaned to her by a Russian duke, staffed it with a fulltime secretary, gardener, butler, maid, and cook, and hosted lavish parties. Still, there were failures mixed in with her success. An effort to turn Marie's fairy tale into a film flopped, despite a generally warm reception from critics. "What makes this production notable is the wonderfully imaginative lighting effects that Loie Fuller has achieved," noted the *London Observer*. "The film is full of fine fantasy and mysticism."

But European audiences evidently liked their mysticism live, and U.S. audiences never got a chance to see the film at all, despite Sam's best efforts. In telegrams to a Cleveland bank to which Loie owed money and which was holding some rare Rodin sketches as collateral, Sam pleaded for an extension of the loan. Her film, he claimed, "is attracting attention I believe it will be highly remunerative." He also wrote Will Hays, president of the Motion Picture Producers Association, trying to persuade Hays to help get Loie's film shown in America. Neither Hays nor the bank was interested. So Sam paid off the loan and took the Rodin pieces for eventual display at Maryhill.

As was her lifelong custom, Loie soon blew through much of the money she had made from her successful enterprises. There was an expensive and time-consuming legal fight with a shady American businessman, and diminishing returns from her dance troupe. But Loie's biggest disappointment was not financial, but personal.

In private, Alma had been effusive in her gratitude for Loie's help in establishing the San Francisco museum. "When it is finished," she wrote her, "I will declare publicly all you have done for it. I would not be worthy of the name de Bretteville if I did not give justice where justice is due." Publicly, however, she never acknowledged Loie's contributions. When the museum was dedicated, Loie was not there, and her name went unmentioned. It hurt. "I never think of my experiences with you without tears springing to my eyes," she wrote Alma. "I believe the pain will never leave me."

Evidently it did. Since Loie couldn't hold a grudge and Alma seldom admitted to being wrong, the two eventually let the issue drop. Besides, Loie had bigger fish to fry: In August 1926, Marie gave her the formal go-ahead to plan the queen's trip to America. In anticipation, Loie had already sent Sam her collection of 26 plaster hands of famous people, made by Eugene Rudier, who had been Rodin's molder. She also sent along a large marble statue for what she envisioned would be part of a sculpture garden outside the museum.

Sam tried to head the queen off, partly because he was up to his neck in his Alabama coal mine venture, and partly because Maryhill was in no shape to entertain anyone. He asked a friend to tell Loie to tell Marie that because other, unspecified, royalty had visited America recently, her trip wouldn't receive the attention it deserved. "Hill believes it would be better for the queen to postpone her trip for a while," the *Oakland Tribune* reported.

Neither the queen nor Loie were swayed. In late September, Loie and Gab arrived in New York with "the advance guard of Queen Marie," which mostly consisted of some of Marie's luggage. Loie was "confined to her cabin all the voyage with an attack of bronchitis and was carried down the gangway to the pier in an invalid chair."

She was met by Alexander Moore, the ex-diplomat who had been romantically linked with Alma earlier in the year. Moore, who had seen Loie's dance troupe perform in Paris, had helped her land an appearance at the U.S. Sesquicentennial celebration that was wrapping up in Philadelphia. A second offer came when a committee hoping to build a women's memorial in Washington D.C. asked Loie to stage a fund-raising performance at New York's Metropolitan Opera House, with Loie to receive half the box office receipts. Marie was slated to attend both performances, guaranteeing their success. Loie was sure the productions would spur other bookings around the country during Marie's trip.

With Sam's reluctant help, meanwhile, Loie and a committee she thought she controlled had lined up use of a luxurious special train for Marie from several of the major U.S. railways. To get around a federal anti-corruption law that prohibited free train rides for political figures, the railroads charged Marie's party of 85 a grand total of $6. Colonel John H. Carroll, a 73-year-old self-important and shady political "fixer" from Missouri, who served as the railroads' chief lobbyist in Washington, was put in charge.

That, however, marked the apex of Loie's involvement, at least in a positive way. To most of the Americans involved in the planning, Loie was a strange old lady and a C-list celebrity at best. To many Romanian officials, she was a potentially sinister and definitely puzzling influence on the queen. "I refuse to serve under a dancer," declared the Romanian Embassy's charge d' affairs, and reportedly resigned. His resignation was later denied by embassy officials, "although it was admitted some irritation had been caused." The "irritation" reportedly led the embassy to hire private detectives to trail Loie.

That wasn't particularly hard, since she was once again stricken by a bronchitis attack. From her sickbed, she dropped out of the planning and issued a statement designed to save Marie any more embarrassment. "I have nothing whatsoever to do with the visit and mission of her majesty the Queen of Roumania except to manifest a lifelong devotion to one whom I consider the noblest woman in the world." Her presence in New York at the same time as Marie's visit, she prevaricated, was "a mere coincidence."

On board the *Leviathan*, Marie, who seldom drank liquor anyway, honored U.S. prohibition laws even though she had been granted an exemption. She toured the engine room; swam in the ship's pool; lunched with Mrs. Woodrow Wilson; ate "American" food such as chicken, baked beans and buckwheat cakes—"one at a time" she answered when asked how many—and kissed a Romanian baby who was traveling in steerage and had been named after the queen.

When the ship dropped anchor in New York Harbor on Oct. 18, the queen adroitly fielded questions from a mob of 150 reporters. She denied Romanian Jews were mistreated, laughed at the suggestion she might star in a movie, and flatly stated her son Carol would not return as crown prince any time soon. She was then escorted by a cavalry troop and 30 motorcycle cops to City Hall, past tens of thousands of cheering, ticker-tape-throwing New Yorkers. Omen or not, it rained steadily on her parade.

NOTES FOR CHAPTER 7

The queen forgot *Time* magazine, Oct. 18, 1926, pp. 15-16.

Since the end Mandache, op. cit., p. 106.

Marie's popularity was Ibid, p. 126.

Marie was both Pakula, op. cit., pp. 317-18.

But not always Elsberry, op. cit., p. 1921.

Plans for a 1921 trip Marie to Loie, May 30, 1921, MMA

"Whenever a queen" *Scranton (Pa.) Republican*, Oct. 21, 1926, p. 2.

At the two-hour dedication *New York Times*, Sept. 7, 1921, p. 12.

"My plans for the" Sam to Loie, Feb. 15, 1923; Sam to Clarice de Bretteville, Feb. 19,

1923; Sam to Clarence Edwards, Feb. 19, 1923, MMA.

For Sam, the cure Sam to Loie, June 1, 1923, MMA.

"I am thinking all" Sam to Loie, June 13 and June 14, 1923, MMA.

By the beginning of Portland *Oregonian*, Feb. 1, 1925, p. 1.

In a long and angry Sam to Klickitat County Board of Commissioners, April 10, 1926, MMA.

The Romanian visit *Honolulu Star-Bulletin*, Oct. 21, 1922, p. 26; Scharlach, op. cit., p. 149.

Her patriotic duty *Overland Monthly and Out West Magazine*, March 1924, p. 103.

But Alma's rise to Scharlach, op. cit., p. 162.

In his will, Adolph *Santa Ana Register*, Oct. 19, 1924, p. 6.

Despite her grief for *Oakland Tribune*, Nov. 12, 1924, p. 9.

The museum's opening *Olean (N.Y.) Times Herald*, Dec. 6, 1924, p. 23.

By the beginning of *Los Angeles Times*, Aug, 24, 1926, p. 7.

Alma was also smart Current and Current, op. cit., p. 312.

However lovely Loie thought Alma to Clifford Dolph, Dec. 24, 1948, MMA.

But neither lungs *New York Times*, July 3, 1920, p. 8.

One production featured *New York Herald*, June 12, 1922, p. 6; New York Herald, July 2, 1922, p. 22.

Even her artistic doodling *Indianapolis Star,* Feb. 1, 1925, p. 84.

For the first time *London Observer*, March 13, 1921, p. 6.

In private, Alma had Scharlach, op. cit., p. 134; Current and Current, op. cit., pp. 300-301.

Sam tried to head *Oakland Tribune*, July 18, 1926, p. 1.

Neither the queen nor *New York Times*, 9-29-1926, p. 25.

That wasn't particularly hard *New York Times*, Oct. 25, 1926.

CHAPTER EIGHT

... Of queens and applesauce
NOVEMBER, 1926

The queen needed a rest room. It was only mid-afternoon, and it had already been a long day: an early rising; her dramatic speech at the strange, unfinished mansion; Loie's grateful tears, and now a slow 30-car motorcade along the splendid Columbia River Highway that Sam had played such a key role in building.

So when the procession of brand-new Lincoln touring cars stopped at a viewpoint called the Vista House, Marie excused herself to visit the ladies' facilities while a crowd waited outside. Just before she emerged, a newspaper photographer exclaimed "Listen folks, a royal flush!"

It had been that kind of trip. "What is difficult for us to conceive is the publicity of everything—each word, each gesture is commented upon, broadcast, read, repeated, criticized, discussed," Marie wrote her husband. "… Everything is a subject of interest to them (Americans) and they want to know, and if they are not told they try to find out."

The American furor over Marie's visit was loud enough to be heard across the Atlantic. "We have not yet heard that by some marvel of engineering the Statue of Liberty has been made to curtsey as Marie of Rumania passes," sniffed the *London Evening Standard.*

If the queen was bemused by all the fuss America was making over her, she consistently kept calm about it. When the New York Mayor Jimmy "Beau James" Walker hesitated before pinning a medal on her bodice, Marie said "proceed, Your Honor, the risk is mine." "And such a beautiful risk it is," the mayor smoothly replied. But even the roguishly handsome and charming Walker blushed crimson when during the motorcade someone in the crowd shouted "Hey Jimmy, you made her yet?" "Tell him yes," Marie smilingly advised.

The queen thought the mayor was "slim and elegant." President Calvin Coolidge, however, was "a thin, dry, waxy-faced little man," who talked "in short sentences, as though words were a pain to him." For his part, "Silent

Cal" was highly suspicious of the motives behind Marie's visit. The president and the queen, both of whom were suffering from nasty colds, got off on the wrong foot, and stayed that way.

Coolidge's aides were annoyed when a lady-in-waiting sent thanks for the welcome bouquet sent to Marie by Mrs. Coolidge, rather than the queen herself. Marie's aides were piqued that American protocol demanded she go to the White House first, rather than the president coming to the Romanian Embassy—and then the Coolidges didn't even answer the door themselves.

Coolidge was furious when against his express wishes, Marie allowed photographers to take pictures during his subsequent, protocol-driven reciprocal visit to the embassy. And Marie was miffed when after a short "state dinner"—the first time a reigning queen dined at the White House—the president excused himself and retired with the male guests to another room for cigars and brandy.

When the dinner was over, Grace Coolidge noticed her husband peering out an open window. "I just wanted to see if the queen had gone," he explained. For her part, Marie shrugged off the whole thing. "No offense was meant," she said. "Why should I be offended? Besides, they just don't have the same kind of manners we have."

Marie was less understanding when it came to relations with the media. During her trip, she was publicly gracious and queenly. Privately, she seethed at what she considered "the odious, trivial press." While she treated reporters "in a friendly, comradely spirit," she recalled a decade later, "they gave back evil for good."

Part of the trouble was Marie's own doing. The queen had signed a lucrative contract with the North American Newspaper Alliance, a consortium of 60-plus newspapers in the U.S. and Canada. Under the contract terms, she agreed to write a series of articles about her travels, and limit her contact with non-alliance media. That naturally raised the ire of those outside the syndicate. But part of the trouble was American journalists' traditional suspicion of—and cynicism toward—anyone or anything that was popular, even when they were largely responsible for whipping up the popularity. And Marie was wildly popular.

In Pittsburgh, "Queen Marie turbans" were "enthusiastically acclaimed by matrons." In Lincoln Nebraska, beauty shops assured women they could have their hair "permanently waved" and still maintain their dignity, because Marie had done so. In Indianapolis, there were ads for "royal Rumanian handbags." In Oakland California, a department store assured its patrons that red was the color du jour because Marie had "set the New York style papers agog" by wearing it. And in Louisville, $49.75 would buy a "Queen Marie dinner ring," which contained "three genuine diamonds" and was "an astonishing value."

Even as they avidly accepted such advertising, more than a few newspapers editorially tsk-tsked at the Marie mania. "When the modern publicity engine, which dotes on moving-picture-version queens, is actually confronted with a queen who, of her own accord, has become a motion-picture-version queen because she dotes on publicity, the lid is off and anything can happen," the *New York World* snarkily noted. "Applesauce flows thick and fast." The *Brooklyn Daily Eagle* was slightly more introspective: "The last thing in the world that a queen ought to be from the romantic American point of view is practical. Queen Marie is just that. And so some of us are a wee bit disillusioned."

Some were a bit more than disillusioned. The Kokomo Indiana Women's Christian Temperance Union wrote to Marie, asking her to publicly deny that she smoked (which in 1926 was still illegal for women to do in U.S. train dining cars.) "We deplore the rumor that Rumania's honored and beautiful queen is a smoke addict, and we are loath to believe that she does not understand the penurious effects of smoking." Marie was apparently unmoved by the request. For her birthday, celebrated as her train moved between the Canadian capital of Ottawa and Winnipeg, her son Nicky gave her an enameled cigarette lighter. Daughter Ileana gave her a silver cigarette case.

After leaving Washington, Marie spent a few days back in New York City before departing on what was supposed to be a leisurely two-month tour through parts of Canada and virtually every section of the United States. Her traveling party was ensconced on what the *New York Times* called the "most elaborate train ever put on rails." Decorated with U.S. and Romanian flags on its exterior, the "all-steel" train included a fancy dining car, two baggage cars, three Pullman sleepers and two private cars, one of which was occupied by Marie and Ileana.

Marie's car was essentially a two-bedroom hotel suite, complete with brass beds, a mahogany dining table for six, marble bath tub, drawing room, office, and small kitchen. The queen also had a glass observation car, equipped with "a powerful searchlight to throw its beam on Western scenery as the train sweeps by." The rest of the passengers had to make do with such amenities as a barber shop, ladies' lounge, two cardrooms and a small soda fountain. No matter how comfortable the train was, however, Marie's route hit one bump after another, many of them created by her closest American friends, particularly Sam and Loie.

Alma wasn't much of a problem, mainly because she wasn't around for much of the trip. After initial indifference to Marie's visit, Alma's enthusiasm grew, especially after Sam asked her to be the official hostess for the Northwest portion of the tour. She rented a private railroad car, filled it with 64 friends and servants, and took off for Minneapolis to hook up with the *Royal Rumanian* on Halloween.

When she arrived, however, Col. Carroll, the tour director, informed her it would be against railroad rules to attach her car to the queen's train. Alma and a single maid would be allowed to board, but the rest of her party would have to go home. Embarrassed and furious, Alma told Carroll where he could stick his rules. Then she met briefly with the queen, to ensure that Marie hadn't forgotten some items she had promised the San Francisco museum, and left on her own to meet the tour again in Spokane and take over her hostess duties.

The Pacific Northwest's society matrons did not meet her with open arms. Alma found that she had been frozen out of not only planning events for Marie, but attending them. Worse, her hopes the queen would dedicate a Romanian Room at the Palace of Fine Arts were dashed when the California leg of the trip was cancelled. The state's railroads refused to host the special train at any kind of discount, and the state's governor refused to extend a formal invitation or put any heat on the recalcitrant rail executives.

So Alma, without a word to anyone, went home. When she got there, she gave varying reasons for her departure. "I was in a hurry to return to San Francisco to arrange for a renewing and repairing of some antique Rumanian furniture," she told one newspaper. "I had a touch of tonsillitis," she told another. "… I left without telling anybody goodbye because goodbyes would have entailed endless explanations."

Loie posed a much bigger source of controversy for the queen, even before the train trip started, and even after she had publicly disavowed any role in Marie's visit.

"Loie Fuller, who if she did not invent it, at least popularized the serpentine dance in this country a generation ago, appears as the power behind the throne in the present tour," whispered the *Detroit Free Press*, variations of which were echoed by other major papers. "Her word appears to be law. She has upset diplomatic arrangements and (made) schedules arranged without consultation with the royal visitor in a manner that, to say the least, has proved disconcerting."

The grain of truth in this nonsense was that both Marie and Loie were upset and disconcerted by the flap. "I know you have had a hard time of it, but here I am and it is your work," the queen wrote the dancer shortly after Marie arrived in New York. "One day they'll know it. When and how am I going to see you, make contact with you? Of all people, it is you my love that I want—like a child its mother."

A few days later, Loie did see Marie at the Ambassador Hotel, where the royal party had taken over the entire fourth floor. "Loie appeared and disappeared," Marie noted in her journal, "full of grief and disappointment at the way she had been wickedly ousted of everything and cruel intrigues cooked up against her. Everything she tried to do was opposed and now she is having a hell of a time about the big festivity she wants to give for me at the Metropolitan Opera House."

The "big festivity" Marie referred to was a performance of the queen's *Lily of Life* by 25 members of Loie's dance troupe who had come over from Europe. With tickets ranging from $3 to $100, the event was billed as a fundraiser for a "Mothers' Memorial" to be built in Washington D.C. But newspapers indignantly reported rumors that some boxes were going for as much as $5,000, and the fact that Loie had been guaranteed half the receipts. The event's chairwoman denied the high prices, but admitted Loie's cut could reach $50,000 (more than $700,000 in 2017 currency), if the house sold out.

It didn't. The furor scared off support from many of New York's social elite as well as leading political figures. Even the presence of Marie, wearing "a diamond tiara, sequin-trimmed satin gown, pearl necklace and long ermine coat," failed to draw much of a crowd. Scalpers couldn't even move tickets at below-box office prices. Loie, who was too ill to attend, received about $5,000, which didn't cover her expenses. Coupled with a poor turnout at a performance a few nights earlier in Philadelphia—and the subsequent failure to book any more appearances—the flop at the Met meant Marie's U.S. trip was a financial fiasco for Loie. Crushed by the controversies, Loie decided to cut her losses and stay away from Marie until the queen's train arrived in Sam Hill Country.

Absent the presence of Loie, Alma and Sam, Marie's journey from New York to Maryhill was relatively sedate, and even enjoyable, except for persistent and conflicting reports about the state of King Ferdinand's health. At Maryhill, Marie's eloquence transported the crowd, the royal party and the press beyond the bickering and the building's bare walls, at least temporarily.

"In spite of the bareness and crudeness of the building," one observer wrote in her diary of the queen's Maryhill stop, "the occasion was made unforgettable by the sincerity of the words spoken in it. When we turned our backs on this embryo temple of beauty to descend the hill, I personally had the conviction that something real would come out of the dream."

Within hours, however, the warm and fuzzy feelings generated by the museum's dedication had turned to applesauce.

Sam had initially opposed Marie's visit. But when it became inevitable, he resolved to take charge of at least the portion of it in his domain, the Pacific Northwest. He partially succeeded, but only by greatly embarrassing the queen and himself.

The trouble began even before the train left New York. An associate of Sam's named Fred Moore had been charged with overseeing press arrangements for the tour, and was to function as Sam's surrogate until the train reached Spokane. But when Moore was mistakenly identified in some stories as the tour's manager, Col. Carroll "expressed irritation" at being slighted, and banned Moore from the train. Two days later, Sam sent a telegram to the Portland reception committee, claiming to be in charge of the tour's West Coast leg. On the same day, the committee received a telegram from a member of the queen's entourage, approving the committee's plans but failing to mention either Sam or the planned Maryhill visit.

But the real melodrama began after the queen's party left Maryhill. Its roots were buried in, of all places, Minnesota politics. While working for his railroad tycoon father-in-law James J. Hill, Sam had helped derail the re-election bid of a U.S. senator named W.D. Washburn, who was a rival railroad executive and bitter enemy of Hill's. Washburn's son, Stanley, had been a newspaper correspondent and military attaché in Romania during World War I, and had become a good friend of Marie's. As such, he was along on the tour as her official liaison. Neither Sam nor Washburn were in a mood to let 30-year-old bygones be bygones.

As the queen's motorcade traveled toward Portland, Sam, Washburn, and Oregon Gov. Walter Pierce sat with Marie in her car. At some point, Washburn asked Pierce if he would mind giving up his seat so Marie's bodyguard could be closer to her. The governor readily agreed, but Sam took it as an insult.

When the incident was repeated after a banquet in Portland, Sam exploded. Confronting the diminutive Washburn at a horse show later that evening, Sam threatened to slap his face. When Col. Carroll took Washburn's side, Sam threatened to throw Carroll off the tour. "I'm a wild man," he shouted. "I will tear Washburn to pieces. I will crush him!" Washburn and Carroll beat a hasty retreat to the train, where Carroll told reporters he "was very surprised that a guest of the queen would make such threats. The great ovation paid to the queen at Maryhill Museum and the queen's tribute to Mr. Hill there as an old friend has turned his head."

The newspapers fell on the flap like a pit bull on a porkchop, with headlines such as "Royal Ruckus Rocks Queen's Train" and "Eccentric Millionaire Disrupts Marie Tour." The queen was distraught. "…They torment me very much and make me miserable," she wrote in her journal, "because of all I hate most, it is the quarreling between themselves of people who are my friends."

As it turned out, no one got slapped or crushed. Instead, the combatants declared an uneasy truce for the duration of Marie's visit in the Northwest. Sam escorted her on a tour of Seattle, which included both a tea party and a dinner at his Highland Avenue mansion. Marie found the house "almost as queer and quaint as Maryhill." The tea party was marred when a 52-year-old woman who lived three blocks from Sam dropped dead on the sidewalk while waiting outside his house for the queen to arrive. An Associated Press dispatch attributed the death to either exertion from the uphill walk or excitement about Marie's visit.

Marie also visited Sam's Peace Arch, and even made waffles for those who could crowd into a house Sam had built nearby. In dedicating the arch (the third time it had been so honored), Marie thought "the idea is fine, but the monument itself is of mean proportions, without particular dignity it is out of the Hill-Loïe imaginations, full of big thoughts and just a little grotesque."

But the truce ended when the *Royal Rumanian* prepared to head east. Carroll announced Sam was not welcome to accompany the party, and "if he attempts to come back he will be physically expelled." Carroll also claimed the ban was Marie's idea, which was a blatant lie. "Dear kind-hearted big original thing," Marie wrote in her journal, referring to Sam, when she learned of Carroll's action. "I could've howled!"

The next day, the queen summoned Carroll, Washburn and Loie for a peace conference, at which, according to Loie, she gave orders that Sam be called back to the train. "And they said they would," Loie later wrote Sam, "but they didn't." Instead, pressure grew on Loie to depart too, this time from Romanian officials who hated the idea of the "lowly woman" being a queenly confidant. As in Sam's case, it was made to appear that Marie was the expelling force. "The queen felt," the *New York Times* reported, quoting an unnamed Romanian official, "that much of the discord of recent days had centered on Miss Fuller's presence on the train and she wished her to go, even though she regards her as her friend."

The truth was that Loie had already planned to leave the train when it reached Denver: She had to be in New York in time to finalize details for what promised to be a fabulous $200,000 U.S. tour for her dance troupe in 1927. "I am sorry you will not remain and that you need to get back to N.Y." Marie wrote Loie in a note dated the same day the *Times* story appeared. "… I never thought of dismissing you my dear friend …".

As it turned out, Marie's American sojourn lasted only two more weeks after Loie's departure. While in Chicago, the queen decided the reports from

Romania about King Ferdinand's health were too disturbing to continue her trip for another month. After visiting the Kentucky log cabin where Abraham Lincoln was born and spending a few days in New York, she sailed for home on November 24th.

"When I am gone," she said in a radio broadcast the night before her departure, "don't let anything tarnish that remembrance you have of me. I did not come on business. I did not come for the sake of politics. I came for nothing but to just make friends with you."

The *New York Times* estimated her trip covered 10,087 miles, "one of the most strenuous journeys ever undertaken by a public personage." She had been seen by perhaps six million Americans, and heard on radio by millions more. Among the souvenirs she collected were a lawn mower and an ice-making machine. "The official functions were strenuous of course," she noted diplomatically, "but I've met some lovely mayors."

When Marie got home, most of her problems were relative—or rather, relatives. There was disapproval from her cousin, King George V of England, who found the controversy over her U.S. trip unseemly. "I did what I thought right for my country," Marie wrote him. "You in your beautiful old traditions cannot fairly judge. I am not a conventional queen, I must admit. I must often make your dear old royal blood curdle. But my heart is in the right place, Georgie dear." More troubling were the persistent rumors that her oldest son Carol, who had given up his birthright for his mistress, was plotting a coup. Despite his entreaties from his Paris residence—which happened to be across the street from Loie's villa—Marie refused to see him as she passed through France on her way home.

Worst of all, King Ferdinand was dying of intestinal cancer, and Russia and Hungary were poised to try and reclaim territory they had lost to Romania after the war. "All is tragedy in my life," Marie wrote Loie, "but deep within me, my faith and hope are still green. There is an invincible something which I am built upon, which cannot, will not, despair."

In order to stabilize the government, Ferdinand appointed 63-year-old Ion Bratianu to be premier, the Romanian equivalent of prime minister. This was the same oily and dictatorial politician who had been upstaged by Marie at the Paris Peace Talks, and who once famously told a reporter "I try to put off until tomorrow the mistakes which people tell me I ought to make today." Despite his prickly personality, Bratianu had been premier 11 times in his career, and knew how to hold things together.

On June 19, 1927, Ferdinand died. He left $10 million to be divided among his five children. "The queen gets all the palaces," a Romanian banker told the U.S. financial journalist Clarence Barron, "and half the former annuity of the king from the government, so she is well-fixed, which means $100,000 pocket money ($1.4 million in 2017 dollars), and in Rumania, that is quite a lot."

He also left the crown to his grandson Michael. At six years old, Michael's greatest asset was the ability to fix a smile on his face on entering a room, and keep it there. He was not considered particularly articulate, even for his age, but he did know how to drive a car. To help him with other royal duties, three regents were appointed: his Uncle Nicky; the patriarch of the Romanian Orthodox Church, and the chief justice of the Supreme Court. Marie was not asked, nor did she want to be, a regent.

She nonetheless remained an influential figure in the government, a fact that came into focus five months after the king's death, when Bratianu unexpectedly died and was succeeded by his ineffectual brother. Sensing an opportunity, Carol began to bombard his mother with requests to help him return and take the throne from his young son. "Oh, Mama dear," he wrote her, "let us have only loving relations between us." While Marie pondered the plea, Carol plotted and schemed.

Given all that was going on in Romania—and had gone on in America—it was hardly surprising Marie gave barely a thought to the museum she had dedicated. But she did recall her visit in what amounted to a self-absorbed pep talk to Loie. "That day at Maryhill, standing in the unfinished hall of Samuel Hill's museum, I tried to make them understand what Loïe Fuller had meant in my life," Marie wrote. "… For a short moment I held the scoffers that morning, even the most cynical and indifferent heard the ring of truth in my words, in my voice Carry on faithful Loïe, grit your teeth, do not waver, do not give way, your spirit is stronger than your tired body!"

If Marie was telling Loie to hang in there, however, Alma was telling her to hang it up. In a letter a few weeks after the queen's rah-rah missive, Alma said she wanted to forget all about Marie's U.S. visit, and advised Loie to do the same: "I had enough of the whole thing, and I should think you would settle down in Paris, and think of Paris and the people there who love you and understand you as a great artist." She also turned down Loie's request for a $2,000 loan, claiming that "because of perhaps additional inheritance taxes I must conserve every penny."

A few days later, Alma wrote Loie to tell her she had decided to give Maryhill the Gold Room furniture she had received from the queen on their first meeting. "This is a very great present that I am giving to Sam and really to the people of the Northwest," Alma stated with Marie-like immodesty. "But you know, Loie, I am always ready to do for others; it is the only thing that makes life worthwhile."

In reality, Alma's generosity was motivated by the fact that she had tried to give the furniture to the Palace of Fine Arts in San Francisco, and it had declined the offer. Moreover, her generosity wasn't all that generous: She wanted Sam to pay the $40,000 Alma had promised Marie for the never-delivered backdrop that was supposed to have been built by Romanian craftsmen for the furniture's display.

Loie was aghast. "You cannot ask Mr. Hill to pay that for you," she wrote. "He would be paying for a present you must either give it outright, without condition, or not offer it at all." She also advised Alma not to risk ruining her relationship with Marie by refusing to pay the money, "even if you go with one fur coat less, or one diamond bracelet or a carpet or something like that."

Alma decided to split the difference. She eventually gave Maryhill the furniture and did *not* give Marie the money. She reassured Loie it was just business, nothing personal. "I want you to know Loie that I love you with all my heart," she wrote. "Nobody but you and I understand the friendship. I am yours forever."

Emboldened by such sentiments, Loie urged Alma to help her get the Maryhill museum completed. "You, Alma, must become a part of that work with me for the benefit of our country. The West is your country! The queen will help you because she wants her visit out there to be justified. And she believes in the museum as a great future monument to our civilization."

But Alma wasn't buying it. Soon after Loie's letter arrived in September

1927, Alma took off for an extended stay in New York City. She took a suite at the Ritz-Carleton, partied with Broadway celebrities, played high-stakes poker with business and industry leaders, and pretty much forgot about civilization's future monuments.

While Alma was enjoying the Big Apple, Sam was digging his way out of a coal mine and on to a golf course. After several fruitless years of trying to make his investment in an Alabama coal operation pay off, Sam gave up a few months after Marie went home. "We had no winter in the South," he wrote Loie. "We sold no coal. It has been all outgo in Alabama—no income." So he turned his attentions 2,700 miles northwest.

The idea for a golf resort had its origins in the Peace Arch—and Prohibition. In building his border-straddling monument, Sam became acutely aware that while Canadians could enjoy a cocktail or two when so inclined, the U.S. Constitution's 18th amendment forbade Americans from doing so. This offended him. "I do not find in the recorded pages of history any instance where an enlightened nation was, by force, compelled to change its food and drink," he indignantly noted in a speech. "… It can be modified and regulated, but not suppressed."

Indignation aside, the situation also piqued his businessman's instincts. A nice liquor-offering resort near the arch might lure more than a few thirsty Americans to cross the border. In 1923, he formed Ye Olde English Restaurants Ltd., with his cousin Edgar as a partner and manager. Over the next five years, he bought slightly more than 150 acres of brushy swamp just over the border in British Columbia. The land cost about $35 an acre, and clearing it cost about 25 times that. By the time the queen had come and gone, Sam had built the Semiahoo ("crescent moon" in a local Indian language) Club.

It consisted of a hotel, an auto camp, two restaurants and several lunch wagons. In 1928, a nine-hole golf course opened, followed by an additional nine holes a year later. Green fees were $3, and duffers could count on losing two dozen balls per round, since the fairways were exceedingly narrow and the rough exceedingly choked with thick ferns and blackberry bushes. A plan to enhance the resort's allure by building a replica of the cottage of Anne Hathaway, Shakespeare's wife, was seriously considered, then prudently dropped.

"Tourists want three things," Sam told his journalist friend Fred Lockley in explaining why he got into the resort business: "a good road to drive on, something worthwhile to see and something worthwhile to eat." He left out "something worthwhile to drink," but that was taken care of, since the club had the only liquor license in the area.

Despite that advantage, the complex was expensive to operate, and never made much money. "If I break even I will be more than satisfied," Sam told Lockley. "It is my contribution toward establishing and maintaining the good will of the people who travel back and forth between our country and Canada."

Sam was decidedly less enthusiastic about finishing the museum at Maryhill. Two months after Marie's impassioned speech at the site, Washington Gov. Roland Hartley announced Sam had written him declaring his intention to leave Maryhill to the state. On the same day, Sam, who was in San Francisco on his way to Chicago for a good roads convention, was asked if it was true he planned to attach a $1 million endowment to the gift. "I'm not ready to make a statement yet," he said. "Yes, I do expect to take care of it in proper style, but haven't decided how extensively." How serious Sam was in making the offer is conjectural. But its potential evaporated a few months later, after Sam met with Hartley and legislative leaders and failed to convince them to complete the North Bank Highway to Maryhill. No road, he reiterated, no museum.

With Marie distracted, Alma disinterested and Sam disillusioned, that left Loie—and Loie was tired. "Have you ever been so tired you could not even undress to go to bed?" she wrote an acquaintance. "Well, I am just that way all the time, except when some activity spurs me on. Then, when the moment is over of mental activity, it all comes back again—and the tired feeling hurts me so that tears come in spite of me. Isn't it dreadful?"

For Loie, most of the year after Marie's visit to America was pretty dreadful. The contract she had signed for two companies of her dancers to tour the United States for most of 1927 was not honored. While waiting in vain for it come through, Loie turned down offers in Europe, she wrote Sam, "and in waiting, I got deeper and deeper in debt."

Mostly forgotten in her own country before Marie's visit, Loie's controversial role in the tour resulted in cruel characterizations of her in the U.S. media, such as *Time* magazine's "once tolerably notable," and "a now-decrepit ballet mistress." It was the kind of publicity that made American promoters think twice about booking Loie's troupe. Worse, an autobiography by the dancer Isadora Duncan, a one-time Loie protégé, all but outed Loie as a lesbian. Loie threatened to sue, but Duncan died in an accident before Loie could stop publication.

Undaunted, she tried making another movie, and even attracted a few financial backers. Based on a story by the German writer E.T.A. Hoffmann, "The Man Who Lost His Eyes" was chock-full of special effects and trick photography: "a man walking upside down, walking on the sky. A tornado cyclone, funnel shape, sweeps twirling and whirling across the screen, taking up inside it everyone and everything the spirit leaves the body and goes back into it again; monsters that become invisible before your eyes and visible instantaneously. A tremendous jump over the moon!" But Loie's ill health, bad weather for filming and an eviction from her borrowed villa meant the film was never finished.

All of her setbacks, however, failed to diminish her dreams for Maryhill. "I hope to come to America this autumn, to go out to the museum and make some speeches there about it, and get the public interested to support it, which they certainly will do when they see how much has been done for them for nothing," she wrote an acquaintance who had offered to donate a collection of sheet music covers. "That museum will enrich the state beyond anything they can dream of, because there will be things in it that everybody will want to go and see, sooner or later."

Loie's plans ranged from the grand to the grandiose. She continued to collect items, even when she couldn't afford to crate and ship them: a silk portrait of the Belgian theologian Désiré-Joseph Mercier; a bayonet from the Battle of Verdun; a painting by the French symbolist artist Eugéne Carriére; more plaster hands, a lock of Queen Victoria's hair.

When she learned Sam's coal career was over, she urged him to get into the museum business. In a 13-page letter, she diagrammed her ideas for a European auxiliary to Maryhill, known unblushingly as the "Loie Fuller Museum." It would be in Paris, on land donated by the French government. It would include 50 to 60 apartments for artists and celebrities—such as Queen Marie—and a "living part," which apparently would consist of a residence for Loie that people could visit and observe Loie being Loie. "Best of all, it will keep Maryhill before the world as the one great international museum." She estimated the whole thing wouldn't cost more than $100,000, and Sam could either borrow the money from New York banks at 4 percent interest, or solicit $20,000 investments from wealthy friends.

When Sam failed to do either, Loie switched her focus back to Maryhill itself. Throughout the summer, she wrote Sam long letters, outlining her plans, and occasionally asking to borrow some money. The railroads should be urged to run special excursion trains direct to Maryhill. A Serbian portrait painter named Paul Yoanovitch has agreed to become the museum's first director. A Romanian official named Dimancesco is in line to become his country's counsel for the Pacific Coast, and Loie thinks he can be convinced to establish the consulate at Maryhill "and work with me there for the museum besides doing his duty as counsel."

"I think that as soon as possible I shall complete everything here and migrate to Maryhill and remain there and work from there until the museum is opened," she wrote. "And if Dimancesco is behind me as Roumanian counsel, and he and you together in the foreground covering up my activities, we could get the work done and open the museum a year from this autumn."

But Loie didn't have a year. For the last three months of 1927, she was confined by chronic illness to her hotel room overlooking the Seine River. In December, her bronchitis turned to pneumonia. On New Years Day, 1928, she died. She was two weeks short of her 66th birthday.

Her death was noted in America, but mourned in France. "Columns of the (Paris) afternoon papers were filled with descriptions of the beauty of her dancing and the famous troupes which she sent around the world," the Associated Press reported, "along with almost ecstatic references of joy which her use of color and light gave to the eye of the spectator." "A butterfly," noted one of the French papers, "has folded its wings."

With Loie's death, plans for the museum at Maryhill sputtered to a halt. Sam, who didn't think of any one place as "home," nonetheless shifted his base of operations to Maryhill in 1928. He installed his Seattle housekeeper and cook (with the Dickensian names of Clara Carter and Lucy Leatherby) in the Meadowlark Inn while he moved into the cottage/office next door.

Either as a gesture of neighborliness, or due to remonstrations from the families of the local war dead, he announced in October 1928 that his Stonehenge war memorial, which had languished for a decade, would finally be finished. "The delay has been occasioned by the failure to build the North Bank Highway from Lyle through to Pasco," the *Goldendale Sentinel* reported, "according to Mr. Hill." It was formally dedicated on Memorial Day, 1929. Sam did not attend.

He also kept up his carrot-and-stick pronouncements that as soon as a paved, automobile-worthy highway to Maryhill was completed, he would finish the museum. At a Portland banquet feting his 71st birthday, he claimed to have the pledges of "forty distinguished citizens and monarchs of European countries" for art works. Beyond such rhetorical flourishes, however, his heart wasn't in it.

In March, 1929, Sam met with Washington state officials and offered them a new deal. A few years before, he had offered the state his unfinished mansion. Now he offered to give his art collection, if a 27-mile stretch of road linking Maryhill to the town of Lyle was built, and if the gift was tax-exempt. The Associated Press story on the offer, which described Sam as being from "Seattle, Blaine and Maryhill and other places," estimated the cost of the road at $1 million ($14.5 million in 2017).

In an editorial the next day, the Portland *Oregonian* conceded "it might seem a fantastic scheme to invest $1,000,000 in a road to reach a museum in the wilderness." But, the paper, argued, if Sam's offer "induces them to authorize prompt construction of the road, it will be worthwhile. The highway will be built eventually anyway, so that the legislature may consider it advisable to take the present offer." Of course it was easy for an Oregon newspaper to suggest ways to spend Washington taxpayers' money, and Washington lawmakers would commit only to begin survey work and entertain construction bids on a seven-mile stretch of the road. But Sam declared victory anyway and boldly predicted the highway would be completed within two years.

He also hit the road again. In the spring of 1929, he made his 51st trip across the Atlantic, in part to host a luncheon in Paris honoring his pal General Joffre. In the fall, he went to New York to take control of the Areocrete Corporation of America, a company that manufactured low-density lightweight concrete.

He was there in time to observe the financial fallout from the stock market crash that would help plunge the country into the Great Depression. "The town is still pretty badly upset," he wrote a friend. "… What with dodging the automobiles on the corners, (and) looking up so as to dodge men jumping from the windows, one appreciates a residence at Maryhill or Goldendale more."

While Sam was dodging cars and suicidal stockbrokers, his own reputation was being assaulted in Washington D.C. Col. John Carroll, the railroad lobbyist who had overseen Queen Marie's tour, had been called to testify before a Senate committee investigating corruption and influence peddling involving the sugar industry. Dodging questions about his own involvement, Carroll instead regaled the committee with stories from Marie's trip. He portrayed Sam as a pompous buffoon and Marie as a naïve dupe. Carroll described the Maryhill dedication as "perfectly ridiculous," adding "I was never so embarrassed in my life."

The Pacific Northwest waited for an eruption of indignation from Sam. "Friends of Mr. Hill predicted that he would catch a fast train and rush off to the national capital to defend himself against what they said he would term as an insult," the *Oregonian* noted. For whatever reason, Sam instead shrugged it off. But the furor sparked the newspaper's curiosity as to the status of the museum dedicated three years before, and it dispatched a reporter and photographer to Maryhill.

The resulting Page One story was depressing, faintly derisive, and devastating to the prospects of Washington politicians taking seriously Sam's offer to swap a museum for a highway. The reporter was requested by Sam's caretaker to refer to the mansion as "the museum, not 'the castle.' Mr. Hill doesn't like to have it called 'the castle.'" The request was ignored, as was the warning to stay out of the building itself. Both of the *Oregonian's* men climbed through a broken window to have a look.

The crude wooden dais used by Marie for her eloquent dedication speech was still in place, with bits of faded bunting still attached, but the rest of the main floor was empty. The crates of art the queen had brought with her were stored in the garage below. Other objects for the museum were cached in bank vaults or at Sam's Seattle house and the golf resort in British Columbia. The mansion's interior was still rough concrete. Here and there, metal lath stuck through the walls. There were dozens of small, windowless rooms with only one entrance. Swallows had built scores of nests along the ceiling.

"The stairs and floors were thick with the refuse of rats," the reporter wrote. "From somewhere above came strange moaning sounds so sudden that the photographer and I looked at each other and shivered. If Mr. Hill allows his castle a few more years of loneliness, it will develop into a haunted place in reality."

Although the Goldendale town council fired off an angry letter about the article, Sam did not respond publicly. His mood swings, always unpredictable, seemed to widen. "I don't expect to be here many more years, and so I am trying to crowd in as much work as I can during the remaining years," he told his journalist friend Fred Lockley in January, 1930. Two months later, he was complaining to his attorney Zola Brooks about the $1,426.02 property tax bill on the Maryhill mansion. "Perhaps I am cross as I am dictating this in bed, but I do feel, Zola, that the limit is about being reached." Three months after that, he was back in New York City, trying to launch something called "the Century of Progress Excursion."

In early February, 1931, Oregon officials invited Sam to address the state legislature on the subject of good roads, and as a way to honor him for his invitation to them to see his demonstration road at Maryhill 18 years before. Enroute to Salem, Sam was stricken by what the press called "intestinal influenza" but was in reality an abscessed pancreas or colon. After emergency surgery in Portland, he lingered for three weeks before dying on Feb. 26, at the age of 73. The death certificate grossly understated his occupation as "lawyer and capitalist."

Sam's death was noted in lengthy and generally accurate obituaries across the country. Many of them struggled to capture the essence of his mammoth personality. One referred to him as "a man whose every undertaking was a hobby and whose every hobby was an enterprise." Another said that "in some respects, he never lost the attributes of childhood. Those who understood him recognized the sincerity of his desire to aid his fellow man, which was so often veiled by the screen of self-glorification."

In accordance with his wishes, Sam's ashes were placed in a crypt he had built on a ledge just below his Stonehenge, overlooking the Columbia River. The inscription was an epitaph he had written himself: "Samuel Hill: Amid

Nature's great unrest, he sought rest." But if the restless dreamer had at last found rest, his museum was just beginning its struggle to survive.

NOTES FOR CHAPTER 8

So when the procession Tuhy, op. cit., p. 245.

It had been that Queen Marie, *America As Seen by a Queen*, p. 170.

If the queen was Pakula, op. cit., pp. 346-47.

The queen thought the Queen Marie, op. cit., p. 41.

When the dinner was Ishbel Ross, *Grace Coolidge and Her Era,* 1962, p. 199; Elsberry, op. cit., p. 200.

Marie was less understanding Hector Bolitho, *A Biographer's Notebook*, 1950, p. 40.

Even as they avidly accepted *New York World*, Oct. 26, 1926, p. 10; *Brooklyn Daily Eagle*, Nov. 4, 1926, p. 8.

Some were a bit more *Decatur (Ill.) Herald*, Oct. 31, 1926, p. 18.

After leaving Washington *New York Times*, Oct. 21, 1926, p. 6.

So Alma, without a *Oakland Tribune*, Nov. 6, 1926, p. 1; *San Francisco Examiner*, Nov. 6, 1926, p. 1.

"Loie Fuller, who, if" *Detroit Free Press*, Oct. 24, 1926, p. 60.

The grain of truth Current and Current, op. cit., p. 315.

A few days later Queen Marie, op. cit., p. 58.

"In spite of the" Morris, op. cit., pp. 128-130.

The trouble began before *Miami News*, Oct. 25, 1926, p. 2; *Santa Ana Register*, Oct. 28, 1926, p. 1.

When the incident was *Santa Ana Register*, Nov. 5, 1926, p. 1; *Asbury Park (NJ) Press*, Nov. 5, 1926, p. 1.

The newspapers fell on Queen Marie, op. cit., p. 104.

As it turned out Ibid., p. 102; *Asbury Park (NJ) Press*, Nov. 5, 1926, p. 8.

Marie also visited Queen Marie, op. cit., p. 106.

But the truce ended *Oregon Daily Journal*, Nov. 7, 1926, p. 1; Queen Marie, op. cit., p. 108.

The next day the queen Loie to Sam, June 23, 1927, MMA; *New York Times*, Nov. 9, 1926, p. 12.

The truth was that Marie to Loie, Nov. 9, 1926, MMA.

The *New York Times* *New York Times*, Nov. 21, 1926, p. 1.

When Marie got home Pakula, op. cit., p. 359.

Worst of all Elsberry, op. cit., p. 216.

On June 19, 1927 Clarence Barron, *More They Told Barron*, 1931, p. 319.

Given all that was Marie to Loie, March 15, 1927, MMA

If Marie was telling Alma to Loie, March 31, 1927, MMA.

A few days later Alma to Loie, April 3, 1927 and April 12, 1927, MMA.

Loie was aghast Loie to Alma, April 26, 1927, MMA.

Alma decided to Current and Current, op. cit., p. 325.

Emboldened by such Scharlach, op. cit., p. 197.

While Alma was enjoying Sam to Loie, April 4, 1927, MMA.

The idea for a golf course Richard Clark, *Sam Hill's Peace Arch*, 2006, p. 384.

"Tourists want three things" Tuhy, op. cit., p. 257.

Sam was decidedly *Oregon Daily Journal*, Jan. 4, 1927, p. 5.

With Marie distracted, Current and Current, op. cit., p. 330.

Undaunted, she tried Loie to Sam, April 4, 1927, MMA.

All of her setbacks Loie to Julius Witmark, June 15, 1927, MMA.

When she learned Loie to Sam, March 27, 1927, MMA

When Sam failed Loie to Sam, June 3, 1927, MMA

"I think that as" Loie to Sam, June 6, 1927, MMA.

Her death was noted *Baltimore Sun,* Jan. 4, 1927, p. 9.

He also kept up *Portland Oregonian*, May 15, 1928, p. 16.

In March, 1929 *Portland Oregonian*, March 1, 1929, p. 8.

In an editorial *Portland Oregonian*, March 2, 1929, p. 5.

He also hit Sam to Robert McCrow, Nov. 15, 1929, MMA.

The Pacific Northwest *Portland Oregonian*, Nov. 21, 1929, p. 4.

The resulting Page One *Portland Oregonian*, Nov. 24, 1929, p. 1.

Although the Goldendale *Oregon Daily Journal*, Jan. 20, 1930, p. 4; Sam to Zola Brooks, March 3, 1930, MMA.

Sam's death was noted *St Paul. Pioneer Press*, Feb. 27, 1931, P. 1; *Portland Oregonian*, Feb. 27, 1931, P. 1.

CHAPTER NINE

"A wanton dissipation of the assets"
MARCH 1932

They got $25 for Sam's old Locomobile. Another $37 from the railroad when a train hit one of the cows. Then there was the 75 cents an hour from renting out a cement mixer that had been used to help build Stonehenge. It wasn't much, but this was the Great Depression—not a terrific time to start a museum—and every little bit helped.

With Sam and Loie interred, Marie in Romania and Alma uninterested (at least for the present), it fell to a new group to carry on the Maryhill dream. Only one of the museum's original five trustees remained: Edgar Hill, Sam's cousin and sometime-business associate. Along with Sam and Loie, Sam's friend Charles Babcock was dead, and Albert Tirman, the French government official, had resigned from the board.

Zola Brooks, who like his father before him had been Sam's attorney, replaced Babcock. Loie's place was taken by Hazel Dolph Clark, a Philadelphia socialite and arts patron whose pioneering Portland family had known Sam for years. Sam's place was taken by Raymond Auzias de Turenne, a pal of Sam's who was a former French cavalry officer, horse-breeder, author, Alaska land speculator and France's consul-general in Seattle. No one replaced Tirman, apparently because no one in America knew he had resigned. Only Edgar, as president, and Zola, the sole trustee to live within 200 miles of Maryhill, had any real sense of the obstacles that lay before them.

Edgar Newlin Hill was neither as impetuous nor as imaginative as Sam. He was also shorter and balder, and only slightly less rotund. The cousins nonetheless had much in common. Like Sam, Edgar "was a hardheaded conservative, and a very delightful and enjoyable personality." He was also ambitious, stubborn and bossy, with a catholic interest in business. Born in 1861, four years after Sam, Edgar stayed close to his hometown of Carthage Indiana for most of the first four-plus decades of his life. With his brother, he opened a hardware store and bought and sold real estate. He became general manager of a company that manufactured boards and paper for boxes and book covers. He was both a director and president of the Bank of Carthage.

Then in May 1905, his cousin Sam came for a visit. Within a few months, Edgar boarded Sam's private railroad car for a month-long tour of the Pacific Northwest. Within a few years, Edgar was splitting his time between Indiana and Seattle. He invested $25,000 in Sam's various enterprises, and eventually took over operation of Sam's golf resort straddling the U.S.-Canada border near the Peace Arch.

Just how intertwined his life became with Sam's was exemplified in May 1928, when Edgar married a pregnant woman named Mona Bell. The woman, whose colorful career had included stints as a circus performer, newspaper reporter and country singer, was also Sam's mistress. He had built her a 22-room mansion on a 35-acre parcel above the Columbia River, not far from Maryhill. He had established a trust for her unborn child (one of four Sam set up for various mistresses and children who may or may not have been his.) But just who fathered Mona Bell's child was to be a hotly disputed subject.

In later years, both Mona Bell and her son (named Samuel Bettle Hill, after Edgar's father) claimed Sam was the father. The marriage to Edgar, they contended, was orchestrated by Sam to ensure the boy had the Hill family name. In his will, Edgar, who divorced Mona less than a year after the wedding, seemed to buttress the claim by stating he had no children.

But Edgar included a curious codicil: Anyone who could prove he or she was his offspring was entitled to $50. When Edgar died in 1945, leaving behind a sizeable estate, Samuel Bettle Hill claimed Edgar was really his father and he was entitled to not just $50, but to Edgar's entire fortune. After a six-year legal battle, Sam B. Hill settled for $46,000—and he and his mother went back to claiming he was the son of Sam after all.

Whatever the truth was, the soap-opera episode demonstrated Edgar's unassailable loyalty to Sam, and helped explain his determination to ensure the museum's survival. "The success of the museum depends entirely upon you and myself," Edgar wrote Zola Brooks, "and I do not want to make a failure of it."

At their first meeting, about a year after Sam's death, the trustees unanimously agreed that the first hurdle to clear was settling Sam's estate. His holdings ranged from one share of the Seattle Horse Show Association to 4,735 acres of Alabama coal land. There was the Seattle mansion; the golf resort in British Columbia; property in Montreal and Minnesota; several thousand shares of preferred stock in the Great Northern Railroad—and the hotel, the cottages, Stonehenge and the rest of the 5,000-plus acres at Maryhill. Altogether, it came to an estimated—and surprisingly paltry—$500,000 (about $7.9 million in 2017 dollars).

Sam's eight-page will, drawn up three months before he died, called for half his estate "to be applied to the equipment, operation and maintenance of" the Maryhill museum. The other half went to the U.S. Trust Co. in Seattle, which Sam had founded and of which Edgar was president. The trust was to provide for the care of Sam's institutionalized daughter Mary, and pay $12,000 a year to his son Jimmy.

His estranged wife Mamie was to get nothing. Sam pointed out that she had kept the $200,000 in stocks and bonds her father J.J. Hill had given the couple on their wedding day; that she had received plenty more when her father died, and that Sam had been faithfully paying her $1,000 a month since their separation. Still, the will stipulated that if Mamie spent through her fortune, the $1,000 monthly stipend would be resumed.

Mamie and Jimmy were not pleased. In May 1933, they filed suit to void the will, contending that spending anything on the museum was "a wanton dissipation of the assets." They also contended that the plans for the museum were "the expression of wholly fanciful, impractible, intangible, unreasonable, irrational and unenforceable ideas imposed upon the testator's mind until they amounted to an obsession and undue influence thwarting the testator's true intent." In layman's terms, the museum was a nutty idea concocted by a looney who had been abetted and encouraged by equally crazy people.

Outsiders predicted the suit amounted to the museum's death knell, even if Sam's will was upheld. "Certainly, half the estate, when the courts and lawyers and heirs have finished with it, would not be sufficient to complete the building and grounds and build up a great treasure house," the Portland *Oregonian* editorialized. "Sam Hill bit off more than he could chew."

Not only was the museum not completed, the paper noted, it was steadily deteriorating: "The place has been left to the storms and the patter of rats. Now the roof is warped and leaking, and $5,000 is needed for that repair. It is a ghostly place the dream is there, but a new Sam Hill is needed to revive it." There was no new Sam Hill. But there was a Zola Brooks.

Zola Olds Brooks liked to tell visitors to his West Main Street office in the small southern Washington town of Goldendale that "I was born (in 1892) within 50 feet of here and lived most of my life not 200 feet in the other direction." He was known around town as "Z.O."—and the handsome, curly-haired Z.O. was very well-known around town.

He was smart and hard-working, graduating from the University of Washington law school at the age of 22. He was gregarious and civic-minded, playing saxophone in the town band, helping to plan both Goldendale's first golf course and first hospital and serving as a founding director of the chamber of commerce. He was also a born lawyer: According to a popular story, when his mother caught him with jelly-smeared hands and face as a child, Zola calmly explained he had been helping her search for her lost sewing scissors, and they weren't in the jam jar. His subsequent legal practice included stints as a criminal defense lawyer, county prosecuting attorney and counsel for various utilities and corporations.

Zola's roots went deep with both the region and Sam Hill. His father, Nelson B. Brooks, had been mayor of Goldendale and a Klickitat County judge. Most of the buildings on Main Street, including Zola's office and house, were made of bricks from the Brooks masonry company. Nelson Brooks was the man Sam Hill enlisted to help him acquire his Maryhill acreage and handle his local legal affairs. As a youth, Zola had worked summers on construction crews building Sam's cherished Columbia River Highway. And Sam's litigious son Jimmy had even lived with the Brooks family during one of his exiles from boarding school.

So when Nelson Brooks died, Zola was a natural choice to succeed him in handling Maryhill's legal matters. He was not only a museum trustee, but also secretary of the U.S. Trust Co. and Sam Hill, Inc., which oversaw the Maryhill ranch property. And since he was the only local resident among the museum's apostolate, it fell most heavily on Zola to keep the operation's life-support system functioning.

It would have been difficult to pick a worse time in American history for undertaking such an enterprise. It was the height, or more properly, the nadir, of the Great Depression. By 1933, nearly 25 percent of the nation's entire civilian labor force was unemployed, and nearly 30 percent of Americans had no income at all. It was estimated as many as half of home mortgages were in default. For each immigrant entering the United States, three were leaving. A widely reported story put a human face on the misery: A West Virginia school teacher told a sickly child to go home and eat something. "I can't," the child replied. "This is my sister's day to eat."

No one at Maryhill was starving. But there were piles of bills to pay, and as the legal fight over Sam's will dragged on, Zola scrambled to make ends meet. Traditional agricultural products were the main revenue producers: fruit, particularly peaches; alfalfa and grain hay, and especially cattle. "There've probably been a lot of cattle barons who've put up art museums," Zola noted, "but Maryhill is the only art museum that owns a cattle ranch."

The cattle business was no sure thing. At one point, Zola mortgaged the ranch herd at 8 percent interest, gambling that beef prices would rise before the note came due. It proved to be a good bet. The next year, he changed tactics, selling off the spring calves rather than having to feed them all summer. That also freed ranch hands to work on the grounds and museum.

Zola seemingly tried to squeeze money out of every Maryhill stone. The cottages and some other unused buildings were rented, for $50 a month. He sold rusting road-construction equipment for scrap. The never-used Quaker meeting house was torn down so cattle stalls could be built from the lumber. He planted 21 acres of grapes on the hillside below the mansion, with the idea of someday selling them, and perhaps wine, to museum visitors—thereby planting the seed for the award-winning wineries that would someday prosper near Maryhill. When the state of Washington finally got around to building the highway past Maryhill, Zola sold them a parcel of land for the road. (The $3,467 was put into government bonds until the estate lawsuit could be settled.) Then he sold water and gravel to the road building crews.

In addition to running the ranch, Zola had to contend with scores of tourists and travelers who poked around, and sometimes vandalized, Stonehenge, Sam's crypt and the mansion itself. He hired a caretaker to live on-site at the mansion and provide security, and wheedled a $2,700 loan from the estate—with the grudging consent of the plaintiffs—to make repairs on the mansion "and get the entire area within Stonehenge oiled and graveled so that it would be free of weeds and not give an appearance of an abandoned place."

There was also the constant battle with the pilfering of anything that wasn't nailed down. Even Clara Carter and Lucy Leatherby, Sam's elderly former cook and housekeeper who had been granted lifetime residency at the Meadowlark Inn, from time to time helped themselves to furniture from the hotel and cottages. They would sell it to secondhand stores in Goldendale; Zola would resignedly buy it back.

"This is a very serious charge against them if anyone cared to push the charge, as you well know, and they should be told. We have been very lenient with the girls, which is as Samuel would have had it, but they do not seem to understand," Edgar lectured Zola in a letter, after learning of the women's light fingers. Zola tartly replied that "possibly on your next trip here, we should jointly have a more definite understanding with them, making it clear."

While relatively trivial, it was precisely the kind of thing that irritated the bejabbers out of Zola. He was devoting an inordinate amount of his time and energy to Maryhill, while the other trustees restricted their roles largely to that of Monday morning quarterbacks. Edgar in particular annoyed Zola by issuing demands or carping about Zola's management. "Money seems to be getting scarce with us and we must be as economical as we can until we get squarely on our feet," Edgar scolded Zola after Zola had sent a wish list for items for the museum ranging from a $50 vacuum cleaner to several $6.50 picnic tables.

Another trustee, Raymond A. de Turenne, the haughty French counsel in Seattle who was the museum board's treasurer, proclaimed at one point he would not attend any more board meetings until Zola produced financial statements for the ranch and museum, as well as minutes from previous board meetings. "I have asked four times the secretary (Zola) for these, without receiving a single answer," de Turenne wrote Edgar. "I am sure that you would agree that it is not possible for a director or trustee to vote intelligently in the absence of such minutes and audits."

The truth was Zola wasn't particularly interested in record keeping. It took valuable time, and when it came to Maryhill matters, he wasn't getting paid nearly enough for his. "I have always felt and understood that I would be fairly cared for in the settling of the estate," he wrote in 1934 to John P. Garvin, who was the estate's lead attorney in the lawsuit. "… Through the years I have given a great deal of time without adequate pay I have had no feeling but that the board would be fair, but have wondered if they realized the time that has been given."

Nearly two years later, he was still waiting. "I don't expect to be reimbursed for being a director," he complained to Edgar in September 1936, "but the time spent in construction supervision and all of the legal and detail matters should be paid for, as it is unfair to my (law practice) partner, and I can't neglect other matters to this extent."

Zola estimated he had received less than $300 a year since 1932. He asked the board to pay him another $1,500 for the time he had put in, which, he said, would average about $50 a month for three years. "I believe that considering all, that should be a modest sum." The trustees agreed, eventually. But Zola, apparently having made his point about his value to Maryhill, magnanimously—albeit a bit theatrically—told them he would wait to be paid until the museum was established and prospering. That would be awhile.

In May 1936, more than five years after Sam's death, the combatants in the war over his estate decided to call it a draw. Son James and daughter Mary received assets totaling about $200,000 ($3.6 million in 2017 dollars). The state of Washington and the federal government took $79,650 in inheritance taxes. Settling several outstanding legal claims against the estate cost another $35,000 or so. The museum got what was left.

What was left wasn't much: the land and everything on it at Maryhill; the British Columbia property; the Seattle house and most of its contents; 1,440 shares in the Great Northern Iron Ore company; 2,000 shares of Great Northern Railroad preferred stock (which in the Great Depression stock market was preferred by almost no one), and $15,987.86 in cash. The trustees promptly decided to give the British Columbia property to Edgar in lieu of $25,000 that Sam had left him in his will. Since Prohibition had ended, the resort wasn't making much money anyway.

"Your letter of June 15th has come with the splendid news that the estate of our friend Mr. Hill has been finally settled," began a letter Zola received from museum trustee Hazel Dolph Clark. It ended with "I congratulate you on all the fine work you have done to date." In between were three pages of suggestions about what Zola should do next. But Zola was already on the move.

Even before the estate was settled, he had enlisted the parks superintendent of the city of Spokane to help devise a landscaping plan for the grounds around the mansion. Within a month of the estate settlement, Zola began assessing what needed to be done at the museum. "I am pleased to report that the heating still appears to be in excellent shape," he wrote Edgar. "… The plumbing, however, was not drained apparently, and was frozen and broken in many places, so many in fact that it looks to me as if it would be advisable to forget all of that now and put in new plumbing."

With the board's assent, Zola hired a Portland contractor to oversee repairing, restoring—and finally finishing—Sam's chateau on the Columbia. The outdoor to-do list was lengthy: plastering and painting the exterior; grading the short-but-steep road from the highway to the museum; planting trees as a windbreak; and a host of finishing touches such as decorative vases along the entrance ramp and a garden fountain. Inside, there was plastering, painting and plumbing to be done. Public restrooms had to be built in the basement.

Initial progress was encouraging. "I wish you could see the maze of pipes all over the place now," Zola reported in October, "for when they are covered no one will ever believe it. Hope to have all underground wiring and plumbing ready this week so that cement can be poured on basement floors...the museum looks like someone is interested in it, at last."

But an assortment of aesthetic, engineering and economic problems began to pop up. Try as they might, the painters couldn't find the right color for the building's exterior. "We have tried a dozen samples, and none are the cream color we talked about," Zola wrote. "If something better does not show up in the next day or two, we will have to use the best color now available, as the outside work must not be held up on account of coming weather." In the end, they settled on a hue that looked good in sunlight, not so good in shade.

More serious—and more expensive—was trouble with the top floor's flooring. Because of flex in the building's steel-beam structure, the concrete floor kept cracking. After several patching attempts failed, the entire floor was replaced, the concrete covered with a mastic, and the mastic covered with high-quality oak planks, at three times the original estimated cost.

With renovation costs closing in on $30,000 ($530,000 in 2017 dollars), money was becoming even more of a problem than usual. The problem was compounded in 1937 by the weather: A freak 90-mph windstorm wiped out the ranch's peach crop, and the hay crop was lost to "more rain this past week than ever known here." To cover the lost income and pay the renovation bills, the trustees reluctantly sold some of the railroad stock they had hoped to keep intact as part of the museum's endowment fund. "Go slow as to expenditures," treasurer de Turenne warned from Seattle. "We have only a few hundred dollars left here."

One of the most vexing problems for Zola was Edgar's pig-headed reticence to electrify Maryhill. Electric power was as rare in the rural America of the 1930s as a quiet congressman. Only 10 percent of the country's hinterlands had electricity in 1935. But as the federal government's Rural Electrification Administration's programs—part of President Franklin Roosevelt's "New Deal"—took hold, Maryhill had several chances to hook up to the grid, only to have Edgar balk each time at the cost.

At one point, fearing future legal liability, he even objected to granting an easement to a utility company to install lines across part of the Maryhill property. "To grant them a right of way easement could not (legally) endanger us," Zola exasperatedly replied, "… (and) there would be no question about them furnishing the museum with power. We certainly will save money by having electricity." Edgar finally agreed, and the lights went on at Maryhill in the winter of 1939-40.

Electrification was only one of the nagging issues, large and small, that needed to be addressed. In July 1939, Zola put together a list of 26 items, ranging from installing a cattle guard to keep errant cows out of the garden if someone left the gate open, to procuring a good large-type typewriter for making exhibit-information cards and labels. The cattle guard was installed; the typewriter was deemed too expensive. But with the museum building nearing completion, a vital question remained unanswered: What were they going to put in it?

In terms of its collections, Maryhill was destined to be eclectic. Its founders had vastly differing tastes and cultural backgrounds. Its spectacular-but-isolated setting preordained that its visitors would be driven by curiosity more than appreciation for any particular art form. And its poverty required it to take what it could get.

Just what it had in the years before it opened was something of a mystery, even to the museums trustees—and finding out was a source of contention. There were 75 sealed crates languishing in the mansion's basement, the contents of which had been brought by Queen Marie on her visit or collected by Loie, Sam and others.

Trustee de Turenne, who had the soul of a bureaucrat, wanted them opened immediately and everything precisely inventoried. "I do think we should start this inventory now," he wrote Zola in September 1934, "as I am asked time and time again what we have for the museum." Edgar was just as adamant that the boxes be left alone until closer to the museum's opening, fearing their contents might be damaged. Zola was caught in between.

The impasse was broken in early 1935, when de Turenne sent his son, an out-of-work Seattle gas station manager, to Maryhill unannounced and with instructions to make an inventory. With Edgar back east and incommunicado, Zola acquiesced. What they found was a mixture of the interesting and the underwhelming.

There were sculptures, busts, paintings, bowls, chairs and bronze medals. There was an oil painting of Sam and a photo of Marie's parents. One crate held a six-foot marble statue of Diana, goddess of the hunt; another nothing at all. There were works by Rodin, and an advertising poster that implored readers to "Hippety-hop to the Souvenir Shop." There was a worm-eaten wooden rack and a moth-eaten American flag. There were Roman Catholic and Russian Orthodox icons and some cigarettes of a brand apparently favored by Marie. There was a plaster model of Loie's hand. It was broken. All in all, it was a bit of a dispiriting start to filling the museum.

Fortunately, there were other caches of art besides the basement booty. The Rodin drawings Sam had ransomed for Loie from the Cleveland creditors were in a Seattle bank vault. Sam's collection of 135 Native American baskets was at the golf resort in British Columbia. And there were books, photographs, furniture, art pieces and other belongings at the mansion in Seattle.

The Seattle house had stood empty after Sam's death, until three homeless people broke in and squatted for a few days. After they were discovered and evicted, Sam's nephew, Dan B. Hill, moved in while the place was offered for sale. Being in the midst of the Great Depression, it took four years to find a buyer. It finally sold in late 1936 for $7,500, less than a fifth of what it cost Sam to build it. In February 1937, four large moving vans carried most of its contents—including a 19th century Studebaker carriage and a Japanese rickshaw—to Maryhill.

Zola was also faced with an array of outside offers to sell, lease, loan or give various objects and collections to the museum. One fellow offered a "very ancient" violin he was pretty sure was a Stradivarius. Another had a collection of rosaries. A third offered his uncle's petrified wood collection, although it was uncertain whether his uncle knew about it. The Pioneer Society of Klickitat County was eager "to fix up a room to resemble one of the (local) pioneer bedrooms." The U.S. Forest Service and Washington State Department of Labor and Industries wanted to sponsor exhibits.

Even Zola occasionally got caught up in the idea of a museum full of esoterica. "We have a chance to get a very wonderful collection of animal heads from England," he excitedly wrote Hazel Dolph Clark, "containing all of the known animals throughout Africa and the rest of the world."

But for the most part, he was prudently dubious about most of the offers. In a letter to the Smithsonian Institute seeking museum-running advice and possibly the loan of an exhibit or two, Zola noted that "with the rather limited funds at present, some effort should be made to center upon some particular phase of museum work, and not allow (Maryhill) to become a collection of everything dumped upon it." In a similar vein, he wrote to Hazel that Maryhill "should specialize in some one particular field of popular interest in order that it should eventually become noted as having the best of something, even if it was not a large collection."

What that "particular field of popular interest" should be was a topic of sometimes-heated debate among the trustees. Zola was keen that the museum's focus be on Native American artifacts and the ethnology of the Pacific Northwest. Edgar had in mind a sort of shrine to the life of his cousin Sam. De Turenne was most interested that Maryhill had all the accoutrements of a European museum, with fountains, and gardens and other opulent trimmings. Hazel was okay with some Indian exhibits, but only if combined "with objects of art, as Mr. Hill's original idea was to make Maryhill a fine arts museum." And the fifth trustee, who had been appointed in 1935 when the board realized Albert Tirman had resigned three years before, wanted a museum where she could dump some furniture and throw her weight around again.

Alma Spreckels had become something of an unwelcome visitor at "her" museum in the decade or so since San Francisco's Legion of Honor had opened. For one thing, she routinely ignored the museum's no-smoking signs and lit up whenever and wherever she felt like it. For another, she sometimes "borrowed" art pieces without asking anyone, displayed them for awhile in her Pacific Heights mansion, then returned them for something else. And her candor could be disconcerting. When the museum's director brought the newly elected board president to meet Alma for breakfast at her home, she greeted them with "Guess what? I just found my cook in bed with the butler!"

Whatever her shortcomings as an art patron, however, it was undeniable that Alma had been a close friend of Sam and Loie. So Maryhill's trustees offered her the vacant seat on the museum board with little hesitation. Besides, she had other attributes quite attractive in a trustee.

"She is a woman of great wealth and could do much for Maryhill if she chose," Hazel wrote to de Turenne. "However, she is temperamental and may or may not do something for us. She seemed interested when I talked to her—really enthusiastic I might say—and led me to believe when the time came she would make some sort of contribution."

Just how temperamental Alma could be was illustrated by the saga of the Gold Room—the custom furniture Marie had given her back in 1922. After the Palace of Fine Arts declined it, the furniture resided in Alma's home, where, she told her brother, "it is only in my way." Maryhill seemed to be the perfect alternative. So she wrote Zola in February 1937 announcing "I have decided to loan my fine collection of gold furniture and other objects (including a coronation robe and copy of Marie's gold crown) from the palace of the Queen of Roumania, if you would like to have it."

Zola did. It arrived in March, followed by a procession of letters from Alma dictating just how it should be displayed in its own precisely designed (by Alma) "Queen Marie Room." Ever the diplomat, Zola explained that he planned to put it in Maryhill's reception hall. "That will give it the main place of honor in the building, and I believe that it will be very striking." Miffed at the failure to follow her instructions to the letter, and in delays in opening the museum, Alma decided she wanted the furniture and other things back.

"Their loss to us at this time will be serious," Zola mournfully replied, "for without them I am afraid we will be unable to open this summer." Alma relented; the collection of Marie memorabilia stayed put.

Marie, however, did not. In late July 1938, word reached Maryhill that the queen of Romania was dead, at the age of 62. "It was most unfortunate from our standpoint," Zola somewhat coldly wrote Edgar, "as we were just getting ready to correspond with her" regarding the things Alma had donated.

It may have been just as well: The items had been a sore point with Marie for years. It was her contention that someone—probably Alma—owed her money for them, along with some Rodin pieces. "Everything was taken from me on sentimental grounds," she wrote Alma in 1935, "but none of what was to come to me ever came...I am not a millionaire. Loïe came and swept my house of enumerable treasures forgive me for my being so outspoken."

Alma readily forgave her, but didn't send her any money. Instead, she told her brother and financial adviser not to pay any future claims from Marie. "I don't think she will ever claim anything," she said, "but still you never know. She (Marie) never lived up to her agreement (about providing a backdrop for the Gold Room), and she was more than paid for her furniture."

It was not the biggest disappointment of Marie's last decade. In 1930, her eldest son Carol returned from exile, deposed his own young son Michael, seized the Romanian throne, and placed Marie under virtual house arrest. Contact with close friends and most travel was restricted. Her mail was censored and her inheritance from her late husband confiscated. True to her nature, she did not endure it quietly. "I may be forced to accept your rules and orders, but I do it under protest and this protest I shall not silence," she wrote her son. "… I am not a slave and shall never consent to being one!"

But she was a writer. Over 1934 and 1935, she published *The Story of My Life,* a three-volume memoir that covered her life up until the end of World War I. It was a smash international best-seller, translated into eight languages and well-received by the critics. "Queen Marie," noted the famous English novelist Virginia Woolf, "can write."

She could also forgive and forget. Despite their differences over the furniture, Marie had invited Alma to visit Romania. When the trip fell through, Marie expressed her regret they wouldn't have a chance "to have a heart-to-heart talk about the Hill museum. I certainly do appreciate your thoughtfulness and that of the trustees in making a Roumanian Room to commemorate my visit to the United States and in remembrance of my friendship for that great idealist Samuel Hill, a true dreamer's heart and a great friend too."

At the time of the letter to Alma, Marie was already dying, of cirrhosis of the liver. Its cause baffled her doctors, since the queen very rarely drank any kind of liquor, and gave rise to speculation that her son had had her poisoned. Her death, on July 18, 1938, was global front-page news. But she had written her epitaph 10 years before, in a letter to Loie. Musing about her own mortality in the third person, Marie wrote "Perhaps she was heroic. She certainly had a quixotic courage for lost causes. And was she not a remnant of a class that was destined to pass away?" She was also a romantic to the last, and even beyond. At her request, her heart was removed from her body, and placed in a small chapel at her sanctuary residence by the Black Sea.

While everyone regretted Marie's death, not all of the trustees were excited about preserving her memory by making her contributions to Maryhill the museum's centerpiece. "I cannot help feeling that we are not a Roumanian museum, and the less of that material spread over the first floor, the better," Hazel Dolph Clark wrote Zola. She added that to do so risked having "the first floor of our fine museum look like a scene from a Balkan comic opera.

Being a lifelong friend of Mr. Hill and the second generation (of her family) to love and admire him, and having put a great deal of money in the past to the Maryhill dedication, I feel, as a trustee, a right to voice my sentiments."

Hazel, who was a graduate and trustee of, and a generous donor to, Mills College in California, and a prominent supporter of the symphony and art museum in Philadelphia, did not overstate her connections and contributions to Maryhill. The Dolphs were early settlers in Portland. Hazel's uncle had been a U.S. senator from Oregon, and her father the Portland city attorney. The entire family had been close to Sam. Despite living across the country, Hazel had made several trips to Maryhill to consult with Zola, and extensively sought advice from museum experts around the United States about lighting, exhibit staging and, most important to her, finding a suitable director.

Moreover, while Edgar frequently excused himself from museum work because his siblings were ill and needed his attention, Hazel carried on despite the unexpected death of her husband in late 1939, and despite the fact that at 54, she was battling breast cancer.

"I hope you know my sincerity and appreciation of your earnestness and remarkable accomplishment," she wrote Zola in apologizing for her testiness about the Romanian collection. "I myself am eager (to help), but handicapped by distance and (a) great burden of detail which goes to a new widow—especially hard for one recovering from illness."

In fact, the more things began to fall into place at Maryhill, the more nervous all the trustees became. The nervousness threatened to grow into paralysis. "Each one is very careful about not doing anything without being sure the other ones know it," Zola admitted. Much of their uncertainty stemmed from a fear that opening the museum before it was truly ready would do it permanent damage. Initial negative, or even tepid, public reaction could put Maryhill on a short, steep decline into oblivion.

Their fear was compounded by the persistent wild rumors and speculation that had surrounded Maryhill—"fortress," "gift to royalty," "shrine to dead wife"—since its inception. The extraordinary romanticizing of Sam and his chateau, in its splendid isolation, threatened to minimize Maryhill's merits as a museum and reduce it to a mere curiosity. "We have had quite a time with that (publicity)," Zola wrote Hazel. "...We will need it, from a practical standpoint, and in any event, cannot stop anyone from writing anything after it is open. I am doing my very best, however, to see that it is dignified."

In the summer of 1939, the trustees' collective cold feet scuttled a plan to open the museum for a six-week trial run. Instead, they set their sights on the following spring. The delay gave Zola time to observe the reactions of people who previewed the museum over the winter, "people who have had considerable experience and training in museums." What he noted was that the "varied and unusual exhibits," such as Queen Marie's furniture, were precisely what captured their interest. Maryhill's unique story, he realized, was reflected in those exhibits, and the story was as important an element in its attractiveness to the public as any of its sculptures or paintings. "The fact is that we must recognize that while no one desires to make any 'circus stunt' of it, we are uniquely placed," he wrote Hazel a few weeks before the opening.

The delay also provided time for fine-tuning things. Hazel's nephew, a 37-year-old fellow from Seattle named Clifford Dolph, who had been temporarily hired in July 1938 to build exhibit cases, was kept on over the winter to help ready the museum. Hazel wasn't crazy about the idea, first because she wasn't asked about it prior to his hiring, and second because she wanted to ensure that a competent, experienced person was found to run the museum, and not a succession of handymen like her nephew. But since Cliff's position was strictly temporary, she went along.

Loans of paintings were secured from museums in New York, San Francisco and Philadelphia. Zola bought a $12.50 model kit of the *Mayflower* to gussy up the display of the hunk of wood that Sam had claimed was from the original ship. It was decided to charge 25 cents admission, "enough to keep out the rabble and give us a small (profit) margin," as Hazel put it. She also reminded Zola to hire security guards and make sure there were paper towels in the ladies' room.

With paintings borrowed, *Mayflower* model assembled, paper towels stacked in the ladies' room—and 4,930 days after Queen Marie's dedication speech—the Maryhill Museum of Fine Arts opened on May 13, 1940. It would have been Sam Hill's 83rd birthday.

NOTES FOR CHAPTER 9

Edgar Newlin Hill *Blaine (Wa.) Journal*, Jan. 17, 1946, p. 4.

Whatever the truth was Edgar to Zola, Jan. 30, 1932, MMA.

Mamie and Jimmy were *Goldendale Sentinel*, Aug. 10, 1933, p. 1.

Outsiders predicted Portland *Oregonian*, Aug. 19, 1933, p. 8.

Zola Olds Brooks *Goldendale Sentinel*, Jan. 7, 1960, p. 2.

No one at Maryhill *Northwest Ruralite*, Vol. 5, No. 6, June 1958, p. 1.

"This is a very" Edgar to Zola, Aug. 27, 1939; Zola to Edgar, Aug. 29, 1939, MMA.

While relatively trivial Edgar to Zola, April 9, 1940, MMA.

Another trustee, Raymond Raymond A. de Turenne to Edgar Hill, June 3, 1939, MMA.

The truth was Zola Zola to John P. Garvin, Jan. 7, 1934, MMA.

Nearly two years later Zola to Edgar, Sept. 2, 1936, MMA.

Zola estimated Ibid.

"Your letter of June 15th" Hazel Dolph Clark to Zola, June 29, 1936, MMA.

Even before the estate Zola to Edgar, June 15, 1936, MMA.

Initial progress was Zola to Edgar, Oct. 6, 1936, Oct. 18, 1936, MMA.

But an assortment Zola to Edgar, Oct. 6, 1936, MMA.

With renovation costs Zola to de Turenne, June 24, 1937; de Turenne to Zola, 11-9-1937, MMA.

At one point Zola to Edgar, Aug. 29, 1939, MMA.

Trustee de Turenne De Turenne to Zola, Sept. 21, 1934, MMA.

Even Zola occasionally Zola to Hazel Dolph Clark, April 22, 1938, MMA.

But for the most part Zola to Smithsonian Institute Board of Directors, Dec. 10, 1935; Zola to Hazel Dolph Clark, Dec. 20, 1936, MMA.

What the "particular Hazel Dolph Clark to Raymond A. de Turenne, Dec. 2, 1936, MMA.

Alma Spreckels had Scharlach, op. cit., p. 224.

"She is a woman" Hazel Dolph Clark to Raymond A. de Turenne, Dec. 2, 1936, MMA.

Just how temperamental Alma to Zola, Feb. 2, 1937, MMA.

Zola did. Zola to Alma, Nov. 19, 1937, MMA.

"Their loss to us" Zola to Alma, Feb. 9, 1938, MMA.

Marie, however, did not Zola to Edgar, July 20, 1938, MMA.

It may have been Scharlach, op. cit., p. 205.

Alma readily forgave her Ibid, p. 206.

It was not the Pakula, op. cit., p. 409.

She could also forgive Marie to Alma, Aug. 11, 1937, MMA.

At the time of the Elsberry, op. cit., p. 283.

While everyone regretted Hazel Dolph Clark to Zola, April 21, 1940, MMA.

"I hope you know" Ibid.

In fact, the more Zola to Drake, Wyman and Voss, Jan, 6, 1938, MMA.

Their fear was compounded Zola to Hazel Dolph Clark, April 17, 1940, MMA.

In the summer of 1939 Ibid.

Loans of paintings Hazel Dolph Clark to Zola, April 5, 1940, MMA.

CHAPTER TEN

"A top hat in the jungle"

AUGUST 1940

On a warm clear day in the summer of 1940, a fellow from New York City stopped by the Maryhill Museum of Fine Arts. He paid 25 cents to go inside, and signed the guest book. His name was B.J. Eldridge; he worked for the Frosted Foods Co.; he was traveling with his wife from Spokane to Portland, and he was reckoned to be the 30,000th visitor to Maryhill since it opened three months before.

Exactly what Mr. Eldridge thought of the museum is lost to history. But if he agreed with the general consensus of the 29,999 visitors before him, he was probably happy with what his quarter bought him. "I know you are anxious to learn of the opening," Zola wrote Edgar, who had missed the May 13 festivities because of a sick brother in Indiana. "It went off very well...the reaction of the public was exceptionally fine...without exception they were all very enthusiastic about the building, its furnishing, arrangement and the exhibits...without exception they expressed the intention of returning many times."

The opening ceremonies had been attended by 242 invited guests, which was about half the number of the cattle grazing in the fields surrounding the museum. Alma unveiled a bronze plaque that commemorated Maryhill's 1926 dedication and bore a quote from Queen Marie's eloquent address. Several dignitaries from Oregon and Washington spoke, as did museum trustee Raymond A. de Turenne.

"In that building made of concrete is something which cannot be seen physically along with the objects of art and other treasures," he said. "It is a dream that was held 14 years ago by the late queen of Roumania and her friend, the late Samuel Hill."

What could be "seen physically" was a diverse assortment of art and oddities that ranged from a painting by the 17th century Dutch portraitist Peter Lily to a small watch containing a lock of Queen Victoria's hair. In the basement was a room full of World War I memorabilia, including the massive artillery shell given to Sam by Belgian King Albert, and a collection of French propaganda posters donated by Alma. On the other side of the basement was what the Portland *Oregonian* described as "the most comprehensive exhibit of Northwest Indian art ever assembled."

The main floor featured gifts from European royalty, including Marie's furniture and classic Greek vases and other items donated by Marie's daughter Elizabeth, who had briefly been queen of Greece. There were separate rooms dedicated to religious icons, the Rodin collection, and Queen Marie. One room contained various things that had belonged to, or were related to, Napoleon. On the third floor, the library featured a valuable collection of superbly bound volumes loaned by one of Zola's cousins, and documents signed by George Washington, Thomas Jefferson, James Madison and Abraham Lincoln. There were two very rare silver medals, donated by the daughter of a Native American tribal leader. The medals had been given by Thomas Jefferson to Lewis and Clark, to be handed out to Indian chiefs on the duo's expedition across the North American continent. There were paintings by the American impressionist Frederick Childe Hassam and the Mexican muralist Diego Rivera. And there was the wood chunk purportedly from the *Mayflower.* The collection's breadth, noted the director of a California art museum, made Maryhill less an art museum and more a history museum with lots of art in it.

The press was generally impressed. "Its great iron-barred doors swung open on one of the strangest museums ever conceived," the *St. Paul Pioneer Press* reported. "Many of its art treasures are mementoes of its builder; others will delight connoisseurs." *Time Magazine's* take was clever, if snarky. In an article titled "Sam Hill's Folly," the magazine faintly praised the collection, lauded the view from the roof, and said Maryhill stood out in its surroundings "as incongruously as a top hat in the jungle," and was easily "the world's most isolated art museum."

The *Oregonian*, which only a few years before had predicted certain doom for the place, cheerfully reversed its forecast: "The days of mystery and seclusion are ended, and the castle has come to fulfill the dream of its builder...the rooms are bright; the floors polished; the walls spotless. Sun streams through the tall windows and all is warmth and welcome."

By mid-June, attendance had topped 15,000, and doubled that figure by mid-August. With the region's sometimes-nasty winter weather looming, Zola decided to shut down the museum's first season on Nov. 1. Attendance had gone over 45,000, with visitors from 44 of the 48 states and at least eight foreign nations. The attendance number becomes more impressive in light of the facts that it accrued in only six months, that a quarter was still valuable enough in 1940 that it could get you three cans of peas or two pounds of pork sausage, and that the total combined population of the two states closest to Maryhill, from where it drew the bulk of its visitors, was fewer than three million.

To collect all those quarters and keep those "great iron-barred doors" polished had required a museum staff. So, it was happily fortuitous that Clifford Dolph had five children.

Throughout the four years between the settling of Sam's estate and the museum's opening, the trustees had been painfully aware that the museum needed a hands-on, on-site, full-time director, who would work cheap and would not mind life in the boondocks. Their search had been hampered in part by the low salary and out-of-the-way location, and in part by a philosophical split over the job's prerequisites.

Alma, Hazel, and de Turenne wanted someone with a background in the arts and experience in museum work. "We must choose our custodian carefully," Hazel wrote de Turenne, "and select a man who will be fit to preside over a fine arts museum." Edgar and Zola were more pragmatic. "Our choice will probably have to be between some party such as an elderly man on the downgrade," Zola wrote, "or a young man not too much tied down with tradition."

Since it was the midst of the Great Depression, there was no dearth of applicants. Some had plausible credentials: an art professor from Reed College in Oregon; an art historian from Austria, a division curator at Chicago's Museum of Science and Industry. Others were less qualified: a Washington state prison inmate; a woman claiming experience as a "hostess," a man willing "to learn history or whatever is needed to run a museum." None of them got the job. Instead, strictly as a temporary measure, Edgar sent

Cliff Dolph, the adopted son of Hazel Dolph Clark's older brother Joseph, to Maryhill in July 1938 to help Zola ready the museum for opening. Zola was delighted.

"I believe that he is going to work fine in every way," Zola reported to Edgar. "... in all his suggestions (he) seems to keep economy first in his mind...(he) has very good ideas in case work and display, and shows a rather complete knowledge of art works for one who does not claim to be an expert in that line."

Not being an expert was precisely what seems to have rankled Hazel about her nephew. Acknowledging, and then ignoring, the fact that Maryhill could not afford to pay the $250-a-month salary that more qualified applicants were seeking, she politely but repeatedly pressed for hiring "someone with recognized museum training." Cliff, she conceded, could stay on as an underling as long as he did "not consider himself above the duties required of him. I presume we must also have someone to do such things as your present man (Cliff) is now doing on the place, take care of the lawns, janitor service, etc., and who in addition might do guard duty in a pinch."

But if the museum couldn't afford an experienced director, it certainly couldn't afford an experienced director *and* a full-time jack-of-all-trades. In a long letter to Hazel a year before the museum opened—and 10 months after Cliff had arrived for his "temporary" employment, Zola firmly said he intended to keep Cliff on.

"His suggestions have all been fine, and he shows a really fine knowledge of display (and) good taste, and knows how to handle the exhibits. His knowledge of art and its history is rather extensive. I believe this myself, and to check it, several museum men who have been here voluntarily expressed to me their opinion we had a good man. I would much rather continue on this summer with him than to chance a second-rate man who is new."

Hazel reluctantly acquiesced, and the board voted to let Cliff bring his family to Maryhill to live in one of the cottages near Stonehenge through the winter months before the museum opened—and then through the first season.

"I find that with Mr. Dolph there, things are running smoothly," Zola wrote Edgar two months after Maryhill opened. "... He has proven very good his daughter is exceptionally satisfactory at the door, is very pleasant with visitors, accurate and dependable. I have the boys doing the cleaning on alternate days, they are OK, quiet and dependable. Without such help living there, we would have quite a problem, for we would have to pay sufficient to ensure good people to drive back and forth, or board." In addition, Zola pointed out, the kids worked cheaper than adults.

Just when—or even if—the board formally named Cliff to be Maryhill's director is unclear. What is clear is that he was definitely in the right place at the right time. Within six months of the museum's opening, both Raymond de Turenne and Hazel Dolph Clark, the two trustees who were most opposed to an inexperienced director, were dead. Alma, who had also been reluctant, was charmed by Cliff on meeting him at the dedication ceremony. She told Zola "that she liked Mr. Dolph and that we were very wise to have a man who could look after things and 'work with his hands.'"

The two men appointed to the board to replace Hazel and de Turenne were Daniel B. Hill, a cousin of Sam's who had worked for him at Maryhill as early as 1906 and was a manufacturer's agent, and Douglas A. Shelor, manager of the Automobile Club of Washington and a longtime friend of Sam's. Both lived in Seattle. Neither expressed problems with Cliff's pedigree, or lack thereof. Edgar was initially in favor of letting Cliff go, but was quickly swayed by Zola's enthusiastic endorsement of Cliff's work.

The result was that as Maryhill approached its second season, Cliff was its de facto manager. He was a poor choice for most American art museums. He was a life-saver for Maryhill.

Clifford Robert Dolph loved chess and hated Picasso. He was exceedingly clever with his hands, and excessively set in his ways. He was thrifty in his personal life, and downright parsimonious when it came to business. He was plain-spoken, and Machiavellian. And he came to be as much a part of Maryhill as any of its possessions.

He was born in Chicago in 1901, and that is about all that is known of his early life. Relatives said Cliff never talked about his childhood, or how he came to be adopted by Joseph Dolph. But census records indicate that by the age of 19, he was using the Dolph surname. After three years at the Art Institute of Chicago and some time working at the Walker Art Gallery in

Minneapolis, Cliff moved his wife and five children to Seattle, where he eked out a living designing and building exhibit cases for retail stores and other businesses. But times were tough, and in mid-1938 he jumped at the offer of even a temporary position at Maryhill.

"He has been dependable, steady, and I am told that his financial affairs have improved greatly," Zola wrote to Hazel about a year after Cliff arrived at the museum. "He is in no financial trouble here, and has lived carefully at all times."

Living carefully was a necessity when trying to feed a family of seven on what was initially a salary of $1,800 a year (about $32,000 in 2017.) So it helped when the Dolphs were allowed to move from the cottage near Stonehenge into a narrow-but-rent-free apartment in the museum's basement after Maryhill's first season. The apartment ran almost the length of the building, but was no more than 18 feet wide. Across the hallway were storage, work and utility rooms. "Because of the historically tight budget, it was comfy, but not what anyone would call a luxury apartment," recalled Vada Dolph, one of Cliff's daughters-in-law. "Access to it was from the museum interior. No strictly private entrance."

Living carefully suited Cliff, whose character description often included words like "introspective" and "methodical." He was tall and unremarkable in his appearance save for slightly oversized ears, and a rather sharply pointed nose on which rested his dark-rimmed glasses. When he spoke, which was more occasional than often, it was with a deep resonant voice that became gravelly in his later years. His skill set ranged from painstakingly nurturing roses to adroitly wielding a hammer, and because he had been hired basically to do manual labor, it was easy to dismiss him as something of a glorified handyman.

But there was more to Cliff Dolph than hammers and pruning shears. He loved poetry, sometimes reciting Shakespeare and other writers to family members while sitting in his sage green armchair. His musical tastes ran to Mozart, Beethoven and Hayden. He was an avid student of history. And he was obsessed with the game of chess. He entered tournaments throughout the Pacific Northwest, with mixed results. "His greatest interest in the mail," recalled his namesake grandson, "was the possibility that someone might have sent a return move in one of the chess-by-mail games that he carried on."

He had a wry sense of humor. For a while he kept a journal of the goofy things he saw and heard while mingling with museum visitors: "Did the birds build those nests?"; "The place was kept up better when Mr. Hill lived here;" "A man asked if the dog house was an elevator down to the river." In a letter to a board member, he drolly noted that his new grandson "shows little promise of being a prohibitionist; in fact, he is definitely not a 'dry.'"

He could be a nails-tough negotiator. When the company that was hired to replace Sam Hill's deteriorating crypt with a monument informed Cliff it needed to raise its quoted estimate by $65, he had a ready counter: The company should do the extra work for free and make it a tax-deductible donation to the museum. "Or, if you like," he further suggested, "we could discuss the matter with the help of a fifth—first one under the table loses." The company dropped the extra charge.

And he could be devious and manipulative. He became adept at playing the trustees off each other to get his own way. He encouraged years-long efforts by Dan Hill to get rid of Zola, or at least strip Zola of his control of the museum purse strings. But in a letter to Alma about Dan, he opined that "the kindest thing that one can say about him is he is not very bright." When a New York art dealer offered to sell the museum a rare Ceylonese chess set as part of a back-door deal involving some of Maryhill's Native American collection, Cliff replied "I will contact the trustees and let you know as soon as I can. Confidentially, I can juggle my budget accounts (a few hundred here and a few hundred there), but not anything higher."

But whatever his foibles, Cliff's strengths were a perfect fit for Maryhill. For one thing, he was willing to live in a snug basement apartment surrounded by thousands of acres of grain and sagebrush. For another, he was a tireless worker. "Dolph is a jewel," Zola enthused in a letter to Dan Hill, "doing all the outside work on grapes, pruning etc., and making cases in bad weather."

He was not avaricious. His highest annual salary, after 30 years of work at Maryhill, was $8,940 (about $52,000 in 2017), and he very rarely complained about the pay (although in the mid-1940s he did point out that he was making $53 a month less than deckhands on the Maryhill ferry.) And while his artistic tastes were regrettably static and narrow for an art museum director, he recognized that Maryhill's uniqueness—its soul—sprang from its history and the stories of Sam and Loie and Marie and Alma as much as its ancient Greek vases or Rodin sculptures, and he worked hard to preserve their presence in the museum.

"I practice every economy possible to keep the museum self-supporting," he wrote to Alma in 1948, "putting up with less compensation than I could earn in other lines, because I have the place and the idea behind it close to my heart...perhaps we can discuss this when you visit Maryhill. It is usually best here in September. I sincerely hope you will find it possible to make the trip then, or anytime."

Alma dealt with the Great Depression mainly by ignoring it. She did grudgingly agree to cut her allowance from the trust Adolph had set up for her from $25,000 a month to $12,500. But the reduction didn't slow her down much. She continued to throw lavish parties and travel extensively. She also continued to flaunt her unbridled personality in the faces of San Francisco's blue bloods. Sitting at the head table at a dinner sponsored by the Palace of Fine Arts, she grew bored with a dull and windy speaker. In a loud stage whisper, she murmured a phrase in Danish, then translated for her dining companions: "Light a fire up your ass!"

Speeches, however, weren't all that bored Alma. Cut off from any meaningful say at "her" San Francisco museum and still shunned by the city's social leaders, Alma sporadically looked for something into which she could pour her formidable wealth and energy. She briefly considered building a museum dedicated to Queen Marie at the Spreckels ranch in California's Napa wine country. But the idea fizzled, in large part because of Marie's long illness and death.

She took a fancy to a decaying Santa Barbara hotel called Samarkand, with the idea that it might help her slide into a top spot among the region's upper crust. So she bought it and poured more than $200,000 into restoring it to its former opulence. She also got married, to a dashing and gregarious polo-playing cowboy.

His name was Elmer Awl, He was a ranch manager and a popular fixture at Santa Barbara rodeos, parades and other festivals. He was also nine years younger than Alma and not particularly well-to-do, and he readily accepted her suggestion in February 1939 that they elope to Nevada. The elopement, for which Alma chartered a United Airlines plane, was as entertaining to the Bay Area as her first marriage had been. A ribald query soon made the rounds: "What did Alma give Elmer when Elmer gave Alma his Awl?"

One of the things she gave him was the responsibility of getting rid of her newly acquired hotel. Santa Barbara society matrons, it turned out, disliked Alma almost as much as their San Francisco counterparts, and the chill killed her interest in the area. So Alma decided to sell the hotel, and sent her 27-year-old Danish niece, Ulla de Bretteville, to help Alma's new husband with the sale while Alma stayed home. Ulla turned out to be something else Alma gave Elmer, since the two began an affair. Within a few years, Alma was not only rid of the hotel, which she traded for a Northern California dairy farm, but also of her husband and niece. And she turned her attentions back to Maryhill.

Her first target there was Zola. In April 1941, Alma's secretary requested, with some acidity, that Zola promptly, and regularly thereafter, send Alma the museum's up-to-date financial records, attendance figures "and any other relevant facts. Mrs. Awl makes it a practice to be actively interested in any enterprise with which she becomes associated." In June, however, Alma was still waiting for Zola to respond, and in exasperation she resigned from Maryhill's board of trustees.

That lit a fire up Zola's procrastination. In a long and somewhat whiny letter two days after Alma's resignation, he explained he had been "personally under a very severe strain." His law partner was recovering from heart trouble; his secretary had mislaid correspondence, the death of board treasurer de Turenne had added to Zola's workload. And oh yes, he hadn't been paid for all his work, neglecting to mention that he had voluntarily postponed taking the money the board had agreed to pay him several years before. In fairness, he also didn't mention that he was continually tasked with mundane tasks such as finding a second-hand blower for removing sawdust from the cabinets, buying lighting tubes and finding a flagpole.

"I knew Mr. Hill very closely for many years," he explained, "and he always told me that he expected me to carry out this project. I have really tried to carry the load through many years when the matter was not encouraged by the others. It has been by hard work, litigation and much personal sacrifice that we have been able to complete the work. Much delay was caused by a too-conservative viewpoint, I am afraid, and some did not believe that it was in any way possible (to open the museum). We have now proven that it is appreciated, will succeed and can be made better as the time goes on."

Zola implored Alma not to quit. "It is my earnest hope and request that you reconsider your membership...I do hope so much to secure those who believe in museum work, who believe in trying something a little different and who have visions that such an institution as ours can really be worthwhile, even if unique in history and location." Alma was mollified, for the time being, although she did have her secretary write to point out that "Spreckels" was spelled wrong on the museum's official stationery.

The museum, meanwhile, was humming along quite nicely through its second season. During the winter, Cliff and Zola had completed interior decorating of the top floor, added more cases and spiffed up the landscaping. In addition to the first year's collection, Zola had wrangled the loan of 18 "fine pictures" from museums in San Francisco and New York He hadn't been too particular about what he was seeking. "We would suggest that the pictures be reasonably large," he wrote the San Francisco Museum of Art. "As to the subject matter, any worthwhile subjects would fit in fine with our exhibit." Attendance was brisk enough that Zola reported admission receipts would cover the museum's operating costs, with something left over.

Back at the ranch, the cattle were doing well, the grape harvest yielded 15 tons, and the hay crop was the best ever. Plus there was the 15-cents-a-crate rental income from the museum's Coca-Cola machine. "I feel that with conservative handling, it (the museum) should carry itself at all times, and build up a reasonable sum annually for betterment," Zola wrote.

But Maryhill's future, like the rest of America's, was sidetracked on a Sunday morning in December 1941. The country's entry into World War II meant gasoline and tire rationing, travel restrictions and a paucity of labor for "unnecessary" enterprises like museums. Although Maryhill opened in 1942, it soon shut down for the duration of the war. Its wartime contributions were limited. It offered West Coast museums that were rattled by the possibility of Japanese bombings to store their best stuff at its isolated and relatively protected location, and it donated the rubber wheels off Sam's old rickshaw to the war effort. The contributions of Zola and Cliff were more significant: Both had sons who were seriously wounded while fighting in Europe. After a bit more than two years of life, Maryhill once again went into hibernation.

The war ended in 1945, and so did Edgar Hill, at the age of 84. The last member of Maryhill's original board of trustees, Edgar's primary contributions to the museum had been his devotion to seeing his cousin Sam's wishes were carried out, and his penchant for pinching pennies. Although irksome, his enthusiasm for saving money was an effective brake on Zola's tendency to spend now and worry about it later. Edgar's penurious attitude toward Maryhill extended beyond the grave: While he left a sizeable estate to his siblings, he left nothing to the museum.

Edgar's place on the board was taken by Warren H. Berry, a Seattle banking executive who had been a friend of Sam's. Berry soon joined the Anti-Zola Brooks Club, whose members included all the other Maryhill trustees, plus Cliff. Their chief complaint was an old one. Zola consistently ignored any and all requests for information regarding the museum's finances and operations.

"I am a trustee of the Maryhill Museum," Alma wrote in 1943, "and as such I am entitled to know what is going on. I feel a financial statement should be sent to me. If that is not done, I will resign." It wasn't, and she did, only to be talked into changing her mind by the other trustees. Alma's third try at resigning from the museum's board came in 1946, and this time she succeeded. Dan Hill, who had replaced Edgar as board president, persuaded her to remain on the museum's stationery as honorary chair, but her official responsibilities were over. Thus freed, she immediately embarked on an almost-manic four-year campaign to "fix" Maryhill.

Her first act was to give Maryhill the larger-than-life portrait of herself that she had posed for in 1923, sitting on the "coronation throne" Marie had given her. Alma's sole condition, which the Palace of Fine Arts in San Francisco had refused to meet, was that Maryhill keep it prominently and permanently on display. Acting for the board, Dan Hill readily assented, and until it was placed in storage in 2017, many visitors to the museum mistook the imposing woman in the scarlet and sable wrap, in a room surrounded by displays of Romanian furniture and artifacts, as Queen Marie.

Her portrait was only the beginning. Over the next five years, Alma gave, loaned, or arranged to have loaned or given, more than 330 items to Maryhill, from kitchen appliances and table ware (and a $15,000 dining set) for entertaining at the museum, to the Gallé glass collection she had bought on her first trip to France in 1914. There were framed miniature oil portraits of Louis XVI and Marie Antoinette on ivory; signed and framed photographs of celebrities and near-celebrities, and an entire gallery of pieces by the noted French sculptor Théodore Rivière.

For a "Gallery of Dance" that Alma envisioned as a permanent exhibit, there were 11 bronze pieces by the American sculptress Malvina Hoffman, a marble figure of Loie by Rivière, and bronze figure of Loie by Pierre Roche. "It was Loie Fuller who really interested Sam Hill to make the museum at Maryhill," Alma reminded Cliff, "and for that reason I feel it is particularly fitting that the bronze be installed as a memorial to that great woman."

The best of show was a painting Alma "indefinitely" loaned Maryhill in 1949. The painting, by the American master James McNeill Whistler, had a backstory as colorful as the museum's. It began in 1876 when Whistler was commissioned by a fabulously wealthy British shipping magnate named Frederick R. Leyland to finish decorating the dining room in Leyland's opulent mansion. The resulting "Peacock Room," as it became known, appalled Leyland, who refused to pay for it. Two years later, Whistler was forced into bankruptcy.

Making things worse for the artist, his chief creditor was none other than Frederick Leyland, the aforementioned shipping tycoon. But Whistler enjoyed a modicum of revenge. When Leyland's auditors began examining Whistler's assets, they found "The Gold Scab," a 55-inch-by-73-inch painting that depicted Leyland as a hideous peacock, sitting on Whistler's house while crouched over a piano, extending his bony claws to the keyboard. The painting's colors mirrored those used in the "Peacock Room."

Alma had first bought the painting in 1915, sold it in the late 1920s because she deemed it "too ugly," then re-purchased it in late 1948 and sent it to Maryhill. It was a huge hit. "It has made a name for Maryhill, with people coming here from many parts of the country to see it," Cliff wrote Alma. "You were so right when you said it would be an extremely valuable exhibit for us."

At least one of the trustees worried Alma was giving too much. "I think it is about time we were combing carefully the things offered for display at the museum," Doug Shelor cautioned Cliff. "We should not let any one person dominate the material displayed at Maryhill. We want variety." But Cliff was not about to discourage anyone from giving or lending to the museum, especially since such offers were neither numerous nor dazzling. In 1948, for example, Maryhill's exhibits included "The Artist in Social Communications," which was a display of greeting card art put together by a card company as a recruiting pitch for prospective illustrators.

"It can safely be said that the average visitor to a museum does not concern himself with who gave what," Cliff wrote to Shelor. "… The policies of a museum should be governed by consideration not of a few years but of a space of time covering generations. It may be expedient at one time or another to emphasize a certain aspect, which, as time goes by, can later be deemphasized."

Still, Alma's largesse did not come without strings. In a slanted, sprawling hand, she bombarded the other trustees and Cliff with suggestions, concerns, demands and complaints. "Mrs. Spreckels writes me almost every day, sometimes oftener, but her letters are welcome," Dan Hill observed diplomatically, "and I learn much from them."

Among the things he learned from Alma were that Maryhill needed a guidebook with a brief history of the museum. It should have a freight elevator; heating in the basement galleries; a gift shop, and a café or lunchroom. It should increase the admission prices; take out part of the lawn and replace it with some fruit or vegetable the museum could sell visitors; get rid of the expensive hand-tufted Austrian rugs that Sam had left, because museums don't have carpets, and maybe name a gallery after her family.

Maryhill, according to Alma, should also establish an auxiliary organization to help raise funds, and expand the board of trustees to include people like her. "I am not even a high school graduate," she said. "What I know (I am humble about it and have much to learn) has been acquired by reading and travelling. I think that Maryhill has a great future. My idea is to let the public feel they are part of it."

Most of Alma's suggestions were sound, with the possible exception of her request for a two-bedroom, two-bath apartment to be provided at the museum for her use on her only post-opening visit to Maryhill in August 1948. (She eventually agreed to stay at the Meadowlark Inn.) But the trouble with many of her sounder ideas was the dollar signs attached to them. "She is very generous and surely has the welfare of the museum at heart, but seems to think we have much money, which is not so," Dan Hill understated to Cliff.

In fact, despite continued good attendance figures during its eight-month season, Maryhill was financially just treading water. In 1947, for example, the museum took in about $9,950 and spent about $10,000 on operations. The ranch, which was designed mainly to support the museum, also seemed to hover at the break-even mark. And the "endowment" of railroad and iron ore stocks that Sam had left had never paid a dividend or crept back anywhere near their pre-Depression value.

Even so, Cliff was guardedly optimistic that, in time, Maryhill would prosper. "The museum so far has paid for its operation costs," he wrote Alma, "... (but) needless to say much is left undone...".

High on Alma's fix-it list was getting rid of Zola, and for this she had company. Maryhill's other directors had complained for years about Zola's habit of routinely ignoring almost every question or request. As his law practice grew—encompassing everything from representing regional utility companies to defending accused rapists—and his civic duties expanded—from running the area's wartime blood drive to promoting tourism—his interest shrank in responding to questions about things he was already dealing with at Maryhill. For his part, as Cliff gained confidence and experience at the museum, he became resentful of having to share directing operations at Maryhill, and at Zola's control of the museum and ranch purse strings.

The other trustees periodically sparred with Zola, but had avoided a showdown, for several reasons. One was Zola's seniority; he had been on the board far longer than the others. Another was Zola was still the only trustee who lived anywhere close to Maryhill. A third was Zola did get things done, in his own way and on his own time. And a fourth was that the museum's by-laws provided that board membership was for life, and they feared any attempt to remove him would be met with a lawsuit.

By July, 1948, the bad feelings seemed to be bubbling toward an explosion. "There is a good chance that there will soon be an end to the bottleneck which has been holding up many things," Cliff wrote to Alma. "All of the trustees are tired of being insulted and ignored by the Goldendale office (i.e. Zola.) This is in confidence, but necessary things will be done which have been arbitrarily vetoed and blocked for years."

Cliff was overly optimistic. Warren Berry, the Seattle banker who had replaced Edgar as a trustee and whose financial acumen had been counted on to look into Zola's bookkeeping for the ranch and museum, died suddenly in September. And Doug Shelor, who had been privately vociferous in his displeasure with Zola, got cold feet about an open fight with him. "Mr. Shelor firmly believes that Mr. Brooks was greatly responsible for whatever success Maryhill now has," Cliff wrote Alma. "He cannot bring himself to sever the connection. (It does not help matters that I am even more firmly convinced that a moron could have done as well, or better.)"

Ten months later, Cliff's anger had intensified. "They (the trustees) have no knowledge of what a museum should be and they don't want anyone around that might show up their ignorance," he wrote Alma. "I don't care whether you keep this in confidence or not. I would resign at once except that I know it would do Maryhill no good."

Alma, while sympathetic, didn't share Cliff's sense of fidelity. "I am tired of telling the trustees what to do. I wouldn't do anything only for 3 people gone to (the) great beyond and because I respect and admire you and Mrs. Dolph," she wrote Cliff in February 1949. A few months later, angered by Dan Hill's rejection of someone she thought would make a good Maryhill trustee, she demanded her name as honorary chairman be taken off the letterhead. "I mean it," she wrote Cliff, "I am through. I feel sorry for you and I wonder what would happen to M.H. if there was not a Mr. Dolph."

But there was a Mr. Dolph. While Alma's departure from an active role in Maryhill affairs was a blow to the museum and to Cliff personally, both the man and the museum would persevere, and leave an indelible stamp on each other.

NOTES FOR CHAPTER 10

What Mr. Eldridge thought Zola to Edgar, May 16, 1940, MMA.

"In that building" *Oregon Daily Journal*, May 14, 1940, p. 14.

The press was generally *St. Paul Pioneer Press*, May 19, 1940, p. 4; *Time Magazine*, May 20, 1940, p. 22.

But the Oregonian Portland *Oregonian*, May 15, 1940, p. 10.

Alma, Hazel and De Turenne Hazel to de Turenne, Dec. 2, 1936; Zola to Edgar, Feb. 27, 1937, MMA.

"I believe that he" Zola to Edgar, July 15, 1938, July 22, 1938, MMA.

Not being an expert Hazel to Zola, May 17, 1938, Sept. 22, 1938, MMA.

"His suggestions have been" Zola to Hazel, May 22, 1939, MMA.

"I find that with" Zola to Edgar, July 27, 1940, MMA.

Just when—or even Zola to Edgar, May 16, 1940, MMA.

He was born in Chicago While personal information about Cliff Dolph is scant, some insights were provided to the author by one of Cliff's daughters-in-law, Vada Dolph; her daughter, Kathleen Irwin, and Cliff's namesake grandson, Cliff Dolph.

"He has been dependable" Zola to Hazel, May 22, 1939, MMA.

Living carefully was a Email from Vada Dolph to Kathleen Irwin, Jan. 12, 2018.

But there was more Email from Cliff Dolph to the author, Jan. 14, 2018.

He had a Cliff to Dan Hill, Sept. 12, 1946, MMA.

He could be a Cliff to A. W. Neu, Dec. 15, 1954, MMA.

And he could be Cliff to Alma, Oct. 9, 1949; Cliff to Jules Carlebach, April 28, 1961.

But whatever his Zola to Dan Hill, Feb. 25, 1944, MMA.

"I practice every" Cliff to Alma, July 19, 1948, MMA.

She also continued to Scharlach, op. cit., p. 224.

His name was Elmer Ibid., p. 252.

Her first target there Cecilia McCue to Zola, April 9, 1941, MMA.

That lit a fire up Zola to Alma, June 25, 1941, MMA.

"I knew Mr. Hill" Ibid.

Zola implored Alma not Ibid.

The museum, meanwhile Zola to San Francisco Museum of Art, March 8, 1941, MMA.

"I am a trustee" Alma to Cecilia McCue, April 29, 1943, MMA.

For a "Gallery of Dance" Alma to Cliff, March 2, 1947, MMA.

Alma had first bought Scharlach, op. cit., p. 304.

At least one of the Doug Shelor to Cliff, Sept. 2, 1948, MMA.

"It can safely be" Cliff to Doug Shelor, Sept. 4, 1948, MMA.

Still, Alma's largesse Dan Hill to Cliff, Jan. 22, 1949, MMA.

It should also establish Alma to Dan Hill, Sept. 7, 1948, MMA

Most of Alma's suggestions Dan Hill to Cliff, Jan. 11, 1949, MMA.

Even so, Cliff was Cliff to Alma, July 19, 1948, MMA.

By July 1948 Cliff to Alma, July 3, 1948, MMA.

Cliff was overly Cliff to Alma, Dec. 18, 1948, MMA.

Ten months later Cliff to Alma, Oct. 1, 1949, MMA.

Alma was sympathetic Alma to Cliff, March 25, 1949; Alma to Cliff, April 29, 1949, MMA.

CHAPTER ELEVEN

Castle Cliff

AUGUST 1957

Arthur W. Dake was no longer ranked the third-best chess player on Earth. In fact, the 47-year-old grandmaster, who had won three gold medals at the World Chess Olympiads in the 1930s and once defeated the legendary Russian/French world champion Alexander Alekhine, no longer even competed. He had long since given up his chess career for a considerably-less-glamorous-but-decidedly-more-secure job with the Oregon Department of Motor Vehicles.

But he was still pretty good. So when Cliff Dolph—and 25 other people—challenged Dake to simultaneous matches on a warm Sunday afternoon, after he had given a lecture at Maryhill on the game, he readily accepted. He got a bit careless in one of the matches and was battled to a draw by a Danish engineering student, but handily won the other 25. The real winner, however, was Maryhill.

"Eight hundred people attended the museum that day," the chess-loving Cliff later told Maryhill's trustees, "which figure topped any previous single (day)...seeking loans for the exhibit brought Maryhill to the attention of many American and foreign museums and private individuals throughout the globe."

The exhibit to which Cliff referred was a collection of 60 sets of rare, novel and antique chessmen and boards gathered together for the first such show ever on the West Coast. There was an early 19th century "spiked" set from France, depicting the forces of Napoleon against those of Britain's George III, and meant to be played at beaches on boards drawn in the sand. There was a set carved from walrus ivory by Alaskan Eskimos. And, especially for the show, a popular Oregon artist named Ed Quigley whittled a whimsical wooden set that arrayed Northwest "pioneers" against Native Americans.

To put the exhibit together, which took more than a year, Cliff wrote to embassies and consulates of 81 countries, requesting loans of chess sets that reflected their histories and cultures. Sweden came through with three sets,

India with two. Iran, Greece and Spain sent sets. The Carlebach Art Gallery in New York sent 23 sets, and the New York Metropolitan Museum of Art sent 10.The exhibit proved so popular, Cliff extended its 1957 run twice, and the publicity was so favorable that Maryhill began receiving gifts of chess sets from the game's fans all over the world: Cantonese ivory, Danish ceramic, Mexican obsidian, Hungarian hardwood. A foundation in Philadelphia even sent $2,000 in cash so Maryhill could buy more sets.

"Carved chessmen are a form of decorative art dating back many centuries," Cliff told the trustees two years after the original exhibition, in successfully pitching his plan to make it a permanent Maryhill feature. "... We have found the collection has brought in many newcomers and much favorable comment. I suggest that a few hundred dollars be set aside each year to add to this collection."

The museum's permanent chess collection, which would eventually grow to more than 350 sets, exemplified three important aspects of Maryhill's existence in the 1950s and 1960s. The first was that to stretch its nearly nonexistent acquisitions budget, it had to be innovative. The second was that to cope with its isolated location, it had to cater to popular tastes without denigrating into the kind of roadside tourist trap that parked a covered wagon on the lawn and sold grape Slushies at the ticket booth. And the third was that Maryhill, by and large, was Cliff Dolph's museum.

Cliff's ascendancy was marked by several of the same factors that had contributed to Zola's reign over Maryhill in its infancy. Both men were competent. Like Zola before him, Cliff willingly took on nagging tasks and unexpected problems that arose. After years of trustee uncertainty about where to put a dedicatory plaque to Sam, for example, Cliff finally took it upon himself to pick a spot, to the left of the museum entrance, and had it installed. He took over replacing Sam's crumbling crypt with a granite memorial, oversaw construction of outdoor restrooms on the picnic grounds outside the museum, and made vitally needed repairs to the Meadowlark Inn. In a letter thanking Cliff for his above-and-beyond work at the hotel, Dan Hill acknowledged "you probably have found that the more you do for us, the more you are asked to do."

Like Zola, Cliff also benefited from being onsite, while the rest of the museum's principals were more than 200 miles away. And like Zola, Cliff had a keen sense of responsibility to make real the future for Maryhill that Sam, Loie, Marie and Alma had dreamed it would have.

But Cliff also had the example set by Zola of what not to do. Zola's management style was to generally ignore Maryhill's other trustees, which was neither unrecognized nor appreciated. "The trustees are losing all patience and are tired of being insulted and ignored by Zola," Dan Hill wrote Cliff in 1948, "and will take some drastic action."

Cliff's style, on the other hand, was to promptly respond to nearly every question and suggestion. And when Dan Hill proposed expanding the Board of Trustees from five members to seven, as well as stripping Zola of his control over day-to-day museum and ranch finances, Cliff quickly and heartily agreed. Referring to Dan's boast that he would celebrate Zola's demise with a drink of champagne, Cliff suggested, with just a touch of sarcasm, that "if—IF—you earn the drink, I think you should also have the privilege of breaking the glass in our fireplace, if we had a fireplace."

The first step in the *coup d'Zola* was to find, in Dan's words," "desirable trustees" who lived "a reasonable distance from Maryhill" and who could thus eliminate Zola's advantage of being the only local board member. "I look at desirable trustees in two ways," he joked in a letter to Cliff. "A younger man might put some pep in the board, but an older man might die and leave some money to the museum."

Who they got to fill the spots vacated by Alma and the late Warren Berry were neither particularly young nor rich, but they were local, and relatively prestigious to boot. Harold E. Wolverton was mayor of Goldendale, the closest town to Maryhill, and also the local representative for Standard Oil. As the former, he was well-plugged-in to the area's movers and shakers, such as they were. As the latter, he operated the service station that was closest to the museum and which sat on museum land. The second trustee, Dr. Thomas E. Griffith, was a longtime practicing physician in The Dalles, an Oregon town about 22 miles from Maryhill. He was not only a decorated World War I hero, but president of the Oregon State Medical Association—and considered an expert on the diets and cooking methods of the mid-Columbia River Native American tribes.

Once Griffith and Wolverton were in place, the board appointed them, and Zola, to a three-person "executive committee" to oversee operation of the ranch, which was still the museum's biggest revenue producer. "Gross mistakes, due to procrastination and mismanagement, have been made in the past, but I feel that a more positive action on the part of the board may help in the development of a policy which will render more profitable the ranch, upon which the museum must largely depend for its operation," Dr. Griffith wrote to Dan Hill, after Griffith had toured the ranch. Griffith recommended that among other things, the board should immediately establish petty cash funds to be controlled by Cliff and Clare Blanchard, the ranch manager, rather than Zola. The other trustees—except Zola—agreed.

In May 1952, the other trustees overrode Zola's objections and voted to expand the board to seven members. They then promptly elected James G. Scripps, whose family owned a nationwide chain of newspapers, to one of the new seats. Trustees also changed the museum's bylaws to allow the board's secretary—who kept track of minutes, correspondence and budget reports—to be a non-trustee, and then immediately appointed Marshall Nelson, an accountant from The Dalles, to the post. Zola was thus stripped not only of his role as the sole ranch overseer, but of his 26-year position as board secretary.

In 1953, after the death of Doug Shelor, two more trustees were appointed: an attorney named Arthur G. Dunn, who was from a well-known Seattle family, and Captain Arvid "Slim" Leppaluoto, a 6'-6"-tall shipping executive who had attained legendary status for his exploits piloting immense barges up and down the Columbia River.

Zola accepted his de facto demotions gracefully. In his last years as a trustee, he was sometimes the lone dissenter on board votes, and sometimes the source of an idea the other trustees embraced. There are no known letters or recorded comments that reflect any bitterness or anger on his part. He dutifully remained on the board until his death in late December 1959, 32 years after he had begun his role in the Maryhill saga.

"While he was highly endowed and greatly admired, a brilliant man who possibly could have become a national figure," his hometown newspaper remarked after his death, "he was a very human person, and chose to have a simple life in the surroundings he loved."

Cliff attended Zola's funeral, subsequently telling Dan Hill it was "a beautiful service, well-conducted," and that "many judges, lawyers (and) most of Goldendale's businessmen" attended. And in later years, Cliff acknowledged Zola's work for Maryhill as key to the museum's survival. He was far less gracious, however, in the months after Zola's death. "That Zola Brooks retarded our progress for so long!" Cliff wrote to Alma. In another letter, he noted that "the trustees are a fine group now, most understanding and thoughtful in promoting the museum."

Even before the diminution of Zola's authority and the rise of Cliff's, Maryhill trustees had generally deferred to Cliff when it came to museum acquisitions. It was a deference based at least as much on pragmatism as on admiration for Cliff's tastes: They were too far away to weigh in on a regular basis. As Cliff himself observed, "most museums have a committee on acquisitions, which judge such things. I wish it were possible for us to have some such arrangement, but I have no idea how it could be done, (since) our isolation and the distance and expense seem to make the idea prohibitive."

The deference extended even to items trustees knew about and didn't like. When Cliff bought a painting from an artist he particularly admired, Dan Hill sniffed that "I would not tolerate it in my home personally I would not give a dime for it, but you say the public likes it, and they are the ones we want to please." In another letter, Dan acknowledged that "the fact that the attendance at the museum is holding up so well shows that you know what the public likes."

For his part, Cliff viewed the board's acquiescence to his accession decisions as a mixed blessing. "I have never claimed to be an art expert," he complained to trustee Doug Shelor. "I am convinced there is no such thing—and even the 'experts' are forever arguing among themselves. Can you figure out a way I could be relieved of either accepting or rejecting material offered to Maryhill by anyone? I would prefer far less responsibility for the total and final decision." Shelor's reply was succinct, if not exactly what Cliff wanted to hear: "As far as I am concerned, and I think I speak for the balance of the board, we are depending on your judgement as to what should be placed in the museum and as to how it should be displayed."

Still, the trustees' faith in his decisions gave Cliff extraordinary control over museum accessions and exhibits—and he used it. As much as he loved chess, for example, he hated "modern art." He was an equal-opportunity hater: neo-Dadaism, pop, minimalist, conceptual, abstract expressionism, all were anathema to Cliff. Between 1946 and 1973, he bought or otherwise acquired more than 200 paintings for Maryhill, for prices ranging from $75 to $5,000 (for "The Wedding Feast," by the 17th century Flemish artist Gillis van Tilborgh.) None of them were modernist or reflected post-war trends. In 1964, in fact, he bragged to trustees that "a large and beautifully cast bronze set of chessmen" that had been donated to Maryhill was "the only abstract work of art in the museum, except in our Indian collection."

What Cliff liked when it came to paintings was what he termed "classicist" works, from European artists of the 17th through 19th centuries, as well as later American artists who emulated them. "For a number of years," he wrote to an acquaintance in 1964, "we have aimed to provide some recognition and encouragement to the relatively few artists capable of producing a well-painted picture. Often today such paintings are totally ignored, or sneered at, by many museums. We have avoided works of art which require a lengthy explanation to be understood."

Thus while other museums, most critics and much of the media doted on Pablo Picasso, Salvador Dali and Jackson Pollock, Cliff admired "exceptionally realistic" artists, especially those from what was known as The Boston School. The group, which had its roots in late 19th century American Impressionism, stressed technical skills, adherence to natural shapes and colors, and realistic use of perspective and light.

Cliff's admiration was encouraged by art dealers anxious to unload works from out-of-favor artists. "I am sure that now is a wonderful time to buy the work of our best American artists," Boston gallery owner Robert C. Vose wrote Cliff in 1950, "while the fool public is being swindled with the absurdities produced by Picasso and company. The market has been so absorbed with 'non-objective' and other radical art that the big sincere artists are forgotten, making it a wonderful time for ridiculous bargains."

But Maryhill couldn't afford even "ridiculous" bargains, as Cliff noted to a sympathetic donor. Classicism, he wrote, "will someday come back into favor. When that time comes, some of the daubs and abstract works which pass for art today will be relegated to the attic. I am only sorry that Maryhill can spare so little cash to purchase fine paintings…". If he lacked funds, however, Cliff didn't lack for lucky breaks. The first came in 1949, in the form of a loaned exhibit from an artist who freely acknowledged he was a better teacher than he was a painter.

Robert Hale Ives Gammell was born into a wealthy Rhode Island family in 1893. Trained in Boston and Paris in the tradition of 19th century painters, Gammell evolved from a landscape and portrait artist to focus on paintings heavy with biblical, mythological and poetic scenes and figures. His art, noted a critic, brings "the past into the present by virtue of his selection of incidents which involve human reactions and emotions which are timeless. His paintings are technically superb."

They were also largely unwanted by museums, galleries and the art-buying public. But Cliff liked Gammell's work. "His traditional style of painting is not popular with the great majority of museums today," Cliff noted, "though I think his figure painting is the best of living American artists." When Gammell offered in 1948 to "indefinitely" loan Maryhill 40 of his paintings, Cliff jumped at the chance.

It was a lucky jump for Maryhill, Gammell, and the Boston School artists in general. Running the entire summer and fall of 1949, the exhibition helped draw more than 53,000 visitors to the museum. Gammell, the Portland *Oregonian* reported in a frontpage story, "may be the entering wedge in a swing back toward good painting. The public attention given his Maryhill exhibition proves, at least, that it has an insatiable appetite for art that looks like art."

Over the following two decades, Gammell loaned, sold or gave Maryhill more than 60 pieces. Moreover, the museum became a favorite showplace for other Boston School artists, including Gammell's mentor, William McGregor Paxton, and Gammell's own students, including Robert Douglas Hunter and Richard Lack, who coined the term "classical realism" to describe the group's style. While none of them rocketed to international stardom as a result, their style resonated with Maryhill visitors—and cemented museum trustees' faith in Cliff's stewardship.

Cliff followed up the successful-and-no-cost-to-Maryhill Gammell show with another lucky break the following year. This one came in the person of a mercurial Romanian physician named Oscar K. Cosla. A professor of medicine at the University of Bucharest, Cosla, who was Jewish, had been relegated to a forced labor gang by the Nazis during World War II, and apparently escaped death only because he was a prominent heart specialist and was deemed potentially useful to the conquering Germans. After the war, he and his American wife relocated first to San Francisco, and then to New York. Moreover, they managed to bring with them most of the vast and impressive art collection Cosla's family had been collecting for almost 200 years.

In 1950, Cosla made an "indefinite" loan of 53 painting to Maryhill, in part because of the museum's links to Queen Marie. The collection included works by masters such as Thomas Gainsborough, Peter Paul Rubens, Jan Breughel, Frans Hals and Anton Van Dyck. Like the Gammell show the year before, the exhibition was a smash hit. Maryhill's attendance for the season reached 58,872, more than 5,000 larger than the previous year's record crowd. "The Cosla collection," Cliff proudly told a reporter, "equals the fondest dreams of the museum's founders." The exhibit, which remained at Maryhill until 1963, was ensconced in the "Oscar Cosla Gallery."

In 1959, a Cosla-owned collection of French drawings that Cliff valued at "at least a quarter of a million dollars" was loaned to Maryhill. It included works by more than 40 artists, including Paul Gauguin, Auguste Renoir and Edouard Manet. Cosla reclaimed them temporarily, then in 1968 returned them to Maryhill, where they remained until 1976.

After visiting Cosla in New York in 1968, Cliff had high hopes the doctor would bequest at least part of his collection to Maryhill. But in keeping with the museum's tradition of attracting unusual personalities, Dr. Cosla was decidedly eccentric. After being gently turned down by Cliff on requests to have his collection on permanent display at Maryhill and to be made a trustee, Cosla asked for something else: "Dr. Cosla," Cliff told the board, "wants his ashes to be near his collection, and I have agreed on behalf of the museum that such will be arranged if his paintings are given to Maryhill."

Cosla, however, eventually changed his mind and took most of his collection to Baldwin-Wallace University, a small liberal arts school near

Cleveland. There he struck a deal where for $20,000 a year, he was to live on campus and curate his own collection. The deal ultimately fell apart when it was revealed that some of Cosla's most prominent paintings were forgeries, and that appraisals he provided to the university were greatly inflated. The bulk of Cosla's collection was ultimately sold after his death in 1975 or was given to Montclair University in New Jersey. In the end, Maryhill got neither the ashes nor the art.

Far more important to the permanent stature of Maryhill than the Boston School painters or the Cosla collection was an assemblage of dolls that had languished for five years in the basement of a San Francisco department store.

The Théâtre de la Mode rose from the ashes of World War II. For four years, the French fashion industry had thwarted efforts by Germany to relocate the global capitol of haute couture from Paris to Berlin. When the Germans were driven out of Paris by the Allied Forces in August 1944, however, French designers needed a way to prove they were still on top.

They didn't lack for ideas, but they sorely lacked materials. Even with the German retreat, France was forced to ration basic necessities such as coal and bread, and when it came to clothing, most Parisians were wearing the same underwear they had on in 1940. The idea of producing lavish evening gowns or smart cocktail dresses was absurd—at least full-sized ones.

But miniature versions were a distinct possibility. And the idea of doll-sized fashions had worked before: In the 19th century, a British couturier named Charles-Frederick Worth had used small mannequins to advertise his fashions in various European capitals—so successfully that he became known as "the Father of Haute Couture."

So in the fall of 1944, a professional association representing the top French designers agreed to an exhibition of very well-dressed *poupées*, standing 27.5 inches tall and constructed on wire frames so as not to resemble children's dolls. The idea was to not only signal the viability of one of France's most important industries, but also to raise money for French war relief efforts. A who's-who of 53 designers contributed, among them names like Schiaparelli, Lanvin, Hermès, Paquin and Nina Ricci.

Using materials from cutting-room scraps to parachute silk, the dolls were draped with exquisite detail. Handbags had working clasps and contained miniature wallets and handkerchiefs. Hats were adorned with real ostrich and bird of paradise feathers, and real diamonds and other precious gems were used in the jewelry created by the likes of Cartier and Van Cleef and Arpels. And unlike most Parisians, the dolls sported new underwear beneath their fashions.

But that was just the beginning. To stage the exhibit, the crème de la crème of France's creative talent was enlisted. Film directors and stage designers put together theatrical backdrops depicting street scenes, the opera, even a bombed-out garret with a witch flying overhead. The settings were painted by leading artists, the dolls posed by ballet choreographers, and composers created special background music.

The result, when the show opened at the Louvre in March 1945, was "a universe of enchantment," in the words of one of the designers. "… People walked from set to set talking in whispers. It was almost like a church, a chapel."

After being viewed by tens of thousands in Paris, the 12-set, 300-doll show moved to London, Barcelona, Stockholm, Copenhagen and Vienna. "Haute Couture has lost none of its inspiration," noted a reporter at the London showing, "and the miniature models show that the present material shortage has been counterbalanced by a richly imaginative and ingenious vein, and that Paris is making a bid to hold her position as leader of the world of fashion."

The Théâtre moved to America in 1946, after another set was added and some of the fashions were updated. More than 100,000 people paid to see it in both New York and San Francisco. "Even to those whose interest is not professional, the exhibit holds great charm," the *St. Louis Post Dispatch* reported. "To the woman who has loved dolls all her life, it is a wonderland."

By mid-1946, however, the dolls' fashions were no longer fashionable, and the expense and logistics of moving the exhibit were deemed too formidable to continue the tour. The French fashion industry had made its point and a great deal of money had been raised for war relief. So the jewels were sent back to Paris, the sets dismantled, and the dolls, dresses and accoutrements abandoned in storerooms beneath the aptly named City of Paris department store in San Francisco.

In 1950, the store's owner, a genial fellow named Paul Verdier, hauled them up to the store's display windows to help celebrate the 100th anniversary of the store's Gold Rush-era founding by his family. Afterwards, he pondered what to do with them—and shared his pondering with his longtime close personal friend and neighbor, Alma Spreckels. Alma knew just where the dolls should go. "I saw Mr. Verdier," she wrote Cliff in September 1950, "and he is going to see if he can get you a gift."

The following year, Verdier received permission from the French designers group to ship the dolls to Maryhill, at his expense. The museum's principals were giddy with the prospect of an exhibit that was novel, artistic—and free. "… The collection is about the most outstanding collection of its kind anywhere and will be an important factor in the reputation of the museum," Dan Hill gushed to Cliff. "Perhaps I am over-enthusiastic about it, but it seems to me that these marvelous dolls will appeal to more people than paintings, statuary or the type of exhibits usually in museums."

Ever-thrifty and practical, Cliff enlisted four local high school girls to help assemble and dress the dolls. Working around the Dolphs' dining room table, the girls rummaged through boxes of numbered dresses, shoes, hats and other accessories. "We spent at least two days sorting through these piles," one of the girls recalled decades later, "matching numbers, outfits and dressing the (dolls') frames, and thinking what rich fabrics and strange designs."

Without their theatre sets, the dolls were relegated to glass cases. Even so, they proved popular enough to become a permanent display. "… The Théâtre de la Mode is still the stellar attraction for our feminine visitors," Cliff wrote Alma in 1960, "and (it) each year brings more and more students of dress design to see the wonderful show." The dolls would also prove to be a key ingredient in legitimizing Maryhill's status as a serious, if decidedly eclectic, museum of art.

Alma's small but key role in steering the Théâtre de la Mode to Maryhill proved to be a fitting capstone to her long connection with, and sizeable contribution to, the museum. Although she stayed in touch with Cliff and occasionally offered advice—"organize a Friends of the Museum Society," "get out of the cattle business," "interest some rich Jews in the museum"—Alma's active role at Maryhill was over. Instead, she poured her time and money into establishing a maritime museum in San Francisco.

Like so many of her enterprises, the undertaking left a bittersweet taste in her mouth. The museum was a success, but Alma's role, at least in her mind, was overlooked and underpraised. She followed it with an unsuccessful effort to create a museum of dance, as a memorial to Loie Fuller.

Alma mostly filled the last years of her life smoking, drinking and eating whatever and whenever she wanted; swimming nude in her large heated pool, with or without guests; battling illness and doctors with equal ferocity, and alternately charming and shocking everyone who came in contact with her. That number grew smaller after 1961, when her only son—a brutish lout who married six times and once kept a photo of Adolph Hitler on his desk—died in a sleazy Phoenix motel bar from a blow to the head. It was never determined whether it was an accident or intentional.

The blow also seemed to take most of the life out of Alma. She became a virtual recluse, but in her own inimitable style. Her daily routine became to climb into the back of her chauffeured Buick, wearing her nightgown and a mink stole, and drop off envelopes of cash to various friends and relatives, and a "Perry Mason" or other paperback mystery to another friend. She stayed in the car, with the windows rolled up, while her driver or a nurse did the deliveries. In 1968, she broke a hip, then contracted pneumonia. In August, she died at the age of 87. She was down, it was reported, to her last $1 million. Alma left the money to her grandchildren; her two daughters got the Pacific Heights mansion.

"Alma de Bretteville Spreckels deserves a novel, an opera even," wrote preeminent California historian Kevin Starr, "capable of reflecting the will, the self-determination, the self-invention of a displaced aristocrat who used her sexual magnetism to parlay her way back into the upper class, if not quite to the complete respectability that had eluded her."

Cliff truly mourned Alma's death and was deeply appreciative of her benefactions to Maryhill. "It is impossible to estimate the value of Mrs. Spreckels' gifts," he told the board after Alma's death. "Without the exhibit material she initially sent, there would have been no Maryhill Museum. Later contributions added greatly to the museum's development. The record shows forty-six years as a trustee (mostly in an honorary role.) There is no way to gauge such service." But he pragmatically, if somewhat coldly, also pointed out the bright side of her passing. "A good part of Mrs. A.B. Spreckels' collections had never been legally given," he reported to the trustees. "Her will completed our title to all antiques and objects of art she delivered to Maryhill. "Any anxiety on that score was thus happily relieved."

Alma was not the only link to Maryhill's past to come and/or go during Cliff's tenure. In 1958, fire destroyed the Meadowlark Inn, which had hosted Queen Marie and housed various visiting dignitaries during Maryhill's early years. The inn, which had been vacant and periodically vandalized for two years at the time of the fire, was virtually the last vestige of Sam Hill's vainglorious effort to establish a permanent community on his vast acreage. Museum trustees had been contemplating whether to try and lease it out again or tear it down; the fire made the decision for them.

In 1961, almost 35 years to the day after her first visit, the woman once known as Princess Ileana of Romania returned to Maryhill. Now she was Ileana Issarescu, the wife of a Massachusetts physician who was a researcher in atomic medicine. The mother of six, Ileana had left Romania after communists took over at the end of World War II, and occasionally toured the United States giving anti-communist speeches. At Maryhill, just before it closed for the year and just after giving a talk in Yakima Washington, about 90 miles away, Ileana wandered past photos and paintings of her family and herself, and mementoes of her mother. "This is heart-warming," she said.

In 1962, Daniel Hill resigned as the museum's president due to failing health, and died the following year at the age of 84. The last of Sam's blood relatives to be associated with Maryhill, Dan had served on the board since 1941 and as president since 1946. Even before the first shovel of dirt was turned to build Sam's mansion, Dan had assiduously, if ultimately fruitlessly, worked to see his cousin's dream of a thriving farm community at Maryhill become reality. Despite living most of his life in Seattle, Dan's widow asked that his ashes be placed next to Sam's. Museum officials decided it would be too expensive to open Sam's granite memorial. Instead, Dan was buried in a small cemetery below Stonehenge that had once served the forgotten town of Columbus. The museum paid the $85 cost of the grave marker. "He was a very long and faithful servant (to Maryhill)," Cliff wrote Alma, "and we shall miss him."

And exactly one year after Ileana's visit—and more than 50 years after Sam Hill first proposed it—a 2,567-foot-long bridge over the Columbia River opened below Maryhill. It linked Oregon and Washington, put the existing ferry service out of business, and made access to the museum far more convenient. The $2.4-million span was formally named the Samuel Hill Memorial Bridge. "But, we fear, the name comes too late," the *Bend (Or.) Bulletin* editorialized. "The new span, so far as the public is concerned, will be known as the Maryhill Bridge. The castle on the hill will remain as the true memorial to Samuel Hill."

Despite the new bridge, Sam's "true memorial" remained unique among museums for both its isolated setting and the logistical hurdles its location caused. While it shared problems like acquisition, preservation and exhibition faced by all museums, Maryhill also dealt with dilemmas undreamed of at the Louvre or the Smithsonian. What other art museum in the world, for example, had to worry about eradicating invasive yellow star thistle from its alfalfa fields?

Its short open season, dearth of wealthy patrons and deep-pocketed trustees—and Cliff's inordinate fondness for the status quo—kept Maryhill on an economic treadmill. The admission charge for adults rose from 25 cents in 1940 to 75 cents in 1972, matching almost precisely the rate of inflation over that period. But while attendance rose fairly steadily (if slowly), the museum's income rarely covered its operating costs. "We are about one thousand dollars ahead of last year," Cliff wrote Alma in mid-1960, after the adult admission charge had been raised from 30 cents to 50 cents. "If this keeps up, we may manage to break even for the season—the first time in many years."

Trustees—notably Zola—had been reluctant to diversify the modest endowment in railroad and iron ore stocks that Sam had left, and as a result the nest egg's growth ranged from sluggish to nil. Sometimes there would be a bit of a windfall—selling a few acres for a right of way or easement, or extra revenue from the ranch's gravel quarry. Once in a while there would be a sizeable gift. In 1958, trustee Jim Scripps donated five shares of stock in his family's newspaper chain, worth $6,000 ($51,700 in 2017 currency.) And as the museum board's membership evolved, the endowment's portfolio was broadened.

But for the most part, Maryhill had depended during its first two decades of operation on income from its ranch to support the costs of running the museum—and ranching is a risky business. In good years, the orchard might produce a bumper crop of Hale peaches, which the Fred Meyer supermarket chain snapped up and advertised as "Maryhill Museum" peaches. In bad years, state agricultural officials might quarantine the herd of 400 cattle because of a leptospirosis outbreak. The vagaries of weather and crop size eventually pushed Maryhill out of the peach business, beef prices rose and fell unpredictably, and Zola's dream of a vineyard at the museum's doorstep had long since withered.

So when a fellow named Paul Dooley offered to lease the Maryhill Ranch in 1966 for $10,000 a year ($77,100 in 2017 dollars), trustees did the math: The annual average net ranch income from 1961 to 1965 had been $2,710. After taxes, insurance and miscellaneous expenses, it was reckoned income from the lease would be $4,100 a year. Dooley got his lease.

While leasing the ranch alleviated some of the board's headaches, efforts to put Stonehenge on someone else's shoulders came to naught. The World War I memorial generated no revenue and was a pain to keep clear of weeds and trash. In 1962, Klickitat County officials proposed to take over Stonehenge and establish a local history museum nearby, along with recreational facilities. Two years of tentative negotiations went nowhere however, and a similar proposal by the Washington State Parks Commission a decade later met the same fate. The "fantastic and weird ruin—a symbol of the prehistoric past—" as one news service put it, remained a concrete millstone around Maryhill's neck.

Even with the perennial paucity of funds, museum trustees still managed to make at least some of the improvements and repairs that Cliff steadily urged. An elevator was installed in 1962 (the first such conveyance in the history of Klickitat County.) Both the interior and exterior water systems were improved. Incandescent lighting in the third-floor gallery was replaced with more energy-efficient and less painting-damaging fluorescent lights.

After the museum's first case of vandalism—repairable scratches to two of the Cosla Collection paintings—the alarm system of bells and push buttons was extended. More picnic tables were added to the lawns; a large storage shed and tractor-mower were purchased. Two of Cliff's loftier suggestions, however, would be implemented only after he was long gone: a museum café, and a building addition to the museum itself.

There was a temporary addition in 1963 that reflected both Maryhill's remoteness and the uneasy Cold War climate of the times. Trustees agreed to a government request that the museum serve as a fallout shelter and a Pacific Northwest defense command headquarters, should the need arise. "A large supply of hardtack and 22 small barrels for storage of water, and two portable toilets" were moved to Maryhill, Cliff reported, with a radio transmitter soon to follow. Fortunately, the need never arose.

While needed repairs and improvements were made, Maryhill's collections generally stagnated after the Gammell and Cosla loans and the acquisition of the Théâtre de la Mode. There were a few exceptions, such as the indefinite loan of a Charles Russell painting, and the gift of 11 pieces of Gallé glass. But Cliff's chief criterion for picking permanent additions or temporary exhibits was the cost, and he much preferred "free." As a result, museum visitors were treated to amateur painting contests, a collection of tables made from petrified wood, and "a very fine example" of a wreath made of human hair, for which Cliff proudly made a special display case.

The exception to this accumulation of mediocrity was in the museum's Native American collection. Starting with the 150 or so objects that Sam had left, Maryhill had amassed more than 4,000 items by the mid-1970s, ranging from late 19th century baskets to paleolithic rock carvings. Two donated collections in the 1950s alone contained a total of more than 1,500 items, worth an estimated $10,000 to $15,000 ($93.500 to $140,400 in 2017).

"It is growing not only in breadth but in quality," the *Oregon Journal's* art critic wrote in 1970, "and Maryhill has achieved quite a reputation for its fine examples of basketry from the Southwest as well as the Northwest coastal tribes. Contributions continue to arrive from people living up and down the Columbia River. Viewing the array, the writer was surprised that so many people have decided to give or lend artifacts to Maryhill rather than to a public collection more easily reached…".

Cliff wasn't an especially big fan of the collection, at one point lumping part of it in a gallery with Maryhill's "Old Gun" exhibit (the weapons collection was deaccessioned by the museum in 2016, netting just over $35,000). But he recognized the collection was unmatched by any other museum in the Pacific Northwest, and had few equals anywhere else. Plus, he seldom turned down a proposed donation, especially if it came with no strings attached and he could trade it for chess sets or paintings he fancied.

In one such exchange, Cliff sold "surplus" Indian baskets so he could buy a large painting called "Solitude" by the British Victorian artist Frederic Lord Leighton. Cliff paid $1,075 for it in 1965. It became the museum's most popular painting and was valued at more than $2 million in 1989.

It was a practice that, while not unheard of, was at best an ethical and legal gray area and deeply repudiated by responsible museums. Trading items that the donor had not specifically designated as "unconditional donations" was seen as betraying a trust. And even when the gift was unconditionally given, Cliff sometimes didn't bother to get a formal okay from Maryhill trustees when he made trades or sold museum items.

Worse, instead of seeking legal counsel or asking the board to set a clear museum policy for such transactions, Cliff turned for advice to a New York art gallery owner with whom he did business. "Anything which has been given outright to the museum can be sold to your (the museum's) benefit, without you asking anybody about it," the dealer, Julius Carlebach, suggested. "As long as the price is approximately the same as the one of the appraisal, you can right now sell anything to your benefit. It is only if you cannot reach (agreement) about the price that you should wait a longer time, preferably five years. By that time, you have no hamstrings whatever, and can sell anything you like, at the best price you can get."

Apparently satisfied with Carlebach's answer, Cliff didn't pursue the issue with museum trustees. This may have been due at least in part to a feeling that after decades of service to Maryhill, he needn't be all that accountable to trustees who seldom even visited the museum. It already rankled him that every year he had to ask for modest pay raises for himself and the small staff, and that the board ignored his requests that a cost-of-living wage scale be established.

Cliff must have been further irritated in 1971 when the board hired a CPA firm to audit the museum's books. In 1973, the board also laid out new procedures that including requiring all museum purchases to have a purchase order, time cards to be more consistently used by museum employees, and expenses to be reviewed monthly. The changes appeared to have been motivated more by a desire for greater efficiency than because of a lack of confidence in Cliff. They also knew that at 72, Cliff's days as Maryhill director were numbered. He had already signaled his intention to soon give up caring for Rodin busts and Romanian artifacts in favor of tending roses and playing chess. Trustees reasoned that his successor, lacking Cliff's experience at the museum, would need a more structured organization.

The board established a mandatory retirement age of 65 for every employee except Cliff, approved a $350 ($1,900 in 2017 dollars) monthly pension for him—when he was ready to retire—and offered to retain him as a paid consultant for a year past his retirement. They also asked him to think about who should replace him. Cliff suggested his son Norton, who lived on the museum grounds in a mobile home, supervised maintenance of the grounds and ran things when Cliff was away.

On Jan. 1, 1974, after spending not quite half his life at Maryhill, Cliff officially announced his retirement, to take effect in June. Just before he and his wife moved to the coastal town of Depoe Bay, Oregon, Cliff was honored with a reception at the museum. "He was here since the way was cleared to complete the museum," said trustee Harold Wolverton. "It owes a large part of its being—after Sam Hill—to him." Wolverton also suggested the museum board consider installing a plaque in Cliff's honor. Instead, the board would consider suing him.

NOTES FOR CHAPTER 11

"Eight hundred people" Director's Report, May 17, 1958, MMA.

"Carved chessmen are" Director's Report, May 21, 1960, MMA.

Cliff's ascendancy was Dan Hill to Cliff, June 20, 1948, MMA.

But Cliff also had Dan Hill to Cliff, June 20, 1948, MMA.

Cliff's style, on the Cliff to Dan Hill, Sept. 5, 1951, MMA.

The first step in Dan Hill to Cliff, Aug. 11, 1952, MMA.

Once Griffith and Wolverton Thomas E. Griffith to Dan Hill, Aug. 12, 1950, MMA.

"While he was highly" *Goldendale Sentinel*, Jan. 7, 1960, p. 2.

Cliff attended Zola's Cliff to Dan Hill, Jan. 7 1960**;** Cliff to Alma, Feb. 26, 1962; Cliff to Alma, July 1, 1960, MMA.

Even before the diminution Cliff to Doug Shelor, Sept. 4, 1948, MMA.

The deference extended Dan Hill to Cliff, Aug. 23, 1949; Dan Hill to Cliff, Oct. 12, 1950, MMA.

For his part, Cliff Cliff to Doug Shelor, Sept. 4, 1948; Doug Shelor to Cliff, Sept. 7, 1948, MMA.

Still, the trustees' faith Director's report, May 23, 1964, MMA.

What Cliff liked Cliff to M. Harbeson, Jan. 7, 1964, MMA.

His admiration was Robert C. Vose to Cliff, Sept. 25, 1950, MMA.

But Maryhill couldn't Cliff to Agnes J. McDonald, June 11, 1953, MMA.

Robert Hale Ives *Portland Oregonian*, July 31, 1949, p. 7.

They were also largely Cliff to Agnes J. McDonald, Dec. 14, 1951, MMA.

It was a lucky jump *Portland Oregonian*, Sept. 25, 1949, p. 1.

In 1950, Cosla made *Roseburg (Or.) News Review*, May 15, 1950, p. 3.

In 1968, a Cosla-owned .... Director's report, May 17, 1969, MMA.

The result, when the show *Seattle Post-Intelligencer*, March 13, 2006, p. D-1.

After being viewed by *The Age (Melbourne, Au.),* Dec. 18, 1945, p. 5.

The Théâtre moved to *St. Louis Post Dispatch*, May 14, 1946, p. 27.

In 1950, the store's owner Alma to Cliff, Sept. 22, 1950, MMA.

The following year Dan Hill to Cliff, April 4, 1952, MMA.

Ever-thrifty and practical Judith St. Pierre, *Dreamers and Workers: The People Who Built Maryhill Museum of Art,* unpublished manuscript, 2012.

Without their theater sets Cliff to Alma, July 1, 1960, MMA.

Alma's small but key Director's report, June 2, 1962, MMA.

"Alma de Bretteville Spreckels..." Kevin Starr, *The Dream Endures: California Enters the 1940s,* 1997, p. 153.

Cliff truly mourned Director's report, May 17, 1969, MMA.

In 1961, almost *Albany (Or.) Democrat Herald*, Nov. 2, 1961, p. 3.

In 1962, Daniel Hill Cliff to Alma, March 11, 1963, MMA.

And exactly one year after *Bend (Or.) Bulletin*, Nov. 2, 1962, p. 4.

Its short open season Cliff to Alma, July 1, 1960, MMA.

While leasing the ranch *San Bernardino County (Ca.) Sun*, July 3, 1966, p. 24.

There was a temporary Director's report, May 23, 1963, MMA.

"It is growing not" *Oregon Journal*, Aug. 28, 1970, p. 4.

On Jan. 1, 1974 *Goldendale Sentinel*, June 6, 1974, p. 1.

CHAPTER TWELVE
"Cultural abuse"
FEBRUARY 1975

Peacocks, thought Maryhill's new director, were just the thing to dress up the well-maintained-but-otherwise-nondescript lawns around the museum. The birds were colorful. They had long been an artistic symbol of beauty, wealth, and rebirth. They were especially popular in the Art Nouveau era where Loie and her luminous dancing had reigned supreme. Illustrator Aubrey Beardsley, glass master Louis Comfort Tiffany, and furniture designer Eugène Gaillard all embraced peacock motifs in their work.

Best of all, they were free. On his way to the county dump with a load of museum rubbish, Bob Campbell had encountered some people willing to trade their birds for some of his surplus plywood. "We have eight new inhabitants at Maryhill," Campbell told trustees, "four pairs of peacocks at no cost. They're in the chicken house behind the shop while they get used to it here, and then out on the lawn for the summer. They are beautiful indeed."

In succeeding decades, the birds would learn to eat out of visitors' hands, kill rattlesnakes in the garden, inspire popular peacock-related items in the museum gift shop, make good watchdogs—and also demand comestible tribute from picnickers, peck children, produce lots of extra peacocks and make sitting on Maryhill's grass a risky proposition. But for now, giving the museum the birds was just another great Bob Campbell idea.

There was no paucity of those. Even before formally taking over as director on Dec. 30, 1974, Campbell had been a whirlwind of creativity. He successfully applied to have Maryhill designated as a national historic landmark, opening the door for a myriad of potential federal, state, and private grants and loans. One such grant, from the National Endowment for the Arts, led to a reorganization of Maryhill's Rodin collection into a gallery evoking the sculptor's workshop. Campbell secured three workers paid for under a federal job training program to help clean out the museum's overflowing storerooms. "Most waste has been removed from the museum building," he told the trustees. "There was so much junk in storage which has been thrown away, we now have adequate storage space for museum-owned material."

The peripatetic director set up a docent program to lead museum tours; established an arts advisory committee to help steer museum acquisitions; began work on a Maryhill guidebook; and hired a Portland architectural firm to restore the museum grounds to Sam's "original plans" (even though there actually were none.) He even suggested the board hire a friend of his, at up to $10,000 a year, to run a fulltime fund-raising effort for Maryhill.

"There is a tremendous upsurge of interest under the inspiration of free-swinging new director Robert Campbell," reported a local periodical. "His enthusiasm in reinventing the museum has inspired many persons to volunteer their help in a variety of ways." Among those inspired were a wealthy couple from nearby White Salmon Washington, Bruce and Mary Stevenson. They donated handsome hemlock paneling for two of Maryhill's galleries—a gift that would eventually sprout into a decidedly more substantial role in Maryhill's future.

The locals weren't the only ones dazzled by Campbell. "The Maryhill Museum has all the makings of greatness—the art, the size, the location, the eccentricities," proclaimed a Stanford University art professor named Albert E. Elsen. Seated on the replica of Queen Marie's summer palace throne, which had been donated by Alma, Elsen told a Saturday evening gathering of wives of trustees and former trustees at the museum in February 1975 that Maryhill was "an eccentric, unique museum and Bob Campbell wants to play up its eccentricities. Right on. Amen. Too many museums could be anywhere, are interchangeable, have no identity." At Maryhill, "even the things in the storerooms are enough to blow your minds."

Campbell did indeed have some definite ideas on how to integrate Maryhill's unique history into its present. He began work to turn the gallery Sam had originally envisioned as his library into a "replica' of a room that had never really existed, filling it with memorabilia related to Sam. He proposed spending $1,000 for an acrylic mannequin and dressing it with Marie's coronation gown, robe and crown, and selling Marie tee-shirts and Sam cookbooks in the gift shop. And he paid an artist friend $900 to paint a portrait of Sam's daughter, Mary, from two photographs, "because visitors constantly ask to see a picture of Mary Hill." Unfortunately, the photos turned out to be of someone other than Mary and the portrait was so horrible it was appraised at $75 and never exhibited.

The botched portrait and the Marie mannequin weren't the only ideas that fizzled. Campbell proposed a sale of some of the museum's surplus Indian baskets, charging $1 admission to get into the museum for the sale. "We will take in 40-50 grand from the baskets when they are sold, plus admissions," he told the trustees. The funds, he said, would be more than enough to purchase a collection of Columbia River bone sculptures, for $20,000, "and that is a bargain. The bone sculptures are very important works of art. Each one is a masterpiece. Maryhill must own them." The idea fell through, however, when a pre-sale appraisal of the baskets' worth came to a collective not-much.

None of the setbacks slowed Bob Campbell or his numerous enthusiastic supporters. "Maryhill Museum of Fine Arts, one of the most colorful, romantic old characters in the American museum world, is starting its 1975 season like a frisky young debutante," the Portland *Oregonian* gushed in a full-page, photo-laden article. In another long *Oregonian* story 10 days later, Campbell made clear the "new Maryhill" would not only reflect its past, but his vision of its future. For one thing, the Boston School paintings Cliff Dolph had so admired were relegated to stairwells, hallways and in one case, the women's rest room.

"They are very weak," Campbell explained. "Placing them in the stairwells was a matter of making use of a bad investment, as you can't seriously exhibit them." The "demotion" of the paintings, he said in words that would in hindsight drip with irony, was in furtherance of his main goal for Maryhill: "To develop a reputation for integrity."

Robert W. Campbell was 51 when he became Maryhill's second director. He wore his thick silver hair stylishly long, and dressed younger than his years or paunch would dictate for most men. He was sometimes accompanied as he strolled around the museum by a parrot perched on his shoulder. The parrot, much to both the amusement and chagrin of staff, was not particularly well house-trained. Campbell was charming, charismatic and a natural salesman. A Portland resident, he was a stockbroker by profession. But his passion was collecting Native American and indigenous African art, which he bought, sold, traded—and occasionally gave—to various museums, including Maryhill.

Campbell had no experience as a museum administrator, although he did have a bachelor's degree and two years of graduate study in anthropology at Oregon State University and had served as a trustee for several years at the Portland Art Museum. He was well-acquainted with Maryhill and Cliff Dolph. He had been a generous donor to the former, and a sometime-trader with the latter. Cliff, in fact, had staunchly defended Campbell in 1969 when Campbell was accused of giving Maryhill several fake pieces—which Cliff had appraised at $4,500 ($31,800 in 2017 dollars)—possibly in order to gain a significant tax write-off.

"His donations to Maryhill extend back many years—beautiful pieces all," Cliff wrote to Campbell's accuser. "… I've never had cause to question his sincerity, his good faith. He really is not a dunce in appraising artifacts of this region." Cliff's faith in Campbell's good intentions was vindicated when the items were authenticated—and the IRS okayed the tax deduction.

It was therefore more than a bit of a surprise when Campbell began lobbying for Cliff's job in mid-1973 by bad-mouthing him to the Maryhill trustees. Cliff, he told them, had been selling and trading museum items out the backdoor for years with various dealers and collectors, including himself. Campbell stopped short of accusing Cliff of feathering his own financial nest, however, and the trustees initially shrugged off the issue. The 1971-72 audits had found nothing alarming, and while sometimes a bit cranky, Cliff had always struck them as straightforward in his conduct and devoted to Maryhill.

Instead of confronting Cliff or launching an investigation, the board waited until Cliff formally announced his retirement on Jan. 1 1974, then named his son Norton as interim director, to take effect when Cliff actually left the job in June. Norton, who was the only other person besides Campbell to apply for the job, had lived most of his life at Maryhill as his father's top assistant and seemed the logical choice for a smooth transition.

But Campbell was as tenacious as he was loquacious. At the board's annual meeting in May, he told the trustees he knew how to pull in grant money, generate publicity, attract financial support and volunteers, and generally shake off the dust and cobwebs that Maryhill had gathered under Cliff's—and by extension, Norton's—watch. Impressed or worn down, or both, trustees decided unanimously a few months later to hire Campbell as an "administrative consultant." They placed him over Norton in the museum pecking order and paid him $1,000 a month, more than Cliff had ever earned in his 36 years at Maryhill. Within two months, Norton resigned and Campbell was named director. "The senior trustees concede that Robert Campbell has persuasive capabilities," trustee James Scripps later ruefully noted. "He persuaded them to hire him."

About the same time they were handing Maryhill's reins to Campbell, some trustees began to get nervous about the claims that Cliff may not have always been on the up-and-up with his handling of museum property. In November, executive committee members ordered a total and immediate inventory and a change of the museum's locks. They stopped short of hiring an outside counsel to take legal action against Cliff, but "did express great concern" about the allegations: "It was the committee's feeling," the meeting minutes recorded, "that someone must talk to Cliff and Ruth Dolph about the problem and clear the air in this unexplored area."

Unfortunately for Cliff, Campbell was put in charge of the inventory. He promptly enlisted untrained volunteers, gave them copies of an inventory Cliff had begun in 1972, and told them to look for "anything strange." More than 100 items were found to be missing.

Although it was unclear at the time, several different explanations for the unaccounted-for items eventually surfaced. Some had been recorded as gifts to Maryhill but were never actually given. Some were things Alma had given and then taken back, such as Whistler's "The Gold Scab" painting. Some were on display at Maryhill but were somehow overlooked by the volunteers. Some had been discarded by Campbell during his cleanup. Some Campbell had given to the volunteers or other people associated with the museum. And some items, mostly Indian artifacts, were actually missing.

Shortly after the inventory was begun, Campbell also began looking at museum copies of correspondence between Cliff and various dealers, donors and private collectors. His ostensible purpose was to see if there were explanations for some of the items being missing. What he produced, however, were a couple of "books" in which Campbell snipped parts of letters that seemed to incriminate Cliff. "As it is," one such snippet read from a 1962 letter to a New York gallery owner, "my petty cash account is in such a mess!

I take amounts out of it—not only with you—for things I have no business doing. If the auditors ever catch up, I'll be known as the (Billy) Sol Estes in museum circles," a reference to the Texas financier who was in the headlines as an accused swindler. In another letter, Cliff asked "can you use some very fine Indian baskets? We have them in all sizes, in excellent condition…".

While Campbell was compiling his dossier, Cliff began to fire back. In a letter to trustee James Scripps, Cliff said he had been visited by a Francis Newton, who was the Portland Art Museum's director while Campbell was a trustee there. "Dr. Newton warned that Campbell will ransack the storerooms, getting away with everything he can. He strongly warned to watch out when he starts to make inventories." Scripps passed along Cliff's warning to the other trustees, who largely ignored it just as they had initially ignored the warnings about Cliff.

The next plot twist in the melodrama came in late August 1975, when a burglar or burglars made off with 48 Indian baskets worth an estimated $8,000 (about $36,800 in 2017). "The burglars knew exactly what they had entered the museum to steal," Campbell told reporters. "… It's a sad thing." Given the way the museum was entered—through a basement window that had been left open—police suspected an inside job. Given that the thieves took only baskets from three specific tribes that were highly coveted by collectors, police also suspected they knew a good deal about Native American art. And given that Campbell refused to take a lie detector test, they also suspected him. But no one was ever arrested and no baskets were recovered. Bars were placed, after the fact, on unprotected windows. A German shepherd named Jim was brought in to do night patrol. And the war of words among Cliff, Campbell and the trustees resumed at full force.

Trustee Scripps, who neither liked nor trusted Campbell, grew tired of the increasingly public innuendos about Cliff's honesty and stewardship of Maryhill. In a memo to Campbell and board president Slim Leppaluoto, Scripps complained Cliff was being convicted without a fair trial. "Cliff Dolph, to my positive knowledge, operated under an extremely penurious budget," Scripps wrote. "… It is my firm belief that Cliff Dolph did the best he could with what he had." To make up for the damage done to Cliff's reputation, Scripps suggested the museum install a plaque recognizing his decades of service to Maryhill.

But Leppaluoto wasn't buying it. Instead, the board president asked the museum's attorney, John B. Moore, to sit down with Cliff and go over the issues raised by Campbell and his excerpted "evidence." In a 10-page report in April 1976, Moore summarized his meeting with Cliff at a Portland hotel: "At the conclusion of my interview, I felt that I had been talking to an honest man, who had attempted to do a good job for Maryhill, but had not protected himself and the museum at all times."

Moore itemized Cliff's explanations for many of the missing items. In some cases, he emphatically denied selling or loaning them. In others, he said the items had been reclaimed by the donors or approved for sale by one or more of the trustees. And in some cases, he just did not remember what happened to them. "I felt that he honestly operated on the basis that he had been there for so long that he felt he had discretion on much of the action taken," Moore wrote, "or that he had board approval either directly or by implication."

In a follow-up letter, Moore recommended the board let the issue go. He pointed out that A) proving a case against Cliff would be lengthy and expensive; B) even if the board won a case, Cliff's pockets were exceedingly shallow and the museum would gain little or no compensation, and C) the resulting publicity would do great damage to Maryhill's reputation. Moreover, Moore said, suing Cliff would be a tacit admission by trustees that they had done a lousy job of overseeing the museum. "Because of the problems," Moore concluded, "it seems to me that the most desirable program to be followed now is to set up proper procedures, checks and balances to prevent a situation such as we now have from ever again arising. In this regard, the past would be forgotten insofar as Dolph is concerned …".

While the board took Moore's advice, Cliff's reputation had taken a beating. "I fully realize and appreciate the part you, Cliff, and your good wife played in building from scratch the fine institution that has gained nationwide recognition," a sympathetic trustee wrote. "…What a shame that we have such people in this world who would question your honesty after so many years of dedicated service." Cliff did not get his plaque. He died in 1979, at the age of 78. As far as the Byzantine histrionics surrounding Maryhill were concerned, he was at last off the hook. The museum most definitely was not.

⊷

While Campbell's creativity and energy were undeniable, his administrative skills were lacking, and his art conservation abilities worthy of a Three Stooges movie. Mishaps at Maryhill seemed to occur with assembly-line regularity. In one case, windows were left open and garden sprinklers drenched several paintings and caused extensive damage. Pima Indian baskets were routinely used as trash cans. Some Romanian medals clad in precious metals were polished so much the gold and silver were worn away. When museum workers had no success with a screwdriver in trying to dismantle an antique ebonized cabinet to transport it to Maryhill, they tried using a hammer. They succeeded in smashing it to splinters—in front of the doubtless horrified donor. An estimated $20,000 worth of trees, shrubs and other plants were torn out in anticipation of the landscaping makeover that never happened.

Then there were the parties that Campbell threw at the museum. Employees damaged Indian clothing and a Romanian robe when they wore them as costumes. Antique plates and silver chalices donated by Marie were used to serve food and beverages. A guest put an elbow through one of the paintings Campbell had hung in a stairwell. Other guests posed for photos hugging and clowning around on sculptures.

Naturally none of this made Maryhill trustees happy. On March 25, 1976, 15 months after he was hired as director, Campbell was fired. Although no public explanation was given by the board, Campbell told reporters "it would appear that I took actions which offended the Board of Trustees." He also graciously added that "Maryhill is a great institution, and I wish it well. I've gone back to the brokerage business." He also asked for a severance package that included vacation pay and moving expenses. The board declined his request.

But there was more to Campbell's dismissal than his haphazard management style. Behind the public pronouncements of new and exciting programs, a web of power politics had been woven that would have given Machiavelli a migraine. It began with the aforementioned Stanford art professor Albert

Elsen, and his thirst for revenge against Cliff Dolph for a slight Elsen had suffered in 1972.

According to Elsen, an intense and irascible sort who was recognized as one of the world's leading experts on Rodin, Cliff had promised Elsen he could borrow some of Maryhill's Rodin drawings for an important exhibition Elsen was staging at the National Gallery of Art in Washington D.C. Then Cliff reneged, citing safety concerns for the drawings. "This last-minute turn-down crippled the show and almost forced us to cancel it," Elsen wrote Bob Campbell in August 1974, in response to a query from Campbell concerning restoration of Maryhill's Rodins. "If Dolph is still director there, this is the end of our correspondence."

With Cliff gone, however, Elsen and Campbell soon became pen pals. Responding to a photo Campbell sent him of a Rodin sculpture Cliff had attempted to repair, Elsen snorted that it resembled "a poultice made by a witch doctor. My God—what level of intelligence did Dolph have?" Campbell, in turn, began unburdening himself to Elsen about his relations with the Maryhill board. "It becomes increasingly apparent that some of the trustees on the board at Maryhill should never have been elected in the first place," Campbell complained in a letter, he took pains to point out, he was sending without his signature. "The thought of them being a lifetime millstone would tax the patience of Job. How do we go about changing to a rotating board, and what political pressure can we use?"

Elsen had some ideas. He and a colleague, the highly esteemed Stanford law professor John H. Merryman, were keenly interested in shining a spotlight on what they regarded as a national problem: the lack of government oversight of private museums. Such institutions, like Maryhill, were often recognized as "charitable trusts," mainly for tax purposes. As such they were theoretically supposed to be monitored by the state, although in practice they seldom were. "Most attorneys general have neither the staff nor the active expertise for such supervision," Merryman observed. "The result is that there is little effective legal regulation of museum trustees. The law is on the whole clear. It is just not enforced."

To Elsen and Merryman, Maryhill seemed like the perfect specimen to make their case. But they were relying strictly on Campbell's perspective and characterizations. While Elsen had visited the museum once, Merryman confessed he didn't even know where it was.

Elsen suggested that Campbell talk the Maryhill board into abolishing its lifetime-tenure policy for trustees in favor of a system of rotating and finite terms, and at the same time expand the number of trustees. The presumed effect of such changes would be to dilute the clout of trustees and increase the museum director's. "I'd suggest talking to the attorney general of Washington," Elsen added. "You could work it so that the trustees are aware that if they didn't make changes they may be investigated by the state A.G. They are still liable for past negligence and mismanagement, unless I am mistaken." Campbell liked the idea. But before he could act on it, someone beat him to it.

Mary Hoyt Stevenson was in some ways a composite of Maryhill's founders. She had Loie's enthusiasm, Alma's impatience, Marie's determination and some of Sam's self-importance. She also loved the museum, which in the long run would prove invaluable but in the short run helped spark a scandal.

Born in Spokane in 1920, Stevenson was a quintessential doer: homecoming queen at the University of Washington, mother of three, Republican Party activist, Girl Scout troop leader, avid dancer and bridge player and ardent art lover. Her husband Bruce, to whom she would be married for 65 years, co-founded a lumber company in the Columbia River town of White Salmon Washington, about 33 miles west of Maryhill. The company prospered; the Stevensons became rich and influential.

In 1969, after the couple had made a sizeable campaign contribution to Gov. Daniel Evans, Stevenson was appointed to the Washington State Arts Commission. About the same time, she offered her services and support to Maryhill. But Cliff, who apparently wasn't quite sure what the state arts commission was, brushed her off. She had better luck with Bob Campbell, who appointed her to the acquisitions advisory committee he formed soon after taking over for Cliff.

"Maryhill Museum is undergoing a great new look under the directorship of Robert Campbell," she wrote to Gov. Evans while inviting him to serve as honorary chairman of a planned gala ball to celebrate the 50th anniversary of Queen Marie's 1926 museum dedication. "… It has been a total amazement to me to learn that the museum has high-quality art and artifacts and memorabilia from the 1920s that have never been displayed or preserved properly."

In March 1976, Stevenson applied for one of two vacant seats on the Maryhill Board of Trustees. "In the past I have always had an interest and pride in the Maryhill Museum," she wrote in her application, "but my enthusiasm has blossomed in the past year under the directorship of Bob Campbell. The museum has come alive and is becoming (an object) of attention from all over the West. I feel that Maryhill trustees should have a woman on its board, and that I am qualified for that position."

Her stated enthusiasm for Campbell, however, was ill-timed: He was fired by the board two weeks after she applied. Worse, she grossly overestimated the trustees' appreciation of candor. If elected to the board, she told a board meeting in May 1976, she would "work toward changes in the bylaws that would limit the number of years a trustee could serve." Moreover, she revealed that she and her husband had gone to the state attorney general's office some months before "to report their concerns regarding rumors that exhibits were not authentic, items were sold and Maryhill had become a dumping ground for items not worthy of exhibit."

Unsurprisingly, Stevenson was not even nominated. The vacant seats went to a Pepsi-Cola distributor from Portland and a Goldendale veterinarian who specialized in horses, cows and other large animals. Stung, Stevenson resigned as co-chair of the museum's planned 50th anniversary gala—and went back to the attorney general. While Attorney General Slade Gordon was not particularly interested in the issue, he was also not interested in alienating wealthy and politically active potential campaign donors, especially since he had plans to run for a U.S. Senate seat.

So Gordon assigned an assistant attorney general named Rod Carrier to the case. Carrier promptly began dragging his feet, apparently hoping the issue would be taken care of by Maryhill trustees or simply run out of steam on its own. It didn't. Frustrated by Carrier's indolence, Stevenson formed a volunteer "advisory committee" consisting of herself, Stanford professors Elsen and Merryman and several Campbell enthusiasts. The committee's main purpose was to keep the heat on the attorney general's office to act.

"We made it clear that we would not go to the press with information of this scandal so that you could bargain for resignation of all the trustees," Elsen threatened Carrier at one point. "... Unless I am given an up-to-date report on what is happening, as soon as possible, I for one will go to the press with all that I know."

Meanwhile, several non-Campbell enthusiasts—namely the Maryhill trustees—decided to sue their former director, alleging he "negligently and willfully caused substantial monetary loss to the museum" through his slapdash management. Campbell shrugged off the allegations. "I view (the) churlish charges with pliant good humor," he said. "When a responsible new board of trustees has been named I am confident they will seriously review these interesting allegations and respond to them from a proper perspective."

In February 1977, the trustees and Stevenson's advisory committee met to work out details of a compromise proposed by the attorney general's office. Under it, the trustees would agree to change Maryhill's bylaws to limit board tenure to two successive three-year terms and expand the size of the board. In return, no charges of mismanagement would be filed against trustees or Cliff. An interim board composed of current trustees and members of Stevenson's committee would be established until a permanent board could be picked.

But the deal fell apart when the advisory committee rammed through a plan that would in effect have given Campbell supporters the authority to pick the permanent board. The trustees were able to block the maneuver through a legal technicality that required the current board president, longtime trustee Arvid Leppaluoto, to sign new articles of incorporation, which he refused to do.

With the deal a dead duck, a legal war erupted. On April 4, 1977, the board filed suit against the attorney general's office, alleging it had reneged on a promise not to stack the interim board with Campbell's friends and supporters, or "anyone else who might have some preconceived notion (for or against) on museum operations." The next day, the attorney general countersued, seeking to oust the trustees and recover damages for various acts of mismanagement that ranged from not conducting annual audits to trustees buying or borrowing museum items to decorate their homes.

As the suits inched painfully through the courts, a war of words raged in the Pacific Northwest press. Elsen, who only two years before had declared

Maryhill had "the makings of greatness," now sneered that it was "a pit stop, a place to go to the bathroom between Portland and God knows where." Mary Stevenson, who had kick-started the legal fight, contended that "if there can legally be such a thing as family abuse and child abuse, then the situation at Maryhill could really be characterized as cultural abuse."

Museum trustees countered by releasing a long list of missteps and blunders they said had occurred under Campbell. They also characterized Attorney General Slade Gordon as a bully trying to intimidate one of the state's cultural and historical treasures. "If they want us to leave," declared board president Leppaluoto, "they'll have to pack us out on stretchers before we'll turn the museum over to that committee."

It took a year, but as it turned out no stretchers were needed. Mindful of the enormous legal costs piling up, trustees agreed to a settlement with Gordon, who was mindful of the political fallout piling up. In April 1978, it was agreed, among other changes, that Maryhill would henceforth be governed by an expanded board of at least nine trustees, who would be elected by dues-paying public "members of the museum."

"As far as the state is concerned, the questions which prompted the lawsuit(s) have been completely and fully resolved," Gordon wrote in an open letter to Maryhill attorney John Moore. "...In short, I believe that Maryhill is presenting a very great asset to Washington culture and deserves the public's enthusiastic support."

In September 1979, a month after Cliff's death, the board settled with Campbell. While denying the allegations, he agreed to put in writing that "I regret any acts on my part which may have given the museum cause for concern." He also agreed to pay Maryhill $10,000, all of which was covered by contributions from his supporters, including Mary Stevenson. "I feel that Bob did more good for the museum than any amount of harm shown by the board in their suit," she said in a note to trustees accompanying her check. "I believe that time will prove this to be true."

While Maryhill trustees, California professors, state lawyers, dismissed directors and various art lovers were jousting over bylaws and missing baskets, someone was making sure the museum's doors opened each day on time. Her name was Dorothy Brokaw, and she fit snugly into what had become a Maryhill tradition of unlikely directors.

A soft-spoken woman who wore oversized eyeglasses and 60s-style hair-dos, Brokaw was a native of nearby Goldendale. She had worked for the city as a coordinator of volunteer programs before becoming a receptionist and secretary at Maryhill in 1972. Impressed by her diligence and organizational skills, Campbell made her his administrative assistant. When he was fired, trustees asked her to take over as interim director. Quickly realizing the job could overwhelm her if she tackled it alone, Brokaw recruited her brother and a friend of his to help out. Her brother, Harvey Freer, was an elementary school teacher with experience in antiques and art restoration, and a knack for exhibit display. David Coomler was an avid and talented researcher. None of them had a background in museum administration.

But they did have determination, enthusiasm and at least in Dorothy's case, loads of self-assurance. "My initial uneasiness has changed to confidence as I have seen the chaos that was Maryhill take form and order under my management," she wrote to board president Leppaluoto just four months after replacing Campbell. "When I first began, my task was to hold the museum together; that goal was long ago reached and passed, and now I am in the process of improving the museum in many areas; my efforts have already begun to bear fruit." Brokaw asked that the board give her at least one full year in the job to prove herself. "I do not think this is a return to the 'Dolph Days,'" she said. "I prefer to think of us as having 'Dorothy Days.'"

"Dorothy Days" stretched into seven years, and Maryhill slowly began its evolution into modernity that had been promised under Campbell. The collections—which were in such shambles that a between-floors crawlspace was found crammed with Indian baskets and the workshop attic with everything from Pierre Roche plasters to the lower jaw of a mastodon—were reorganized and cataloged. An anthropologist from the University of Washington was hired to sort out the Native American collection. "Everything was so mixed up, she couldn't really see what she was working with," Freer related to a reporter. "But as she groped through the collection and was able to group the pieces stylistically, she got more and more excited. She ended up calling it one of the finest in the country—if not the finest—for its quality and breadth."

With Freer and Coomler, Brokaw visited the Palace of Fine Arts in San Francisco in an effort to get back some of the items Alma had given Maryhill and then taken back. They struck out on retrieving Whistler's "The Gold Scab," but did score several other pieces, including a Pierre Roche painting of Loie. Brokaw transformed what had been basically a postcard kiosk at Maryhill into a full-fledged gift shop. A $50,000 state grant was obtained to patch the museum's aging concrete, and a National Endowment for the Arts grant paid for redesign and restoration of galleries and showcases. Marie's coronation gown, long a favorite with the public, was restored and displayed in a special case built by Freer.

The improvements were duly noted by the press. "The museum has never looked better, more professional and more prepared to welcome yet another season's worth of souls adventurous enough to make the trek," the *Oregon Journal's* art editor wrote in March 1980. "In the past four years, Maryhill's tiny but hard-working staff has made a valiant effort …".

Annual numbers of "those adventurous enough to make the trek" were fairly impressive through the "Dorothy Days," despite the bad publicity stemming from the museum's breathlessly-reported legal strife. From 1975 to 1982, annual attendance averaged about 65,000, which was not bad for a rural museum that was closed four months of the year.

The museum's board was mindful that to keep the crowds coming, Maryhill had to maintain its unique eccentricity and not overreact to the charges it was more a roadside attraction than an art museum. To that end, trustees adopted a new mission statement that the museum "exists to house, preserve, exhibit and interpret the collection given by Queen Marie of Romania, Samuel Hill, Alma de Bretteville Spreckels and Loie Fuller so that the desire of those benefactors to create a museum for the education and pleasure of the general public may continue to be a reality." The board also dropped the "fine" from the museum's self-designation as a "museum of fine arts," noting that "the museum must strike a balance between scholarly and public appeal it should be kept in mind that Maryhill is different in that the historical aspect of the museum is as important to the general public as the works of art; the union of the two should be preserved."

Stung by the "dumping ground" charge hurled by Elsen and others, trustees adopted a formal acquisitions policy. Romanian folk art, Loie-related items, Native American objects, Greek and Russian Orthodox religious icons and Art Nouveau glass were in. Contemporary paintings, antiquities and art not associated with the four founders were out. Additional Rodin pieces were deemed too expensive to seek. And while the chess sets would be kept because of their popularity, new sets would be acquired only if they were gifts.

But with all the progress, there were also inevitable bumps in the road. Some were embarrassing: One of the Rodin drawings was stolen off the wall in mid-afternoon in 1981. (It was returned, unharmed and anonymously, two years later. But the thief kept the cheap frame it was in.) Some were disturbing: The same year as the Rodin theft, a man was stabbed to death at Stonehenge during an annual weekend gathering of motorcycle gangs at the World War I war memorial. But the biggest bumps, inevitably, were financial.

Like most museums, Maryhill sat on a mountain of wealth with only a molehill of revenue to protect, preserve and exhibit its treasures. In 1980, for example, the museum's net assets amounted to an estimated $1.7 million (about $5.4 million in 2017 dollars.) That included the collections, the building and the land, but not the modest equities portfolio representing the remainder of Sam's original endowment. The operating budget was $176,000. But revenues from admissions, gift shop sales, donations and investments came to only $162,000. Moreover, mainly because of its legal bills, Maryhill owed more than $125,000 to a Seattle bank, and just paying the 9 percent interest rate on the note gobbled up more than its stocks-and-bonds investments were making.

Trustees pondered various ways to raise money, including a possible sale of Maryhill's vast acreage. Revenues from the ranch, once the museum's financial mainstay, had become marginal at best. A government reclassification of the land as "open space" had cut property taxes in half, but most of the land was largely unusable for agriculture. In the end, the board decided to hold on to the property, in part because if it was ever developed, Maryhill would lose the sense of "splendid isolation" that was part of its character. It did grant an energy company a lease to explore the land for natural gas and oil, which brought the museum $52,900.

And the board agreed to sell up to 100 annual bird hunting permits for $200 each on a portion of the property. The permits included free admission to the museum. Maryhill thus became the only institution in the world to offer its patrons a chance to view Rodin bronzes and shoot quail and chukar on the same visit.

In January 1982, Maryhill hit a bump at least as painful as its financial problems, when the American Association of Museums turned down its request for accreditation. Few U.S. museums could meet the AAM's lofty requirements, and Maryhill didn't come close. According to the AAM's visiting committee, Maryhill lacked adequate security, had no legitimate inventory of its collection, needed an education coordinator and better storage facilities, and should have its staff become more familiar with modern museum practices by observing other museums. But at the heart of the turndown was Maryhill's failure to explain just what it was and why it was there.

"Something should be done to acquaint the visitor with the unique collection waiting to be viewed before he gets absorbed in collections at hand, and loses, in the process, all sense of what he is seeing," the committee wrote. "Maryhill requires interpretation for the general visitor, explaining the history and significance of the objects on display, as well as the personalities of the people which they reflect."

The AAM rejection hit Brokaw hard, and she began to fulminate privately that some of the trustees were pleased with the result because the association's standards were too exacting and expensive. Like Cliff and Campbell before her, she also complained about what she regarded as the board's passive-aggressive philosophy of governing: Trustees made few positive suggestions but reacted emphatically and negatively to staff proposals. As evidence, she said, they had not approved a single notable acquisition during her tenure, despite numerous staff requests. In fact, the only new major acquisition—ironically given the trustees' formal acquisitions policy—was a collection of antique chess sets valued at $84,000 and donated by a Michigan doctor who chose Maryhill over the Louvre.

"During most of my time at Maryhill, the board has been an obstacle to progress, which we (the staff) accepted," she said when she finally went public with her frustration. "… We accepted their functioning in general as sort of a benign dead weight."

Things came to a head in February 1983. Brokaw, without consulting the board, had elevated David Coomler's position as associate curator from a half-time position to full-time. Board members reacted by eliminating the job altogether, citing budget problems, and did so without consulting Brokaw first. Furious, Brokaw and her brother, curator David Freer, resigned, although Freer later withdrew his resignation and stayed on another year.

"I will be leaving as quickly as my position is filled," Brokaw wrote the board. "I have no choice for I will not continue without the respect due my position as administrator." Maryhill, she said, had received "as much bad publicity as has ever been given to a museum now Maryhill is once again in the public eye, and the old, negative statements are being repeated."

Then the publicity got worse. A few months after Brokaw's resignation, the board faced an election that posed Maryhill at a crossroads. Two informal slates of candidates emerged for four seats on the board. One side was a status-quo faction led by some incumbent trustees. The other side, led by local business and community leaders, wanted to add some razzle-dazzle to the museum and make it a must-see tourist attraction.

"There will be either a perpetuation of the status quo, with some growth and orderly development or there will be some fairly imaginative and perhaps aggressive efforts to increase the awareness of the museum and the real asset that it is," said trustee Keith Mobley, an attorney from The Dalles who wasn't up for re-election and assumed a role of neutrality. "I think that's really the heart of it. Some people would like to see it remain much as it has been; there are others who would like to see more happening."

What happened was the go-slows outmaneuvered the go-fasters. There were 164 dues-paying museum members eligible to vote. That is until someone—most probably trustee Arvid Leppaluoto—paid the $15 annual fee for 418 people just before the election. As a result, all three incumbents up for re-election easily won, along with a fourth candidate who shared their views. "I have no apologies for the deliberate and unhurried fashion in which we are proceeding," said trustee Muriel Hager after the vote.

Seven years after the firing of Bob Campbell, Maryhill was thus right back where it was then: without a director and up to its ears in bad press. "If Maryhill is to pull out of the most recent slump, it must hire a top-flight professional to replace the departing Brokaw, and not simply a rubber stamp for whoever happens to be controlling the board," a regional arts magazine observed. "So far, things look less than promising."

NOTES FOR CHAPTER 12

Best of all, given Director's report, Feb. 17, 1975, MMA.

There was no paucity Ibid.

"There is a tremendous" *Klickitat County Ruralite*, June 1975, p. 21.

The locals weren't the *Goldendale Sentinel*, Feb. 13, 1975, p. 5.

Campbell did indeed Director's report, Feb. 17, 1975, MMA.

The botched portrait Ibid.

None of the setbacks Portland *Oregonian*, March 17, 1975, p. 11.

"They are very weak" Portland *Oregonian*, March 28, 1975, p. 9.

"His donations to Maryhill" Cliff to Emory Strong, April 17, 1969, MMA.

But Campbell was tenacious Draft copy of proposed newspaper ad, April 16, 1977, MMA.

About the same time Executive committee minutes, Nov. 8, 1974; Nov. 20, 1974, MMA.

Shortly after the inventory Cliff to Julius Carlebach, Sept. 6, 1962; Cliff to Carlebach, Jan. 16, 1963, MMA.

While Campbell was Cliff to James Scripps, March 25, 1975, MMA.

The next twist in *Salem (Or.) Capital Journal*, Sept. 9, 1975, p. 19.

Trustee Scripps, who James Scripps to Robert Campbell and Arvid Leppaluoto, Dec. 18, 1975, MMA.

But Leppaluoto wasn't John B. Moore to Arvid Leppaluoto, April 16, 1976, MMA.

Moore itemized Cliff's Ibid.

In a follow-up letter John B. Moore to Arvid Leppaluoto, April 19, 1976, MMA.

The board took Moore's Harold Fariello to Cliff, April 16, 1977, MMA.

Naturally, none of this *Goldendale Sentinel*, March 26, 1975, p. 3; *Portland Oregonian*, March 26, 1976, p. C1.

According to Elsen Albert Elsen to Robert Campbell, August 14, 1974, MMA.

With Cliff gone, however Albert Elsen to Robert Campbell, Nov. 15, 1974; Robert Campbell to Albert Elsen, March 18, 1975, MMA.

Elsen had some ideas "Breaches of Trust: Museums, Ethics and the Law," *ARTnews*, December 1982, p. 52.

Elsen suggested that Campbell Albert Elsen to Robert Campbell, March 23, 1975, MMA.

"Maryhill Museum is" Mary Stevenson to Gov. Daniel Evans, June 27, 1975, MMA.

In March 1976, Mary Mary Stevenson application, March 12, 1976, MMA.

Her stated enthusiasm Board minutes, May 21 and May 22, 1976, MMA.

"We made it clear" Albert Elsen to Rod Carrier, Nov. 7, 1976, MMA.

Meanwhile, several non-Campbell *Goldendale Sentinel*, March 3, 1977, p. 1.

While the suits inched *Vancouver (Wa.) Columbian*, March 6, 1977, p. 1; *ARTnews*, March 1977, p. 84.

In September 1979 Settlement agreement, Yakima Co. Superior Court, Sept. 2, 1979, Item No. 78-2-0412-7; St. Pierre, *op. cit.,* p. 335.

But they did have Dorothy Brokaw to Arvid Leppaluoto, July 21, 1976, MMA.

"Dorothy Days" stretched *Northwest Magazine*, July 12, 1981, pp. 12-13.

The improvements were duly *Oregon Journal*, Match 27, 1980, p. 27.

The museum's board was Maryhill Board of Trustees mission statement and acquisitions policy, November 1977, MMA.

"Something should be done" American Association of Museums to Dorothy Brokaw, Jan. 12, 1982, MMA.

"During most of my time" *Goldendale Sentinel*, May 26, 1983, p. 1.

"I will be leaving as" Brokaw to Board of Trustees, Feb. 23, 1983, MMA.

"There will either be" Portland *Oregonian*, April 3, 1983, p. 12.

What happened was Portland *Oregonian*, May 22, 1983, p. C7.

Seven years after *Northwest Arts magazine*, May 22, 1983.

CHAPTER THIRTEEN

"Resurrection of the Phoenix"

MAY 1990

There was only so much cake to go around, even if it was a pretty big cake, and had cost $1,093. So the fellow serving it to the hundreds of people attending the Golden Anniversary party of the Maryhill Museum of Art had been told to cut it in pieces of no more than two square inches. "It's a gesture," cautioned a board trustee, "not a meal."

Actually, it was more of a miracle. Fifty years after it had first opened its doors to 242 guests, Maryhill was hosting more than 4,000 celebrants of what the cake's frosting-inscription said was "50 years of art on the Columbia River"—and the fact that against formidable odds, Maryhill's doors were still open. Along with the small-but symbolic chocolate confection (the entirety of which had been decorated with a very good likeness of the museum,) guests were entertained by actors portraying Sam, Loie, Alma and Queen Marie; a demonstration of stunt kite flying, and an appearance by a fully restored 1914 Locomobile that had once been owned by Sam himself. The museum's first board of trustees had sold it during the Great Depression to help make ends meet. Now, after changing hands several times over the decades, it had chugged up the east ramp and was parked near the museum's entrance.

"The last few years have shown a considerable upswing," board President Alexander "Sandy" Thomson told the museum's annual members' meeting. "Measured by virtually any parameter, there has been very significant progress. Today we inherit the task of firming the foundation and maintaining the impetus."

Maryhill's "impetus" was measurably impressive. Since the resignation of Dorothy Brokaw and the struggle for control of the board of trustees in 1983, annual attendance had risen from 54,000 to more than 72,000 in 1990. The permanent staff grew from two to 10; the operating budget from less that $250,000 a year to more than $450,000, and the museum's "nest egg" endowment from $995,000 to a bit more than $1.8 million.

Given Maryhill's traditional eclecticism, the key factors behind the museum's rise from the ashes of what was quietly referred to as "the dark days" were suitably varied, from a collection of French poupées to a professor of French history. They also included a fatherly fruit-packing executive, wealthy donors—both unexpected and mistrusted—and a bubbly 26-year-old woman who was, in her own words, "eager, determined, very green and scared to death."

The first time Linda Brady Mountain ever saw even a likeness of the Maryhill Museum of Art was when she opened an envelope one morning in the spring of 1983 at her Columbus Ohio home. Inside was a gray piece of stationery with the museum's silhouette on its letterhead. The letter acknowledged the museum had received her application, along with those of 19 other people, to become its next director.

Although she had grown up in Eugene Oregon, only about 200 miles from Maryhill, Mountain (who eventually remarried and changed her name to Linda Brady Tesner) had never heard of the museum prior to learning of the job opening and applying. Friends warned her that as a self-described "city girl," she would grow to hate living in so isolated a location. And even with her master's degree in art history from Ohio State University and experience as assistant director of the university's art gallery, "I was so young and so green I knew I wouldn't get it anyway," she recalled in a 2015 interview.

Still, she applied for the job because she wanted to return to the Pacific Northwest. She figured that at worst, applying would help her begin networking with museum people in the region. On a visit to her parents in the spring of 1983, Mountain met with a Maryhill board member, talked on the phone with another, attended a meeting at the museum—and in November 1983 officially became the fourth director in the museum's history. Her starting salary was $20,000 (about $43,500 in 2017 dollars). She and her husband, who worked for Ohio State and traveled continually, were given a house to live in on the museum grounds. The house came complete with mice in the walls, wildlife—and the occasional cow—that wandered through the yard, and a few decorative touches left by Bob Campbell, such as a stripe of black tire paint circling the living room.

"It was the best place I ever lived and the best job I ever had in my life," she said years later. "(But) the museum was in absolute tatters from the top down. Everything had to be redone, because everything had been done so unprofessionally."

News of her appointment was met with cautious optimism. "Maryhill had not what you would call a good track record," said Glen Mason, director of the Cheney Cowles Memorial Museum in Spokane. "I think a lot of people who had seen what was going on from a distance breathed a sigh of relief when they finally had a professional director." Before the museum's 1984 annual meeting—Mountain's first—Portland *Oregonian* art critic Alan Hayakawa noted "the remote museum's friends and supporters must be hoping that better times are ahead for the institution."

Mountain and board president Herb Frank ensured better times, at least for the annual meeting: Instead of the long and acrimonious rhetorical fireworks that had marked the 1983 gathering, the business portion of the 1984 meeting was kept to 30 minutes, after which attendees were offered box lunches and a choice of behind-the-scenes tours of the museum's collections or the ranch lands.

"Herb was my savior, my mentor, my go-to guy," Tesner said. "The board was very nervous about things and very hands-on. Herb made sure I had room to organize and operate things."

A Chicagoan by birth and civil engineer by training, Herbert L. Frank settled in Washington's Yakima Valley in 1947 and bought an apple orchard. Eventually he opened a fruit-packing and storage facility that became one of the largest in the region. Laid-back and likeable, he was chosen by Maryhill's board as president in May 1983, and promptly gave the trustees a pep talk in the form of an anatomy lesson. Noting the difference between a pat on the back and a kick in the butt was about 18 inches, Frank made a suggestion: "Let's raise our sights 18 inches."

With the backing of Frank, who served as board president until 1987, Mountain began making changes. Harvey Freer, the high school art teacher who had been serving as curator under his sister, Mountain's predecessor Dorothy Brokaw, was replaced by Stephen J. Broocks, formerly the executive director of an Illinois art museum. Broocks' chief task was to catalog Maryhill's sizeable and disparate collection, for the first time according to professional museum standards.

To attract repeat visitors, the museum began hosting well-publicized traveling exhibits at least three times a season. The subjects ranged from musical instruments, quilts and wine labels as works of art to dolls' houses designed by some of the world's leading architects, collections of Old West art and life-sized "photo sculptures." A summer concert series was initiated, most often performed in the Queen Marie gallery and featuring music as varied as Baroque chamber quartets, jazz trios and folk-singing duos.

Mountain began a four-to-six-page quarterly newsletter for museum members, with book reviews, background stories on Maryhill art and artifacts, and news about the museum. "The potential to introduce our visitors to the fine arts, to educate, inform and entertain our guests is great," she wrote in the first edition. "Realizing this potential, it is my key goal to make Maryhill a more *interactive* museum, a place where *participation* is an essential ingredient of our success."

To do that, she realized she would need help, particularly in areas where she freely professed to have little aptitude or interest. And finally, after decades of problematic hiring practices, Maryhill began to get lucky.

One of the tasks Mountain hated most was schmoozing—talking to reporters, drumming up publicity and buttering up potential donors. So when she met Ross Randall, it was, in a professional sense, love at first sight. "He was like Sam Hill, a born publicist," she said. "He did things for the museum no one else had ever done before in terms of getting favorable attention and making Maryhill come to life."

A native of nearby Goldendale, the 23-year-old Randall had a freshly printed degree in public relations in June 1985, and an intern's job at the *Goldendale Sentinel.* Mountain convinced him to become Maryhill's first director of public relations—and also work the admissions desk. He would eventually become the museum's first development officer, which translated to chief fundraiser, and after leaving Maryhill in the mid-1990s go on to a long and successful career in museums around the country.

Ten months after hiring Randall, Mountain hired a 28-year-old woman from Corvallis Oregon named Colleen Schafroth. Schafroth had a talent for drawing, a love of art history and a pending masters degree from Oregon State University. A recent outside assessment of Maryhill had concluded that, among other things, the museum needed an education curator. "I interviewed Colleen, and I can still feel myself sitting in my chair and thinking 'oh my God, this is the person," Tesner recalled. "She turned out to be a world-class curator of education."

A signature Schafroth project was creating a "Museum Week," in which school children from the region attended half- or full-day sessions at Maryhill. The sessions included meeting artists who created while they talked to the kids; hands-on workshops where they painted, drew or sculpted, and games that focused on discovering why they liked or disliked particular art objects. The first year drew 400 students; the second 750, the third more than 1,100. "I didn't have a budget of any kind," Schafroth said in a 2016 interview, "so not knowing how much I could spend, if anything, I had to be creative."

She was also put in charge of the gift shop and supervised the museum's volunteer programs. "We would work the front desk on weekends, paint, clean the display cabinets," Schafroth said. "We had one phone when I started, and it was a party line. If you needed to call someone, you had to get on and ask 'are you going to be much longer, I need the phone!' It was a pretty small operation."

It was also the start of a key part of Maryhill's evolution, marking the transformation of a staff from the well-intentioned to the well-qualified. In 1988, a third key hire appeared in the form of an experienced collections manager named Betty Long. An expert in textile arts, Long would have a 22-year Maryhill career.

"Having quality people in all the key positions allowed us to professionalize the way Maryhill operated," Tesner said. "I really think it began to change into a relevant art museum from sort of an historical oddity."

An early contributor to Maryhill's history, if not necessarily its oddness, showed up in November 1986 to help celebrate the 60th anniversary of the museum's dedication by Queen Marie. The queen's daughter, the former Princess Ileana was now Mother Alexandra, abbess of an Eastern Orthodox monastery in Pennsylvania. She nostalgically perused items that had once belonged to her royal family and helped identify some objects. What museum staff had thought was an umbrella handle, for example, turned out to be part of a Turkish smoking device. At the rededication ceremony, which drew a crowd estimated at 2,500, the 77-year-old princess-turned-nun couldn't help but notice there had been some changes made. "Quite honestly, there was not much to see (in 1926)," she remembered. "(But) my mother was a very understanding person. She could see it would become something."

Even so, Maryhill retained a hefty measure of uniqueness. For example, there were the signs in the parking lot cautioning visitors to watch out for rattlesnakes. And new employees were warned that the museum had a life—or lives—of its own. Doors opened and closed, seemingly by themselves. Footsteps were heard on the stairs when no one could be seen walking on them, and the visitor elevator sometimes ran by itself. Operations manager Pat Perry was convinced she had actually seen Sam Hill a time or two, seated at an office desk or disappearing around a corner on mornings before the museum opened. Reminded by a reporter that Sam had once said he expected Maryhill "to be here for a thousand years after I am gone," Perry replied "he's checking things out. I think he's pleased."

Whether it was Sam's perceived presence or the museum's new aura of professionalism, Maryhill began to attract donors in the last two decades of the 20th century, both symbolic and significant. Among the former was a gift from a familiar name: Spreckels. In 1989, an employee of the sugar company was visiting Maryhill when he learned of its deep ties to Alma. When he returned to work and told his boss, the company was moved—although not very deeply: It sent the museum's café, which had opened the year before, a crate of sugar packets.

Other gifts were more substantial. Robert Ives Gammell gave outright 23 of his paintings, bringing the museum's Boston School collection to more than 50, by 12 different artists. A painting by the esteemed Old West artist Charles Russell that had been on indefinite loan to the museum and was valued at more than $400,000 was made an outright gift. Elizabeth Wade, who was widely acknowledged to be one of Sam's illegitimate children, donated her 1,500-volume library of art history books. And a collector of Rodin's art who admired Maryhill's compilation of the master's pieces, gave a rare example of Rodin's early work, a terra cotta sculpture called "The Crying

Lion." Specific gifts were made to finance publication of a richly illustrated book on Maryhill's chess sets, written by Schafroth, and a museum guide replete with photos of the collections and written by Mountain.

There were even hidden treasures. In November 1996, someone figured out how to operate an intricate hidden lock on a chest that had not been opened for at least 25 years. Inside were chunks of old wood—Sam's purported pieces of the Pilgrim ship *Mayflower.*

The most utilitarian gifts, however, were those that could be spent. In 1988, a New York City woman, Irene Bie-Corsani, donated more than a dozen Romanian art objects—and a $200,000 endowment in cash and securities, the largest such gift Maryhill had ever received. Her father had been with Queen Marie at the post-World War I peace conference in Paris, and later Romanian ambassador to the Vatican, which explained Bie-Corsani's affinity for a museum 3,000 miles away.

Bie-Corsani's generous gift was dwarfed four years later by a hefty $1 million, no-strings donation by someone who insisted on remaining anonymous. The mystery donor, it turned out, was an old friend of Maryhill's—or an old enemy, depending on who was assessing the relationship.

After being rejected as a trustee candidate, seeing her friend Bob Campbell fired as director and ending up on the losing side of the fight to take control of the museum board in the 1970s, Mary Hoyt Stevenson had backed off her efforts to "reform" Maryhill. She still occasionally attended the board's annual meetings each May but was either ignored or regarded with suspicion by many of the trustees.

In 1990, however, the Stevensons made an unexpected $5,000 contribution to Maryhill, followed in January 1992 by a $75,000 gift. Six months later, the museum received $500,000 in cash and $500,000 in securities from a donor whose only condition was anonymity. It was pretty much an open secret around Maryhill, however, as to who the donor was.

"I don't know exactly what brought her back," Laura Cheney, Stevenson's oldest daughter, said in a 2018 interview. "But she was a tenacious woman I don't know, in the end, that she actually 'came back' to the museum. I think that everyone realized there had been a big problem, and she brought it to light."

Not coincidentally, Stevenson was elected to the Maryhill board in 1993 and served as an active member for eight years. "Money talks," conceded Cheney, who herself is a museum trustee and generous donor. "But I don't think my mother ever indicated that she wanted to control the place. I think she just wanted to make things right."

The money was desperately needed to fuel far more than Maryhill's expanding payroll. Sam's chateau was falling apart. The mansion's stucco was peeling, the concrete crumbling and entry ramps cracking. In 1989, the board spent $127,000 ($264,000 in 2017) on a major overhaul of the building's exterior. Stucco and concrete were repaired, retaining walls and balustrades replaced and the entire structure painted. The following year, another $50,000-plus was poured into the problem of the porous entrance ramps, which leaked onto the galleries below with alarming regularity.

While Maryhill's body was being rejuvenated, so was its reputation. "I went to my first AAM (American Association of Museums) convention in 1984," Linda Tesner said. "When people looked at my ID badge, they would start to laugh. They were acutely aware of what a shambles the museum was in...it was embarrassing."

Within five years, however, the embarrassment had passed, enough so that she eagerly presented a 26-page paper on Maryhill's history at an AAM conference session with the apt title "Resurrection of the Phoenix." "It has taken a long time and energy of many people to turn Maryhill around," she told the conferees. "… But the museum has evolved we still are the subject of national publicity, but now it is overwhelmingly positive."

While the museum's turnaround could be attributed, as Mountain did, to the "time and the energy" of the staff and board, the favorable national publicity was due in large part to the serendipitous combination of an Ohio university professor, a Paris-based magazine editor, and the collection of French fashion mini-mannequins Maryhill had salvaged from a San Francisco department store basement.

The professor was Stanley N. Garfinkel, who for more than 30 years taught French history at Kent State University. Garfinkel was also a film documentarian. In 1984, while working on a film about the legendary French designer Christian Dior, Garfinkel heard a rumor that a small Washington state museum had a collection of French fashion dolls from the 1940s. Intrigued, he visited Maryhill—and was flabbergasted by what he found. Garfinkel shared his "discovery" with Susan Train, who was the Paris editor for Conde Nast Publications, which produced the fashion periodical *Vogue*. Train visited Maryhill the following year—and was equally flabbergasted.

"It was like a miracle," Train said. "I'd heard about the dolls before, but nobody seemed to know where they were." Soon an idea began to sprout. The mannequins, the Portland *Oregonian* noted, "have stood poised on wire frame legs in plain glass cases, a frozen moment of fashion history since the mid-1950s. But recently, they've been rediscovered by the European designer community, and rumors of putting the mannequins on the road again have begun to ripple across the Atlantic."

It was more than rumors. In 1988, the Maryhill mannequins were on their way to Paris. A collaboration that included the museum, the French government, the New York Metropolitan Museum of Art, a Tokyo art gallery and the editors of *Vogue* had agreed the dolls deserved a makeover. "Imagine going 40 years without a coiffure," quipped the fashion editor Train.

Betty Long, Maryhill's newly hired collections manager and a fabrics expert, carefully cataloged, photographed and packed the fragile mannequins into 10 crates and sent them off—with Linda Mountain's accompaniment—to Paris. There, they were over the course of a year lovingly groomed with tiny vacuums, their hair restored, their costumes mended and cleaned. Nine of the original 15 sets were rebuilt, some of the work overseen by the original designers.

The curtain rose on the reborn Théâtre de la Mode at the Louvre in the spring of 1990. After a triumphant stint, the exhibit moved to New York and equally large crowds and rave reviews. "The clothes and designs can scarcely be believed, with details exact to the tiniest button," wrote the *Baltimore Sun*. "This exhibit is magnificent in its smallness." Other cities followed Paris and New York: Tokyo, Portland, Baltimore, Honolulu. The mannequins finally came home in 1996, although there were occasional smaller-scale loans after that.

Maryhill made little money from the tour, but the non-cash returns were huge. "The consideration to Maryhill was the substantial increase in value of the collection by the re-creation of the sets, the cleaning and restoration and the attendant public notice and recognition for the collection and the museum," a staff report noted. Left unsaid was the accompanying cleaning and restoration of Maryhill's reputation in the museum world.

"The future looks very bright for Maryhill Museum," Mountain wrote in the Spring/Summer 1991 museum newsletter. "The promising growth of the museum audience, the international importance of the Théâtre de la Mode project, the development plans to improve and expand our physical facilities and programs are all very exciting together we hold the potential that will make us all proud of our association with Sam Hill's dream."

But Mountain's dream-association was about to end. The theatre tour had been a major triumph in what would be a long and distinguished museum career. But it was not enough to keep her at Maryhill. Neither was the doubling of her salary in 1990 to $40,000 ($79,000 in 2017 dollars), nor her election to a second term as president of the Washington Museum Association. Her marriage had foundered, and Maryhill's isolation had worn her down. After a short-lived effort—with the board's support—to commute from Portland to the museum, Mountain resigned as Maryhill's director in March 1992. The museum's bright future had clouded over, again.

For Josie De Falla, Maryhill was a land of fire and ice. Slightly more than a month after taking over as the new director in June 1992 and moving into the charming-but-run-down cottage behind the museum, De Falla had been roused by firefighters in the middle of the night and evacuated from the roaring flames of a wildfire that scorched a thousand acres and swept within a few hundred feet of the museum.

Five months later, Maryhill's steep entry road was so frozen the museum's ancient Subaru couldn't make it up the drive. Staff members took turns shoveling snow from the steps. Space heaters brought in to help boost the museum's fixed—and chilly—closed-season heating system overloaded the electrical system and shut down the computers.

Even so, the 57-year-old De Falla had had worse jobs in what had been a 30-year museum career that encompassed stints in Colorado, New York, California, Oregon and Peru. Her background even included working on a llama ranch where, she smilingly told Maryhill trustees, "I learned how to mend fences." Unsaid was the fact that the Maryhill job was something of a consolation prize. De Falla, one of 55 applicants to replace Linda Mountain, had wanted to head the Bowers Museum in Southern California, where she had been assistant director for several years. But apparently sensing she would not get the job, she withdrew a month before it was filled citing "other job opportunities." Those turned out to be Maryhill, where she won a two-year contract at a salary slightly higher than Mountain had been getting.

Quiet to the point of secretiveness—some of the Maryhill staff didn't even know if she was married—De Falla nonetheless brought a wealth of experience, confidence and determination to the post. Most of the key staff she inherited stayed on, although publicist/development officer Ross Randall left soon after Mountain. He was replaced by Lee Musgrave, an artist and veteran museum man from Los Angeles who for nearly 15 years would function not only as Maryhill's chief spokesman, but as its curator.

But while most of the staff remained, much of Maryhill's stuff moved. Items that were more curiosities than art, such as a life mask of Sam Hill and the gun collection, were put in "visible storage" areas, where they were out of the way but could still be seen by visitors peering through small windows into the room. The Rodin collection, which had been on the third floor, was moved to the bottom floor galleries. "The top floor vibrates and some of the sculptures were developing hairline cracks," a museum spokesman explained. "The main floor is concrete and there is no vibration."

Unfortunately, the collection was also right next to the museum's small café, which meant "The Thinker" competed for attention with the whir of the espresso machine. The good news was that moving the Rodins made room for displaying three of the wildly popular Théâtre de la Mode sets. "We've received so much publicity from that collection," the spokesman said. "It has put us on the map, more so than our Rodins."

The Rodins, however, weren't the only things cracking. As bad as the museum's exterior had deteriorated, its interior was worse. Both the labyrinthine plumbing and electrical systems were dangerously out of date, and the building did not comply with federal disability access laws. Some interior walls needed to be removed to improve sight lines. Paint was peeling off the walls and buckets to catch dripping rainwater in the galleries under the entrance rotundas were a common sight. Museum staff and board trustees knew renovation and repairs that extensive would mean closing the museum, perhaps for an entire season—and would be very expensive. It was estimated just moving things out of the way would cost $100,000. "We have no time frame (for starting the work)," De Falla glumly told a reporter in early 1996. "We have lots of money to raise."

How much was open to question, and earnestly debated by the board. Anticipated costs started at $2 million, then ratcheted up to $2.6 million, then $3.6 million. Some trustees wanted to approach the makeover incrementally; others favored getting it over with at once. The get-it-done trustees prevailed, and Maryhill launched its first-ever construction capital campaign. De Falla, who had an aversion to asking people for money, nonetheless spent three solid weeks lobbying legislators at the state Capitol in Olympia and wrangled a $500,000 grant from the state of Washington as seed money. But Maryhill would only get the money if it raised at least $1 million on its own. Another $250,000 came from a new source for Maryhill, the M.J. Murdock Charitable Trust. Based in Vancouver, Washington and founded by electronics entrepreneur Jack Murdock, the deep-pocketed trust was to become a major source for funds for the museum.

It took longer than hoped, but the rest of the money was found. In the spring of 1998, the museum was ready for its facelift. "We want to prepare Maryhill for the next hundred years," said spokesman Musgrave. Plans were made to shut down the museum for the 1999 season. Then the project's engineers took another look and realized they had grossly underestimated the amount of work needed and would have to re-evaluate their plans.

So Maryhill opened after all in March 1999, only with not a lot to see. Most of the Rodin collection had been loaned to another museum, and no traveling exhibits had been scheduled. But heeding the adage that desperation is a close relative of invention, curator Musgrave created a display out of a part of the mess. It consisted of a section of a decades-old spaghetti of wires and fuses—and the first electricity meter ever installed in Klickitat County—which had been exposed when a wall was removed. "This is a museum piece itself," Musgrave said with a grin. "It scares electricians to death. They look at it and turn green."

The shocking bit of "art electro" stayed on display until the end of the

2000 season, when Maryhill's interior makeover was finally completed—for just a bit more than $3.6 million. The museum opened for the 2001 season two months later than usual but with better lighting, more reliably flushing toilets, and much calmer electricians.

Other nearby Sam Hill creations also needed work. Stonehenge had deteriorated to the point that rebar showed through its concrete "stones." And the 10-mile "Loop Road" Sam had completed in 1912 to demonstrate the wonders of asphalt highways was riddled with potholes and often copiously decorated with cow poop.

Fixing Stonehenge was relatively simple, though not inexpensive. The museum spent $37,500 in 1995 (about $62,000 in 2017 dollars) to patch the pillars and clear the surrounding grounds of weeds and brush. In the same year, with the trustees' assent, Klickitat County residents completed a war memorial adjacent to Stonehenge that commemorated the county's fallen in conflicts since World War I.

Fixing the Loops Road took longer but cost much less. Using state and federal grants almost exclusively to finance the project, museum officials reopened the road to pedestrians and cyclists in 1999. In succeeding years, it also played host to rallies by both vintage and modern cars and became a world-renowned mecca for gravity sports aficionados on skateboards and street luges. Cattle were banned.

Meanwhile, back at the ranch, the cattle were grazing, crops were growing, hunters were hunting—and trustees were pondering how to make more money from the museum's vast acreage. In Maryhill's early years, board members had directly overseen ranching and farming operations. The cows, pigs, peaches and alfalfa were cared for by museum employees, and the crops and livestock were as much Maryhill property as its paintings and sculptures.

In 1966, however, trustees began leasing the usable parts of the ranch, charging a flat annual fee while still picking up part of the capital improvements costs, such as new fencing. Fifteen years later, the board decided to change its leasing methods. Instead of a flat fee, Maryhill would get an annual fee *plus* a share of the crop, livestock and rock quarry revenues. The museum's ranch income rose from $12,000 a year to between $30,000 and $40,000. The Hunt Club's membership had gradually shrunk as drought and natural predators such as coyotes and mountain lions had depleted the game bird population. But the club still brought in about $5,000 annually. Still, many of Maryhill's trustees, now 17 in number, figured there had to be a way to wring more cash out of all that land.

Ideas came and went, from subdividing and selling parcels, to resurrecting Loie's dream of establishing an artists' colony. There was talk of a golf course, a gas station/truck stop and/or a bed and breakfast inn. A Southern California company proposed taking over management of the property and possibly developing a residential community. An oil company paid a modest sum to do some prospecting for black gold beneath the hills, but nothing came of it.

The most novel proposal—and one that came fairly close to being accepted—was from a local farmer named George Rohrbacher in 1991. A former state legislator and the inventor of a wildly successful board game based on farming, Rohrbacher wanted the trustees to lease him 250 acres of level land just east of the museum, for a nominal sum. On it, he planned to finance and build a hotel, restaurant, amphitheater, gift shop—and an ornate garden that would feature an "English-style" hedge maze on the cliff overlooking the Columbia. It would be "the Disneyland of Mazes," Rohrbacher pitched, and "a gold mine" for the museum, which would share in the profits.

There were two years of on-again, off-again conversation, followed by several weeks of intense negotiations in mid-1993. At one point the board provisionally approved the idea. But ultimately, the deal fell apart. Trustees had too many concerns about an adequate water supply, Rohrbacher's questionable financing and how long the lease should be. Out of ideas, or at least good ones, and also out a few thousand dollars in consultants' fees, the board decided to wait until a good Gorge breeze blew in with a sound and sure money-making use of Maryhill's land.

While trustees considered various plans for outside the museum, they also wrestled with an even more pressing problem: what to do about the museum itself. The extensive repairs and restoration to the building didn't address a major dilemma: the lack of space. With a total of about 20,000 square feet spread across three levels, Maryhill hadn't been built to house a museum. All the painting and patching couldn't make it substantially bigger, even as the collection had grown tremendously.

But expansion was both technically tricky and hugely expensive. Because it was a national historic landmark, there were restrictions on how much the exterior could be changed. Constructing an addition aboveground was less expensive and would provide more space for the money but could change the look of Sam's mansion and would be less energy-efficient. Building underground would have less visual impact and be more eco-conscious but would cost more and would have to be dug out of the basalt rock without explosives, since blasting might damage the existing building.

In 1993, an exuberant Portland architect with long ties to Maryhill presented trustees with plans that would almost double the size of the museum. Gene Callan loved Maryhill. He grew up in nearby Goldendale and had even been married on the museum grounds. Using music, video and slides, he presented computer-generated images of a "once-in-a-lifetime" underground extension. It was replete with storage, gallery space, auditorium, café and outdoor terrace on the edge of the Gorge, and connected to the old museum by a glass corridor that would provide both light and views of majestic Mt. Hood and the Columbia River. Moreover, the addition would not obstruct the view of the original building from either side of the river.

Most of the board liked the design and hated the price tag: $6.7 million. Still, if expansion was inevitable, so were bigger costs the longer it was postponed. Trustees voted to try and raise $12 million by 2000. Mary Stevenson promptly kicked in $500,000 to kick-start the campaign, but the effort withered as almost every available dollar that could be raised during the rest of the decade went to repairs. Moreover, some of the trustees were troubled that even if the herculean task of raising the expansion funds was accomplished, a bigger museum would mean bigger annual operating costs. Those almost certainly wouldn't be covered by admission revenues, gift shop sales and ranch income, no matter how successful the larger museum was.

In fact, Maryhill had already become a victim of its own success. Annual attendance had averaged about 79,000 during the 1990s, and total operating revenues were up nearly 10 percent. The museum was brighter, safer, cleaner and more interesting. New visitor participation programs had been launched and more and better exhibits exhibited. But driven by expanding payroll costs, the museum's operating budget had risen from about $450,000 in 1990 to more than $825,000 in 1999, an 83 percent increase. Simply put, Maryhill was thriving artistically and withering financially.

"The museum cannot operate without drawing funds annually from its unrestricted endowment," the board treasurer reported in June 1999. "Draws from the endowment (the museum's nest egg that had been first established by Sam Hill) have increased in the last two years while Maryhill has been earning 11 percent or more annually on its endowment principal, draws at the current levels are actually depleting the principal."

At a September 1999 meeting, trustees voted to limit annual withdrawals from the endowment to no more than 13 percent. De Falla, whose performance as director had been consistently praised "for her outstanding accomplishments in managing people and her unlimited knowledge," warned of dire consequences. She argued that cutting the budget meant cutting staff, and "that even the loss of one person would begin a steady slip backwards." It would be "cutting the institution off at the knees," she said. De Falla pointed out there would always be unexpected costs, such as the $120,000 she needed immediately to replace the museum's elevator, which routinely trapped visitors between floors.

"She further stated," the board minutes noted, "that during the seven years she has been at Maryhill Museum, she had devoted a huge amount of energy, time and affection into understanding how the museum functions, as well as its potential…".

Within a year, De Falla's "energy, time and affection" had apparently run out. The elevator was fixed, but in August 2000, De Falla quit. The stated reason was a desire to move to the Southwest, "an area that has a great appeal to me personally as well as professionally." The board wished her well. The expansion plans went into hibernation.

NOTES FOR CHAPTER 13

"The last few years" *Maryhill Quarterly*, Vol. 7, No. 2, Summer 1990, p. 3.

Given Maryhill's traditional Author's interview with Linda Brady Tesner, Oct. 5, 2015, Portland Oregon.

Although she had grown up Ibid.

"It was the best place" Ibid.

News of her appointment *Spokane Spokesman-Review*, June 24, 1985, p. B1; *Portland Oregonian,* May 18, 1984, p. F5.

"Herb was my savior" Tesner Oct. 5, 2015 interview, op. cit.

Linda began a *Maryhill Quarterly*, Vol. 1, No. 1, Winter 1984, p. 2.

One of the tasks Tesner Oct. 5 2015 interview, op. cit.

Ten months after hiring Ibid.

A signature Schafroth project Author's interview with Colleen Schafroth, Sept. 23, 2016, Maryhill Wa.

She was also in Ibid.

"Having quality people" Tesner Oct. 5 2015 interview, op. cit.

A contributor to Maryhill's Portland *Oregonian*, Nov. 4, 1986, p. B5.

Even so, Maryhill retained *Yakima Herald-Republic*, Oct. 31, 1999, p. E1.

"I don't know exactly" Author's interview with Laura Cheney, June 15, 2018, Maryhill Wa.

Not coincidentally Ibid.

While Maryhill's body was Tesner Oct. 5 2015 interview, op. cit.

Within five years, however Linda Brady Mountain, "The Maryhill Museum Case Study, prepared for the AAM Session 'Resurrection of the Phoenix," June 20, 1989, MMA.

"It was like a miracle" *Bloomington (Ill.) Pantograph*, May 13, 1990, p. C3; Portland *Oregonian*, March 13, 1986, p. B1.

It was more than rumors…. *Bloomington (Ill.) Pantograph*, May 13, 1990, p. C3.

The curtain rose on *Baltimore Sun*, Feb. 11, 1993, p. 1D.

Maryhill made little money Maryhill Board of Trustee minutes, May 17, 1994, MMA.

But while the staff stayed *Vancouver (Wa.) Columbian*, June 25, 1993, p. D-15.

Both the labyrinthine *Hood River News*, Jan. 10, 1996, p. 3.

Finally, in the spring *Yakima (Wa.) Herald-Republic*, March 13, 1998.

So Maryhill opened after all *Yakima (Wa.) Herald-Republic*, March 11, 1999.

The most novel proposal Maryhill Board minutes, May 22, 1993, MMA.

"The museum cannot operate" Maryhill Board minutes, June 8, 1999, MMA.

At a September 1999 meeting Maryhill Board minutes, July 15, 1995; Sept. 18, 1999, MMA

"She further stated" Maryhill Board minutes, Sept. 18, 1999, MMA.

Within a year, De Falla's *Yakima (Wa.) Herald-Republic*, Aug. 29, 2000.

CHAPTER FOURTEEN

"There is a dream built into this place"

JUNE 2018

In the Maryhill Museum of Art's somewhat grandiloquently named "Board Room," tucked behind the Rodin collection, the museum's executive committee has gathered on a balmy, breezy morning for its monthly meeting. The leadoff topic is water—both too much and not enough.

The "too much" is costing Maryhill money. As executive director Colleen Schafroth explains it, the Columbia River is running high this spring. That means the small cruise ships that stop at the museum have to berth further downriver and shuttle passengers via buses back to Maryhill. As a result, fewer people opt to visit. That hurts gift shop sales in particular, she says, because the cruise ship folks tend to buy lots of souvenirs.

The "not enough" part of the water discussion is more serious. Throughout its history, the museum has drawn its water from springs on its vast acreage. But it's a vulnerable source in terms of both quantity and quality. Maryhill has rights to water from the Columbia. To get it, however, means digging a well, pumping water up the steep cliffs and storing it in an impoundment at the site of a dam Sam Hill built almost a century earlier. It will be a complicated process, requiring the approval of a myriad of state and federal agencies. And it will be costly. Schafroth tells the committee there is a chance the state of Washington will pick up part of the tab—if the museum can produce a plan that satisfies legislators. The goal is to have such a plan ready to take to the Capitol in January.

"It's not going to get easier, is it?" sighs trustee Byron Henry, a retired pharmacist from Vancouver. "It never does," replies board president Ian Grabenhorst, a retired educator from Yakima.

Like all of Maryhill's 21 trustees, Henry and Grabenhorst volunteer their time, and often some of their money. Henry, who's been on the board for seven years, first came to Maryhill as a kid in the 1950s, and it helped develop a lifelong passion for Native American art and culture. Grabenhorst, in his eighth year as a trustee, was lured to the museum by his wife's volunteer work there. But his ties go back to Maryhill's birth. His grandmother attended the dedication of the museum in 1926—after bobbing her hair to emulate Queen Marie, much to the consternation of his grandfather.

The board members come from all over the Pacific Northwest (as well as one trustee from Transylvania), and comprise a panoply of backgrounds: business owners and executives, legislators, advertising agency and baking company operators, dentists, doctors, lawyers, chemists and art historians. Given the museum's history, they are also something of an anomaly for Maryhill boards in that they get along. "I've been on a lot of non-profit boards, worked at a lot of museums, and this is the most collegial board I've ever been on," says Jim McCreight, a Portland business executive who has served, in two stints, as a Maryhill trustee for nearly two decades. "I think we all consider each other friends and that's made it worth it to come back year after year."

For the next two hours, the eight committee members present sit around a large conference table in the spartanly furnished room that doubles as the staff kitchen and whose main wall adornment is a large map depicting the museum's sprawling domain. While the meeting continues, trustees jot brief thank-you notes and address envelopes to the 400 or so museum members who pay annual dues to support Maryhill. The idea is that a handwritten note from a board member will encourage members to renew.

Besides water, they discuss topics that range from a fallen tree near the museum's entrance to the current price of a blue-chip stock being added to Maryhill's portfolio. There is good news: Trustee Laura Cheney and her husband are donating more tables and chairs for the café patio. There is bad news: the sound system in the education center has died. Schafroth shares a photograph of a young mountain lion seen on the Maryhill ranch lands near the museum. She also shares her expectation that despite a current operating deficit of $47,317, the museum will still finish the season in the black.

There are plans afoot for $15,000 worth of fixes at the Stonehenge memorial. They include putting in a gate to bar entrance at night, constructing some barriers to keep people from parking too close to the monument and removing several trees that visitors are occasionally using as toilets. The state parks department, which is leasing the old store at the site to host astronomy programs on summer weekends, is going to chip in.

Trustee Jim Foster, who is an attorney from The Dalles, explains a convoluted probate case in Colorado, from which Maryhill might get a bequest of as much as $100,000—or nothing at all. The committee votes unanimously to authorize Schafroth to spend up to $5,000 in legal fees to pursue the matter.

As lunchtime nears, the meeting winds down. Some trustees head home or back to work. Others, as well as Schafroth, rush to grab a sandwich before heading to another museum committee meeting. "Some days it never stops," she explains. "Actually, most days."

She wasn't sure she wanted the job, or that she even wanted to stay at Maryhill. In fact, Colleen Schafroth had seriously considered a move to Idaho, where her sister lived. But when Josie De Falla quit as Maryhill's executive director in August 2000, Schafroth agreed to fill in as interim director while trustees launched a nationwide search for De Falla's replacement.

"When I was made interim director, nobody was sure about me, particularly colleagues I had been working with and now I was their boss," Schafroth said in a 2018 interview. "We were all packed together into the Rodin Gallery because the offices were closed due to reconstruction. I remember there was a trench cut in the floor of the museum, so at night when we left, we had to walk across a little bridge of planks they had laid down. It was a bit of a nightmare."

While Schafroth and the rest of the staff were walking the planks, trustees were looking for a new director. "But six months into the search," said then-board president Jim McCreight in a 2018 interview, "I had found only one person who was even close to being appropriate. At the same time, Colleen had done such a great job. So I went to the board and said 'why are we still looking? Let's go ahead and appoint the director we already have.' And I think we are all happy we did that. I think it was a critical point in the development of Maryhill."

Personally and professionally, Schafroth was perhaps the best fit Maryhill had ever had for its top job. She had the academic background. At the time she was named director in May 2001, she had already been at the museum for 15 years as education curator. She lived in The Dalles, a 30-minute commute from the museum, which meant she was relatively close but free from the sense of isolation that had stressed Mountain and De Falla, her two predecessors who had lived on-site. And while she professed to hate office- and boardroom politics, she was nonetheless adept at dealing with trustees and staff.

All of that came in handy, as Schafroth's assumption of the job came at an inopportune time on a number of fronts. The extensive repairs and reconstruction begun in 1999 crawled to completion in her first months as interim director. That delayed Maryhill's opening by two months in her first season as museum boss, and the delay cut deeply into operating revenues just as the trustees decided to rein in subsidies from the museum's nest egg. The lofty dream of museum expansion had been stalled for seven years and some of Maryhill's financial angels, particularly Mary Stevenson, were getting restless. And De Falla's departure came just as the museum was entering the final throes of completing the tortuous hike to full accreditation by the American Association of Museums.

The AAM (now the American Alliance of Museums) was founded in 1906 to further the common interests of museums and help develop ethical and professional operating standards. In 1971, the AAM began an accreditation process that was designed to help the public, as well as government and private organizations, identify museums that were responsibly run. To become accredited, a museum must meet AAM benchmarks for public trust and accountability; have a clear sense of its mission; possess solid leadership and organizational structures; operate educational and interpretive programs and strive for financial stability.

Within the museum world, accreditation is something akin to the Holy Grail, particularly for smaller and lesser-known museums. Of the estimated 35,000-plus museums in the United States, only 1,070—about 3 percent—were AAM-accredited in 2018. Accreditation validates an institution's work, adds to its prestige, makes it more attractive to potential donors and legitimizes it as a deserving location for loans and traveling exhibits. Achieving it, however, is something of a bureaucratic nightmare.

Maryhill had rashly sought accreditation in the late 1970s and early 1980s and hadn't come close. Over the next 20 years, Mountain, De Falla and Schafroth patiently and painstakingly pushed the museum through the myriad hoops set up by the AAM's process. In July 2000, just before De

Falla resigned, Maryhill got word that it had received "interim" approval. But the AAM held up its final OK for months because it was still dissatisfied with items ranging from adequate climate control to the precise wording of Maryhill's mission statement. On the latter issue alone, a board workshop was held, the mission statements of accredited museums were studied and consultants were consulted.

In late January 2002, after nine months of work, the Board of Trustees adopted a two-sentence, 54-word mission statement that in essence said Maryhill would do its best. Six months after that, Schafroth opened a two-page letter that the museum had awaited for decades. Accreditation had been granted in "recognition of (the) museum's commitment to excellence and high professional standards of operation." The letter was accompanied by two certificates suitable for framing and tips on how best to publicize the honor. The letter also thanked Maryhill for its patience. It did not, however, include any of what the museum most urgently needed: money.

Financially, Maryhill was in a rut. After a decade of mostly sparkling numbers, museum attendance began to sag. Between 1999 and 2004, annual visitor counts dropped 12.5 percent, from 56,000 to 49,000. The possible reasons were both numerous and conjectural. Gasoline prices rose 62 percent over the period, making the 200-mile roundtrip trek from the Portland-Vancouver metro area more problematic. Two natural history museums opened west of Maryhill, one on each side of the river, creating new competition for the tourist dollar. One year, the Columbia's system of locks was shut down, meaning the small cruise ships that visited Maryhill couldn't navigate the river.

Whatever the contributing factors were, Schafroth was forced to cut the staff and trim, patch and juggle the operating budget, which shrank from $1.1 million to $925,000. Meanwhile, there were unexpected bills that popped up on a frustratingly regular basis. A 2001 drought resulted in no field crops from the ranch—and thus no revenue. The museum's septic tank had to be replaced, at a cost of $100,000. The caretaker's cottage burned down. "The museum's operating financial picture is much the same as it is every year at this time," Schafroth told trustees in March 2004. "The museum is running at a deficit."

Maryhill's survival had always depended on its trustees and directors finding revenue sources undreamt of at any other museum in the world, from cattle ranches to car commercials to skateboard races. Now it needed a new source—and found it blowing in the wind.

If there is an aspect of the Columbia River Gorge as constant and pervasive as its impressive scenery, it's the wind. In fact, it is one of the windiest places in the Pacific Northwest. The Gorge slices through the heart of the Cascade Mountains, compressing and funneling the air along paths created by differences in atmospheric pressure. It makes the region ideal for kite-flying, world-class windsurfing—and generating electrical power.

Klickitat County officials began studying the area's potential for wind farms as early as the 1970s, and Maryhill officials were approached several times in the 1990s by companies interested in locating towering turbines atop the hills on the museum's ranchlands. In 2002 and 2003, they even signed short-term deals to allow site exploration. But it wasn't until a San Diego company showed up in 2005 that things got serious.

Founded in 1979, Cannon Power Group was a relatively small company with a big reputation. It had had launched close to 30 wind power projects in North America and Europe. For the Gorge, it envisioned a $1.2-billion wind farm involving 88 turbines over a 90-square-mile area, eventually generating as much as 500 megawatts of electricity, or enough to power 250,000 Southern California households for a year.

The aptly named Windy Point Project would place 15 of the 420-feet-high tri-bladed towers on Maryhill property. The museum would annually receive a percentage of the revenues generated over the life of a 20-year lease, with an option to renew for another 20 years. As a sweetener, the company offered a $25,000 upfront signing bonus.

Museum trustees were intrigued, hopeful, enthused—and cautious. They retained an attorney well-versed in windpower leases. They questioned the company's financing, the potential environmental and aesthetic impacts, and how much the museum might realistically expect to make. "There is no guarantee that the turbines will properly work," conceded trustee Mark Macnab, who had led the board's study of the Cannon company's pitch. "That is the risk for both sides. However," he argued, "we must have faith in the process."

In May 2006, the board took a leap of faith and unanimously approved the deal, with some conditions. Cannon agreed to mitigations that ranged from protecting raptor nests and archeological sites to restoring and preserving a wetlands region on the ranch. Then the company quickly began installing the bright white 40-story-tall towers on Maryhill's sunbaked hilltops, in the process donating $20,000 worth of concrete for curbs, walkways and a new parking area at the museum.

By mid-2009, the first of the turbines were up and running. By 2011, Maryhill was reaping annual wind-generated revenues of $220,000 to $250,000, or roughly a fifth of its total operating budget. Like so many episodes in Maryhill's history, the deal was one of a kind. "We've never had a situation even close to this," Cannon president Gary Hardke told the *New York Times* in 2012. "It really put a floor under their annual revenues."

While the turbines certainly added to the mythos of Maryhill, it did end another unique aspect of the museum: Because of potential liability issues created by the presence of the wind towers, Maryhill's Hunt Club, in which members paid to shoot birds and deer on the ranch and visit the museum for free, was discontinued.

Still, as Schafroth puckishly put it, the new arrangement was a "wind-win" situation. "It will keep the museum open and thriving," she told a reporter as the first towers were being erected. "It will lay a foundation for the museum to continue what it's doing now and preserve that into the future ... it ensures the museum is here for the next 20 years."

The windfarm deal also gave Maryhill's leaders *almost* all the confidence they needed to believe the museum could not just survive but grow. The rest came from the spirit—and estate—of Mary Stevenson.

Since her "return" to the museum in the early 1990s, Stevenson had been unflagging in giving both time and money to Maryhill. "She was a great encouragement to the board to think big and not just be content with the status quo," said Jim McCreight, who served as a trustee with Stevenson.

But a decade into her efforts, and entering her 80s, Stevenson was growing impatient with the pace of Maryhill's progress, particularly when it came to the long-delayed expansion plans. In 2003, she went to see Schafroth for a serious talk. Soon after, Schafroth had her own serious talk with the board of trustees, and soon after that, trustees formed an "expansion committee," headed by trustee Art Dodd, who happened to be an architect.

Dodd, himself a generous and enthusiastic Maryhill supporter, favored building a third rotunda that would appear like a part of the original building. But state officials scotched the idea because historical building regulations required any new structures to be clearly delineated from the old structure. Instead, trustees re-hired GBD Architects of Portland, the company they had dealt with a decade earlier, and revived the design presented then by the firm's Gene Callan.

Callan, who sometimes favored vision over budget practicalities, pushed for pushing the addition to the very brink of the Gorge, with an outdoor terrace that would allow visitors unparalleled views of the river below and imposing Mt. Hood to the west. "There was a lot of juggling, planning this, revising this, giving up this," Schafroth recalled 15 years later. "But in the end, I think it (Callan's design) was a piece of genius."

It was, however, genius with a hefty price tag. By the time the plans were tentatively finalized and agreed upon in October 2006, a fundraising consultant hired by the board estimated it would cost the staggering total of $17.4 million—about 15 times Maryhill's annual operating budget—to complete the expansion. The consultant added that given the museum's isolated location and history and the condition of the current economy, Maryhill could realistically expect to raise no more than $2 million.

Then economic conditions got worse. Maryhill was born in the Great Depression. Now it was trying to grow in the Great Recession, which began in 2007 and proved to be the deepest and most stubborn of the 10 recessions America had endured since World War II. Fortunately for Maryhill, its money managers had been relatively prudent with the museum's portfolio, which lost only 11 percent of its value while the stock market as whole dropped 39 percent. Unfortunately, the museum's water system required $800,000 worth of repairs and improvements. It appeared that once again, the expansion would be thwarted by the exigencies of the old building.

But in 2008, the museum was the sad beneficiary of two deaths. Elizabeth

Wade, who was generally regarded as one of Sam Hill's illegitimate children, and who had donated items to Maryhill from time to time, died at the age of 94. Under conditions of the trust Sam had set up for her, the $142,415 balance in the trust reverted to the museum upon her death. And on Nov. 7, Mary Hoyt Stevenson died at the age of 88. At her memorial service, Jim McCreight suggested that while Sam had named his empire after his daughter and wife, both named Mary, *Mary* Stevenson "should be part of that (heritage) too, because of all she did for the museum."

Stevenson's giving continued after her death. In 2009, it was announced she had left Maryhill $2 million to be used any way the trustees saw fit. After some debate, they decided to use it—and another $600,000 Stevenson and her husband Bruce had given earlier—to jump-start the fundraising drive for expanding Maryhill. "If she hadn't left us that money, it would have been very, very hard to pull it off," Schafroth said in 2018. "Still, it was very, very tight."

The first step was to scale back the scope of the project. Forgoing a moveable wall for the education center, for example, saved $40,000 by itself. The cutbacks sometimes came despite the entreaties of architect Callan and Craig Schommer of Schommer and Sons, the Portland-based company that had been founded three years before Maryhill opened and was the expansion's lead contractor.

"Craig Schommer was our Sam Hill," Schafroth smilingly recalled. "He had a hundred thousand ideas and we just didn't have the money for them. He'd bang the table and say 'we gotta do this,' and we'd say 'we can't.' But he was a sweetheart about it. He would bring the staff lunch all the time."

With project costs whittled to between $9 million and $10 million, Schafroth and Jill Baum, Maryhill's capital campaign director, hit the road in search of funds. They roamed up and down the Interstate 5 corridor between Portland and Seattle, with repeated stops at Washington state's capitol in Olympia. By February 2010, the project was half-funded. By June, it was up to 90 percent.

In addition to the $2.6 million from Mary and Bruce Stevenson, a foundation the couple had established contributed $500,000. The state of Washington kicked in $1.5 million. The Vancouver-based M. J. Murdock Charitable

Trust, which had donated to Maryhill's restoration drive in the 1990s, gave $700,000. The Cannon Power Group donated more than $150,000 as did the Stevensons' oldest daughter and her husband, Laura and John Cheney. About 50 other individuals gave $5,000 or more each. As a result, when construction began in 2011, the expansion was all but paid for, without the burden of loans. In the midst of a recession, for a museum in a county whose population comprised 0.3 percent of its state's population, it qualified as at least a minor miracle.

Callan had generally followed the design he came up with in 1993. Most of the 22,000 square-foot project was built underground, with a ground-level glass-enclosed gallery acting as a corridor from the existing building. There was room for an education center; a collection storage center and library; a large outdoor terrace and a café. In addition, the museum store and ground-level gallery were renovated. The extension was also environment-conscious in its design, eventually earning a gold rating from the U.S. Green Building Council.

"From an architectural point of view," Callan said, "the addition had to be quiet and respectful of the old building." The Portland *Oregonian* deemed Callan's effort a success: "The design is crisp and frankly contemporary, making it clear that the addition is a product of its own time the addition is clearly subservient to the original building, and clearly designed for low visible impact." In fact, the expansion couldn't even be seen from the highways passing Maryhill on either side of the river.

Building an "invisible" building wasn't easy. Despite Maryhill's vast acreage, construction crews had to operate as if they were in the cramped confines of downtown Seattle, because the museum stayed open during the work and parking lots and grounds were off-limits to the builders. They also faced the challenge of timing the delivery of building materials because virtually everything except concrete had to come from a long way off.

"We're removing the basalt without blasting, but since it is rock, it takes some significant equipment to do that mechanically," said Bob Schommer, one of Schommer and Sons' sons, during construction. The deck along the cliff "is all cast-in-place concrete and pouring it will be challenging. It's hard to access and we'll be pouring concrete almost into mid-air."

The gravity-defying challenge was met. Maryhill's appropriately named

Mary and Bruce Stevenson wing was formally opened on May 13, 2012, which would have been Sam Hill's 155th birthday. Reviews were generally positive. "The panorama alone (from the terrace) is worth a pilgrimage to this eastern Gorge landmark," a Portland magazine noted. "Combined with Maryhill's art collection, it practically demands it."

But just as the wind turbines had killed the museum's quirky Hunt Club, the new wing meant the end of another of Maryhill's charmingly odd features. Over the years, the museum's peacocks had become increasingly aggressive, chasing children, harassing picnickers and even scratching several visitors. Now the male birds were seeing themselves in the addition's glass walls—and charging headlong into them in an effort to challenge an imagined rival. To preserve both glass and bird brains, the peacocks were deported to an animal sanctuary.

In a narrow storage area that is all but hidden in Maryhill's large and startlingly impressive Native American gallery, Steve Grafe is looking at too much of a good thing. Grafe is Maryhill's curator of art. Crammed onto a table before him are more than 150 newly acquired California Indian artifacts, donated by an elderly collector whose prospective heirs have no interest in the items, and who fears the collection would be broken up after his death. There are exquisitely woven baskets, intricate boxes and an arrow quiver that is more than a century old but looks as if it were finished yesterday.

"God knows where we are going to put it," Grafe tells a visitor, "but we couldn't say no, because the best of it is in pristine condition we'll have to do something creative." One idea is to make more room in the existing exhibit cases by replacing the explanatory cards that accompany each piece with small letters or numbers. These would correspond with information in booklets attached to the outside of the cases. That way, Grafe explains, visitors with historical curiosity could read about the objects' background while those more interested in the objects' artistic qualities might be less distracted—and more could be put in each case.

"I'd like to display this Native American art as art," he says, "because we are an art museum and not a natural history museum. But at the same time, we don't want to display in a vacuum."

An Oregon native, Grafe came to Maryhill in 2009 armed with a doctorate in art history from the University of New Mexico, a decade's experience in curatorial work and a reputation as an expert in Native American culture. He also came with a pragmatic approach to the job.

"We're a small museum, obviously with limited resources," he says. "My idea has been to evaluate what we did and what we could continue to do, and because we don't have the resources of a major metropolitan museum, we have to continue to play to and develop our strengths." As Grafe sees it, one of Maryhill's primary strengths is its eclecticism. In fact, "'Eclectic' is not a pejorative" is the title of a talk Grafe often gives to various groups and at museum association conventions and seminars.

Playing to Maryhill's strengths and eclectic traditions helps explain why on this particular day, the museum's exhibits include a large and striking 2005 painting by the Midwest artist Stephen Gjertson, titled "Fall of Samson." Grafe says Gjertson "is the first Classical Realist painter in his generation." He is following the trail laid down by R.H. Ives Gammell, Richard Lack and others whose works have been collected at Maryhill over the decades. In words that would warm Cliff Dolph's heart, Grafe says "I would be delighted if we can continue to collect American Classical Realist paintings."

There are other examples of the museum building on its strengths. One area is devoted to works by leading contemporary Native American artists who sometimes work in non-traditional art forms. There is a growing collection of pieces by Pacific Northwest artists. And Grafe muses wistfully about the recent offer of 500 hats. The hats, he says, could, with the Théâtre de la Mode and Maryhill's extensive assemblage of Romanian clothing and textiles, create a new niche for Maryhill as a museum of fashion as well as art.

But 500 hats take up space, and despite the 2012 expansion, Maryhill doesn't have a lot of space for its collection of more than 16,000 items—not including the California Indian pieces or the hats. With a painful grimace, Grafe laments that the museum's world-class collection of art glass is still displayed in what Sam Hill originally planned as a closet. Grafe points out that with 5,300 acres at its disposal, there is plenty of room for Maryhill to build more storage. "We need to plan for 50 or 100 years out, and the only way to do that is to have the available storage now."

Whether there will be a Maryhill Museum of Art, or indeed any similar museums, in 50 or 100 years is far from certain. Art museum attendance in the United States seemingly peaked in the early 1990s, thanks to the confluence of a good economy, government support of the arts, the maturation of the Baby Boomers generation and the relatively meager scope and size of the World Wide Web at the time. Between 2002 and 2015, however, the National Endowment for the Arts reported, overall attendance at U.S. art museums dropped 16.8 percent, a slow but steady decline. Moreover, Maryhill has hurdles few, if any, other museums must cope with: its remote location, small population base, relatively paltry endowment and the fact it's only open eight months a year.

Part of the reason for the attendance decline experienced by art museums is undoubtedly technological. Phillipe de Montebello, the longtime director of New York's Metropolitan Museum of Art once observed that "a museum is the memory of mankind." But mankind's memories are increasingly being reduced to ones and zeroes and stored on thumb-sized metal-and-plastic devices, each of which can hold more images and information than a hundred Maryhills. On a single Google-run website, one can view and learn about more than 400,000 pieces of art from 1,500 museums around the world.

Competition from cyberspace, developments in virtual reality and the inescapable ubiquity of mass media are only some of the challenges faced by art museums. Another is the economic paradox built into their operation. While they may hold immensely valuable stores of physical assets, they are ethically, morally and often legally merely custodians, rather than owners, of their treasures. As such, most are faced with a constant struggle to raise enough money each year to keep going. At Maryhill, for example, adult admission was $12 in 2018. But it cost $30 per visitor to pay the staff, maintain and repair the facility and above all preserve and enhance its collection. "We have to make up that gap somehow," said executive director Schafroth, "and some day there may not be a Mary Stevenson or a wind farm to count on but somehow, we keep going."

Perhaps the reason is in Maryhill's very bones. Next to the museum's entrance there is a plaque containing a quote from Queen Marie's dedication speech. It reads in part: "There is much more in this building made of concrete than we see. There is a dream built into this place. Some may smile and scoff, for they do not understand, but I came in understanding for these dreamers would say 'good things are not only for this life, but for beyond.'"

NOTES FOR CHAPTER 14

In the Maryhill Museum The first section of this chapter comes from the June 15, 2018 meeting of the museum's executive committee at Maryhill.

"When I was made" Author's interview with Colleen Schafroth, June 18, 2018, Maryhill.

While Schafroth and Author's interview with Jim McCreight, June 15, 2018, Maryhill.

In January 2002 Thomas Livesat to Colleen Schafroth, Aug. 1, 2002, MMA.

Whatever the contributing Board minutes, March 31, 2004, MMA.

Museum trustees were intrigued Board minutes, May 13, 2006, MMA.

By mid-2009, the *New York Times*, May 19, 2012, p. C1.

As Schafroth puckishly Portland *Oregonian*, July 7, 2009, digital edition.

Since her return to .... McCreight interview, June 15, 2018, Maryhill.

Callan, who sometimes Schafroth interview, June 18, 2018, Maryhill.

Stevenson's giving continued Ibid.

"Craig Schommer was our" Ibid.

"From an architectural" *Seattle Times*, June 30, 2012, digital edition; Portland *Oregonian*, Oct. 4, 2010, digital edition.

"We're removing the basalt" *Daily Journal of Commerce, Oregon*, March 3, 2011, digital edition.

The gravity-defying challenge *Portland Monthly* magazine, May 25, 2012, digital edition.

"God knows where we" This and other comments by Grafe in this section are from an author's interview, June 18, 2018, Maryhill.

Part of the reason for "A history of museums, the 'memory of mankind,'" National Public Radio broadcast, Nov. 24, 2008.

Competition from cyberspace Schafroth interview, June 18, 2018, Maryhill.

Perhaps the reason *New York Times*, Nov, 4, 1926, p. 1.

SELECTED BIBLIOGRAPHY

Atwater, Issac (ed.). *History of the City of Minneapolis, Minnesota* (two volumes). New York: Munsell & Co., 1893.

Barron, Clarence W. *They Told Barron: Conversations and Revelations of an American Pepys in Wall Street.* New York: Harper and Bros., 1930.

Boia, Lucian. *Romania: Borderland of Europe* (translated by James Christian Brown). London: Reaktion Books, 2001.

Bolitho, Hector. *A Biographer's Notebook.* New York: The MacMillan Co., 1950.

Brands, H.W. *Woodrow Wilson.* New York: Times Books, 2003.

Cammaerts, Emile. *Albert of Belgium: Defender of Right.* New York, The MacMillan Co., 1935.

Carter, Robert B. *Buffalo Bill Cody: The Man Behind the Legend.* New York: John Wiley & Sons, 2000.

Clark, Richard. *Sam Hill's Peace Arch: Remembrance of Dreams Past.* Bloomington, Ind: Authorhouse, 2006.

Cleland, Robert Glass. *California in Our Time (1900-1940).* New York: Alfred A. Knopf, 1947.

Cullen, Frank. *Vaudeville Old and New: An Encyclopedia of Variety Performers, Vol. I.* New York: Routledge, 2007.

Current, Richard Nelson and Marcia Ewing Current. *Loie Fuller: Goddess of Light.* Boston: Northeastern University, 1997.

Daggett, Mabel Potter. *Marie of Roumania: The Intimate Story of the Radiant Queen.* New York: George H. Doran Company, 1926.

Duncan, Isadora. My Life (restored edition). New York: Liveright Publishing Corp., 2013.

Elsberry, Terence. *Marie of Romania: The Intimate Life of a Twentieth Century Queen.* New York: St. Martin's Press, 1972.

Feldstein, Martin (ed.) *The Economics of Art Museums.* Chicago: University of Chicago Press, 1991.

Flanner, Janet. Paris *Was Yesterday: 1925-1939.* New York: Viking Press, 1972.

Florescu, Radu R., and Raymond T. McNally. *Dracula: Prince of Many Faces, His Life and Times.* Boston: Little, Brown and Co., 1989.

Fuller, Loie. *Fifteen Years of a Dancer's Life.* Boston, Small, Maynard and Company, 1913.

Gelardi, Julia P. Born. *Born to Rule: Five Reigning Consorts, the Granddaughters of Queen Victoria.* New York: St. Martin's Press., 2005.

Gilbert, Martin. *The First World War: A Complete History.* New York: Henry Holt and Company, 1994.

Gordon, Winifred. *Roumania, Yesterday and To-Day.* London: John Lane Company, 1918.

Grunfeld, Frederic V. *Rodin: A Biography.* New York: Henry Holt and Co., 1987.

Harris, Margaret Haile. *Loie Fuller: Magician of Light.* Richmond: The Virginia Museum, 1979.

Harrison, John H. *A Woman Alone: Mona Bell, Sam Hill and the Mansion at Bonneville Rock.* Portland: Frank Amato Publications, 2009.

Holbrook, Stewart H. *Rivers of America: The Columbia.* New York: Rinehart and Co., 1956.

Keegan, John. *The First World War.* New York: Alfred A. Knopf, 1999.

Kendall, Elizabeth. *Where She Danced: The Birth of American Art-Dance.* Berkeley, Ca.: University of California Press, 1979.

Lewis, Oscar. *San Francisco, Mission to Metropolis.* Berkeley, Ca.: Howell-North Books, 1966.

MacMillan, Margaret. *Paris 1919: Six Months that Changed the World.* New York: Random House, 2001.

Malone, Michael P. *James J. Hill: Empire Builder of the Northwest.* Norman, Ok.: University of Oklahoma Press, 1996.

Mandache, Diana (ed.) *Later Chapters of My Life: The Lost Memoir of Queen Marie of Romania.* Thrupp, England, Sutton Publishing, 2004.

Marie, Queen of Romania. *The Story of My Life.* New York: Charles Scribner's Sons, 1934.

Marie, Queen of Romania. *America Seen by a Queen.* Bucharest: Romanian Cultural Foundation, 1999.

Martin, Albro. *James J. Hill and the Opening of the Northwest.* St. Paul, Minn.: Minnesota Historical Society Press, 1976.

McCarthy, Anne L. *The Hill Family of Chowan County, North Carolina.* Edina, Minn.: McCarthy Publications, 1990.

Moore, Lucy. *Anything Goes: A Biography of the Roaring Twenties*. New York: The Overlook Press, 2010.

Morris, Constance Lily. *On Tour With Queen Marie.* New York: Robert M. McBride and Co., 1927.

Neils, Selma M. *So This is Klickitat.* Goldendale, Wa.: Metropolitan Press, 1967.

Newsom, Barbara Y. and Adele Z. Silver. *"The Art Museum as Educator."* Berkeley, Ca.: University of California Press, 1978.

Pakula, Hannah. *The Last Romantic: The Life of the Legendary Marie, Queen of Roumania, the Most Famous Beauty, Heroine and Royal Celebrity of Her Time.* New York: Simon & Schuster, 1984.

Peterson, Ruth Jordan. *This Land of Gold and Toil.* Caldwell, Id.: Caxton Publishing, 1982.

Plotts, Lois Davis. *Maryhill, Sam Hill and Me.* Self-published, 1979.

Randolph County Historical Society. *Randolph County, 1779-1979.* Winston-Salem, N.C.: Hunter Publishing Company, 1980.

Rodger, Gillian. *Champagne Charlie and Pretty Jemima: Variety Theater in the Nineteenth Century.* Urbana, Ill.: University of Illinois Press, 2010.

Ross, Ishbel. *Grace Coolidge and Her Era: The Story of a President's Wife.* New York: Dodd, Mead & Co., 1962.

Sagala, Sandra K. *Buffalo Bill on Stage.* Albuquerque: University of New Mexico Press, 2008.

Schafroth, Colleen. *Sculptures in Miniature: Chess Sets from the Maryhill Museum of Art.* Goldendale, Wa.: Maryhill Museum of Art, 1990.

Scharlach, Bernice. *Big Alma: San Francisco's Alma Spreckels.* Berkeley: Fine Arts Museums of San Francisco/Heyday Books, 2016.

Starr, Kevin. *Inventing the Dream: California Through the Progressive Era.* New York: Oxford University Press, 1985.

Tesner, Linda Brady. *Maryhill Museum of Art.* Portland, Or.: Arcus Publishing, 2006.

Train, Susan (ed.) *Theatre de la Mode. Fashion Dolls: The Survival of Haute Coutre.* Portland: Palmer/Pletsch Publishing, 2002.

Tuhy, John E. *Sam Hill: The Prince of Castle Nowhere.* Bend, Oregon: Maverick Publications, Inc., 1991.

Walhimer, Mark. *Museums 101.* Lanham, Md.: Rowman & Littlefield, 2015.

Wilson, Edith Bolling. *My Memoir.* Indianapolis: Bobbs-Merrill Company, 1939.

ACKNOWLEDGEMENTS

Dr, John Tuhy, the Maryhill Museum trustee and biographer of Sam Hill, once observed that the only people who read a book's acknowledgements page were those expecting to see their names listed. Notwithstanding the sagacity of Dr. Tuhy's remarks, and despite the near-certainty that I will leave deserving people out, I'd like to thank the following folks:

First, my wife Ceil, for all the usual reasons and because she always gets listed last in my acknowledgements. That's not only backwards, it's just wrong. Ditto to my daughter Erin.

I owe a deep debt to Dr. Judith St. Pierre. Judith, who worked for many years at Maryhill as a volunteer, generously shared her own research and insights into the museum. Maryhill's executive director, Colleen Schafroth, was equally generous with her time, her memories and her perspective, as well as graciously affording me access to the museum's materials and its staff. Collections manager/registrar Anna Goodwin exhibited extraordinary patience in putting up with unceasing questions and unreasonable requests, and never failed to dig up what I was looking for from the museum's archives. Curator of Art Steve Grafe not only gave me a taste of what it's like to keep a place like Maryhill fresh and relevant, but shared his views on the vital role museums play in our society.

My deep appreciation also to several people who read the manuscript as it waddled toward completion. They provided cogent critiques, asked relevant questions and above all encouraged me to keep going: Rob Gunnison, Bobbie Metzger, Steve Capps, and Steven and Sue Boudreau. Thanks, folks.

Former Maryhill director Linda Brady Tesner not only consented to a long interview, but sent me her copies of the museum's quarterly newsletter produced during her tenure. Several of Cliff Dolph's relatives—Vada Dolph, Kathleen Irwin and Cliff Dolph—all shared nuggets of what living at Maryhill was like.

A huge thanks to Bruce Bortz at Bancroft Press, not only for his counsel and guidance, but for helping to keep alive an endangered idea in publishing:

that a good story is worth sharing, even if it doesn't fit neatly into a niche. Also thanks much to Tracy Copes, for her fine cover and interior design.

Finally, thanks to Sam and Loie and Alma and Marie—and all those people who have shared their dream. They remind us that no place is too out of the way for striving to remember the past and enhance the future, through the preservation and exhibition of art. It's a damn fine idea.

ABOUT THE AUTHOR

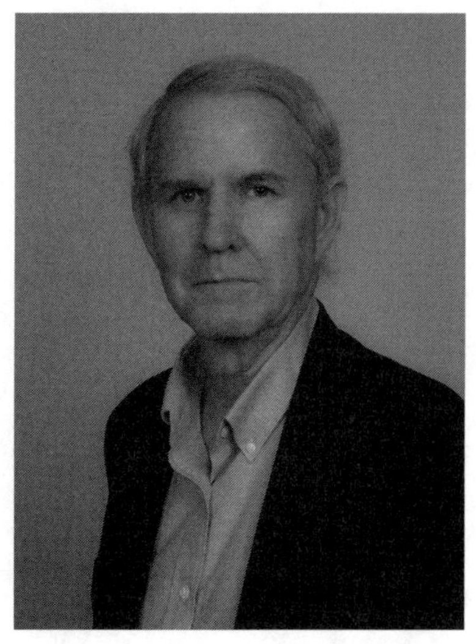

Steve Wiegand is an award-winning journalist and history writer. His 35-year journalism career was spent at the *San Diego Evening Tribune,* where he was chief political writer; *San Francisco Chronicle*, where he was state capitol bureau chief; and *Sacramento Bee*, where he was a special projects writer and politics columnist.

Wiegand is the author, co-author, or contributing author of eight books, including *U.S. History for Dummies,* which is currently in its fourth edition and has been published in both Chinese and German; the *Mental Floss History of the World; Papers of Permanence*; *Lessons from the Great Depression for Dummies;* and *The American Revolution for Dummies.*

He is a graduate of Santa Clara University, with a bachelor's degree in American history and literature, and has a master's degree in mass communications from San Jose State University.

He lives in Arizona.

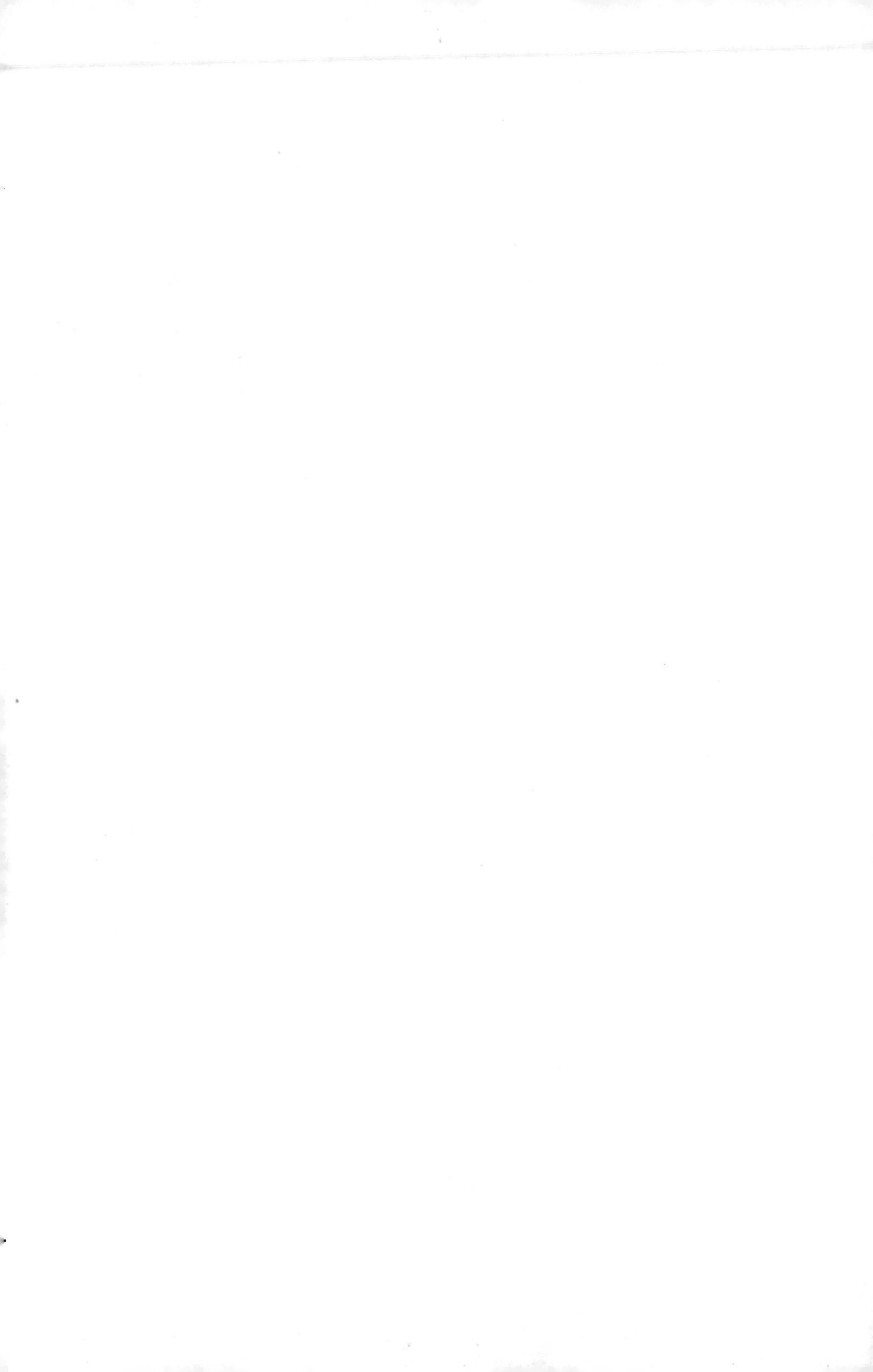